Choice, Persuasion, and Coercion

Choice, Persuasion, and Coercion

Social Control on Spain's North American Frontiers

EDITED BY
JESÚS F. DE LA TEJA AND
ROSS FRANK

UNIVERSITY OF NEW MEXICO PRESS ❧ ALBUQUERQUE

LIBRARY OF CONGRESS CATALOGING-IN-PUBLICATION DATA

Choice, persuasion, and coercion : social control on Spain's North American frontiers
/ edited by Jesús F. de la Teja and Ross Frank.

p. cm.

Includes bibliographical references.

ISBN 0-8263-3646-9 (pbk. : alk. paper)

1. Spaniards—North America—Politics and government.

2. Social control—North America—History.

3. Frontier and pioneer life—North America.

4. Ethnicity—North America—History.

5. Indians of North America—Government relations—To 1789.

6. Indians of North America—Government relations—1789–1869.

7. North America—Ethnic relations.

8. North America—Social conditions.

9. Spain—Colonies—America.

10. North America—History—Colonial period, ca. 1600–1775.

I. Teja, Jesús F. de la, 1956– II. Frank, Ross, 1957–
E49.2.S7C47 2005
303.3'3'0970903—dc22

2005009952

Book design and type composition by Kathleen Sparkes

Book is typeset in Janson 10/13.5; 26P

Display type is Bernhard Modern

Contents

FOREWORD
DAVID J. WEBER   vii

INTRODUCTION
JESÚS F. DE LA TEJA   xi

CHAPTER ONE
Who Controls the King?
ALFREDO JIMÉNEZ   1

CHAPTER TWO
Social Control on Spain's Contested Florida Frontier
JANE LANDERS   27

CHAPTER THREE
Spanish Control over a Multiethnic Society:
Louisiana, 1763–1803
GILBERT C. DIN   49

CHAPTER FOUR
"They Conceal a Malice Most Refined":
*Controlling Social and Ethnic Mobility in
Late Colonial New Mexico*
ROSS FRANK   77

CHAPTER FIVE
Subverting the Social Order:
Gender, Power, and Magic in Nueva Vizcaya
SUSAN M. DEEDS   95

CHAPTER SIX
Social Control and Native Territoriality in
Northeastern New Spain
CECILIA SHERIDAN,
TRANSLATED BY NED F. BRIERLEY   121

CHAPTER SEVEN

Beyond Their Control:

Spaniards in Native Texas

JULIANA BARR   149

CHAPTER EIGHT

The Común, Local Governance,

and Defiance in Colonial Sonora

CYNTHIA RADDING   179

CHAPTER NINE

Racialized Hierarchies of Power in Colonial Mexican Society:

The Sistema de Castas *as a Form of Social Control in Saltillo*

JOSÉ CUELLO   201

CHAPTER TEN

Colonization and Control:

The Case of Nuevo Santander

PATRICIA OSANTE,

TRANSLATED BY NED F. BRIERLEY   227

CHAPTER ELEVEN

Social Control within Missionary Frontier Society:

Alta California, 1769–1821

JAMES A. SANDOS   253

GLOSSARY   277

ABBREVIATIONS   287

BIBLIOGRAPHY   289

CONTRIBUTORS   321

INDEX   325

Foreword

This collection of essays grew from a seed that Jesús F. de la Teja planted in June 1999. Frank, as he is known to his friends, and I had attended the Fifth Annual Conference of the Omohundro Institute of Early American History and Culture, held in Austin, Texas. The Clements Center for Southwest Studies at SMU, which I direct, had cosponsored that conference, which brought historians of the Spanish colonial experience together with historians of French and English America. This was a rare occasion. Scholars working on these different colonial empires seldom meet in the same room. Frank observed, however, that even historians interested in Spain's North American Empire had little direct communication. Historians of Spanish colonial Florida and students of Spanish California history addressed similar questions, but seldom talked to one another. Neither had much occasion to meet with experts on the history of today's north Mexican states—or vice versa. The Clements Center for Southwest Studies, Frank suggested, should host a meeting of historians who study the Spanish past in different locales, from California to Florida, and across the northern tier of present-day Mexican states, from Tamaulipas to Sonora.

Although founded in 1996 and still in its infancy, the Clements Center had already developed a distinctive model for encouraging such scholarly conversations. Our plan was to hold an annual conference that would address a broad question and meet in two different venues to explore the answers. In the autumn we would invite participants to SMU's Fort Burgwin campus at Taos, New Mexico. There, having read drafts of each essay in advance, the invited scholars would critique one another's work. How well did each essayist answer the question and how well did their essays articulate with one another? The next spring, the Clements Center would bring scholars to the SMU main campus in Dallas. They would again meet privately to talk about the revised essays, but also present synopses of their work in a conference open to students, faculty, and the general public. Then, the scholars would do final revisions of their essays under the direction of a general editor who would prepare the final manuscript for publication.

When Frank de la Teja and I talked in June 1999, the Clements Center had completed the first of its annual conferences; the University of New Mexico Press published the essays in 2003 as *The Culture of Tourism, The Tourism of Culture: Selling the Past to the Present in the American Southwest,* edited by Hal Rothman. The Center had a conference planned for the next year as well—the results of which also appeared as a book in 2003, published this time by the University of Oklahoma Press, *The Future of the Southern Plains,* edited by Sherry Smith.

Frank's idea, then, had to wait until the 2001–2002 academic year. In the meantime, however, we needed to identify a scholar who would pose the central question, identify the historians who could best answer it, preside over the two meetings, and edit the essays. Two historians agreed to share those responsibilities—Frank de la Teja and Ross Frank, who had been part of the initial discussion in Austin in June 1999. In October 1999, the three of us met again. We decided to examine how "social control" functioned in various regions of Spanish North America, and Frank and Ross agreed to identify historians who could do that.

Social control was central to understanding Spain's vision for its American empire. In Spain's ideal universe of that era, God was in his heaven, humans on earth, and saints and other intercessors occupied an intermediate position—as numerous religious paintings attest. The earthbound were supposed to know their place in the social order, and stay in it. In America, Indians and Spaniards were to live apart, in separate spheres or *repúblicas,* but those spheres had to revolve around fixed communities. Neither Indians nor Spaniards were to live in isolation, scattered throughout the countryside like "wild" Indians or Anglo-American "pioneers," who seemed one in the same to urban Spaniards. Within Indian and Spanish communities, clear hierarchies were to reign. In Spanish towns the rich and the well born were to govern local society and occupy homes close to the main plaza, itself an orderly rectangle set amidst a grid of streets and house lots. The plaza would be the site of the church and its clerics, who dispensed moral laws emanating from an ecclesiastical hierarchy that reached to Rome. The town hall also stood on the plaza, housing government officials who enforced earthly laws that the king and his council issued from across the Atlantic. In Spanish and Indian towns alike, men were to rule women, and fathers were to rule children.

Historians knew, of course, how the system was supposed to work in theory, but how did it function in practice? What variations would one find in the distinctive human and physical geographies of frontier regions located far from the seat of viceregal power in Mexico City?

Charged with answering that broad question, our team of historians met first in San Diego in September 2001, rather than at SMU-in-Taos. The enterprising Ross Frank had obtained grants from several sources at the University of California, San Diego: the Department of Ethnic Studies (where he teaches), the History Department, the Center for the Humanities, and the Center for U.S.-Mexican Studies, which opened its wonderful ocean-front facilities to us. Ross Frank expertly led a thought-provoking, day-long conversation. Our discussion was enriched by the presence of David Holtby, a senior editor at the University of New Mexico Press and a Latin American specialist, whom we had invited to guide us in making essays accessible to student readers as well as professional scholars. Eric Van Young, UCSD's genial and insightful historian of colonial Mexico, also contributed to the exchange of ideas.

In April 2002, our group reassembled at SMU under the auspices of the Clements Center for Southwest Studies. After a stimulating day of public and private conversations, scholars revised their essays yet again, with Frank de la Teja providing editorial guidance if not social control. The results appear in this remarkable collection.

I am grateful to "the two Franks," as we came to call them, and to all of the participants. All took time from their own book-length projects to meet and think in concert about an important question. The results of their thinking will be of interest to professional scholars, and the care they took in crafting these essays makes them accessible to college-level scholars.

David J. Weber, Director
William P. Clements Center for Southwest Studies
Southern Methodist University, Dallas, Texas

Introduction

JESÚS F. DE LA TEJA

In the conquest of Mexico Hernán Cortés proved himself a consummate practitioner of social control. Through persuasion and coercion the conquistador managed to maintain the upper hand in almost every situation he encountered with his followers and his opponents (both European and indigenous). Without effective agencies and mechanisms of social control, which Cortés was quickly able to identify and effectively apply in a given situation, a few hundred Spaniards could not have become the overlords of millions of Indians. So effective were these various tools of social control— missionaries, *encomienda*, land grants, royal sanctions—that they became important features of colonial life long after the Spanish Crown imposed its own controls on Cortés himself. For the next three centuries Spanish methods of social control effectively sustained an imperial system that included millions of inhabitants spread out over much of two continents. Only in marginal areas, where Spanish institutions of social control were relatively weak, was Spanish control consistently challenged. What better place, then, to examine colonial methods of social control and their consequences than on the northern peripheries of Spain's American empire?

In commenting that Cortés employed persuasion and coercion in implementing social control, I want to make it clear that controlling a society, or any group within a society, involves more than the use of force. Social control as a tool of historical analysis has long emphasized the use of force, or coercion, particularly in regard to what dominant groups consider "deviant behavior" among subordinate groups.[1] However, when addressing persuasion—voluntary participation in a system of social control—historians have avoided employing the term. Thus, the editors of *Rituals of Rule, Rituals of Resistance: Public Celebrations and Popular Culture in*

Mexico avoid the terminology even as they describe it: "successful rulers throughout history have understood that their dominion rests on much more than force alone. Persuasion, charisma, habit, and presentations of virtue serve as familiar techniques and exhibitions of authority."[2]

Our survey of social control on Spain's North American frontier begins by looking precisely at the role of the monarchy in establishing and maintaining control over the empire. In the first chapter Alfredo Jiménez provides an expansive introduction to the imperial system and its various agencies of social control in "Who Controls the King?" As the title implies, Jiménez is ultimately concerned with demonstrating that Spanish monarchs were not entirely independent agents. The elaborate structure of the empire, together with competing economic, political, and racial interests, placed great pressures on the monarchy to take the concerns of all its subjects seriously. In effect, Jiménez asserts, the various groups that composed colonial society exercised their own control over the Crown.

The two chapters that follow discuss the workings of social control in Spain's first colony and one of its last. Chapter two, Jane Landers's survey of Spanish Florida, "Social Control on Spain's Contested Florida Frontier," emphasizes the difficulties that any conquest society has in maintaining control when faced with continuous aggression. Along with the successful resistance from the native peoples of the southern part of the peninsula, and periodic revolts by Indians under Franciscan tutelage, Spanish policy makers had to contend with rising levels of violence from groups it did not control—Indian slave raiders organized by English colonials in the Carolinas, English military forces bent on displacing Spain on the Atlantic seaboard of North America, Anglo American frontiersmen determined to incorporate the region into the nascent United States. Despite the challenges, Spanish officials tried to combine black fugitive slaves, the quickly dwindling number of natives, and an assorted international cast of colonials into the semblance of Spanish society.

In chapter three, "Spanish Control over a Multiethnic Society: Louisiana, 1763–1803," Gilbert C. Din addresses many of Jiménez's themes within a specific case study. In Louisiana, a considerably mature colony when Spain acquired it in 1763, the Crown faced special problems arising from its unique mix of non-Hispanic Euroamericans, Indians, and people of African descent. Quickly abandoning coercion as a primary tool of control, Spanish officials were instructed to be flexible and conciliatory in adapting traditional Spanish institutions to meet the needs of government.

As a result, the province's black, Indian, and French-descent populations found the Spanish yoke mild; so much so that Louisianans were dismayed by the transfer of the colony to the United States in 1803.

It was not just the actions of rulers, authorities, or elites who sought to effect social control. Ethnic groups, classes, and castes also exercised control within their respective societies. Likewise, institutions such as the Church, schools, fraternal organizations, and the family taught patterns of behavior to their members through which individuals understood their place in society and their relationship to every other member of society.

Social control, then, is a broad concept encompassing the myriad ways in which a society attempts to maintain order by persuading, coercing, or educating individuals to accept and behave according to the principles and values—norms—of the group of which they are members, want to become members, or have been compelled into membership.[3] Another way of understanding social control is by looking at its purpose: "to bring about conformity, solidarity, and continuity of a particular group or culture."[4] Social control is so powerful a force that it works on the individual even in the absence of the group. A well-integrated member of a society, social group, or institution adheres to the rules even when alone. An individual who is not well integrated or who becomes disaffected from society may elect to disregard or subvert social norms intentionally, bringing about the group's disapproval and the label of deviant or eccentric. When entire groups choose to subvert or disregard social norms, or when the values and standards of a society are in a period of transition, the group or society's behavior might be termed chaotic, decadent, rebellious, or revolutionary.

Consider the case of Governor Fernando de la Concha, as does Ross Frank in chapter four, "'They Conceal a Malice Most Refined': Controlling Social and Ethnic Mobility in Late Colonial New Mexico." As a professional soldier who expected to find order and adherence to Spanish law and policy, de la Concha was dismayed to encounter the Spanish population of New Mexico apathetic if not downright hostile to everything he understood to be proper behavior. Frank describes a situation in which local society, faced with unique frontier circumstances, developed its own set of norms, which while based in general on Spanish values responded to local needs. Set in their ways, Nuevomexicanos collectively countered the various mechanisms of social control that late-colonial governors attempted to impose on them.

While the broader society, or as in the above case local society, can instruct, encourage, threaten, or compel the individual to observe a given set of norms, the individual is left with a range of responses. In *The Devil in the New World: The Impact of Diabolism in New Spain*, Fernando Cervantes provides a clear example of this type of situation. Father Alonso Hidalgo presented himself to the Inquisition in 1613 to confess his crimes against God and the Church "in deed as well as in word, from the earliest day I can remember until the present ... denying all the precepts of our holy faith ... having renounced ... the Holy Trinity, and our Lady, and the whole of the celestial court, and having denied the authority of the pope, believing myself to be greater than God and rendering obedience to the devil."5 In other words, Father Hidalgo, racked by guilt for having long violated the norms of Christian life, which given his clerical status made his disobedience all the greater, chose to come clean by throwing himself at the mercy of one of colonial society's chief agencies of social control, the Church's branch for dealing with deviant moral behavior.

In chapter five, "Subverting the Social Order: Gender, Power, and Magic in Nueva Vizcaya," Susan M. Deeds probes the cases of two women who in different ways attempted to gain greater control over their lives by transgressing gender roles, manipulating supernatural powers, and employing their sexuality. The different ways in which these women exercised their choices to subvert gender roles and Catholic tenets are examined by Deeds to address how the colonial state and its chief institution, the Church, understood threats to the social order from ethnic and economic underclasses. At the same time, Deeds reveals how frontier Nueva Vizcaya—a vast semidesert territory punctuated by mining camps, agricultural estates, and few urban centers and occupied by a diverse population of Spaniards, mixed-bloods, resettled Indians from central New Spain, and recently subjugated natives—provided greater latitude for individual subversion and reconstitution of the social order.

It was not just on an individual basis that acceptance or rejection of social norms took place, however. In a conquest situation, such as existed throughout Spanish North America, conquered groups might or might not accept the new norms that the conquerors attempted to impose. Returning to Cortés's conquest of Mexico for a moment, Miguel León-Portilla points out the complexity of the post-conquest world, in which rival Indian groups had not only allied with the Spaniards against the Aztec overlords, but had maintained their rivalries long after they had all been incorporated into the Spanish orbit. In a 1560 letter complaining of excessive tribute levies against their town, the Indian council of Huetjotzingo chose to appeal to the king's mercy by contrasting their own loyalty to the Crown with Tlaxcaltecan treachery: "[The people of] many towns were forced and tortured, were hanged or burned, because they did not want to leave idolatry.... Especially those Tlaxcaltecans pushed out and rejected the fathers, and would not receive the faith, for many of the high nobles were burned, and some hanged, for combating the advocacy and service of our Lord God. But we of Huetjotzingo, we your poor vassals, we never did anything in your harm, always we served you in every command you sent or what at your command we were or-dered."[6] We have, in effect, circumstances in which one group—Spaniards—was able to convince another group—Huetjotzingos—to change its modes of behavior to the point that the latter group totally identified with the former, even at the expense of other groups—Tlaxcaltecans—with which it might otherwise have had a commonality of interests.

The range of native group responses to the Spanish invasion in central Mexico was repeated over the course of the next three centuries as the Spanish frontier moved northward. The chapters by Cecilia Sheridan and Juliana Barr explore the ways in which autonomous Indian groups on the frontier negotiated with Spaniards, sometimes in the creation of alliances, sometimes in preservation of their independence. Sheridan's contribution, "Social Control and Native Territoriality in Northeastern New Spain," concerns the world of nonsedentary groups that inhabited a large portion of today's northeastern Mexico and southern Texas. Mobile, flexible, and adaptable, many of these groups altered their patterns of behavior as well as their territories, some to the degree of forming new identities in order to accommodate themselves to the presence of Spaniards. This "ethno-genesis," or cultural birth, proved a power tool for resisting Spanish conquest, creating a situation in which Spaniards could claim only limited control over the region under discussion.

In chapter seven, "Beyond their Control: Spaniards in Native Texas," Juliana Barr takes the Indians' ability to resist Spanish control one step further. She argues that it was the native peoples the Spaniards encountered in Texas who had the upper hand, and that it was the Euroamericans who had to learn and accept Comanche and Caddo ways in order to remain in the region. Although Texas Indians traded with Euroamericans and incorporated aspects of European material culture into their societies, they held fast to their cultural and social norms, creating an effective barrier to further Spanish penetration into the interior of North America.

This is not to say that Spanish social control mechanisms were not capable of bringing about the incorporation of frontier areas in which

Indians themselves would become the main components of Spanish colonial society. We do not have to wander from our area of interest to see this type of analysis at work. In his groundbreaking study "The Mission as a Frontier Institution in the Spanish American Colonies," Herbert Bolton explained how the Spanish quickly determined that "if the savage were to be converted, or disciplined, or exploited, he must be put under control." He then acknowledges that the natives resisted the exploitation through flight, requiring that they be gathered into settlements, "pueblos," where they could be effectively transformed into Spanish subjects. "The pueblos were modeled on the Spanish towns, and were designed not alone as a means of control, but as schools in self-control as well."[7]

Not all Indians required congregation in villages organized by the Spanish. In chapter eight, "The *Común*, Local Governance, and Defiance in Colonial Sonora," Cynthia Radding explains how Spanish authority in the vast territory of the Intendency of Sonora relied on the continuation of pre-existing village culture. In effect, although the Spanish introduced European forms of social and political organization, they were forced to place these in the hands of native leaders whose agendas might or might not coincide with those of their Spanish overlords. Even more intriguing, the Indian villagers on whose labor the system depended had their own means of controlling the actions of their leaders.

Likewise, studies of the *encomienda* system, of the *sistema de castas*, of the role of the Catholic Church in general, and of the family have all addressed issues of social control. Lesley Byrd Simpson, in his classic work on the encomienda in colonial Mexico, makes clear that although it was an instrument of social control, it was not so on the commonly accepted terms. Rather than serving as the vehicle through which Indians were educated "in proper (Spanish) norms of conduct," throughout its first half-century of existence in Mexico, it "was looked upon by its beneficiaries as a subterfuge for slavery." Only through the ceaseless efforts of the Dominican defender of the Indians Bartolomé de Las Casas and others was encomienda "reduced to some semblance of a social system. Indeed, the metamorphosis of the encomienda, which achieved lasting notoriety for its shocking wastage of labor, into a kind of benevolent paternalism is one of the most curious phenomena of colonial history."[8]

The elaborate racial structure that the Spaniards developed in the first decades of colonial rule, the sistema de castas, was likewise an instrument of social control, as numerous studies make clear. On the one hand, as

Patrick J. Carroll in his study of the Afro-Mexican population of colonial Veracruz points out, racism/ethnocentrism was a willful division of "non-white and non-Hispanic peoples from one another, thereby inhibiting united opposition to European rule."[9] On the other hand, as Cheryl Martin stresses in her work on colonial Chihuahua, "in new communities where an individual's personal history could not be checked, physical appearance furnished a convenient means of distinguishing those presumed to be virtuous from those who clearly were not."[10] The conquerors, in other words, needed a quick if imperfect way of distinguishing themselves from the conquered, the elite from the plebe.

The uses of race and ethnicity for social control are the subject of José Cuello's chapter for this volume, "Racialized Hierarchies of Power in Colonial Mexican Society: The *Sistema de Castas* as a Form of Social Control in Saltillo." He maintains that the *casta* system was an effective instrument of social control because it was fluid and flexible. Working census and other colonial demographic records, Cuello identifies the ways in which racial categorization was tied to real-world social and economic position. In particular, he maintains that the system worked because it kept Spaniards in a distinctly superior position, severely limiting the access of the castas (mixed-bloods) to prestigious places in society. At the same time, because it worked imperfectly it allowed some people to slip through the cracks and so released tensions that might have exploded into rebellions.

Control of labor, whether of slaves or wage workers, has also received attention as a social control mechanism. In her study of plantation societies in St. Domingue and Cuba, Gwendolyn Midlo Hall points out that colonial officials themselves understood the power of religion as a means of controlling a slave population. She quotes one mid-nineteenth-century Cuban government agent on the social control aspects of catechizing slaves. The slave revolts that once had to be contained by force during the colonial period, he said, were now "completely unknown, because religious instruction is the most efficacious remedy for the inconveniences which follow from slavery."[11] R. Douglas Cope points to the role of labor relations as an instrument of social control in colonial Mexico City. "Employers bore the brunt of the day-in, day-out task of social control." Unlike in rural New Spain, where parish priests and native officials maintained control over the Indians, "poor castes and Spaniards had greater freedom from supervision and control—in the eyes of the elite, the kind of freedom that led to lasciviousness, thievery, and disorder. The only curb on their social irresponsibility was the need to earn their daily bread."[12] In the latter part of the eighteenth century the Crown itself entered the realm of social control through labor management, as Susan Deans-Smith points out. The royal tobacco factory "provided a miniature of the Bourbon project to reform and control the populace by inculcating habits of disciplined work and ordered behavior. It emphasized submission to and respect for authority."[13]

Economic aspects of social control dominate Patricia Osante's chapter for this collection, "Colonization and Control: The Case of Nuevo Santander." Focusing on the Gulf of Mexico region above Tampico and south of Texas, Osante examines how powerful regional economic forces combined with imperial strategic needs to establish one of the last of Spain's North American colonies. José de Escandón, the Spanish official chosen to carry out the occupation and development of Nuevo Santander, turned out to be a master of social control, persuading wealthy landowners to invest in his project through offers of large grants of land and municipal and military offices while coercing Indians into the labor pool through military intimidation. He also bullied yeoman Spanish families to remain in the colony by threatening to deny them land. The thousands of families he attracted to the colony did have choices, however, and they complained of Escandón's behavior to royal authorities, who forced him to meet his obligations.

Patriarchy as an instrument of social control is the subject of chapter eleven, James A. Sandos's contribution to this volume. In "Social Control within Missionary Frontier Society: Alta California, 1769–1821," he contrasts the successful resistance of an elite woman—a governor's wife—to patriarchal order with an Indian woman's successful negotiation of a place in Spanish society in order to escape the greater oppression of mission Indian status. The first of the two cases sheds light precisely on the increasing tension between Church and State over the moral norms of society, while the second case explains how an Indian's acceptance of Spanish patriarchal and religious norms might be seen as a case of "adaptive ingratiation" rather than defeat.

The paternalism of the Spanish monarchy was simply a reflection of the Christian Mediterranean civilization from which it sprang. It was a dynamic process, however. While the Spanish Hapsburgs relied on the Catholic Church to instill the values of respect and loyalty for the monarch as "father" of his racially and ethnically diverse "family," the Bourbons inherited a mature colonial system, in which the Church's role in establishing social control had diminished. Rather, the Church could be treated as one among various agencies of control at the disposal of a more activist monarchy. This transformation in philosophy is clear, according to Ramón Gutiérrez in his study of New Mexican society, in the actions that Charles III took to restrict the powers of the Church over civil society, while reinforcing popular respect for the king. "The terrestrial community increasingly was no longer viewed as a mere reflection of the celestial order. Rather, the patriarchal household became the natural and analogical symbol of good government. As a father exercised his authority and domination within the household over wife, children, servants, and retainers, so the king viewed the state as his private domain."[14]

The present collection of essays attempts to survey the multiple ways in which social control can be used to study the Spanish experience in North America. To Anglo Americans, Spanish North America means the United States Southwest and, perhaps, Florida. Restricting the definition to those portions of the present-day United States that were once under even nominal Spanish rule requires an expansion of coverage to include Louisiana, and the Atlantic seaboard above what is today the state of Florida as far as the Carolinas. Yet this definition remained too constrictive to the three of us who devised the project between 1999 and 2001, Ross Frank, David Weber, and Jesús (Frank) de la Teja. We agreed that the political boundary created by the Treaty of Guadalupe Hidalgo in 1848 artificially divided what was very much a single cultural unit. Consequently, the geographic scope of this collection encompasses northern Mexico as well as the southwestern and southern United States. The question that surfaced as an organizing principle for such a disparate assemblage was, how did Spain manage to maintain control over it?

The answers from the various scholars we asked to contribute to the collection are as diverse as the geographic and cultural landscapes they traverse. As discussed above, some essays place the question of social control on the policy-making or imperial level while others look at how local colonial society functioned—or dysfunctioned in the eyes of imperial officials—or how individuals negotiated their place within the colonial system. Some of our scholars look at the question of social control from the outside in, focusing on how native peoples responded to Spanish efforts at controlling their lives and transforming their societies or on the ways in which Spanish authorities attempted to exercise control over non-Hispanic populations.

Every author has abandoned some of the older, sometimes hackneyed descriptions of Spanish North America. The complex ways in which different racial and ethnic groups combined, the ability of Indian peoples to negotiate their relationships with Spaniards, the flexibility and adaptability of policy makers and institutions, all work against stereotypical portrayals of the empire. The "Black Legend" is revealed a myth; the "monolithic empire" becomes an assemblage of distinct cultural and economic regions; Spanish America as a "zone of inclusion" is transformed into a zone of cultural interactions ranging from complete acceptance to total rejection of European norms. Through the prism of social control, Spain's frontier in North America becomes a vibrant, complex world of negotiated social roles and diverse cultural identities.

NOTES

1. John A. Mayer, "Notes towards a Working Definition of Social Control in Historical Analysis," in *Social Control and the State*, ed. Stanley Cohen and Andrew Scull, 22 (New York: St. Martin's Press, 1983).

2. William H. Beezley, Cheryl English Martin, and William E. French, eds., *Rituals of Rule, Rituals of Resistance: Public Celebrations and Popular Culture in Mexico*, xiii (Wilmington, Del.: Scholarly Resources, 1994).

3. The following discussion of social control as a concept is based on Joseph Roucek, *Social Control*, 2nd ed. (repr., Westport, Conn.: Greenwood Press, 1970), 3–14. See also David and Julia Jary, "Social Control," in *The HarperCollins Dictionary of Sociology*, 449 (New York: Harper-Collins, 1991).

4. Kimball Young, *Sociology* (Cincinnati: American Book Company, 1942), as quoted in Roucek, *Social Control*, 7.

5. Fernando Cervantes, *The Devil in the New World: The Impact of Diabolism in New Spain* (New Haven, Conn.: Yale University Press, 1994), 98.

6. Miguel León-Portilla, ed., *The Broken Spears: The Aztec Account of the Conquest of Mexico* (rev. ed.; Boston: Beacon Press, 1992), 157.

7. Herbert E. Bolton, "The Mission as a Frontier Institution in the Spanish American Colonies," in *Bolton and the Spanish Borderlands*, ed. John Francis Bannon, 190 (Norman: University of Oklahoma Press, 1964).

8. Leslie Byrd Simpson, *The Encomienda in New Spain: The Beginnings of Spanish Mexico*, rev. ed. (repr., Berkeley: University of California Press, 1982), xiii.

9. Patrick J. Carroll, *Blacks in Colonial Veracruz: Race, Ethnicity, and Regional Development* (2nd ed.; Austin: University of Texas Press, 2001), 86.

10. Cheryl English Martin, *Governance and Society in Colonial Mexico: Chihuahua in the Eighteenth Century* (Stanford: Stanford University Press, 1996), 126.

11. Gwendolyn Midlo Hall, *Social Control in Slave Plantation Societies: A Comparison of St. Domingue and Cuba* (repr., Baton Rouge: Louisiana State University Press, 1996), 45.

12. R. Douglas Cope, *The Limits of Racial Domination: Plebeian Society in Colonial Mexico City, 1660–1720* (Madison: University of Wisconsin Press, 1994), 94.

13. Susan Deans-Smith, "The Working Poor and the Eighteenth-Century Colonial State: Gender, Public Order, and Work Discipline," in *Rituals of Rule, Rituals of Resistance: Public Celebrations and Popular Culture in Mexico*, ed. William H. Beezley, Cheryl English Martin, and William E. French, 50 (Wilmington, Del.: Scholarly Resources, 1994).

14. Ramón A. Gutiérrez, *When Jesus Came, the Corn Mothers Went Away: Marriage, Sexuality, and Power in New Mexico, 1500–1846* (Stanford: Stanford University Press, 1991), 317.

CHAPTER ONE

Who Controls the King?

ALFREDO JIMÉNEZ

From the earliest days of the Spanish conquest of the Americas, the Crown attempted to exercise direct control over its new dominions. All political, social, and even religious relationships were constructed around the premise that the kings of Spain had absolute power in the New World. Just how did the Crown achieve control over its empire, particularly that remote and peripheral region of North America known as the Spanish borderlands? Is it possible that colonials employed social, political, and economic mechanisms to gain as much control over the Crown as the Crown had over them? In this chapter, I will employ the analytical tools provided by cultural anthropology and social control theory to advance some answers. My final objective will be to explore how Spaniards succeeded in controlling the Crown. An analysis of who controlled the king, and how they did so, adds a new dimension to the typical top-down perspective of social control research.

This study focuses on New Spain's northern frontier and is based on the following assumptions. First of all, I argue that the northern provinces of New Spain fit within a larger system—the Spanish overseas empire. Therefore, most of what can be said about the frontier can be applied to any other major area within the empire, and vice versa. For this same reason, the Spanish North shared in the prevalent Spanish culture of the time. Second, I understand the so-called "Spanish enterprise in America" as a joint venture of Crown and Church. This collaboration—unique in the history of modern empires—was both a consequence and a manifestation of a value system sincerely shared by everyone, starting with the king and extending downward to the least of his subjects. Cultural values influenced all aspects of behavior, from ordinary actions in daily life to significant decisions, including those related to achieving an afterlife in heaven. Finally, the close relationship between Church and State engendered a permanent source of conflict that affected social control.

Social Control and Spanish Colonial Society

Sociology and social anthropology gave birth to social control theory. Its empirical basis has been the result of field work conducted on complex, modern societies or on simple ones, which are sometimes labeled "primitive." In other words, social control studies have either focused on western societies or on "exotic," faraway peoples or groups. Hispanic American society—and the Spanish North for that matter—is complex but not "exotic" because it conforms to the western tradition, and is "far away" only in terms of time. Yet, the analysis of this and of any other historical phenomena from the perspective of sociology or anthropology calls for more than extensive archival research. Among other things, it is necessary to adapt social science theories to the historical past and be familiar with the cultural background of the society in question. The second requirement consists of what anthropologists call *ethnography*, the knowledge and description of a cultural system. Only with sufficient ethnographic background can one understand essential aspects of a culture no longer like one's own because the passage of time has removed the scholar, or the lay reader, from the context of his subject matter. The importance of ethnographic knowledge holds truer for historians and anthropologists of different cultural traditions studying the pasts of others—for example, those within the Anglo-Saxon, Protestant tradition of England studying people of the Hispanic, Catholic tradition.

Until the very end of the colonial period, Spanish America was a preindustrial society not organized into social classes—as classes are understood today—but made up of two major groups (the elite and the common people), plus a number of marginal groups. Race, ethnicity, language, and religious beliefs added to the complexity of Hispanic American society. The elite attempted to obtain royal favor by behaving properly, or in ways approved of by the Crown and Spanish society in general. The Crown, in turn, encouraged

and defended the social order by ideological means rather than by the traditional use of force or the threat of force. The Crown also encouraged its
subjects to send information directly to the king, confirming the aphorism
that information is power. As discussed below, the passage of time combined
with geographic distance served the Crown as an amazingly effective mechanism for the achievement of its own goals. Apart from the revolts of poorly
integrated native groups and attacks by frontier nomads, serious conflicts and
deviations from established norms came generally from the elite, or members of the privileged social group, which exercised power delegated to them
by the king. When *criollo* members of Spain's colonial military and intellectual elite (many of whom were educated in Europe and/or were influenced
by the Enlightenment), deviated from traditional beliefs and values, the colonial system collapsed. Indeed, it was the criollo elite that headed the movements that led to the emancipation of Spain's American colonies. But before
these movements took shape, Spanish America experienced a long history of
social stability, and of elite loyalty to the Crown.

The Spanish Empire

It was not easy to build and maintain the Spanish overseas empire. The settling of a continent and its administration demanded both a unique and
flexible complex political system. The system also had to be dynamic and
capable of taking into consideration the varied conditions and the changing circumstances present in Europe and in the Americas during the more
than three centuries of colonial rule. Without engaging in value judgments
of any kind, it can be substantiated that the Spanish colonial enterprise
reached an unprecedented scale. In the words of J. H. Elliott, "no European society until this moment had been faced with an administrative task
of such magnitude and complexity." In order to establish its American
empire, "Spain had to export people—people to convert the Indians to
Christianity, to found cities, and to settle the land. But these new territories, once conquered and settled, had also to be governed."[1]

The American territories were divided into political-administrative
units, from viceroyalties to Spanish cities, towns, and Indian villages.
Although viceroys did not hold their positions for life, they served as overseas proxies for the king. For more than two centuries there were only two
viceroyalties, New Spain (1535–1821), with its capital in Mexico City, and
Peru with its capital in Lima.[2]

The viceroyalties were divided into judicial-administrative units called *audiencias*. The audiencia functioned as a high-ranking unit of Spanish bureaucracy, administering justice through judges, or *oidores*. A president headed each audiencia, exercised governmental responsibilities, and also met with oidores to deal with matters of political administration. In this way, the audiencia filled the dual role of political organism and high court of justice, and this duality conformed to the prevalent belief that above all else, Spanish royal officials had the obligation of administering the king's justice.

Gobernaciones (kingdoms or provinces) functioned as another level of territorial and administrative unit. The viceroy of New Spain was the president of the Audiencia of Mexico, while the president of the Audiencia of Guadalajara was also the governor of the Kingdom of Nueva Galicia, one among several kingdoms on the northern frontier of New Spain. *Corregimientos* and *alcaldías mayores* were minor territorial divisions. *Corregidores* and *alcaldes mayores* functioned as political and judicial authorities in cities that were not the seat of an audiencia or gobernación. These officials held jurisdiction over extensive territory, which included numbers of Indian villages. The *cabildo* or *ayuntamiento* (municipal council), each with a number of *regidores*, or councilors, functioned as political authorities in cities and towns. Regidores elected *alcaldes ordinarios*, or magistrates, in ways that would seem rather democratic for the time.

The Crown acted in the New World through the *Real y Supremo Consejo de Indias* (Supreme Royal Council of the Indies), which answered only to the king. The Council of the Indies exercised from Madrid full responsibility over matters of governance, justice, economics, and Church-State relations, and even decided religious and moral questions.[3] Through the council, despite the vast distance separating the New World from the Old, the Crown made its presence felt in the most remote corners of the empire. It was the Council of the Indies that received and answered the myriad correspondence from the Americas. Yet, the king remained ever present in the minds of his subjects, and people believed that he answered their requests and complaints personally. Elites felt close to the king, and consistently addressed petitions, letters, and *relaciones* (narratives of important events) to him personally. Letters from the elites appeared in their wording as a dialogue, or conversation, with His Majesty. Some letters contained paragraphs of congratulation or of condolence related to birth, sickness, or death within the royal family.[4] Rarely, however, did secretaries take correspondence from the Americas to the king for consideration.

Besides the king, the other effective power in Spanish America was the Church, which worked in parallel, and sometimes above, the Crown. Since the discovery of the New World, the Crown justified its right to rule by highlighting Spain's moral obligation to evangelize and educate the Indians. This was the substance of the early agreement between the Pope and the Spanish Crown. Although the Church saw to the indoctrination and acculturation of the indigenous population, the Crown assisted by contributing money, providing military protection for missionaries, and approving legislation promoted by the clergy on behalf of the Indians. As the settling of new territories continued, the Church created its own organization of governance. For example, the territory covered by the first two gobernaciones in northern New Spain (Nueva Galicia and Nueva Vizcaya) virtually overlapped with the bishoprics of Guadalajara and Durango. Territorial expansion into the frontier during the colonial period led to the establishment of new gobernaciones and, to a lesser extent, other bishoprics. New Mexico, for instance, although established in 1598, belonged to the Diocese of Durango until the mid-nineteenth century.[5]

The close and intense relationship between Crown and Church made it at times difficult to discern a division between secular and religious authority. By virtue of the *Patronato Real*, the Spanish king served as head of the American Church, and therefore exercised authority delegated to him by the Pope (presenting, for example, candidates for ecclesiastical positions). The Church, in turn, participated in matters that extended beyond the evangelization of the Indians, as well as in temporal issues that involved royal officials or civilians. An example of the singular relationship between the political and ecclesiastic power is that some bishops served as interim governors or viceroys, sometimes functioning in these positions for years.

Church and Crown consistently came into conflict, however, principally over indigenous policy and the abuse of Indians by royal officials, ecclesiastics, and civilians. Conflicts over the right to hold jurisdiction over cases related to legal and moral infractions were also frequent. Often, it was only the authority of the monarch that could reestablish peace and order. The power to appoint, transfer, and dismiss viceroys, audiencia members, provincial governors, bishops, and other secular and religious officials at any time, before conflicts reached unmanageable proportions, served to back up the king's moral authority.

The great deal of detailed correspondence that the Crown received from the American provinces allowed royal officials in Madrid to overcome the wide limits of geography and to retain a high degree of control. In allowing his subjects to write directly to him, the king also made himself fundamentally responsible for the maintenance of order in the American dominions. The Council of the Indies often answered complaints and demands with requests for more information, and this meant delays and the continuous movement of paperwork across the Atlantic. In short, the system rested on an intricate combination of royal authority, power and responsibility, mutual rights and obligations, doggish loyalty and fervent obedience to the king, confidence in God and the throne, and the freedom to demand, complain, and defend oneself. After having attempted to resolve disputes in a number of ways, subjects generally had no other recourse but to wait patiently for the king's verdict, and to hope for a favorable, magnanimous decision.

So far I have commented only on the social structure and political and ecclesiastic organization of the Spanish-American empire. Something should now be said about the culture and the system of values that characterized the ruling apparatus of the Crown and Church and that structured social relations in the colonial world. I will begin by highlighting an obvious point: For Spaniards, religion constituted much more than a body of beliefs, and its influence extended far beyond the domain of the individual. Religious beliefs and values shaped a way of life both in Spain and in Spanish America. The term "value" can be defined as that which is conceived of as desirable and that which provides criteria for decision making.[6] Values are ranked along a hierarchical scale of options, and these priorities help guide decision making during critical moments. Values also function as a constant guide for proper behavior and are the most significant and defining elements of any culture.

The Spanish value system was primarily based on the belief in an almighty, righteous, and merciful God, and a life after death. Religion affected all aspects and events of social life including, but not limited to, appropriate business dealings, correct political behavior, family life, and sexual behavior. Honor, probably the paramount value of traditional Spanish culture, was essentially a virtue.[7] The fidelity of wives, the virginity of daughters, the respect of sons, and the courage and loyalty of men guided individual and group conduct and reflected one's honor. Any violation of proper conduct constituted more than a breach against cultural values, it represented a sin against God. Needless to say, many people occasionally or consistently violated the rules of behavior prescribed by Spanish culture, but transgressors could not claim ignorance of the rules. A difference existed between ideal and actual behavior—as in any human society—but Spaniards firmly shared and accepted the dominant values of the time.

New Spain's Northern Frontier

Composed of a number of generally arid regions, the northern provinces of New Spain had a widely dispersed native population. Colonization brought into the area Spaniards from other American regions, immigrants from the Iberian Peninsula and the Canary Islands, civilized Indians from central Mexico, and black slaves. Miscegenation helped to rapidly produce a racially complex frontier society. Censuses referred to European Spaniards (*españoles europeos*), American-born Spaniards (*españoles americanos* or *criollos*), *mestizos* (persons of Spanish-Indian parentage), *negros* (persons of pure African descent), *mulatos* (persons of Spanish-black parentage), and other mixed racial groups generally known as *castas*.

Frontier authorities communicated constantly with the Mexican and Spanish metropolises, although distance, geographic obstacles, and a chronic state of Indian warfare delayed correspondence. Remoteness and marginality favored, rather than hindered, a policy of effective control, however. Indeed, the Crown had a strong interest in the northern frontier because of its silver mines and because of its borders with Spain's rival powers.[8] The Great Spanish North—as defined above—fell at one time or another under the gobernaciones of Nueva Galicia, Nueva Vizcaya, Sinaloa and Sonora, Baja California, Alta California, Nuevo México, Coahuila, Texas, Nuevo León, and Nuevo Santander. With the exception of the northeastern provinces, assigned to the Audiencia of Mexico, this huge territory depended on the Audiencia of Guadalajara from the jurisdiction's creation in 1548 until Mexican Independence. In the late eighteenth century the threat of attack by hostile Indians and rival powers brought about the establishment of a special jurisdiction—the Commandancy General of the Interior Provinces. This political innovation placed the North directly under the Crown's control.[9]

The establishment of towns and cities was an early and permanent goal that conformed to one of the highest principles of Spanish policy, the settling of the land. Given the large areas of virtually empty land characteristic of the northern provinces, the countryside dominated over the few and scattered towns in the region.[10] The social structure of the frontier basically mirrored that of other regions within Spanish America. The elite was composed of members of the audiencia, governors of kingdoms or provinces, high-ranking military officials, bishops, and the heads of provincial religious orders, such as the Franciscans and Jesuits. Below these high-ranking secular and religious authorities came lesser royal officials who saw to the Crown's economic interests or served in minor bureaucratic posts. If Crown and Church occupied different corners of an inverted sociopolitical triangle, the lower corner belonged to cabildos or ayuntamientos. These were presided over by elected alcaldes ordinarios and consisted of a number of regidores who came from the pool of *vecinos*, or household heads, within a town or city. Besides the bureaucratic and religious elite, Spanish frontier society was composed of a few "*hombres ricos y poderosos*" (rich and powerful men), some *médicos*, or physicians, *escribanos*, or scribes, other educated professionals, owners of haciendas, merchants and artisans, and farmers, ranchers, and laborers who worked in *el campo* or countryside, or in the urban milieu. From the imperial perspective mining was the most important economic activity, followed next by ranching and agriculture. Hombres ricos acquired power through their ownership of both mines and large estates.[11]

As a frontier, Spanish society in northern New Spain contained a number of distinctive features. The captains of the many *presidios*, or forts, that served as the line of defense against hostile Indians became typical figures on the frontier, as did the *presidiales*, or soldiers, who manned the forts. Indians were supposed to live in pueblos in order to facilitate their christianization and the collection of tribute, and to provide labor for Spaniards. New Spain's northern provinces also served as a home for communities of hispanicized Indians like the Tlaxcaltecans, descendants of the Indians who helped Hernán Cortés in his war against the Aztecs. The Crown brought Tlaxcaltecans and other native groups from central Mexico into the frontier as colonizers and to serve as models of civilized life for the "*indios bárbaros*."

The Crown could hardly apply its general Indian policy on the frontier, where cultural differences were so great that the social integration of the natives proved to be virtually impossible. It was a matter of levels of social complexity, or the stark difference between an advanced, expanding society and tribes of nomads, or small-scale agriculturalists. In many areas of the frontier, the situation lasted for centuries, and was refueled by the late-colonial intrusions of Apaches and Comanches. Even Indian groups that had been living for generations under the Spanish colonial system sometimes rebelled, as the Tepehuanes did in 1616, and as the

Tarahumaras did at mid-century. The Pueblo Revolt of 1680 forced Spaniards to abandon New Mexico for a decade. Revolts often took the form of nativistic, millenarian movements, which, consequently, cannot be defined as social deviance, but rather as clashes of cultures. These Indian rebels were acting from outside the system; they either had not been integrated into Spanish society or had maintained their traditional beliefs hidden from the eyes of religious and secular authorities. Spanish officials had to subject the native population to *military control* before they could subject them to *social control*.

Social life on the frontier conformed to the basic features of Spanish-American society. Yet, danger, isolation, hopelessness, and poverty reached the extreme levels commonly associated with frontier life elsewhere. Complaints and denunciations arose from secular officials, members of the Church, and vecinos, addressed to the Council of the Indies, the organization that represented the king for American subjects.

Social Control on New Spain's Northern Frontier

The story of Spanish political deviance on the North American continent began with Hernán Cortés and his conquest of Mexico. Cortés had studied at the University of Salamanca and used his astute intelligence and knowledge of Spanish law to evade the authority of Governor Diego Velázquez of Cuba, whose orders he disobeyed when he departed for Mexico. By founding Veracruz on the Mexican shore, Cortés transformed himself from an insubordinate soldier into the founder of a new town. This maneuver allowed Cortés to evade the strict royal policy on exploration and conquest, while allowing him to continue declaring his loyalty to the king. In 1520 (when the Aztecs had not yet been defeated), he wrote a letter to Charles V, stating that "one might call oneself the emperor of this kingdom with no less glory than of Germany." Cortés alluded to the young king's position as heir of the Holy Roman Empire.[12]

The earliest Spanish conqueror in the Mexican north was Nuño Beltrán de Guzmán, the great enemy of Cortés and founder of Nueva Galicia—a man known for his extreme cruelty against the Indians. Despite having gained the office of president of the audiencia, his American adventure ended with his arrest and deportation back to Spain for crimes against the native peoples. Francisco Vázquez de Coronado (1540–1542), and Juan de Oñate (1598–1609) made well-known and well-studied expeditions into the present-day United States. Both men suffered long inquiries and each received some punishment for mistreatment of the Indians.[13]

Aside from the best known cases, during the sixteenth century the far Spanish North saw two serious cases of disobedience that ended tragically. In 1590, Gaspar Castaño de Sosa, lieutenant governor of Nuevo León, marched into New Mexico with several hundred men, women, and children, but without royal authorization. His three years in the Río Grande area began when he deserted his post in Nuevo León, leaving the Crown no other choice but to punish this act of insubordination. The viceroy ordered Castaño de Sosa's apprehension, and he was found guilty and exiled for a period of six years to the Philippine Islands, the most remote region in the Spanish empire. Francisco Leyva de Bonilla's *entrada* into the area beyond the Río Grande in 1593 was also illegal and also ended badly. Desertion immediately placed Bonilla outside the law, but, unlike Castaño de Sosa, the Crown never received an opportunity to punish him. Bonilla's companion, Gutiérrez de Humaña, murdered him, and shortly after died at the hands of a group of Plains Indians.

Most cases of deviant political behavior were not as dramatic as those mentioned above, and those involved were not adventurers, but people fully integrated into the system. These are the cases that really count because they reflect aspects of everyday life on the northern frontier. The men involved were neither heroes nor villains, but people moved to act by common human drives. Indeed, most challenges to royal control and established social order came from secular and religious authorities; that is, from within the power apparatus. Common vecinos appear to have been more respectful of social order, or they had not the need or the opportunity to challenge the colonial system directly. In any case, their infractions or rebellious outbursts usually had less to do with politics than with a desire to satisfy basic needs. In 1785, Juan Velázquez, the interim governor of Nueva Vizcaya, wrote to the Minister of the Indies, José de Gálvez, explaining how Durango was threatened by the famine that had been raging throughout the province, and how in the mining district of Cuencamé there was a sort of popular uprising. He wrote: "The mining camp of Cuencamé is in revolt, and its women have mounted a protest against the *alcalde mayor*. Before the men who incite them join in . . . I have dispatched General José Ximénez Caro, with the people we have been able to muster and with only twelve lances, which are the only weapons it has been possible to acquire for such a difficult situation." A week later, the governor wrote again: "From the reports that Captain don José Ximénez Caro has sent me, I am relieved of the worry that the insurrection at Cuencamé camp caused me ... which had its origin, not in a lack of loyalty to the king, but in the extreme hunger occasioned by the delay in acquiring corn. And, as I had the good fortune to learn my lessons in our great school, Spain in the year 1767, all my actions have succeeded and all is calm."[14]

Popular uprisings were infrequent affairs that rarely challenged the established order. The elite, however, protested so much and made so many subtle threats to the Crown that from an outsider's perspective the colonial system might appear barely functional. Yet, archival records testify to the imperial system's capacity for survival, despite the endemic conflict and general dissatisfaction that characterized colonial society. I hold that conflict acted in a positive way in Hispanic America and that, on the frontier in particular, feelings of hope and confidence in achieving eventual success through the king's beneficence moderated the impact of horizontal and vertical confrontations among contending parties. Although the colonial system displayed many weaknesses, the possibility of triumphing in a legal dispute maintained a vital tension that kept the system functional.[15]

Although the king represented the best hope for justice on earth, desirable outcomes could not be achieved without the help of Divine Providence. Indeed, success or failure depended on one's relationship with the Divine, and heavenly assistance could be denied in case of wrongdoing. Writing about the calamitous situation in the far north during the years of Juan de Oñate, lieutenant governor of New Mexico Sosa Peñalosa wrote: "to whom can one impute guilt but to our own sins?" Spaniards of that time typically explained failure as divine punishment, reflecting the fatalistic character of Hispanic culture.[16] In 1788, Bishop of Durango Esteban Lorenzo spoke of "the plague, famine, and war that for three continuous years these provinces have suffered. ... The mortality was general, taking with it more than half the clerics and religious of my diocese. This blow from the just hand of God for our sins reached visibly and most rigorously to my venerable chapter and all its prebendaries."[17] A very common argument used to pressure the king was to warn him that "*la tierra*" (the land from which, or about which, the author was writing) was in danger because of a lack of military protection or some other kind of royal assistance. Consequently, the land would have to be abandoned, adversely affecting not only revenues of the royal treasury, but also the Christian faith of the Indians. This typical threat combined economic arguments with religious ones in an attempt to reinforce action; sincerely and sagaciously, petitioners played on the king's conscience and stirred feelings of guilt.

The king knew, however, that there were limits to his moral authority, which made necessary the use of instruments of social control other than those based on pure ideology. Time generally worked in favor of the Crown. While waiting for a decision from Madrid, drastic action on the part of litigants rarely occurred because creating disruption was not advisable while awaiting a verdict. During the wait, hostilities could cool, litigants could be transferred or dismissed, or one of the parties could die. The king and Council of the Indies also used positive sanctions to defuse tension or to reinforce loyalty, and these strategies included sending members of the elite words of appreciation, and promoting Crown officials to other posts. In some cases, successful viceroys of New Spain were promoted to the rich viceroyalty of Peru. Lower-level officials in the northern provinces also frequently asked the king for a transfer to Mexico City in order to escape the harsh climate and the many inconveniences of frontier life. Other possible royal favors included: creating new bishoprics; founding churches, convents, hospitals, and colleges; building a cathedral; sending more missionaries from Spain and settlers from the Peninsula or the Canary Islands; establishing more presidios; and raising the salaries of bureaucrats and military personnel. To receive any of these favors corporations and/or individuals needed to be on good terms with the king.

Royal officials tried to fatten their *curriculum vitae* by the accumulation of merits for services to the Crown. The king had a long memory and for this reason, individuals and corporations needed to avoid creating stains on their records. Conquerors, public servants, and vecinos were routinely promoted, and in due time included a *probanza de méritos y servicios* (record of merits and services) based on testimony given by witnesses during court proceedings. Every witness had to respond to a list of questions related to the life of the petitioner, and the testimony of the people acquainted with the petitioner served to prove the person's merit and to substantiate his services to the Crown. Obviously, a person with a known history of deviant behavior would not promote a probanza as a basis for royal favors. The eventual need of a probanza served as a permanent incentive for people to conform to societal codes of proper behavior. In 1636 treasurer Ambrosio Espinosa de Porres wrote to the king to inform him about various economic matters, especially those related to silver mining. At the end of the letter he included a personal request based on his merits: secretary of accounts at the principal castle of Perpignan; paymaster of Flanders fleet of 1602; inspector and superintendent of the Cuenca mint; administrator of records of the council of state of the Count of Villalonga; accountant of the royal treasury of the island of Margarita in 1613, treasurer of the royal treasury of Guatemala in 1620; and, lately, commissary and inspector of Nueva Vizcaya.[18] In his request to the Crown on behalf of his own personal interests, Governor of Nueva Vizcaya Luis de Valdés also mentioned to His Majesty his thirty-eight years of service in Spain, Africa, Flanders, on the Island of San Martín, and in Nueva Vizcaya.[19]

A more prosaic and direct, and by no means less effective, mechanism of control was the application of royal justice by one of the various colonial courts. Judicial records quite often refer to deviant behavior as crimes against God, and to the subsequent punishment as heavenly justice. However, most transgressions were perceived as offenses against both majesties, God and the king. It is the inseparable connection between religion and government that produced a peculiar binomial of deviance and punishment. Typical punishments included fines, incarceration, and flogging. Governor of Nueva Vizcaya José Carlos Agüero (1767–1768), came into conflict with Bishop Pedro Tamarón y Romeral (1758–1768) over various matters, one of them the application of corporal punishment. The bishop complained to the king about a man who had been in jail, where he stabbed another inmate, and while he was under bond (*caución juratoria*) took refuge in the church. After having the man pulled from the church, the governor ordered him punished with two hundred lashes.[20] Agüero, in an attempt to justify this harsh measure, told the king about the deplorable state in which he found the province at his arrival. "The greatest disorder, the most rooted custom and more public vice was thievery. With such abandon and little fear of God and Your Majesty's royal justice, that neither the churches, nor the houses, nor the haciendas, nor even the roads and streets were exempt from their effronteries, from which resulted some killings, rapes, drunkenness, fires, and other transgressions and the gravest offenses to His Divine Majesty. All of this is the result of that abominable crime, which is rooted in these people." In consequence, the governor had ordered "that anyone caught stealing would be branded on the shoulder with the word 'DURANGO' after being flogged, asking the king that this punishment of flogging and branding remain the exclusive law of this land."[21]

Transfer to less convenient places, demotion, and dismissal were penalties applied to both civilian and military personnel. Some high-ranking military officers paid visits to, and administered justice in, the long line of presidios that peppered the frontier. Bishops also corrected the behavior of priests and missionaries during their mandatory *visitas* (general visitations) of their dioceses. Military inspectors and bishops dealt with matters other than those purely political or religious in nature, and included in their diaries denunciations, recommendations, and critical comments of various kinds. Of course, it was in the field of morality—where no clear line separated the secular from the profane—that deviant behavior and appropriate measures of social control concerned both military and religious inspectors.[22] The *juicio de residencia*, the judicial review of all government officials from the viceroy down to lower-level functionaries, also served as an instrument of social control routinely used by the Spanish administration. The Crown prohibited people under review from abandoning their place of residence until the *juez de residencia* had completed a trial that usually took several months. The process was part public and part secret. Some witnesses were summoned, but an announcement publicized in advance invited anyone, including Indians, to come forward to testify. Although an imperfect instrument of social control, the residencia played a dual role in prevention and punishment. The anticipated fear of royal justice at the end of one's term, and the knowledge that everyone had the opportunity to testify during a residencia, made officials less inclined to commit egregious infractions and made the residencia an instrument of *backward social control*.[23]

The Church had its own specific mechanisms of control, which contributed directly or indirectly to the maintenance of social order. The sacrament of penance not only served as a form of psychological relief for the faithful, it also functioned as an important instrument of control. While capital sins, such as adultery or murder, involved the threat of eternal damnation, confession and repentance restored peace of mind and encouraged good behavior in the future. Sermons, novenas, and many other kinds of religious rituals not only helped to break the monotony of social life on the frontier, but also served as instruments that fostered social control. The Church's most decisive tool, however, was excommunication, or the cutting off of membership from the body of the Church. Bishops dictated these sentences publicly, and excommunicated individuals who could not appeal to secular authorities. The reasons why bishops utilized this punishment were generally diverse and complicated, and often derived from interpersonal conflicts and the clash of impetuous personalities. Nevertheless, the mere threat of excommunication served to curtail improper conduct, as many wished to avoid public dishonor and disgrace before the king. Again, we find here the component of time playing a decisive role in social control policies. Judicial support from the audiencia, the viceroy, or the king in cases of excommunication took much time to acquire, and did not guarantee that the bishop would change his mind. Meanwhile, the excommunicated person could not attend church or partake of any sacraments, and was thus held up to public scorn.

In the mid-seventeenth century, Bishop Diego de Quintanilla Hevia y Valdés and Governor Diego Guajardo Fajardo of Nueva Vizcaya engaged in a heated confrontation that also involved several groups and individuals. Franciscan friars took the side of the governor, while secular priests supported their bishop. The conflict centered on jurisdictional issues, a consequence of the close relationship between Crown and Church and the blurred line that separated secular and religious authorities. The dispute between the top authorities affected social order and threw into question the Crown's principles on social control. Guajardo Fajardo wrote persistently to the king with evidence and arguments to defend his position. The bishop took a more moderate approach in his letters, but he also kept the Council of the Indies informed of his own point of view and arguments. As the dispute progressed priests and friars participated in violent street encounters, and a priest stabbed an *alguacil* (sheriff). When two black men took refuge in the church after killing an Indian, the issue of immunity within holy sanctuaries became another component in the jurisdictional confrontation. Spanish vecinos were also affected by the general climate of disorder and complained to the king.[24]

The single most dramatic action taken during the conflict was the excommunication of the governor, who wrote to the audiencia, the viceroy, and the king, but to little avail. A careful, in-depth analysis of the conflict, using an *emic* approach, might help us understand why the governor and the bishop behaved the way they did, and eventually discover that both men were right from their own points of view.[25] The Council of the Indies expressed its displeasure with the situation and ordered that rancor (*enojos*) should not be mixed into the process. The council also ordered the viceroy and the Audiencia of Mexico to settle the question of jurisdiction. These higher authorities were also committed to reuniting the region's two *cabezas*, or leaders. The Council of the Indies jotted down the aforementioned rulings in three letters the governor sent to Madrid in September and October of 1649. As evidenced by the notes written upon these letters, the council did not make its decision until April 16, 1651. It may be argued that the affair between the governor and the bishop was more than a social conflict—though it certainly was such a conflict. It is also possible to speak, however, of "hostile attitudes or sentiments," defined by Lewis Coser as "predispositions to engage in conflict behavior."[26] In the history of the Spanish North as a whole, this was but one of many conflicts that affected social order for a time but failed to undermine the system.

To leave out the Inquisition, even in an introductory chapter, might seem to omit one of the strongest coercive institutions in Spanish society. There is no other aspect of Spanish history as negatively, or as strongly, imprinted on the popular mind as the Inquisition. However, the Inquisition was not a Spanish invention, and it operated in European countries centuries before the discovery of the New World. The institution's objective was to combat heresy, as well as such activities as witchcraft and sorcery, and inquisitors worked under the assumption that offenders were enemies of society. In comparative terms, however, the Inquisition mattered less in the New World than in the Old, and was even less important on the frontier.[27] Controls exercised over migration impeded the passage of Jews and Protestants to the New World, while the natives were not subjected to the tribunals of Inquisition on the basis that they were either pagans or newly converted to Christianity. Consequently, witchcraft and other non-Catholic practices by baptized Indians were not considered heresy but idolatry.[28] Nevertheless, the mere existence of the Inquisition engendered fear, denunciations, and dissimulations that functioned as indirect mechanisms of social control. As the prosecution of heresy declined in importance, the Inquisition in New Spain dealt more and more with minor religious offenses and with matters of sexual morality.[29]

One historical event in particular, which occurred in the late colonial period, tested the Crown's capacity to maintain control over its lands and people. In 1767 the Crown expelled the Jesuits from the continent. Although France, Portugal, and eventually the Pope also abolished the Company of Jesus, the expulsion of the Jesuits from Spanish America carried some specific local connotations. The order had become so powerful in the field of education, so economically prosperous, and so influential among sectors of the elite, that many in the government feared the Company of Jesus was becoming a state within the state. King Charles III (1759–1788) and his ministers could not tolerate what might eventually be a dramatic failure in social control, and did not hesitate to act accordingly.

Let us now move away a little bit from serious issues of social deviance. Misdemeanors and unusual modes of conduct account for the majority of cases that draw public attention or arouse scandal, but they do not seriously challenge the system, and may not require further intervention. Northern frontier society was no exception. Archival sources related to more mundane forms of deviance—not necessarily involving interpersonal conflicts—help to create a much more complete picture of frontier society.[30]

Before proceeding, however, let us suggest that societies exercise control over their members largely through the use of informal positive or negative sanctions. Informal negative sanctions were widely applied on the northern frontier, where small communities predominated, and face-to-face relationships characterized daily life. Informal sanctions such as gossip and popular accusations of cowardice, selfishness, greed, witchcraft, inappropriate sexual behavior, neglect of family members, or other behaviors not necessarily punished by judges, have traditionally been very effective in Hispanic society. Although not unlawful, actions that might cause loss of reputation were to be avoided. Similarly, the expectation of positive sanctions could encourage actions that might increase public appreciation. Parties involved in jurisdictional or other legal conflicts sometimes brought crimes, misdemeanors, or simple cases of deviant behavior to His Majesty's attention in order to reinforce their arguments and enhance their own personal achievements. This practice, incidental to the main dispute and designed to discredit the adversary, today provides a source of data and perceptions about aspects of social life and transgressions that occurred in a particular time and place, and which otherwise might have remained unknown to us.

Before Guajardo Fajardo had arrived as governor of Nueva Vizcaya, Bishop Hevia y Valdés complained to the king about government officials within the province, and lamented the uselessness of his efforts to temper "the wrath of God and remove the public and scandalous sins, as Your Majesty has ordered and as is my obligation. However, everything I do amounts to little or nothing, for I lack powers and ministers. So that in order to expel from this kingdom two women of scandalous life has cost me considerable money and drops of blood, for in these kingdoms, Sire, absolute power, without hindrances or obligations resides solely in your ministers, magistrates, and governors."[31] Just two years later Governor Guajardo Fajardo, in one of his many letters to the king about his conflict with the bishop, mentioned the public scandal of a woman who had children with a clergyman.[32] Don Francisco Cuervo y Valdés, lieutenant governor and royal inspector in the Kingdom of Nueva Vizcaya, informed the king in 1686 that Luis de Morales had been involved in the fraudulent resale of *barajas de naipes* (packs of playing cards). He added that for twelve years, Morales had been provoking a public scandal by committing incest with Josefa Gonzalez, the sister of his legitimate wife. Cuervo y Valdés ended his letter by saying, "in view of the little remedy possible for the excesses and faults of these subjects, Your Majesty may determine what action he would find most convenient for the example of others."[33]

In 1721 Bishop of Durango Pedro Tapiz painted the king a gloomy picture of the general lack of morality in Chihuahua, and how social perversion was related to the mining character of the city. "The large and diverse [racially confused] population, combined with the abundance of silver, results in their living with the most licentious liberty and little fear of God. The vices and all manner of sin reign, as is so often the case in such mining camps, as Your Majesty may be served to request that some experts on the country report to you."[34] A visita to Nuevo León brought about several charges against corregidor-elect Antonio Ladrón de Guevara. The viceroy informed the Council of the Indies about the visita, and asked whether Ladrón de Guevara should be obliged to "make a married life with his wife, in the knowledge that his rebellious nature requires that such measures be taken." The resolution of the council was that "with regard to whether or not he should be obliged to live a married life with his wife, the royal prosecutor concludes his last reply by saying that although the file does not make clear that they are living apart, it is always convenient that there being no just reason for a separation, he should not be allowed to abandon her. All of which, he adds, may be made known to His Majesty, in fulfillment of the said royal order."[35]

Some Questions and Answers

After this brief examination of social control on New Spain's northern frontier, placed in the context of the Spanish overseas empire, some questions remain. First of all, how did the Crown manage to control so much territory, and so many people, for such a long period of time? The question is all the more important because the frontier lacked a strong army or a police force worthy of the name—that is, the tools commonly used by rulers to maintain or regain internal control. How then did the State maintain social control over its subjects? How did the Crown acquire collaboration from overseas authorities in fulfilling imperial goals? How did the State convince elites and vecinos to comply with the law, and to conform to the Crown's vision of social order?

Part of the answer can be found in the continuous movement of people across the Atlantic and the consequent enrichment of colonial culture. A permanent stream nourished and refreshed the culture of overseas Spaniards, while the American provinces maintained a constant communication with Spain. Migration to the New World continued throughout the entire colonial period, and most high-ranking secular and religious officials, as well as friars destined for the missions of the North, came from Spain. This permanent influx of people helped to reinforce Spanish political and religious values in core areas, as well as on the periphery. Viceroys, governors, bishops, and missionaries served as primary agents of cultural reinforcement because they formed the upper elite of Spanish colonial society. The Crown customarily appointed *peninsulares* for high offices, even when criollos had increased in number and virtually monopolized commerce and middle- and lower-level appointments within the royal bureaucracy, church administration, and the military. Such long-term control is even more amazing in the face of tensions that existed between the Spaniards born in Spain and those born in America, because of the Crown's preference for European Spaniards at the highest ranks of colonial administration.

In any case, social control on Spain's northern frontier, and elsewhere, should be understood in the context of a dominant value system which, in turn, was deeply embedded in religious beliefs. Spaniards were sincerely loyal to their two majesties, God and king. True social movements of rebellion were rare in Spanish America, and almost did not exist among Spaniards.[36] The first generalized cries of protest in America were not for independence, but for governmental reforms: *Viva el rey y abajo el mal gobierno* (Long live the king and down with bad government). People frequently violated ideal moral principles because of human frailty and not, usually, for political reasons. Deviant social behavior did not contradict the prevalent value system. Throughout Spanish America, and the frontier in particular, circumstances favored improper behavior, disorderly conduct, and abuse of power by royal officials and ecclesiastics. Yet, individual and corporate cases of misconduct do not negate the fact that people widely respected the king's authority and accepted his power to legislate, enforce law, and administer justice. Spanish-American subjects viewed most crimes as sins against God, and believed that by going through confession, the

deity would pardon their sins. Spaniards on the frontier were not puritan-
ical like Anglo-American frontiersmen were supposed to be. Yet, they still
shared clear notions of right and wrong. Because they considered themselves to be spiritually and morally weak, they hoped endlessly for forgiveness and a chance to purge themselves of sin before their death. It was
not a matter of cynicism or hypocrisy but rather of humbleness before an
almighty, but also merciful, God.

doesn't agree w/ missions or encomienda

State and Church used various mechanisms of coercion and persuasion.
I would argue, however, that psychological attitudes favored social control
far more than the threat of any particular kind of coercion. I would stress
conviction rather than fear as the most permanent feeling working in favor
of proper social behavior. Conviction is produced by internalization, or
incorporation of cultural values, mores, and goals by the individual through
a psychological process that makes them an inseparable part of oneself.[37]
Spaniards of all kinds (peninsulares and criollos) were convinced of the legitimacy of the king and the authority of the Church. People knew that royal
officials and members of the clergy made mistakes and committed crimes.
Indeed, this happened so often that denunciations flooded into the Council
of the Indies from every corner of the empire. But the king's honesty
remained always beyond accusation. The blame always fell somewhere below
the king, who was responsible only to God. Nevertheless, it seems amazing
that the Spanish monarchy maintained its control for centuries over a diverse
population scattered across the dual continents of North and South America,
and preserved a huge frontier whose largest part was lost to the United States
only twenty-seven years after Mexican independence.

Certainly, the mammoth colonial bureaucracy—a power within the
supreme power—and the region's many ecclesiastical institutions worked
to ensure the Crown's hold on the frontier and elsewhere in the Americas.
But America also had a population fully confident in royal justice and ever
hopeful to receive a positive answer to its demands, or some kind of favor
from the Crown. People understood that, just like them, the king had a
soul that needed to be saved from eternal damnation. In fact, regardless
of who happened to be the king at the moment, it was the conception of
the monarchy itself, its charisma, which held the pieces of the empire
together and helped maintain the loyalty of Spain's subjects. An individual king at a given time did not mean much by himself to his remote
subjects. The letter, or the report, sent to the court was sometimes received
after the addressee had died weeks or months earlier, and another king was

seated on the throne. Some kings were efficient and basically honest, others were mediocre, and some of them were totally incompetent, if not immoral. No Spanish king ever visited his American empire. It was the institution, not the person, that really counted.

Given that the Crown exercised a significant degree of control over so many aspects of colonial life, I raise a final question: Who controlled the king? The question is important because, although subjects regarded the king's authority as sacred, he was as human as the least of his subjects. The existence of a countercontrol to the Crown's policies completes our picture. It is my contention that social control did not only function from the top down. Any elite person or institution, lesser vassal, or Indian, through an advocate, could write to the king with complaints, denunciations, or suggestions, in an attempt to obtain justice, have improper behavior or mistakes punished, have formal policies reviewed and reformed, and call for a halt to abuses. The voice of the empire's subjects served as an instrument that qualified the power of the king and forced the Crown to take into consideration the expectations of its subjects. Continual, although time-consuming, communication with the king, served as a safety valve, or a mechanism of balance between the absolute power of the monarch and the aspirations and anxieties of his vassals. Letters and memorials to the king never contained the least hint of disrespect or disobedience. All used arguments or formulas that complied fully with the empire's legal culture. The king could not avoid attending to this type of correspondence because if he did not do so, or if he did not ensure that the Council of the Indies did so, he risked destroying the foundation on which the imperial system rested.

Yet, what made the king vulnerable to pressures from below? How did subjects frame their demands and requests to the king? When complaining to or subtly threatening the king, people protected themselves with a short phrase of justification that appears in the thousands within this type of documentation. People customarily wrote that their intention was to "*descargar la conciencia de Vuestra Majestad*" (relieve the responsibility of Your Majesty before God). Those controlled by the Crown made it clear that they obeyed the royal will. Yet, by playing on the king's conscience, they came to control the supreme controller. While displaying concern for the king's eternal salvation—an action the monarch could not refuse, much less disapprove of—his subjects were touching upon his humanity. It is well known that Spanish kings responded to this kind of warning or threat sweetened by subjects with exaggerated words of praise and fidelity.

NOTES

1. J. H. Elliott, *Spain and Its World, 1500–1700* (New Haven, Conn.: Yale University Press, 1989), 13. For general, concise treatments of imperial Spain see C. H. Haring, *The Spanish Empire in America* (New York: Harcourt, Brace & World, 1947) and Guillermo Céspedes, *América Hispánica (1492–1898)* (Barcelona: Editorial Labor, 1983).

2. The *virreinatos* of Nueva Granada (Bogotá) and Río de la Plata (Buenos Aires) were founded in the eighteenth century. The virreinato of New Spain never was divided, and maintained jurisdiction over the Caribbean Islands and the Philippines until Mexican independence.

3. The Council of the Indies was one of several councils used by the Spanish Crown to deal with specific affairs or with certain areas of its domains in Europe. As early as 1524 the *Consejo de Indias* was created to rule the quickly growing empire in the New World.

4. Upon learning of the death of the queen in 1647, the bishop of Durango lamented to the king of "the deepest sorrow and most heartfelt grief that I have experienced in my life, because I realize that it is the greatest loss that Spain has suffered among its queens since their Catholic Majesties don Fernando and Queen Isabel." Guadalajara 63, 14 April 1647, Archivo General de Indias, Seville, Spain (hereafter cited as AGI).

5. Nueva Vizcaya was the central and most significant area in the Great Spanish North. See Oakah L. Jones, *Nueva Vizcaya: Heartland of the Spanish Frontier* (Albuquerque: University of New Mexico Press, 1988).

6. Anthropologist Clyde Kluckhohn as quoted by Paul Sites, *Control: The Basis of Social Order* (New York: Dunellen Publishing Co., 1973), 15.

7. Governor José Carlos de Agüero wrote to Carlos III in 1768 to denounce the appointment of a governor for the minor province of Tepehuana and Tarahumara, which was part of his own province of Nueva Vizcaya. Agüero requested to be heard by a *Consejo* or a *Junta de Guerra* in order to be able to defend the boundaries of his jurisdiction and his honor, which he evaluated "as a gem that I treasure as my only fortune, and which is more valuable than my life." 21 May 1768, Guadalajara 337, AGI.

8. For the organization and administration of northern New Spain see Peter Gerhard, *The North Frontier of New Spain* (Princeton: Princeton University Press, 1982). The most complete and the best interpretive synthesis is David J. Weber, *The Spanish Frontier in North America* (New Haven, Conn.: Yale University Press, 1992).

9. The most comprehensive and documented work on the subject is Luis Navarro García, *Don José de Gálvez y la Comandancia General de las Provincias Internas del norte de Nueva España* (Sevilla: Escuela de Estudios Hispano-Americanos, 1964).

10. If we take into consideration extreme points like Santa Fe in New Mexico, San Antonio in Texas, and Los Angeles and San Francisco in California, New Spain's northern frontier covered as large a territory as Western Europe. The rich mining city of Zacatecas, founded in 1548, became in time the point of departure for the Camino Real (or Royal Highway) to Santa Fe, over a thousand miles away as the crow flies. Governor Ignacio Francisco de Barrutia wrote in 1728, "This kingdom [of Nueva Vizcaya] is of so much extension as France and Spain together." Guadalajara 110, AGI.

11. A man could combine in his life various occupations (explorer, conqueror, government official, land and cattle owner, successful mining entrepreneur), which would make of him a "rich and powerful man." Ibarra and Urdiñola are family names of men who for generations formed the elite of the frontier as descendents of early leading figures. See François Chevalier, *Land and Society in Colonial Mexico: The Great Hacienda* (Berkeley: University of California Press, 1963). See also Peter J. Bakewell, *Silver Mining and Society in Colonial Mexico: Zacatecas, 1546–1700* (Cambridge: Cambridge University Press, 1971).

12. Hernán Cortés, *Letters from Mexico*, trans. and ed. A. R. Pagden (New Haven, Conn.: Yale University Press, 1986), 48.

13. On how the behavior of protagonists like Oñate has been seen and judged, then and now, see Alfredo Jiménez, "Don Juan de Oñate and the Founding of New Mexico: Possible Gains and Losses from Centennial Celebrations," *CLAHR* (*Colonial Latin American Historical Review*) 7, 2 (1998): 109–28. See also Richard Flint, *Great Cruelties Have Been Reported: The 1544 Investigation of the Coronado Expedition* (Dallas: Southern Methodist University Press, 2002).

14. Interim governor to Gálvez, April, May 1785, Guadalajara 302, AGI.

15. In his classic work on the matter, Lewis Coser uses as a point of departure the following definition of conflict: "a struggle over values and claims to scarce status, power and resources in which the aims of the opponents are to neutralize, injure or eliminate their rivals." In *The Functions of Social Conflict* (Glencoe, Ill.: The Free Press, 1956), 8.

16. "For who can be blamed but our sins." In a letter dated 1 October 1601, Mexico 26, AGI. Marc Simmons makes the following final comment on the episode: "Wanly, he concluded that all the colonists' troubles must be attributed to bad luck." In *The Last Conquistador: Juan de Oñate and the Settling of the Far Southwest* (Norman: University of Oklahoma Press, 1991), 167. In this particular case, the translation does not reflect what Sosa Peñalosa really meant.

17. Bishop to the Council of the Indies, 5 March 1788, AGI.

18. Ambrosio Espinosa de Porres to the king, 29 January 1636, Guadalajara 33, AGI.

19. Governor to the king, 28 February 1646, Guadalajara 28, AGI.

20. Bishop to the king, 14 March 1765, Guadalajara 334, AGI.

21. Governor to the king, 24 June 1766, Guadalajara 334, AGI.

22. Several inspections, or visitas, in the eighteenth century were important and of consequence. They were carefully registered in their diaries by Brigadier Pedro de Rivera (1724–1728), Bishop of Durango Pedro Tamarón y Romeral (1759–1763, in four distinct rounds), engineer Nicolás de Lafora (1766–1768), while accompanying Field Marshal Marqués de Rubí in his inspection of presidios (1766–1768), and Fray Agustín de Morfi (1777–1778), who acted as secretary of Teodoro de Croix, the first commandant general of the Interior Provinces.

23. Juicios de residencia followed such a fixed pattern that almost any individual case may serve as an illustration. See Alfredo Jiménez, "El juicio de residencia como fuente etnográfica: Francisco Briceño, gobernador de Guatemala (1565–1569)," *Revista Complutense de Historia de América* 23 (1997): 11–21.

24. The governor wrote to the king as many as twenty-one letters between April 1649 and August 1652, the vast majority concerning his confrontation with the bishop. The bishop was less prolific. In those years both the governor and the bishop resided in Parral, de facto capital of the province, in order to be closer to the area where Indian hostilities were stronger.

25. This perspective is known in cultural anthropology as *emic*, in contrast with the traditional *etic* perspective of ethnographic accounts. See Alfredo Jiménez, "El Norte de Nueva España: Visiones EMIC de una sociedad de frontera," in *Actas del XI Congreso Internacional de AHILA*, ed. John R. Fisher, 4: 143–56 (Liverpool: Asociación de Historiadores Latinoamericanistas Europeos and Institute of Latin American Studies, University of Liverpool, 1997).

26. Coser, *The Functions of Social Conflict*, 37.

27. It bears mentioning that the same circumstances did not obtain in colonial Spanish America as those which prevailed in Spain during the war of reconquest against the Moslems, which ended in 1492, or later on when many Moors and Jews falsely converted to Christianity to avoid expulsion. In any case, the functioning of the tribunals of the Inquisition in Hispanic America should be examined and qualified vis-à-vis its functioning in Spain and other European nations, where coercion based on religious grounds was a common practice.

28. James Lockhart and Stuart B. Schwartz have stated that "[i]n the Indies, far from the large ethnic-religious minorities of Iberia and denied jurisdiction

over the Indians, the Inquisition tended to lack clients. Cases of crypto-Jews and Protestant foreigners were relatively rare, as were executions: a total of some thirty for the great tribunal of Lima over about 250 years, for example." In *Early Latin America: A History of Colonial Spanish America and Brazil* (Cambridge: Cambridge University Press, 1983), 153. In Salem, Massachusetts, twenty men and women were executed in 1692, condemned for witchcraft. The Inquisition, as an agency of control, was used in New Mexico in the seventeenth century. It was a further step against political authorities after excommunication proved insufficient. See David Weber, *The Spanish Frontier in North America*, 131.

29. On the Inquisition in New Spain see Solange Alberro, *Inquisición y Sociedad en México, 1571–1700* (México City: Fondo de Cultura Económica, 1988). Significant aspects of social life in colonial New Mexico are the subject matter of Ramón Gutiérrez, *When Jesus Came, the Corn Mothers Went Away: Marriage, Sexuality, and Power in New Mexico, 1500–1846* (Stanford: Stanford University Press, 1991). Research on deviant behavior necessarily dwells so much on negative aspects that the ensuing bibliography can produce a distorted image of social reality to the inexperienced reader.

30. See the sources and bibliographies in Alberro, *Inquisición y Sociedad en México*, and Gutiérrez, *When Jesus Came*.

31. Bishop to the king, 14 April 1647, Guadalajara 63, AGI.

32. Governor to the king, 14 December 1649, Guadalajara 29, AGI.

33. Cuervo y Valdés to the king, 4 December 1686, Guadalajara 29, AGI.

34. Bishop to the king, 12 December 1721, Guadalajara 206, AGI.

35. Virrey Cruillas to the Council of the Indies, 2 February 1763, Guadalajara 331, AGI.

36. The rebellion of Túpac Amaru in Peru (1780–1781), though a precursor of independence, was fundamentally millenarian in nature and involved— for the most part—native people, criollos, and mestizos. Independence on the continent occurred after more than three hundred years of imperial administration and almost half a century after the American Revolution. Independence movements did not occur until Napoleon's armies invaded Spain in 1808, and after France virtually kidnapped the Spanish royal family.

37. Internalization and socialization are two mechanisms for the enculturation of the individual in society. Internalization refers to beliefs and values, socialization refers to status and roles. The goals and end results of both mechanisms are the acquisition by the individual of the basic aspects of culture, and his or her integration into society according to basic categories such as gender and age. The more complex a society, the larger the number of possible status positions and roles.

CHAPTER TWO

Social Control on Spain's Contested Florida Frontier

JANE LANDERS

Spain's attempts at social control in its frontier Florida colony were imbedded within the more critical struggle to control its territorial boundaries. For three centuries following Juan Ponce de León's "possession" of Florida in 1513, Spain sought to maintain sovereignty over a contested landscape that, in its original conception, stretched along the Atlantic coast from the Florida Keys to Newfoundland and west to the "mines of Mexico." In such a vast expanse, Spaniards were always an embattled minority facing resistance from a wide array of indigenous peoples, their own African slaves, multinational pirates, and assorted European and American challengers. Although territorial sovereignty was Spain's primary goal, a close second was the imposition of a desired social, religious, and political order in Florida, as elsewhere in the empire. These were difficult objectives to achieve, for Florida was always a multiracial, polyglot, ethnically and religiously diverse province. Nevertheless, Florida officials doggedly mounted a variety of responses to the triple threats of imperial competition, religious "heresy," and social deviance. These included defense forces of local militias, professional Spanish soldiers, and navies and coastal patrols manned by "*gente de color quebrado*" (people of broken color); legal structures such as the governor's tribunal, frontier justices, and *comisarios de barrio* (neighborhood commissioners); and religious and social monitoring by parish and regular priests, visiting bishops from Cuba, and members of the community. Although the results were uneven, Spanish law and order did prevail against the multiple challenges, until Florida finally became a territory of the United States in 1821.

Early Spanish Florida

The adventurers who conquered the New World for Spain all knew they were expected to establish well-ordered Catholic settlements wherever they went and in 1565, after others had failed, Pedro Menéndez de Avilés finally succeeded in founding San Agustín and later Santa Elena (in present-day South Carolina). Although these towns predate the other settlements discussed in this volume by more or less two centuries, they share many common features with their more western counterparts. Just as his peers did elsewhere, Menéndez sought to convert the indigenous populations and control their labor and tribute, to explore the interior expanses and economic potential of his province, and to protect it from foreign encroachment. While managing all that he also had to administer the king's justice and good government.[1]

In many ways, early Florida resembled other infant Spanish colonies—strung together by small forts and dotted by rudimentary missions. But Amy Turner Bushnell has highlighted the differences between southwestern and southeastern Spanish frontiers by, among other things, emphasizing the Atlantic and Caribbean orientation of the latter. Florida, she argues, was a "maritime periphery" of the Atlantic world.[2] Given the absence of dense Indian populations and mineral wealth, Florida's significance lay in its strategic location, guarding the passing silver fleets and serving as the northern outpost of Spain's Caribbean defense system. Intimately linked to Cuba, by government, economy, and extended kin and clientage networks, Florida's primary city, St. Augustine, was virtually a suburb of Havana. The Atlantic orientation and geography of Florida and its heterogeneous population shaped both territorial and social control in the colony.

Despite their precarious and often impoverished situation on the fringes of empire, Florida's colonists struggled to maintain a Spanish lifestyle. Like other Spaniards they attached a special value to living a *vida política* (civic life), believing that people of reason distinguished themselves from nomadic "barbarians" by living in stable urban communities. The vast new American colonies such as Florida were surrounded, it seemed, by "savage" and threatening "people without reason" whom Spaniards needed to pacify and, if possible, incorporate into a Spanish world wherein they might be "saved" and exploited at the same time. Spaniards throughout the Americas depicted theirs as a civilizing mission and sought to promote good governance through Spanish law and righteous living through the Catholic Faith.

The primary focus of reduction efforts was always Indians, and in Florida Jesuit, and later Franciscan, missionaries labored to create missions among the Yamasee, Guale, Timucua, Calusa, Ays, Jororo, and Apalachee Indians, to name only some of the largest groups.[3] The pests and epidemics that decimated the indigenous populations of other Spanish colonies also struck the Florida tribes, causing the same demographic crises. The interventions of the zealous friars and the tribute and labor demands of the colonists also provoked Indian revolts in Florida. As they did elsewhere, the Spaniards retaliated with brute force. For instance, in 1587 they put nineteen Indian villages to the torch before abandoning Santa Elena and their northernmost missions along the Atlantic coast. The Crown debated whether to give up on the costly and unproductive colony, but eventually was convinced that its strategic value was worth the expenditures.[4]

With this reprieve, Florida's Franciscans advanced a new mission frontier westward along the Gulf Coast, supported by more small forts. The same constellation of Franciscan missions and military posts is noted by Cecilia Sheridan (chapter 6) on New Spain's northeastern frontier in Coahuila, Nuevo León, and southern Texas and by Cynthia Radding (chapter 8) in Sonora. Although Florida's westernmost mission, San Luis de Talimali (in present-day Tallahassee) was considered a frontier outpost, it nevertheless had a church built to the same dimensions as its match in St. Augustine. The Apalachees themselves selected the site and invited in the Franciscans and soldiers who were to live there. On the face of it, they might appear to have bought into the Spanish "civilizing" project. Like the Ópata about whom Cynthia Radding writes, Apalachees became agriculturalists and took active roles in the church, although they never developed the institution of the *cabildo* that Radding argues proved efficacious as an indigenous instrument of resistance. At San Luis, however, Spaniards were always in the minority and the Apalachees still numerous and prosperous, so the indigenous "converts" were able to maintain much of their traditional life. Archaeologists have found that Apalachees continued to deposit grave goods with their deceased loved ones, despite Church prohibitions against it. And although San Luis's great new Catholic church was impressive, the building sat on the edge of a large circular ball court where villagers hosted sometimes violently energetic games. On the opposite edge of the ball court the *cacique* of San Luis held court in a council house that accommodated 2,000 to 3,000 people at a time. The Franciscan friars, of course, despaired about Apalachee dedication to the games and the old ways, documented them, and tried to eradicate them, but they and the Spanish soldiers posted at the adjoining fort found that they were limited in what they could control at San Luis. Like the Texan groups studied by Juliana Barr, Apalachees continued to exercise a certain autonomy, despite Spanish opposition. Eventually, it was not Spanish repression but the violent raids of Carolinian Indian trader James Moore in 1700–1704 that altered the Apalachees forever. Moore destroyed San Luis along with the rest of Florida's western missions, and thousands of captured natives were subsequently sold as slaves in Carolina or the Caribbean.[5]

Meanwhile, on Florida's Atlantic coast, the Spaniards were beset by a "plague of piracy" in the seventeenth century. The maritime raiders were after loot, but fired by the religious wars in Europe they also saw their actions as an extension of the Protestant fight against papacy. The exposed and poorly defended Atlantic port of St. Augustine was a ready target for French and English raiders, and the most notorious of all, Francis Drake, burned the town in 1586.[6] In 1670 Barbadian planters challenged Spain's impossible claim to the entire Atlantic coast by founding a new colony they called Carolina.[7] From that moment on, Spanish officials in Florida worried not only about controlling Indian "heathens" but English "heretics" on their borders. English entry into the Spanish Southeast triggered a century and a half of territorial, economic, and religious contestation that enveloped not only the European contestants but all the native populations and a sizeable population of African descent.

Small numbers of Africans, free and enslaved, had accompanied all the failed Spanish *entradas* (expeditions) and attempts at settlement in the Southeast. Along the way Africans deserted their Spanish masters and overlords to live among welcoming Indian groups such as the Guale. Black shipwreck survivors also lived among the Calusa and Ays tribes. Royal slaves from Havana, sent to build fortifications and public works, also bolstered the black presence in Florida. And soon after the English introduced African slaves into Carolina, those new Africans began running southward and were admitted into Florida. Responding to this phenomenon, in 1693 the Crown established a religious sanctuary policy that granted liberty to refugee slaves who sought Catholic baptism, thus insuring a steady stream of black immigrants from the north. The English in Carolina denounced Spain's provocative sanctuary policy, but neither diplomatic negotiations nor military action stanched the flow of runaways.[8]

As Gilbert Din also notes, the significant African influence in southeastern Spanish colonies such as Florida and Louisiana and the resulting complexity of the population made them unlike many of the southwestern colonies with a much smaller African component. As black and mixed populations grew, so did Spanish concerns about how these elements would be assimilated into "civilized" society. Yet, despite such worries Spaniards would depend upon Africans in each of those colonies, for both labor and defense.[9]

The Development of Afro-Spanish Florida

By the end of the seventeenth century, the theoretical construct of "two republics" of Spaniards and Indians had given way to a much more diverse reality in Florida.[10] When the auxiliary bishop of Cuba, Francisco de San Buenaventura y Tejada, conducted a *visita* in Florida in 1735, he was horrified by what he felt was the province's spiritual decadence—a judgment that was often associated with racial diversity. For the next ten years the bishop worked to shore up the Catholic Faith in Florida and sparked a religious revival of sorts. Bishop Buenaventura initiated a daily procession of the rosary through the town, tried to root out "indecent" and "forbidden" games and dances, rebuilt the church, opened a school for the religious instruction of the town's young boys, and confirmed 630 Spaniards and 143 blacks, both free and slave.[11]

Of all the challenges facing the church in St. Augustine, the bishop was most concerned about the influence of Protestantism. George Whitefield's tour of the southern colonies in 1740 had "awakened" an evangelical fervor in the region, and Bishop Buenaventura charged that English traders openly preached their Protestant beliefs in the streets of St. Augustine while conducting commerce forbidden by Spain. Moreover, in Carolina enthusiastic proselytizers like Hugh and Jonathan Bryan gathered "great Bodies of Negroes" and before them prophesied about the "Destruction of Charles-Town, and deliverance of the Negroes from their Servitude." Coming on the heels of the 1739 Stono Rebellion during which Angolan slaves killed many whites and headed for St. Augustine, such messages were alarming to all slave regimes.[12]

Many of the Africans then living in St. Augustine had once lived among the Protestants and, therefore, may have been "infected" by both the religious heresies of Protestantism and by the radical social message of men like Whitfield and the Bryans. This double threat and the actual impending war with England may have encouraged Governor Manuel de Montiano to establish the freed and converted refugee slaves into an African village of "new Christians" at Gracia Real de Santa Teresa de Mose. In one move, the governor protected his frontiers and the purity of the Church.[13]

Located on a tributary of the North River with access to St. Augustine, and laying directly north of St. Augustine, near Indian trails north to the St. Johns River and west to Apalachee, Mose was of great strategic significance. Governor Montiano and his successors clearly considered the benefits of a northern outpost against anticipated British attacks, and who better to serve as an advance warning system than grateful ex-slaves carrying Spanish arms? The freedmen apparently understood their expected role for, upon receiving their new homesteads, they vowed to be "the most cruel enemies of the English" and to risk their lives and spill their "last drop of blood in defense of the great crown of Spain and the Holy Faith."[14] The new African subjects of Spain were pragmatists, and their own interests were clearly served by fighting those who would return them to chattel slavery. As a frontier outpost and early warning system for St. Augustine, Mose also served a vital objective of Spanish imperial policy.[15]

Spanish officials considered Mose a village of "new converts" comparable to any other *doctrina*, or mission, of Christianized Indians, and following that model, Florida's governors assigned Franciscan friars to instruct inhabitants in doctrine and "good customs" and to administer their sacraments.[16] They felt it necessary, not only for strategic reasons, but also as a sort of quarantine against the "superstitions" many Africans were introducing into the body politic.[17] Although Florida never instituted an Inquisition such as Susan Deeds discusses in Nueva Vizcaya, its religious authorities also seemed to have viewed natives and blacks as religiously problematic. One Florida friar claimed the natives' lack of Spanish, "evil superstitions," and "the unfaithfulness to which their nature inclines them" were responsible for their continuing abuses (religious errors), and in an interesting linguistic conflation, the priest referred to such Indians as "*Indios bozales*," a term usually reserved for unacculturated Africans.[18] Many of the Mose villagers were just that. No other colonial city imported more slaves than Charleston, and a vast majority of those slaves were imported directly from Africa. After Georgia legalized slavery in 1749, Savannah received large numbers of slaves transhipped from Charleston, so it is probable that many of the runaways who escaped to Florida from either of those locations had been born in Africa.[19] At Mose priests struggled to convert them despite their "bad customs," "crudeness," and the fact that they still prayed in their native African languages.[20]

Despite concerns by government officials and priests about the orthodoxy of the Africans living at Mose, they soon came to rely on their military skills.[21] Considering Georgia to be an illegal colony, Spain planned a major invasion from Havana to eradicate it, but the attack was aborted at the last minute to allow for possible diplomatic resolution of contested boundaries. When the War of Jenkins's Ear finally erupted, it was the Georgians who invaded Florida. General James Oglethorpe led a major expeditionary force against St. Augustine in 1740 that included volunteers from South Carolina and Georgia, approximately six hundred Creek and Uchise allies, and approximately eight hundred black slaves or "pioneers." Seven warships of the Royal Navy sailed up from Jamaica to join the siege and assault.[22] During this invasion, Florida's governor relied heavily on militias composed in equal numbers of Spaniards, Indians, and free blacks, "of those who are fugitives from the English colonies," to patrol the frontier and report on enemy movements.[23] The African runaways from Carolina and Georgia faced some of the very planters who had enslaved them. While slaves in Carolina and Jamaica rose in rebellion and waged maroon wars against the English, Florida's black militiamen fought to protect the Crown that had freed them. All joined in a common effort to withstand the most significant threat to date to Spanish control of Florida.[24] Despite the danger, Florida's tri-racial guerrilla units struck back repeatedly and finally, with hurricane season approaching, the Royal Navy sailed home and the Georgians withdrew.[25]

Provincial militias such as those deployed against Oglethorpe were an important Spanish institution for all involved. Spaniards depended upon them to order, regulate, and defend their borders, but subordinate groups also used them to gain status and create or recreate their own social and political hierarchies. Cynthia Radding shows how the Ópata used titles, symbols such as staffs, and uniforms to enhance their own positions in the community. So did Africans in Florida and Louisiana. Although the highest rank either Indians or Africans gained in the Florida militias was captain, Spanish officials recognized the elected leaders of those groups and the governor referred to other blacks as the "subjects" of the black militia captain at Mose. The incorporation of Spaniards, Indians, and blacks in the same units in Florida was not only an effective military tactic but a significant social statement. It demonstrated that in precarious times, on vulnerable frontiers, the racial and social hierarchies Spain might have wished for gave way to the imperatives of territorial defense.

The Sociedad de Castas in Florida

In the brief peaceful interludes Florida enjoyed in the eighteenth century, Spanish officials struggled to create social order in the polyglot and multiracial city of St. Augustine. Although certain racial restrictions existed on paper, they were rarely enforced in a frontier settlement such as St. Augustine, where more relaxed personal relations were the norm.[26] Everyone knew everyone else, and this familiarity could be a source of assistance and protection for free blacks such as those from Mose, who had acquired at least a measure of acceptability through their military service. Susan R. Parker's study of contemporary "urban Indians" living in St. Augustine shows a similar integration of Indians who left their villages to take up residence in the Spanish city. Historians have commonly assumed that *mestizaje* (racial mixing) involved concubinage and, less frequently, marriage, between Spanish men and Native American women, but Parker has documented Indian men marrying Spanish women, even in one case, the kinswoman of the governor.[27] More common, however, were marriages of free blacks and Indians. Like free blacks, urban Indians also used Church and military connections and interpersonal relations such as godparenthood to break through supposed racial barriers in the "tri-racial" frontier town.

José Cuello's study of the contemporary tri-racial town of Saltillo found similar patterns of race mixture and socially assigned or constructed racial identities. In St. Augustine, as in Saltillo, Spaniards occupied the highest economic and social ranks, while free blacks and Indians worked on government building projects, were sailors and privateers, tracked escaped prisoners, and helped forage for food, wood, and fodder. They also were petty traders, linguists, and artisans and rounded up wild cattle for slaughter and wild horses for cavalry mounts.[28] Men with military ability joined the urban black and Indian militias, as the Ópata did in Sonora, gaining titles, pay, and government grants of land. Although restrictive legislation repeated (and possibly reinforced) popular notions about the degraded nature of *castas* (persons of mixed ancestry), personal and corporate relations were more powerful in a small community such as St. Augustine, where residents could form their own judgments about an individual's character.[29]

Spain's Second Occupation of Florida

After holding Florida for almost two centuries, Spain ceded its colony to Great Britain in 1763 to recover the more prized island of Cuba. A brief twenty years later, as a result of Spain's alliance with France in the American War of Independence, the Spanish resumed occupation of Florida, but Crown officials returned to a province much changed by revolutionary war and colonial transfer.[30] Across the international border of the St. Marys River lay the newly established United States of America, a nation one Spanish border official remarked was "as ambitious as it is industrious."[31] Once again, territorial defense took precedence over social control. The St. Marys proved to be an easily penetrated barrier. Although Spain attempted to enforce its borders with military patrols, and to control trade and immigration with passport and customs regulations, the province was almost impossible to police, and raiding Indians and Georgians entered almost at will. Spanish Floridians considered themselves "victims of the many ambitious characters that infest the major part of the United States, especially Georgia." Nor did Indians respect the international border that whites had negotiated and imposed. Like the Georgians, they were attracted by slaves, cattle, and horses and found the settlements along the St. Marys and St. Johns Rivers easy targets. Settlers complained that they lived "in great dread" of both Americans and Indian raiders.[32]

The heterogeneous nature of Florida's population during this second Spanish period also presented a unique and constant challenge to Spanish administrators. In 1790 the Spaniards, including troops and dependents, accounted for only about one-sixth of the total population.[33] The largest group of non-Spaniards consisted of approximately 460 Italians, Greeks, and Minorcans, remnants of an ill-fated British attempt to establish an indigo plantation south of Florida's Atlantic port and capital of St. Augustine. They were, in the main, Roman Catholics, and although they spoke a variety of languages—Catalán, Italian, Greek, and assorted dialects—they were Mediterranean people and could easily assimilate into Spanish culture.[34]

Also remaining in Florida were many "British"—a designation the Spaniards used to identify English-speaking people of many ethnic backgrounds—English, Irish, Scots, even Swiss. In general they were welcomed by Spanish administrators, for they operated large plantations that helped supply the colony and were a source of credit to the oft-impoverished government. The group included people with useful skills and connections to the American state and national governments, but some of its members also became involved in assorted plots to wrest control of the area from their hosts. Susan R. Parker has called the frontier north of St. Augustine an "Anglo suburb," almost exclusively Protestant, and culturally distinct from the Spanish capital at St. Augustine. To emphasize this cultural difference, a Spanish official described the Anglo settlers living there as men "without God or king."[35]

The other main group of non-Spaniards inhabiting the province was persons of African descent, most of whom were enslaved, but about one-fifth of whom were free. Florida's black population included African-born peoples of various nations, those born in Spanish and French colonies of the Caribbean and South America, and African and country-born runaways from the Anglo-American plantations north of Florida. In an attempt to order the chaotic colony, Florida's incoming governor ordered an accounting of all persons of color remaining in the province. He required any whites "having in their control" blacks or mulattoes, either free or slave, to register them, and "every vagrant black without a known owner or else a document that attests to his freedom" was to report to the authorities within twenty days to clarify his or her status and obtain a work contract. Those failing to report would forfeit their freedom and become the slaves of the king.[36] More than 250 blacks, most of whom had escaped from their owners during the American Revolution and the subsequent British evacuation of Florida, came forward to be registered and legitimate their free status. Florida's archives document the attempts of Carolina and Georgia owners to recover their runaway slaves over the next years and, although the governor worried about their growing numbers and the "noted insubordination" of some, he steadfastly upheld Crown orders not to return them to their former owners.[37] Over the next decades these black immigrants, and others who followed them, played important roles in the defense of the colony and helped Spain hold Florida until 1821.[38]

Informal but important mechanisms for integrating unlike or unequal members in Spanish/Mediterranean society also served to integrate these "foreign" blacks into Spanish Florida. The extended kinship group, or *parentela*, which included blood relations, fictive kin, and even household servants and slaves, and the institution of *clientela*, which bound more powerful patrons and their personal dependents into a network of mutual obligations, were so deeply rooted that one scholar suggested they might have been the "primary structure of Hispanic society."[39] Even the most humble subjects could create support networks of family (fictive and real), friends, and patrons, which might even include that of the highest government officials, and by extension, even the monarch. In St. Augustine, this was as true for Indians and Africans as it was for poor Canary Islanders or Minorcans. In 1796, when a group of former slave rebels from Saint Domingue turned Black Auxiliaries of Carlos IV, arrived in St. Augustine fresh from the most violent race war in the hemisphere, they too were integrated into the community.[40] Despite the increasingly more multilingual, multiethnic, and multiracial nature of the residents and the turbulent geopolitics engulfing the province throughout most of the eighteenth and early nineteenth centuries, government officials attempted to mold Florida to Spanish patterns. Although administering such a disparate citizenry presented unique challenges, Spanish law and religious traditions held sway and generally ordered social relations in the community of St. Augustine.

Law and Order

Florida's governors, like their counterparts elsewhere, tried to legislate proper social conduct by issuing edicts such as the *Bando de Buen Gobierno* promulgated in Florida in 1790. In minute detail this document addressed matters such as the cleanliness of the city, regulation of bread and meat contracts, commerce, and vagrancy. Public edicts also prohibited wearing of masks and carrying weapons, gambling, or racing horses through the streets.[41] An examination of criminal records for the colony indicates the impact of such efforts was probably minimal. They document street brawls between competitors for a woman's favors, curfew violations, abuse of women and of animals, solicitation, and masked balls hosted by free blacks and attended by the governor's slaves.[42]

In many cases the records show a pattern of previous like behavior and demonstrate that unless the offenses became "public and notorious" they were often either ignored or corrected by peer pressure. Both the legal culture and society at large worked to curb behaviors defined as inappropriate or threatening. Neighbors, who were often related or linked by marriage and godparenthood ties, monitored each other.

Florida's governors also appointed neighborhood commissioners who, like the patriarchs, were responsible for investigating and addressing complaints and for maintaining order in their "houses." These commissioners could settle disputes and could require certain actions be taken if the neighbors for whom they were responsible wished to avoid court appearances. This amount of monitoring and intervention often was sufficient to quiet things. If the problem persisted or escalated, however, one of the parties usually initiated legal action in the form of a *causa criminal* (criminal suit). This involved some effort and costs because the complainant had to file a notarized memorial detailing the problem before the governor's tribunal would consider it. The court interrogated all parties to the dispute as well as any witnesses who might offer evidence, including the *comisario de barrio*. Someone who repeatedly violated social norms, exhibited violent or unruly behavior, or frequently disrupted the peace of the community was soon labeled a troublemaker and could count on little support. Repeated incidents of insubordination or notorious behavior could, in a sense, be considered status crimes in Spanish communities, and governors usually responded by sentencing the convicted "nuisance" to a fine, or hard labor, or even banishment.

Such was the case when disgusted neighbors on the Calle Española (Spanish Street) in the Minorcan quarter of St. Augustine finally filed a complaint against a Minorcan woman, Agueda Enrique, for disturbing the whole street with "indecent, denigrating, and injurious words," and "scandalous expressions and gestures." Unfortunately, the delegation of Minorcan men and their wives did not repeat Agueda's exact words or describe in their complaint the gestures she used, but they charged she was always "drunk, furious, and brazen," and they complained her disturbances prevented them from keeping their doors open. Prior to filing their legal complaint, these residents of "the very poorest section of the [Minorcan] Quarter" had tried to settle the problem at the neighborhood level by reporting Agueda's annoying behavior to their comisario de barrio, don José Fernández. Fernández verified that he had repeatedly admonished both Agueda and her husband, Juan Seguí, to no avail, and he recommended that the couple be banished to the countryside. The governor so ordered and forbade Agueda to return to the city except for Mass on feast days.[43] Spaniards valued urban life and considered it a marker of civilization. Only the uncivilized or those lacking in cultural or spiritual attainments lived "beyond the walls." Removing citizens from civic space was, therefore, a critique on their social inferiority as well as a punishment.[44]

As James Sandos and Susan Deeds have shown, conflict generated by women often had a ripple effect in Spanish communities, involving their families and others in sometimes lengthy disputes. María Crosby, who was of Scottish descent, went to court to protest that a Minorcan woman was circulating rumors about her "obscure" background. The very suggestion of a "stained" racial heritage had caused María's husband, the Minorcan shopkeeper Pedro Llul, to throw her out of the house and caused her daughter's fiancé to call off their wedding. María testified that she had always been considered white, and demanded her accusers to present any evidence to the contrary or be silent so that she might resume "a tranquil and harmonious" life with her husband and restore the "honor of the family." José Cuello demonstrates that racial identification was often specious at best, but it was the disjunction between self-identity and the insult to which María objected.

Three years later María's husband, Pedro, argued with a Spanish sailor and his wife about a debt and María publicly threatened to slice open the other woman's belly with a razor if she so much as spoke to her. This graphic threat raises questions about María's earlier claims to live a "tranquil and harmonious life," and its very utterance suggests she may have had some familiarity with physical violence. The earlier racial slur against María obviously had taken on a life of its own for the sailor and his wife both countered by calling María a mulatta. Just as Spanish society held a man responsible for his wife's actions, it also held him accountable for her honor and a public insult against a woman required a public response by her husband—even if he had once thrown her out of the house. Llul pressed criminal charges against the Spanish sailor for "injuring his wife with the expression mulatta." Everyone understood that the insult of his wife actually injured Llul as well. Several witnesses testified they had heard the sailor yell from the street up to the window where María looked out that she was a mulatta and that if he saw her in the street he would cut her tongue out for talking too much (*por ser habladora*). The court finally decided things had gone far enough. Remarking on the repeated nature of the insults, the court ordered the Spanish sailor to pay a stiff fine of twenty-five pesos and threatened worse corporal punishment if there was any more trouble.[45]

The primary objective of judicial administration within Spanish communities such as St. Augustine was the resolution of conflict and restoration of harmony. Historian Charles Cutter has analyzed the "non-adversarial nature" of the Spanish legal culture and the manner in which Spanish authorities deployed written law (*ley*), customary law (*derecho*), and personal discretion (*arbitrio judicial*) effectively to achieve justice (*equidad*), even in peripheral areas of the empire.[46] In a culture that believed that the prime directive of a good government was justice, even frontier administrators strove to apply the law equitably. The care with which Spanish officials in Florida adjudicated cases involving black slaves demonstrated this commitment and must have made a powerful impression on the many "foreign" blacks in Spanish Florida, who would never have had access to the courts in their previous settings.[47]

Accusations or reports of a crime by any member of the community, free or enslaved, triggered an immediate *sumaria* (fact-finding inquiry), in which the court solicited testimony from all witnesses regardless of race, class, gender, or legal status. Because so many residents of Spanish Florida did not speak Spanish, the court employed translators of English, Spanish, and African languages. After witnesses testified, authorities read the statements back to those who gave them and allowed changes or corrections, additions or deletions. The court followed the same judicial procedures in each case, expending just as much time and expense on crimes against slaves as it would against more elite members of the community.[48]

In addition to taking testimony from witnesses, the court made full examinations of crime scenes, weapons, and other physical evidence. The criminal records of Florida include measurements of wells, drawings of guns and knives, estimates on the weights of canes and other weapons, and discussions of weather and other information pertinent to the cases. Highly trained Scottish and French physicians attached to the military garrison even exhumed bodies and conducted autopsies to help arrive at justice. Particularly violent crimes such as murder were referred to Havana, Santo Domingo, Mexico City, or even Spain for superior court review, and sometimes cases dragged on for many years and many thousands of pages of documentation.[49]

Although murders were rare in St. Augustine, even when they involved the enslaved, court officials followed the letter of the law. As husbands were responsible for the actions of their wives, so were owners responsible for those of their slaves, who were extensions of his family.

Elites of the community took this responsibility seriously and advocated for their dependents in court. When the slave Liberty killed another slave in a fight, his owner testified that Liberty had not acted in malice and he asked for compassion for "his client." He also charged that the victim's death was "a punishment of the Almighty for his wickedness and dishonesty." The governor ruled that a death required punishment and condemned Liberty to one year of hard labor on the public works—a light sentence for homicide, and one that probably reflected the influence of Liberty's defender as well as the character of the governor.[50]

When another slave tried to claim self-defense after axing a victim who was halfway out a window and then admitted sharpening the murder weapon prior to their fight, the governor made further inquiries in Havana before ultimately declaring him guilty and condemning him to death. Although sentenced in 1796, Roberto was not executed until six years later, and then he did not die alone.[51] His owner served as his godfather at the condemned man's baptism in the Castillo de San Marcos, members of a religious confraternity consoled him on the eve of his death, escorted him to his death, and prepared his body for burial in their habit the next day.[52] This execution served to reinforce legal norms and remind witnesses of the penalties for crime, but it also underscored that even enslaved murderers could be redeemed and reincorporated into the community via Church intercession. Murders such as those just discussed were rare in Florida, however, and most social correction involved lesser crimes such as theft, disorderly conduct, or alleged immorality. The real violence and disorder came from without.

Conclusions

Despite the best efforts of officials and citizens alike to create a stable Spanish settlement, imperial contests, Indian wars, the American, French, and Haitian revolutions, and various Latin American wars of independence repeatedly destabilized Spanish Florida. Spain was also buffeted by European wars and the Napoleonic invasion and could do little to defend or support its remote and impoverished colony. The United States government saw opportunity in Spain's weakness and not very covertly supported a number of hostile actions against Spanish Florida, including the Patriot War of 1812, a U.S. naval attack on the black fort and settlement at Prospect Bluff on the Apalachicola River in 1815, and Andrew Jackson's devastating raids against black and Seminole villages along the Suwannee River in 1818. Spanish Floridians lived in a sort of perpetual state of siege, and that may have actually served to mediate conduct and unite the many disparate elements of society against a common foe. Ultimately, however, neither externally produced cooperation nor centuries of legal and social control were enough to keep Florida Spanish, and by the Adams-Onís Treaty of 1819 Spain was forced to cede Florida to the United States. As in Louisiana, cession treaties required the incoming government to respect the legal status and property rights of remaining Spanish citizens, including free blacks. Nevertheless, Cuba's captain general encouraged Floridians to emigrate to other Spanish colonies including Texas, Mexico, and Cuba. Most Floridians chose the latter, and the last act of social control of Spanish officials in Florida was to supervise Spain's second full-scale evacuation to Cuba. Spanish sovereignty ended on July 10, 1821, and Florida became a territory of the United States.[53]

NOTES

1. Eugene Lyon, *The Enterprise of Florida: Pedro Menéndez de Avilés and the Spanish Conquest of 1565–1568* (Gainesville: University Press of Florida, 1974), 14–17, 100–130.

2. Amy Turner Bushnell, *Situado and Sabana: Spain's Support System for the Presidio and Mission Provinces of Florida* (Athens: University of Georgia Press, 1994).

3. The historiography on European contact with native groups in Florida is voluminous and is enriched by the close collaboration of historians and archaeologists over many decades of research. See for example Bonnie G. McEwan, *Indians of the Greater Southeast: Historical Archaeology and Ethnohistory* (Gainesville: University Press of Florida, 2000); John H. Hann and Bonnie G. McEwan, *The Apalachee Indians and Mission San Luis* (Gainesville: University Press of Florida, 1998); Jerald T. Milanich, *Florida Indians and the Invasion from Europe* (Gainesville: University Press of Florida, 1995); Jerald T. Milanich and Charles Hudson, *Hernando de Soto and the Indians of Florida* (Gainesville: University Press of Florida, 1993); John H. Hann, *A History of the Timucuan Indians and Missions* (Gainesville: University Press of Florida, 1996); *Missions to the Calusa* (Gainesville: University Press of Florida, 1991); *Apalachee: The Land between the Rivers* (Gainesville:

University Press of Florida, 1988); Bonnie G. McEwan, *The Spanish Missions of La Florida* (Gainesville: University Press of Florida, 1993).

4. Paul E. Hoffman, *Florida's Frontier* (Bloomington: Indiana University Press, 2002).

5. Hann and McEwan, *Apalachee Indians and Mission San Luis*.

6. Kris Lane, *Pillaging the Empire: Piracy in the Americas 1500–1750* (Armonk, N.Y.: M. E. Sharpe, 1998), 29, 52, 102, 165, 168.

7. On the history of Carolina and the English southeastern frontier, see Alan Gallay, *The Indian Slave Trade: The Rise of the English Empire in the American South* (New Haven, Conn.: Yale University Press, 2002); Peter H. Wood, *Black Majority: Negroes in South Carolina from 1690 through the Stono Rebellion* (New York: W. W. Norton, 1974) and Verner W. Crane, *The Southern Frontier, 1670–1732* (New York: W. W. Norton, 1981).

8. Jane Landers, *Black Society in Spanish Florida* (Urbana: University of Illinois Press, 1999), ch. 1.

9. Gilbert C. Din, *Spaniards, Planters and Slaves: The Spanish Regulation of Slavery in Louisiana, 1763–1803* (College Station: Texas A&M University Press, 1999); Gwendolyn Midlo Hall, *Africans in Colonial Louisiana: The Development of Afro-Creole Culture in the Eighteenth Century* (Baton Rouge: Louisiana State University, 1992); Kimberly S. Hanger, *Bounded Lives, Bounded Places: Free Black Society in Colonial New Orleans, 1769–1803* (Durham, N.C.: Duke University Press, 1997).

10. Report of the Visita of Bishop Francisco de San Buenaventura, 29 April 1736, Stetson Collection 5543, P. K. Yonge Library of Florida History, University of Florida, Gainesville (hereafter cited as PKY); John Jay TePaske, *The Governorship of Spanish Florida, 1700–1763* (Durham, N.C.: Duke University Press, 1964), 167–69.

11. Wood, *Black Majority*, 308–26; Harvey H. Jackson, "Hugh Bryan and the Evangelical Movement in Colonial South Carolina," *William and Mary Quarterly*, 3rd ser., 43, 4 (1986): 594–614.

12. Landers, *Black Society*, ch. 2; Montiano followed a model that had been used to "reduce" maroon populations in Panama, Mexico, Hispaniola, and Colombia. Jane Landers, "La cultura material de los cimarrones: Los casos de Ecuador, La Española, México y Colombia," in *Rutas de la esclavitud en África y América Latina*, ed. Rina Cáceres, 145–74 (San José: Editorial de la Universidad de Costa Rica, 2001), and "*Cimarrón* Ethnicity and Cultural Adaptation in the Spanish Domains of the Circum-Caribbean, 1503–1763," in *Identity in the Shadow of Slavery*, ed. Paul E. Lovejoy, 30–54 (London: Continuum, 2000).

13. Fugitive Blacks of the English plantations to Philip V, 10 June 1738, Santo Domingo (hereafter cited as SD) 844, microfilm reel 15, PKY.

14. Council of the Indies, 2 October 1739, cited in Irene Wright, "Dispatches of Spanish Officials Bearing on the Free Negro Settlement of Gracia Real de Santa Teresa de Mose,"*Journal of Negro History* 9, 2 (1924): 178; Council of the Indies, 28 September 1740, SD 845, microfilm reel 16, PKY.

15. Manuel de Montiano to Philip V, 16 February 1739, SD 845, microfilm reel 16, PKY.

16. Juan Joseph de Solana to Juan Francisco de Güemes y Horcasitas, 15 September 1757, SD 846, microfilm reel 18, PKY.

17. Pedro Lorenzo de Asevedo called the Indians living in St. Augustine "Indios ladinos," a term also used for persons of African descent who had learned Spanish and were Christians. Testimonios y autos... entre el cura...y el guardian del convento, 1745, SD 864, Archivo General de Indias, Seville (hereafter cited as AGI).

18. Robert Higgins, "Charleston: Terminus and Entrepot of the Colonial Slave Trade," in *The African Diaspora: Interpretive Essays*, ed. Martin L. Kilson and Robert I. Rothberg, 129 (Cambridge, Mass.: Harvard University Press, 1976); Converse D. Clowse, *Measuring Charleston's Overseas Commerce, 1717–1767: Statistics from the Port's Naval Lists* (Washington, D.C.: University Press of America, 1981), 31, table A-21; Elizabeth Donnan, *Documents Illustrative of the History of the Slave Trade to America* (Washington, D.C.: Carnegie Institution, 1930–1935), 608–25.

19. Black Baptisms, Cathedral Parish Records, Diocese of St. Augustine Catholic Center, Jacksonville, Fla. (hereafter cited as CPR), microfilm reel 284 F, PKY. Governor Melchor de Navarrete promised certificates of freedom once the catechumens had been successfully examined and baptized and asked that he be awarded some title or his family some distinction for his efforts to evangelize the escaped slaves. Melchor de Navarrete to Francisco Cagigal, 2 April 1752, cited in Irene Wright, "Dispatches," 184–86.

20. In the Darien antislavery petition of 1739 Georgian settlers wrote, "The Nearness of the Spaniards, who have proclaimed Freedom to all Slaves, who run away from their Masters, makes it impossible for us to keep them, without more Labour in guarding them, than what we would be at to do their Work." See Harvey H. Jackson, "The Darien Antislavery Petition of 1739 and the Georgia Plan," *William and Mary Quarterly*, 3rd series, 34 (1977): 618–19.

21. TePaske, *Governorship of Spanish Florida*, 139–46; Ricardo Torres-Reyes, *The British Siege of St. Augustine, 1740* (Denver: Denver Service Center [National Park Service], 1972). The Georgia accounts of the siege and its

aftermath can be followed in *General Oglethorpe's Georgia: Colonial Letters 1738–1743*, vol. 2, ed. Mills Lane (Savannah: Beehive Press, 1975), 422–510. On estimates of Indian allies and black pioneers see, *Journal of the Commons House of Assembly, May 18, 1741–July 10, 1742*, ed. J. H. Easterby (Columbia: Historical Commission of South Carolina, 1953), 168–76. The same volume includes a narrative of the expedition by the Carolinians and Oglethorpe's account. Ibid., 93–248. Montiano's account of the same time period can be found in "Letters of Manuel de Montiano: Siege of St. Agustine [*sic*]," vol. 7, pt. 1, *Collections of the Georgia Historical Society* (Savannah, 1909).

22. On 8 January 1740, Captain Pedro Lamberto Horruytiner commanded a group of twenty-five Florida cavalrymen, twenty-five Spanish infantrymen, and thirty Indians and free blacks. Manuel de Montiano to Juan Francisco de Güemes y Horcasitas, 31 January 1740, SD 2658, AGI. On 27 January 1740, Montiano sent Don Romualdo Ruiz del Moral out on a similar mission with "twenty-five horsemen, twenty-five Indians, and twenty-five free blacks." Manuel de Montiano to Juan Francisco de Güemes y Horcasitas, 31 January 1740, *Letters of Montiano*, 36.

23. Ibid., 40–42.

24. Manuel de Montiano to Juan Francisco De Güemes y Horcasitas, 17 January 1740, SD 2658, AGI; Manuel de Montiano to Juan Francisco de Güemes y Horcasitas, 6 July 1740, *Letters of Montiano*, 56–58; Manuel de Montiano to Juan Francisco De Güemes y Horcasitas, 9 August 1740, SD 845 microfilm reel 16, PKY.

25. On the multiethnic nature of the eighteenth-century city, see the essays in *Spanish St. Augustine: The Archaeology of a Colonial Creole Community*, ed. Kathleen A. Deagan (New York: Academic Press, 1983).

26. In larger capitals such as Mexico City, Lima, and Havana discriminatory legislation probably had more impact, but was still largely ineffectual and moderated by personal and corporate relations. R. Douglas Cope, *The Limits of Racial Domination: Plebeian Society in Colonial Mexico City, 1660–1720* (Madison: University of Wisconsin Press, 1994), ch. 1.

27. Susan R. Parker, "Spanish St. Augustine's 'Urban' Indians," *El Escribano* 32 (1993): 1–15.

28. Pedro Sánchez de Griñan to Julian de Arriaga, 7 July 1756, cited in Michael C. Scardaville and Jesús María Belmonte, "Florida in the Late First Spanish Period: The Griñan Report," *El Escribano* 16 (1979): 1–24; Jorge Juan and Antonio de Ulloa, "Eighteenth-Century Spanish American Towns: African and Afro-Hispanic Life and Labor in Cities and Suburbs," in *The African in Latin America*, ed. Anne Pescatello (New York: Knopf, 1975), 106–11.

29. Landers, *Black Society*.

30. Ibid., 68–69.

31. Carlos Howard to Luis de las Casas, 2 July 1791, Cuba 1439, AGI.

32. Residents of St. Marys to Vicente Manuel de Zéspedes, 24 October 1787, East Florida Papers (hereafter cited as EFP) microfilm reel 45, and Residents of the St. Johns River, 8 October 1789, EFP, microfilm reel 46, PKY, cited in Parker, "Men Without God," 151.

33. For the history of this community see, Patricia C. Griffin, *Mullet on the Beach: The Minorcans of Florida, 1768–1788* (Jacksonville: University of North Florida Press, 1991).

34. Report of Nicolás Grenier, 10 November 1784, cited in Lockey, *East Florida*, 307.

35. Susan R. Parker, "Men Without God or King: Rural Settlers of East Florida, 1784–1790," *Florida Historical Quarterly* 64, 2 (1990): 135–55. On the British period in Florida, see Daniel L. Schafer, "'A Swamp of an Investment?': Richard Oswald's British East Florida Plantation Experiment," in Jane G. Landers, ed. *Colonial Plantations and Economy in Florida* (Gainesville: University Press of Florida, 2000), 11–38.

36. Proclamation of Vicente Manuel de Zéspedes, 26 July 1784, cited in Lockey, *East Florida*, 240–41.

37. Manuel de Zéspedes to José de Ezpeleta, 2 October 1788, 3 November 1788, and 14 February 1789; Petition of Don Diego (James) Spalding, 8 May 1788; Cuba 1395, AGI.

38. Census Returns, 1784–1814, EFP, microfilm reel 148, PKY; Landers, *Black Society*.

39. Lyle N. McAlister, *Spain and Portugal in the New World, 1492–1700* (Minneapolis: University of Minnesota Press, 1994), 39–40.

40. Landers, *Black Society*, 75–79, 209–17; Jane Landers, "Rebellion and Royalism in Spanish Florida: The French Revolution on Spain's Northern Colonial Frontier," in *A Turbulent Time: The French Revolution and the Greater Caribbean*, ed. David Barry Gaspar and David Patrick Geggus (Bloomington: Indiana University Press, 1997), 156–77.

41. Bando de Buen Gobierno, 2 September 1790, EFP, PKY.

42. Landers, *Black Society*, ch. 6.

43. Complaints of Bartolomé Usina, María su muger, Pedro Estopa, Miguel García, Antonia su muger, y otros vecinos de la Calle Española, EFP, microfilm reel 174, PKY. Agueda's beleaguered husband, Juan, filed an appeal citing the hardships it would create for him and his children to

have to rebuild his country home but the governor held firm and held both Agueda and her husband responsible for any violation of the banishment. I discuss this case and the following Llul case in "Female Conflict and Its Resolution in Eighteenth-Century St. Augustine," *The Americas* 54, 4 (April 1998): 557–74.

44. Memorial of Juan Seguí and response by Governor Juan Nepomuceno de Quesada, 16 August 1790 and 31 August 1790, EFP, microfilm reel 174, PKY. Griffin found that although Juan Seguí had relatives living elsewhere in the city, he was one of the few Minorcan men not linked by godparent ties to other Minorcans in his neighborhood, and this fact may have contributed to the couple's ostracism. Griffin, *Mullet on the Beach*, 168–69.

45. Pedro Llul versus José Ximénes, for having injured his wife with the expression mulatta, 30 October 1802, EFP, reel 125, PKY.

46. Charles R. Cutter, *The Legal Culture of Northern New Spain, 1700–1810* (Albuquerque: University of New Mexico Press, 1995), chap. 2. Also see McAlister, *Spain and Portugal in the New World*, 24–26.

47. On the topic of honor see Lyman Johnson and Sonya Lipsett-Rivera, *The Faces of Honor: Sex, Shame and Violence in Colonial Latin America* (Albuquerque: University of New Mexico, Press, 1998). For more on the power of insults and conflict among women see Richard Boyer, "Respect and Identity: Horizontal and Vertical Reference Points in Speech Acts," Kimberly S. Hanger, "'Desiring Total Tranquility' and Not Getting It: Conflict Involving Free Black Women in Spanish New Orleans," and Sonya Lipsett-Rivera, "*De Obra y Palabra*: Patterns of Insult in Mexico, 1750–1856," all in *The Americas* 54, 4 (April 1998).

48. Landers, *Black Society*, chap. 6, and Landers, "African and African American Women and Their Pursuit of Rights Through Eighteenth-Century Spanish Texts," in *Haunted Bodies: Gender and Southern Texts*, ed. Anne Goodwyn Jones and Susan V. Donaldson, 205–17 (Charlottesville: University of Virginia Press, 1997). An anonymous British visitor to Amelia Island found this noteworthy and wrote, "The slave may demand compliance with the laws, an infraction of which incurs the penalty of release of service." *Narrative of a Voyage to the Spanish Main in the Ship "Two Friends,"* ed. John W. Griffin (Gainesville: University of Florida Press, 1978), 127.

49. Landers, *Black Society*, chap. 6; Cutter, *Legal Culture*, chap. 5.

50. All material related to this case is found in "Criminales contra el negro Liberty," EFP, microfilm reel 124, no.1, PKY. On Fatio's influence see Susan R. Parker, "Success through Diversification: Francis Philip Fatio's New Switzerland Plantation," in Landers, *Colonial Plantations and Economy in Florida*, 69–82.

51. All material related to this case is found in "Criminales seguidos contra el negro Bob o Roberto," EFP, microfilm reel 124, no. 2, PKY.

52. Baptism of Roberto Jones, 7 January 1802, CPR, PKY.

53. Landers, *Black Society*, chap. 10.

CHAPTER THREE

Spanish Control over a Multiethnic Society

Louisiana, 1763–1803

GILBERT C. DIN

Of the Spanish borderland colonies that today comprise a part of the United States, Louisiana stands alone in several respects. For more than a half century prior to Spanish acquisition, France had owned the province and, aside from Indians, it held both European and African inhabitants.[1] Geographically, Louisiana was Spain's largest borderlands possession, embracing a vast, unsubdued, and largely unexplored expanse in mid-continental North America. Hispanics, nearly all Spaniards who arrived after 1763, comprised only a minority, roughly 15 percent of the 25,000 European residents at the end of the Spanish period, and it was the only borderlands colony where Hispanics constituted a minority among whites. In addition, 5,940 African slaves lived in the province in 1766, and they made up 51.8 percent of the nonindigenous population of 11,476, enough to brand Louisiana as a slave colony.[2] Blacks accounted for slightly more than half of the estimated 50,000 inhabitants in 1803, and their presence posed concerns to whites generally absent elsewhere in the borderlands. The few free blacks of the French era grew significantly during Spanish rule. Iberian policy in Louisiana also differed from other borderlands colonies as Spain welcomed non-Hispanic whites, many of them Protestants, to build up the province's virtually empty terrain, and it elected not to Christianize the colony's Indians, as the mission-presidio system, widely employed from Texas to California and in Florida, was never used here. Finally, among the borderlands possessions, Spain's tenure of Louisiana was the most ephemeral—forty years—and it was the first borderlands colony surrendered and absorbed into the United States, along with its Hispanic residents and settlements.[3]

Contrary to Spanish administration in other borderlands possessions, whites, not Indians, presented greater problems of social control. Spain dealt gingerly with whites since they were powerful in the lower Mississippi Valley, home to 80 to 90 percent of the nonindigenous population. They resided mostly along the numerous rivers and bayous of the lower section of the present-day state, notably the Mississippi, because until the twentieth century waterways provided the most convenient form of travel. Fortunately for Spanish control, whites were not united in interests as they consisted of several groups and classes. Most important were French administrative and military officials, planters, and merchants. Other whites, including French and German farmers brought in by France between 1717 and 1731, had not prospered substantially. They, along with the most recent settlers, the Acadians, or Cajuns, who first entered Louisiana in the early 1760s, constituted the lowest white class. In imitation of the early French and Germans, the Acadians settled above New Orleans on both banks of the Mississippi River and west of the river in the Attakapas district. Not counting soldiers, New Orleans, the province's only city in both the French and Spanish periods, had a disproportionate share of whites, a thousand or more in 1766, who spanned all economic and social classes and included a sprinkling of professionals and artisans.[4]

Louisiana's diverse inhabitants challenged Spain to adapt its traditional forms of social control in order to retain the colony. Its policy—if it can be called that—for maintaining order among the heterogeneous residents was to refrain, if possible, from causing friction. Through its Louisiana administrators, Spain employed several methods for dealing with the populace. It relied primarily upon cooperation, which after 1769, flourished with many of its inhabitants through the remainder of the Spanish era. Many within Louisiana's French community either espoused the Spanish regime or, especially among the lower classes, were passive and indifferent.

Besides cooperation, Spain's juridical system of courts and judges worked to resolve civil and criminal strife. In the years immediately after its acquisition of the colony, Spain sought to impose a form of government similar to that in operation elsewhere in its empire. As the discussions in other essays in this volume make clear, particularly those of Cuello on Saltillo, Landers on Florida, and Radding on Sonora, local government was emblematic of royal authority. Although the Spanish system differed from the French, most judges were French Creoles (American-born Europeans of French descent), and the laws of the two nations bore similarity. In Spanish Louisiana, two members of the New Orleans *cabildo*, or city government, which was erected in 1769, were *alcaldes ordinarios*, or magistrates, who determined cases of individuals not protected by a *fuero* (legal privilege). Because these two alcaldes, who were elected the first of each January by the *regidores* (councilmen) for a one-year term, were not lawyers, a government adviser, who was a university law school graduate, assisted them. The alcaldes ordinarios handled an extensive variety of civil and criminal cases. If a party appealed an alcalde's decision, that same judge and two regidores chosen by the council resolved it by at least a two-to-one vote. The Louisiana governor was also a judge, whose "ordinary" court was equal, and not above, those of the alcaldes ordinarios. In addition, he handled cases for the privileged few protected by a fuero.[5]

Besides these tribunals, several inferior courts resolved disagreements, mostly among the lower classes. New Orleans consisted of wards, where *alcaldes de barrio*, roughly justices of the peace, preserved order and adjudicated minor disputes about goods and services possessing a value no greater than ten pesos. District commandants, who were army or militia officers, also acted as judges and notaries in their jurisdictions. They investigated crimes and gathered evidence, which they usually forwarded to the governor to render judgment. District commandants adjudged civil causes having a value of twenty pesos or less. As Louisiana's population grew, governors appointed or commandants selected syndics to assist them in their districts. The office of syndic, which combined both law enforcement and inferior judicial functions, steadily expanded over the years. In 1795 the governor defined their duties in a variety of areas such as slave control, livestock, crime, and road, levee, and bridge maintenance.[6]

A final method for controlling the inhabitants was the army. Had it possessed a sizable military presence in 1768, Spain could have prevented the civil insurrection (explained below) that occurred that year. But after 1769, when a battalion of soldiers, never numbering more than 500 men, was present, troops were not needed since the dissidents had lost support. Thereafter, Spain rarely resorted to military force to dominate the colony's inhabitants. Instead, the army's presence, which in the 1780s rose to two battalions on the Mississippi, served to proclaim Spanish ownership of the province and defend it against potential aggressors. The army also served as a vehicle for social control by incorporating many middle- and upper-class French Creoles who served as officers in the Fixed Louisiana Infantry Regiment. Their loyalty to the Spanish Crown was never in question.[7]

Spain Attempts to Establish Control in Louisiana

When Spain first acquired Louisiana, it gave little thought to ways to control the inhabitants. Diplomatic pressure from France in the Seven Years' War as well as political reality persuaded a defeated and reluctant Spain to embrace both peace and Louisiana in 1762. With the loss of Canada in the war, France felt no need to retain Louisiana as it lacked value and consumed scarce funds. Spain accepted the colony to prevent its acquisition by the English and to halt their encroachment on older and more valuable Spanish possessions farther to the west along the Gulf of Mexico coast.[8] In relinquishing Louisiana, King Louis XV of France requested that the Spanish Crown preserve its Gallic laws and customs. While Carlos III agreed to do so verbally, it was not written into the treaty that ceded the colony.[9]

Spain initiated its rule in Louisiana by blundering seriously, never anticipating that local whites would resist Iberian control. Among the errors that led to civil insurrection, Spain failed to take immediate and firm possession of the province, devoting its attention instead to implementing military and economic reforms in the more valuable colonies of Cuba and New Spain.[10] That neglect induced Louisiana's French Creole leaders to believe that the cession was temporary. Moreover, they were accustomed to administering the colony *their* way, with only minimal royal supervision, especially in the vital areas of commerce, taxes, and slave control. Merchants and planters alike advocated for freedom to trade where they pleased, both legally and illegally, especially with Spanish colonies. They dreaded the imposition of Spain's stifling mercantile regulations, which funneled colonial trade to the metropolis. Only when the French king permitted his soldiers in Louisiana to enter Spanish service did Carlos III agree to assume control since he had few troops to send there.[11]

These obstacles produced a three-year delay before the first Spaniards arrived in New Orleans in March 1766. They comprised a handful of royal officials and slightly more than one hundred soldiers, all of whom made a less than awe-inspiring entrance. Not surprisingly, naval Capt. Antonio de Ulloa, the first peninsular governor (1766–1768), encountered difficulties from resentful local leaders. In addition, administrative errors by both Ulloa and officials in Spain greatly chafed the provincial inhabitants.[12] Under France, Louisiana's Superior Council, originally a court of law that evolved into the colony's administrative body, represented local interests, and it attempted to retain power despite the Spaniards' arrival. The dissident leaders also tried to persuade Louis XV to reclaim Louisiana because they deplored its transfer.[13]

Ulloa, meanwhile, ignored the French Creole–dominated Superior Council, believing that it lacked authority, and dealt with French royal officials. He abstained from showing the council his patents of appointment, and the council, observing Ulloa's paltry troops and the absence of royal documentation validating the transfer, chose to assume that he had not taken charge. The compelling reason why Ulloa left matters seemingly undisturbed stemmed from the refusal of the colony's French troops to enter Spanish service; many clamored to return home. Had Ulloa "taken control," many of the soldiers would have demanded repatriation and left him pitifully short of troops. He also erred when, in obedience to a royal mandate forbidding innovation, he cut Spanish army wages to match the pittance French soldiers received. His ill-chosen decision disgruntled every soldier, Spanish and French alike. Although he soon rescinded his order, resentment lingered.[14]

Given these problems, Ulloa decided to wait for the arrival of Spanish troops before taking official control. The acting French governor, army captain Charles-Philippe Aubry, technically remained in charge. In reality, however, Ulloa used Aubry as a front to deal with the locals, while the Spaniard exercised authority directly in pivotal areas such as finance, interior and exterior commerce, the military, diplomacy, and the issuance of passports. Although local French officials, mainly in the Superior Council, presided over the colony's everyday affairs, they were relatively unimportant to overall management of Louisiana. Despite this, and most important to the French perspective, the Superior Council projected the illusion to the inhabitants that it retained charge of the colony.[15]

That illusion caused Ulloa serious difficulties. Among them, the council insisted that he redeem the colony's depreciated paper money at full value. The council represented members and inhabitants who speculated in currency and now sought to profit from Spain. Sniffing the possibility of a greater return, they rejected Ulloa's offer to exchange their nearly valueless notes at 75 percent of the certificates' value and pressed for full redemption. Instead of granting it, Ulloa tried to shore up the money in circulation by spending specie, but it quickly disappeared in obedience to Gresham's law (bad money drives out good). Inasmuch as the Crown failed to supply him adequately with specie, the Spanish governor never resolved the paper currency problem.[16]

Revolt of the Creoles

Difficulties in administration and the meager Spanish presence forced Ulloa in early 1767 to appeal to the government for 1,200 troops, which was more than enough to dominate subversive elements and defend the colony. A frugal Crown, however, consented to less than half that number. It then worsened Ulloa's predicament in Louisiana by sending the troops piecemeal to Havana, where they were to remain until all had assembled. Only at that time would they proceed to New Orleans. Word of the battalion's formation and eventual dispatch to Louisiana helped to incite the dissidents who resented Spanish authority.[17]

Spain's decision to impose its rule on Louisiana, both administratively and economically, before it effectively controlled the colony also prompted discord. Dissatisfied with the behavior of the French Superior Council that acted as if it still had charge, Ulloa began exercising judicial powers. The Crown initially had ordered him to abolish the council and establish a new court for the colony when he took formal possession. But in early 1768, after learning about the council's obstructionism, the Spanish government rescinded that order and decreed its immediate abolition and the establishment of a single court for Spaniards and Frenchmen alike. Rather than comply, however, Ulloa left the council intact and created a larger court than what the Crown had prescribed. His unwise decision granted the French Creoles on the council and hostile to Spanish legitimacy time to organize. They led the opposition to Spanish rule as they represented merchants, debtors, and planters, many of whom engaged in smuggling, which heretofore had constituted an integral part of the French colony's economic activity.[18]

They abhorred Spanish mercantile regulations. French Louisiana had imported nothing from Spain, and Spain similarly wanted little or nothing from the colony. Without knowing anything about Louisiana's economy, the Iberian government had ordered its trade to conform to the stringent commercial mandates present in its other colonies. On 23 March, 1768, it rescinded the 6 May, 1766, order that had allowed Louisiana interim trade with France's West Indian colonies and French ships to sail to New Orleans with a Spanish passport.[19] By May 1768 word of the new decree had arrived in Louisiana, causing consternation about its implementation. In October Ulloa increased their anxiety when he announced his intention to enforce the March trade regulation.[20]

His intention to obey the Spanish government's directive restricting commerce became the catalyst that triggered the Superior Council's 28 October, 1768, uprising against him and Iberian rule.[21] Acting French governor Aubry, who was at best a mediocre officer and administrator, failed to act decisively against the council when it mobilized French, German, and Acadian farmers to seize control of New Orleans. The council encouraged them with patriotic rhetoric and generous libations of "the good wine of Bordeaux." Because most of the few troops he had were at new posts far up the Mississippi, Ulloa declined to oppose the insurrection and departed quickly after ordering the evacuation of all Spanish personnel; the rebel leaders, however, retained three treasury officials as hostages to insure payment of debts. Ships that shuttled between New Orleans and Havana kept the Spaniards abreast of events in Louisiana. French Creole efforts to return the colony to France failed as Louis XV, whom the Spaniards had already apprized of their intent to recover the province, refused to meet with representatives from the chronically burdensome former colony. Subsequent rebel attempts to form a viable independent republic and convince the English to assume the colony similarly foundered.[22]

Meanwhile, the Iberian government authorized Lt. Gen. Alejandro O'Reilly on 16 April, 1769, to subdue the rebellion, punish ringleaders, and impose Spanish control and law. Four months later the general arrived in New Orleans from Havana, bringing an imposing force of two thousand troops and peacefully assuming power. Support for the rebel leaders had withered as economic conditions steadily eroded under their direction. Moreover, a substantial population, especially French officials and military officers who put loyalty to the Crown first, had never sided overtly with the insurgents. O'Reilly soon arrested twelve ringleaders and put them on trial for insurrection. The proceedings concluded in October, when two Spanish jurists, Félix del Rey and Francisco Xavier Rodríguez, sentenced six of the accused to death and the rest to prison terms in Havana's Morro Castle.[23]

Reimposition of Spanish Rule

As the trials proceeded, O'Reilly began establishing laws for Louisiana's governance as a typical Spanish colony. The attorneys del Rey and Rodríguez drew up legal summaries that included regulations for a cabildo for New Orleans and for many other facets of local government.[24] O'Reilly issued instructions for district commandants along the Mississippi River and for two important settlements at St. Louis and Natchitoches that emphasized preserving good relations with the Indian tribes inhabiting those regions. He appointed local Frenchmen, who were militia officers, to serve as commandants at various civilian settlements and named six regidores, who were all French and had aligned with the Spaniards before the revolt, to the New Orleans cabildo. Spain, likewise, accepted many French army officers in the Fixed Louisiana Infantry Battalion and about a hundred French troops in the enlisted ranks. O'Reilly expelled merchants who had trafficked illegally with the Spanish colonies, and some additional grumblers voluntarily abandoned Louisiana.[25] Aside from families whose kin had been executed or expelled, Louisiana's Gallic inhabitants accepted Spanish rule, and cooperation in virtually all areas prevailed.[26]

While O'Reilly imposed rigorous economic restrictions on Louisiana, limiting its trade solely to Cuba and Spain, both of which consumed few of its products, economic reality dictated a different course. His successor, Governor Luis de Unzaga (1770–1776), recognized that the Irish-Spaniard, who served as his nation's expert on Louisiana until 1776, had strived to ingratiate himself with court officials and ignored the colony's needs. Unzaga wisely realized that Louisiana could not survive under Spain's mercantile regulations and their enforcement could spark another insurrection. When the British, who engaged in widespread clandestine trade with Spanish colonies, displayed a willingness to do the same with Louisiana from neighboring West Florida (located on the Mississippi's east bank from Bayou Manchac to the Yazoo River and eastward to East Florida), Unzaga permitted it, but within limits. The British served as an alternative to trade with France and the French West Indies, and the commerce continued throughout Unzaga's term. Effectively, Unzaga's flexibility acted as a form of social control by allowing French Creoles to perceive the Spanish Crown as willing to address their specific needs.

Change occurred only when pro-French ministers in Spain assumed power in 1776, and they gradually reopened trade with the French West Indies as well as facilitated commerce between the Spanish colonies.[27]

Unzaga's successor, Governor Bernardo de Gálvez (1777–1782), allowed greater trade with the French West Indies and restricted British merchants to New Orleans, where he could regulate and tax their activities. By the time the Spaniards entered the American Revolutionary War and began the conquest of British West Florida in 1779, resentment about trade from Gallic inhabitants had vanished, and they willingly assisted Spain in the conflict.[28] The war effort engulfed all of Louisiana's inhabitants, and victory over an inveterate common foe elated them. Further improvements in Louisiana's economy occurred as Spain enacted new laws in 1782 and thereafter that steadily expanded trade. Moreover, from 1788 commerce with the United States began in earnest and quickly grew in volume. Spain in the 1790s was often at war, and it allowed neutral nations, including the United States, to trade with Spanish colonies. But tension between Spaniards and a few French Creoles still loyal to the former mother country kindled anew with the start of the French Revolution. As the revolution became progressively radical, it led to the execution of Bourbon king Louis XVI, an act that provoked Spain's own Bourbon sovereign to join the first coalition of conservative monarchies and war (1793–95) on republican France.[29]

During the conflict, a few Gallic Louisianians supported the former mother country, and a handful of French Jacobins, armed with incendiary propaganda, entered the colony to radicalize its inhabitants, particularly New Orleans, the colony's nerve center. While signs of both white and black unrest alarmed Governor Francisco Luis Héctor, Barón de Carondelet (1792–1797), they did not measure up to the exaggerated descriptions he dispatched to superiors in Havana and Madrid. At one point, to quell the agitation incited by a noisy minority of the city's residents, the governor summoned militia units from rural settlements throughout lower Louisiana, and they readily responded. The mere appearance of these armed Acadians, Spaniards, Anglo-Americans, and free blacks in the city immediately silenced the militant Jacobins. Carondelet also illegally expelled agitators from the colony, which earned him a royal reprimand.[30] In general, the episode demonstrated the effectiveness of Spanish social control measures.

Slavery and Social Control

What motivated prominent Gallic Louisianians to side with Spain was the French Republic's termination of slavery and its 1793 decree granting blacks equality with whites. The conservative Spanish government, however, did

no such thing and recently had even capitulated to colonial slave owners
who protested royal slave reforms. Louisiana's Creole planters were generally slave holders, some of whom had major investments in blacks. In addition, planters, as well as other whites in the colony, dreaded the prospect
of being swept up in a bloodbath similar to those that had engulfed the
French in the West Indies. Louisiana's planters supported neither the radical French government nor the abolition of slavery, contrary to the asser-
tions of some historians.[31]

As noted, the province's trade and economy improved significantly from
the 1780s, and new royal decrees at that time commenced the flow of
African slaves to the Spanish colonies. Beginning soon after the American
Revolution, slaves poured into Louisiana. By the early 1790s, even Louisiana
inhabitants and ships brought blacks directly from Africa into the colony.
The slave spigot remained open until early 1796, when an economic down-
turn prompted the New Orleans cabildo, where planters had significant
input, to request the governor to halt the entry of slaves for sale, which he
did. Despite this, the government continued to admit slaves when introduced by planters, who purchased them abroad for personal use, or by new
settlers, who entered the colony for the first time with their property.[32]

When the Franco-Spanish war ended in July 1795, what discord the
war had engendered in Louisiana rapidly evaporated. Revolutionary
France, too, turned conservative and, before long, restored black slavery.
Moreover, fear of an African uprising in the colony because of the 1795
Pointe Coupée slave conspiracy, which occurred a hundred miles up the
Mississippi from New Orleans, dissipated after the slaves involved were
punished. The conspiracy was neither widespread nor did it generate a bru-
tal repression as one recent historian has contended.[33]

Although Spanish authorities in Louisiana encountered some difficulties both with the regulation of slaves and with dissident whites in opposition to peninsular slave policy, neither threatened Spain's control. Signs
of dissatisfaction among some French masters, particularly in the heavily
slave-populated New Orleans district, arose when they repeatedly denounced the "lenient" slave laws that O'Reilly had introduced in 1769.
Earlier, slave owners had also complained about Gallic slave rules and customs. In 1724 France drew up a *Code Noir* for Louisiana, modeled on the
1685 *Code Noir* for the French West Indies, which contained safeguards
for slaves. But Louisiana's officials and masters generally disallowed them
during the French regime. For example, slaves could not complain about

abuse by owners, and manumission required the consent of the Superior Council, which rarely granted it. The French Catholic Church in Louisiana similarly did little for slaves, aside from baptize them. Clerics performed relatively few church weddings for slaves because masters deplored them, as they preferred to sell off black adults singly, not as couples. Similarly, priests denied slaves extreme unction—the final rites—so as to draw a distinction between whites and blacks. Except when overturned by Spanish secular authorities, French church practices toward slaves persisted during Iberian rule.[34]

Once Spanish slave laws took hold in secular matters, blacks had more rights than they had possessed in the French era. Some historians have suggested that Spain did so to render slavery more palatable to blacks born into slavery, who would follow designated paths to freedom rather than revolt or flee. That would help to allay white fears of black insurrection and bolster proper behavior, as only slaves with impeccable conduct qualified for manumission. While these motives were perhaps true, they overlook that Spanish slave regulations arose from practices initiated in the Roman era and modified under King Alfonso VI, when racial distinctions largely did not exist and servitude was not necessarily permanent. Although the enslavement of whites ended in Europe in the late Middle Ages, it persisted in the Iberian Peninsula due to wars between Christian and Islamic kingdoms. Meanwhile, Portugal introduced black slavery in the fifteenth century, which Spain and other Atlantic nations soon imitated. Spain employed African slave labor in the New World in agriculture, mining, ranching, construction, and a multitude of other tasks. With the advent of black slavery, Spain did not modify its laws governing this institution. There were, however, customs within slavery that grew up in the colonies, and the customs and practices in Louisiana emulated those in Cuba; they were more compassionate than either French slave laws or British practices in neighboring West Florida between 1763 and 1781. This, however, should not minimize that individual masters, oblivious to written law or custom, at times behaved monstrously, and examples of inhuman slave owners were present in Spanish Louisiana.[35] While enforcement of Spanish laws generally occurred in the courts of New Orleans, not all cases involving master abuse or evasion of laws found their way to the bar of justice. Spaniards lacked the police power to regulate the treatment of slaves on every plantation; knowledge of sadistic whites abusing slaves occasionally came to light, but no doubt other cases averted detection.

Spanish slave practices mitigated the institution's harshness in Louisiana. Slaves could complain to the authorities about abuse by their owners and compel their sale to another master, who presumably would be kinder. Slaves had free time—Sundays, religious holidays, and after work hours—when they labored for themselves. This practice first developed in the West Indies and has been called an "internal economy." Slaves often grew foodstuffs in their gardens for sale or for themselves since many owners declined to provide them, or they worked for wages for other whites and sometimes even for their own masters. In either case, slaves retained their earnings; masters did not own the property (*peculium*) of slaves. With their money, slaves purchased food, clothing, and even small luxuries. Some fortunate bondspeople either saved or otherwise acquired enough money to purchase their freedom. Spanish law permitted this practice (*coartación*), and slaves could "buy themselves" against the wishes of their masters. Furthermore, they paid only their appraised value, not a price arbitrarily imposed by the owner and designed to frustrate slave efforts to gain their liberty.[36]

Flight was the most frequent problem in controlling slaves. It was a common phenomenon wherever slavery existed because it protested the master's mistreatment and/or the institution that held them in bondage. Flight happened most often when a slave judged the punishment he or she had received as unfair; the master sold a slave who did not wish to be parted from family and friends; or a slave was apprehensive about a new master. Most runaways never strayed far and soon returned since they wanted to remain close to kin and familiar surroundings. Moreover, lower Louisiana, where the preponderance of slaves in the colony lived, lacked suitable refuges for runaways. Life in the wilderness appealed largely to bondspeople who had abusive masters or had committed serious crimes. Few slaves in Louisiana fled to the Indians since they often hunted down runaways. Free blacks also chased maroons for pay. In the early 1770s, masters in the New Orleans district set up rewards, payable through the cabildo, to pursue and either capture or kill fugitives. The cabildo fund eventually collapsed because on 14 May, 1777, the Crown decreed that slave owner participation had to be voluntary, not mandatory as the cabildo had prescribed. It had taxed all slave owners for funds with which to reward captors of slaves and compensate owners two hundred pesos for each runaway killed. Several governors later tried to reestablish the fund, but they failed because masters beyond the New Orleans district adamantly refused to contribute to it. They argued that slaves from the New Orleans district were more likely to abscond than those from elsewhere. For similar reasons, many masters in the province, who had controlled their blacks, refused to compensate Pointe Coupée owners, whose fifty-four slaves were executed or imprisoned for conspiracy in 1795. Although slave owners throughout colonial Louisiana never constituted a unified body on the treatment of blacks, the most vociferous and influential, especially in the New Orleans district, generally made their wishes known, even when they failed to achieve their objectives.[37]

Since the most stringent slave masters were often wealthy and enjoyed distinction in the colony, enforcement of these laws presented a quandary to the Spaniards, who sought their assistance in running the colony. As people of substance, some purchased council seats on the New Orleans cabildo, attended and voted in *cabildos abiertos* (municipal forums open to the colonial elite) that discussed compelling issues, sometimes acted as syndics (assistants to district commandants), and served as officers in militia units while their sons became army officers. Governors only reluctantly crossed swords with these slave owners, although it happened. Carondelet, more than any other governor, raised the hackles of owners when he insisted on enforcing slave rights in several areas and reminding them of Spanish slave laws. But Carondelet also backed down at times in the face of planter intransigence.[38]

Under Governor Gálvez, who tied himself to the planter elite of the New Orleans district immediately upon arriving in the colony, it briefly appeared that planters might eradicate Spanish slave laws and impose their own. Two cabildo members, who were also planters, drew up slave regulations amenable to their cohorts known as the *Code Noir ou Loi Municipale* in 1778–1779. It annulled coartación and restored many of the earlier rigid French slave practices. Gálvez was on the verge of sending the new regulations to Spain for royal approval when he suddenly scrapped them. He did so because the cabildo attempted to infringe upon his prerogatives in supervising New Orleans' Charity Hospital. Furthermore, he belatedly recognized that he was remiss in not enforcing the special instructions his uncle (José de Gálvez, Minister of the Indies) had issued on the treatment of slaves, which designated gentler treatment.[39]

The governor's abandonment of masters in the New Orleans district halted their efforts to secure amenable slave laws for a number of years. They attempted to do so again in 1800, with the support of the acting military governor, the Marqués de Casa-Calvo (1799–1801), scion of a Cuban sugar magnate, but it resulted in a rebuke from the then acting civil governor of Louisiana and legal adviser to the government, Dr. Nicolás María Vidal. He recognized what these masters were trying to do with their "needed" but austere regulations and denied them permission to act. Rebuffed but not defeated, these slaveowners momentarily achieved their objective during the twenty days in December 1803 that France ruled Louisiana. Their victory, nevertheless, proved fleeting because Spanish, not French, slave law remained in effect until 1807 and 1808, when Americans in Louisiana supplanted them with their harsher regulations. Nevertheless, aspects of Spanish slave jurisprudence remained in effect for several more decades.[40]

Despite differences in Spanish and French laws and attitudes toward blacks and slavery, they never constituted a major problem in maintaining social control in the colony. The greatest concern occurred in the 1790s during the French and Haitian revolutions, but the ferment was largely limited to New Orleans, where outside influences entered the colony. Governor Carondelet also exaggerated the strife. Although the efforts to regulate slavery according to their precepts occasionally produced discord, the Spaniards in Louisiana generally resolved problems without resorting to external help.

Another aspect of slavery involved manumission, and free blacks in Louisiana increased conspicuously under the Spaniards, enough so that they have been likened to a class. These free people of color constituted an ethnic element rarely found elsewhere in the borderlands, except for Florida, as Landers' essay so amply illustrates. Unfortunately, the Spaniards in Louisiana never collected province-wide data on free blacks. New Orleans provides more information (gleaned from notarial, church, and census data) where they grew in number faster than in the countryside. Quite properly, coartación has been labeled an urban phenomenon because in New Orleans, more than elsewhere in the colony, black workers could earn the funds necessary to purchase their freedom. It was not accidental that most free blacks were artisans, whose incomes exceeded the wages of unskilled or agricultural slaves. In addition, many were mulattoes or quadroons, whose linkages to whites sometimes had assisted in gaining their freedom and occasionally even money and property. From only 97 in 1771, the number of free blacks in New Orleans rose to 315 six years later. By 1788, they had increased to 820. While no figure is known for free people of color at the end of the Spanish regime, the next census, in 1805, showed that they numbered 1,566. Probably several hundred more lived scattered throughout the province. Free blacks cooperated with the Spanish regime and, for the most part, supported rather than challenged it. They served proudly in black and mulatto militia with their own officers. These units participated in the American Revolution, chased fugitive slaves, and took part in expeditions that sought to capture the adventurer William Augustus Bowles. A few free people of color even became relatively wealthy and the owners of lands, businesses, and slaves.[41] The Spanish colonial political and legal structure contained enough mechanisms for co-opting such individuals that they acted as effective means of social control.

Immigrants and Social Control

Besides Louisiana's black population, growing due to slave imports, whites also entered the colony in burgeoning numbers through the later Spanish era. In this respect only Louisiana and Florida, as Jane Landers explains in her chapter, deviated from other eighteenth-century borderlands provinces in the admission of immigrants, and they constituted another group to control. From its acquisition by Spain, the Crown recognized that the colony's most significant function was as a *barrera*, or barrier, to stop Anglo-American encroachment from the English Atlantic colonies and later United States. To convert Louisiana into a bulwark, Spain needed to build up its population and initially sought settlers from friendly Catholic kingdoms in Europe and individuals and families searching for free lands to countercolonize. These desultory initial efforts, however, secured only minuscule numbers. The first Spanish governors continued to help arriving Acadian refugees from the English Atlantic colonies and French West Indies in their settlement. More significantly, in 1777 Spain agreed to the recruitment of Canary Islanders for a second army battalion stationed in the colony, choosing to conscript married men with families so as to increase Louisiana's Hispanic population. Although only bachelors eventually entered the army, the recruitment of families resulted in approximately two thousand civilian *Isleños* (islanders) arriving between 1778 and 1783. Their entry created several new settlements where the dominant language and customs were Spanish and which represented anomalies in the colony. Needless to say, the Canary Islanders never posed a problem to Spanish control.[42]

Not long after the last Isleños reached Louisiana, the Iberian government brought in sixteen hundred Acadian refugees living in France to bolster the colony's population. From the late French period, the mostly poor Acadians had been entering the province and receiving assistance in their settlement. Similar to the indigent already present, controlling them presented no trouble to the Spaniards. The Spanish government intended initially to assist the needy and uneducated Isleños and Acadians only briefly, but achieving self-sufficiency took longer than expected, and it eventually cost an enormous sum to the money-strapped mother country.[43]

By 1787, Spain determined that it could no longer bear the financial burden. Settlers, nevertheless, constituted an essential element if Louisiana was to remain Spanish and become a barrier to Anglo-American encroachment on the Mississippi. But the government could only obtain them at no cost from the newly independent American Atlantic states. Governor Esteban Miró shifted immigration policy when he proposed using the American adventurer James Wilkinson to further the entrance of settlers. He arrived in New Orleans in 1787, with plans to separate Kentucky or the American West and join the Spaniards in an alliance. Besides this well-known plan, Miró gave Wilkinson a second mission: to send Anglo-Americans to settle in Louisiana, where they could acquire free lands in the Natchez district. British immigrants, who elected not to leave following the Spanish conquest of West Florida in 1779–1781, were already settled there. Although Wilkinson objected to Miró's immigration project as contrary to his original project and sent few colonists, other people, attracted by free and fertile lands, rushed in to claim them.[44] While denying newcomers, who were mostly Protestants, the right to practice religions other than Catholicism, the Spanish government required only an oath of fidelity and observance of Spanish laws from them. In time the Natchez district developed into the largest Anglo-American settlement on the Mississippi. Spain appointed Lt. Col. Manuel Gayoso de Lemos, an English-speaking Spanish officer, as governor and sent Irish priests living in Spain to win them over to Catholicism. Spain endeavored diligently to attract these Anglo-American settlers to Louisiana and build up the colony's defenses against more of their own kind in the United States. Only after Spain ceded the Natchez district to the United States in the 1795 Treaty of San Lorenzo, but whose transfer Louisiana officials delayed because the cession gave away important fortifications, did Americans in Natchez, incited by Protestant ministers, rise up in protests against the Spaniards. In 1798, upon completion of the transfer, the area became a part of the Mississippi Territory.[45]

The Anglo-American newcomers to Spanish possessions, however, did not limit themselves to the Natchez district and settled in many places, including St. Louis, New Madrid, Arkansas, and at different locations in the lower province (the northern portion of present-day Louisiana, which became mainly Protestant as opposed to the predominantly Catholic southern portion). Anglo-Americans never represented a challenge to Spanish rule, since even in 1803 they made up only several thousand in a provincial population of approximately 25,000 white inhabitants. As evidence of this, adult males served loyally in militia units wherever they settled.[46] A few of them, who were militia officers, even served as district commandants.

Controlling the Fringes

Governors relied on army and militia officers to run the districts in Louisiana and maintain control over the local inhabitants. Prime objectives for them included maintaining harmony among the residents and ensuring that they engaged in pursuits that allowed the communities to function economically without government assistance. At older civilian settlements, French Creole militia officers usually commanded. At settlements where a fort was present, often, but not always, an army officer who was either a Spaniard or French Creole served.[47] In most districts, problems in keeping the settlers at work and peaceful were minimal, although on rare occasion turmoil could engulf a community. Such an incident occurred at Natchitoches in 1795–1796, which necessitated sending an army officer with a detachment of soldiers to replace the local militia officer, who had allowed the agitation to boil over. It arose when the eccentric French-born resident priest, Father Jean Delvaux, refused to be reassigned and rallied a dissident fringe of an already fractured community to his support, and it momentarily convulsed the district.[48]

Control of the Indian tribes also constituted a special problem for Louisiana's Spaniards. As Juliana Barr's chapter makes clear, the Louisiana-Texas frontier represented the limits of Spanish dominion in North America in the face of Indian peoples that had successfully preserved their independence. In Louisiana three posts on the Mississippi's west bank figured as hubs for trade and domination of the natives. In descending importance, they were St. Louis, whose jurisdiction contained the largest number of tribes and the greatest trade; Natchitoches on the Red River, which also had many tribes; and Arkansas Post, where considerably fewer Indians lived. Of the tribes, the Osage nation possessed the most numerous hunters and most important trade, but it also posed concerns because of the hostile tendencies of its younger warriors. The aggressive Osages warred on many tribes throughout the present-day states of Missouri, Arkansas, and northwestern Louisiana, in particular against the smaller Quapaw and Caddo nations. Weaker but friendlier tribes constantly exhorted the Spaniards to halt Osage depredations. When curtailing trade failed to subdue the Osages, often because of surreptitious trade, governors confronted a seemingly unresolvable quagmire. One Osage band repeatedly sought goods in Arkansas, which local business-starved merchants craved but governors denied because it undermined control. No other tribe killed as many white hunters and *habitants* as did the Osages, and all without paying retribution. Among governors, only Carondelet advocated battling the Osages, but coordinating from afar a motley military force of Indians, white hunters, and militiamen did not work. What proved more successful was French Creole merchant Auguste Chouteau's construction of a fort in Osage country manned by twenty militiamen.[49]

In general, however, Spanish weakness in both manpower and trade goods seriously crippled efforts to maintain tranquility on the Mississippi's west bank. The Spaniards never resolved the Osage dilemma, but, fortunately for Spanish authorities, their depredations occurred on the fringes of white settlement and involved few settlers. As in Texas, efforts at controlling the Indians lay beyond the realm of social control, in the arenas of diplomatic and commercial relations.

Conclusions

In controlling Louisiana, the Spaniards faced their greatest difficulty in the beginning, when ignorance about the colony, preoccupation with more important possessions, and limited resources, all contributed to making errors. Furthermore, Louisiana's past as a Gallic colony; the presence of French, African, and native inhabitants; and its location on the edge of first the British empire and later the United States made it a potentially unruly place. The most serious dissension sprang from a small but determined subversive element within the French Creole population that engineered a revolt for economic and political reasons. Later unrest resulted from dissident whites over the exercise of slavery and from African slaves who protested the institution that held them in bondage. While these groups created quandaries in administration that demanded resolution, Spanish officials in Louisiana dominated most of the diverse and restless elements and controlled most situations. Meanwhile, the bulk of the inhabitants across the province lived quietly and without raising concerns to Spanish administration. Spain's policy fervently sought cooperation, not opposition, from its inhabitants and strove to avoid antagonizing any faction. When the Iberian nation surrendered the colony, it did so for reasons that emanated from Europe and not because its representatives had lost control to the inhabitants, as happened in the southwestern borderlands.

Spain's shift to dispose of Louisiana began with Manuel Godoy's rise to power as first secretary of state in 1793. Exasperated by burdensome military expenditures to protect the colony from an increasingly militant and encroaching United States, he negotiated the Treaty of San Lorenzo (Pinckney's Treaty) with the republic in 1795 to purchase goodwill. The agreement ceded lands that the United States claimed from its 1783 treaty with Great Britain, but which Spain held through conquest and its own accord with the British. Besides ceding territories with important forts on them, Godoy, out of step with Spanish officials in Louisiana who were committed to its retention, drastically reduced expenditures for the vexatious colony and eagerly sought an opportunity to relinquish ownership.[50]

In 1800 Godoy achieved his objective when he retroceded the colony to France. Godoy had expected the French directorate to assume responsibility for defending the barrera on the Mississippi and protecting Spanish lands beyond it. Although some Gallic residents eagerly awaited France's recovery of Louisiana, Napoleon Bonaparte quickly disillusioned them and Godoy. Once he received the province in 1802, the wily Frenchman promptly sold it to the United States. At the conclusion of the Spanish regime in Louisiana, most French Creoles bemoaned the transfer as they had not anticipated domination by a new and alien power. Despite the hostility that had greeted the first Spaniards in 1766, French Creoles had come to accept Spanish rule. Only the Americans resident in New Orleans cheered the United States' takeover in December 1803.[51]

NOTES

1. On French Louisiana, see Marcel Giraud, *A History of French Louisiana*, vol. 1: *The Reign of Louis XIV (1698–1715)*, trans. Joseph C. Lambert (Baton Rouge: Louisiana State University Press, 1974); *A History of French*

Louisiana, vol. 2: *Years of Transition, 1715–1717*, trans. Brian Pearce (Baton Rouge: Louisiana State University Press, 1993); *Histoire de Louisiane Française*, vol. 3: *L'Epoque de John Law, 1717–1720* (Paris: Presses Universitaires de France, 1966); *Histoire de Louisiane Française*, vol. 4: *La Louisiane àpres le système de Law* (Paris: Presses Universitaires de France, 1978); *A History of French Louisiana*, vol. 5: *The Company of the Indies, 1723–1731*, trans. Brian Pearce (Baton Rouge: Louisiana State University Press, 1992). See also Mathé Allain, *"Not Worth a Straw": French Colonial Policy and the Early Years of Louisiana* (Lafayette: Center for Louisiana Studies, University of Southwestern Louisiana, 1988); Nancy M. M. Surrey, *The Commerce of Louisiana During the French Regime, 1699–1763* (New York: Columbia University Press, 1916).

2.   "Resumen General," (Louisiana census of 1766), MS 569, fol. 107, Museo Naval, Madrid. Ira Berlin's *Many Thousands Gone: The First Two Centuries of Slavery in North America* (New Haven, Conn.: Yale University Press, 1998) contains a good discussion on the development of slavery in the North American English colonies, but his section on the Mississippi Valley is flawed because of his reliance on poorly researched books.

3.   General histories of Spanish Louisiana include Edwin Adams Davis, *Louisiana: A Narrative History* (3rd ed.; Baton Rouge, La.: Claitor's Publishing Division, 1971), and David J. Weber, *The Spanish Frontier in North America* (New Haven, Conn.: Yale University Press, 1992). Spanish acquisition of Louisiana anteceded only upper or Alta California, which was founded in 1769. On the mission-presidio system, see Herbert Eugene Bolton, "The Mission as a Frontier Institution in the Spanish American Colonies," *American Historical Review* 23, 1 (1917): 42–61.

4.   Mathé Allain, "French Emigration Policies: Louisiana, 1699–1715," in *Proceedings of the Fourth Meeting of the French Colonial Historical Society* (Washington, D.C.: University Press of America, 1979), 39–46; Glenn R. Conrad, comp., *The First Families of Louisiana*, 2 vols. (Baton Rouge, La.: Claitor's Publishing Division, 1971); Glenn R. Conrad, "*Emigration Forcée*: A French Attempt to Populate Louisiana, 1716–1720," in *Proceedings of the Fourth Meeting of the French Colonial Historical Society* (Washington, D.C.: University Press of America, 1979), 57–66; Marcel Giraud, "German Emigration," trans. Glenn R. Conrad, in *Revue de Louisiane/Louisiana Review* 10 (1981): 143–57. See also Glenn R. Conrad, *The French Experience in Louisiana*, vol. 1 of *The Louisiana Purchase Bicentennial Series in Louisiana History*, gen. ed. Glenn R. Conrad (Lafayette: Center for Louisiana Studies, University of Southwestern Louisiana, 1995), 106–73.

5.   Gilbert C. Din and John E. Harkins, *The New Orleans Cabildo: Colonial Louisiana's First City Government, 1769–1803* (Baton Rouge: Louisiana

State University Press, 1996), 101–26. Other fuero tribunals were present for ecclesiastical, governmental, and military personnel. Except for those appointed in 1769, subsequent regidores bought and held their seats in the city government until they died or sold them.

6. Ibid., 103–8, 114–15, 117–22; James A. Padgett, ed., "A Decree for Louisiana Issued by the Baron of Carondelet, June 1, 1795," *Louisiana Historical Quarterly* 20, 3 (1937): 590–605. Because Spanish Louisiana had few trained lawyers, intelligent, knowledgeable, and literate individuals could serve as advocates before the courts.

7. Although not entirely reliable, the only book on the Spanish military in Louisiana is Jack D. L. Holmes, *Honor and Fidelity: The Louisiana Infantry Regiment and the Louisiana Militia Companies, 1766–1821* (Birmingham, Ala.: Louisiana Collection Series, 1965). See also Gilbert C. Din, "'For Defense of Country and the Glory of Arms': Army Officers in Spanish Louisiana, 1766–1803," *Louisiana History* 43, 1 (2002): 5–40.

8. Arthur S. Aiton, "The Diplomacy of the Louisiana Cession," *American Historical Review* 36, 4 (July 1931): 701–20. See also Robert L. Gold, *Borderland Empires in Transition: The Triple Nation Transfer of Florida* (Carbondale: Southern Illinois University Press, 1969).

9. King [Louis XV] and the Duke of Choiseul to French Director-General Jean Jacques Blaise d'Abbadie of Louisiana, Versailles, 21 April 1764, in Alcée Fortier, *A History of Louisiana*, ed. Jo Ann Carrigan (2nd ed., 2 vols.; Baton Rouge: Claitor's Book Store, 1966–1972), 1: 149–50.

10. Among works on Spanish reforms after the Seven Years' War, see Arthur S. Aiton, "Spanish Colonial Reorganization under the Family Compact," *Hispanic American Historical Review* 12, 3 (1932): 269–80; Alan J. Kuethe, *Cuba, 1753–1815: Crown, Military, and Society* (Knoxville: University of Tennessee Press, 1986), 24–49; Christon I. Archer, *The Army in Bourbon Mexico, 1760–1810* (Albuquerque: University of New Mexico Press, 1977); and Lyle N. McAlister, "The Reorganization of the Army of New Spain, 1763–1766," *Hispanic American Historical Review* 33, 1 (February 1953): 1–32; Bibiano Torres Ramírez, *Alejandro O'Reilly en Indias* (Seville: Escuela de Estudios Hispano-Americanos, 1969); Herbert Ingram Priestley, *José de Gálvez: Visitor-General of New Spain (1765–1771)* (Berkeley: University of California Press, 1916).

11. Marqués de Grimaldi to Antonio de Ulloa, Madrid, 24 May 1766, Papeles procedentes de la isla de Cuba (hereafter cited as PC) 174B, Archivo General de Indias, Seville (hereafter cited as AGI). See also Eugene W. Lyon, *Louisiana in French Diplomacy, 1759–1804* (1934; repr., Norman, Okla.: University of Oklahoma Press, 1974), 19–33.

12. John Preston Moore, "Antonio de Ulloa: A Profile of the First Spanish Governor of Louisiana," *Louisiana History* 8, 2 (1967): 189–218; and Arthur Preston Whitaker, "Antonio de Ulloa," *Hispanic American Historical Review* 15 (1935): 155–94. A thorough study of Ulloa's administration of Louisiana had not yet been written; see, however, John Preston Moore, *Revolt in Louisiana: The Spanish Occupation, 1766–1770* (Baton Rouge: Louisiana State University Press, 1976), 42–142; Vicente Rodríguez Casado, *Primeros años de dominación española en la Luisiana* (Madrid: Consejo Superior de Investigaciones Científicas, 1942); and David K. Bjork, "The Establishment of Spanish Rule in Louisiana" (Ph.D. diss., University of California, Berkeley, 1923).

13. Jerry A. Micelle, "From Law Court to Local Government: Metamorphosis of the Superior Council of French Louisiana," *Louisiana History* 9, 1 (1968): 85–107.

14. Moore, *Revolt in Louisiana*, 42–59.

15. Ibid.

16. Ibid., 113–16.

17. Gilbert C. Din, "Protecting the 'Barrera': Spain's Defenses in Louisiana, 1763–1779," *Louisiana History* 18, 2 (1978): 191–92.

18. Din and Harkins, *New Orleans Cabildo*, 41–43.

19. Ibid., 43; Antonio Bucareli to Ulloa, Havana, 7 June, 1768, AGI, PC, leg. 1054; Charles Gayarré, *History of Louisiana*, 4 vols., 3rd ed. (repr., New York: Arno Press, 1972), 2: 224–25.

20. Moore, *Revolt in Louisiana*, 131–32; Rodríguez Casado, *Primeros años*, 125–26. The 23 March 1768 economic decree, "Regulation of Louisiana Commerce," is in Lawrence Kinnaird, ed., *Spain in the Mississippi Valley, 1765–1794*, 3 Parts (Washington, D.C.: Government Printing Office, 1949), pt. 1: 45–50. Moore suggests, in *Revolt in Louisiana*, 147, that the rebel conspiracy, to a large degree, consisted of an extended set of family members, many related by marriage.

21. Fortier, *History of Louisiana*, 1: 161–62; Gayarré, *History of Louisiana*, 2: 181–85.

22. James E. Winston, "The Causes and Results of the Revolution of 1768 in Louisiana," *Louisiana Historical Quarterly* 15, 2 (1932): 181–213; Gayarré, *History of Louisiana*, 2: 284–359 and 3: 1–41; Moore, *Revolt in Louisiana*, 143–84; Rodríguez Casado, *Primeros años*, 137–72; Richard Ira Matthews, "The New Orleans Revolution of 1768: A Reappraisal," *Louisiana Studies* 4 (1965): 124–67. See also Carl A. Brasseaux, *Denis-Nicolas Foucault and the New Orleans Rebellion of 1768* (Ruston, La.: McGinty Publications, 1987).

23. Rodríguez Casado, *Primeros años*, 265–91, 319–50; Moore, *Revolt in Louisiana*, 185–215. See also Torres Ramírez, *Alejandro O'Reilly en Indias*, 97–179; and David Ker Texada, *Alejandro O'Reilly and the New Orleans Rebels* (New Orleans: Center for Louisiana Studies, University of Southwestern Louisiana, 1970). Because one of the prisoners sentenced to death had died, only five individuals, including Lafrénière, were executed.

24. "Ordinances and Instructions of Alexander O'Reilly, November 25, 1769," and "Instructions as to the manner of instituting suits, civil and criminal, and pronouncing judgments in general, in conformity to laws of the Nueva Recopilación de Castilla, and the Recopilación de las Indias, . . . November 25, 1769," both in Benjamin Franklin French, ed., *Historical Memoirs of Louisiana from the First Settlement of the Colony to the Departure of Governor O'Reilly in 1770: With Historical and Biographical Notes* (5 vols.; New York: Lamport, Blakeman and Law, 1853), 5: 254–88. On the New Orleans cabildo's economic participation, see John G. Clark, "The Role of the City Government in the Economic Development of New Orleans: Cabildo and City Council, 1783–1812," in *The Spanish in the Mississippi Valley, 1762–1804*, ed. John Francis McDermott, 133–48 (Urbana: University of Illinois Press, 1974). Because New Orleans, in comparison with other borderlands cities, was larger, enjoyed greater commercial activity, and possessed water access to overseas ports that most borderlands provinces lacked, its cabildo had more personnel and functions.

25. Torres Ramírez, *Alejandro O'Reilly*, 115–79; O'Reilly's instructions to the lieutenant governors of St. Louis and Natchitoches, to the commandant of Arkansas Post, and to the commandants in lower Louisiana are in AGI, Audiencia de Santo Domingo, leg. 2594. Instructions to St. Louis are published in *The Spanish Regime in Missouri*, 2 vols. in 1, ed. Louis Houck (1909; repr., New York: Arno Press, 1971), 1: 76–83; and to Arkansas Post in "The First Spanish Instructions for Arkansas Post, November 15, 1769," ed. Gilbert C. Din, *Arkansas Historical Quarterly* 53, 3 (1994): 312–19. See also David K. Bjork's two works, "The Establishment of Spanish Rule in the Province of Louisiana, 1762–1770," and "Alexander O'Reilly and the Spanish Occupation of Louisiana, 1769–1770," in *New Spain and the Anglo-American West: Historical Contributions Presented to Herbert Eugene Bolton*, 2 vols., ed. George P. Hammond, 1: 165–82 (1932; repr., New York: Kraus Reprint Co., 1969); David Ker Texada, "The Administration of Alejandro O'Reilly as Governor of Louisiana, 1769–1770" (Ph.D. diss., Louisiana State University, 1968).

26. Many documents in the Spanish archives attest to the French residents of Louisiana who cooperated with the Spaniards. See, in particular, Din and Harkins, *New Orleans Cabildo*, passim, and Din, "For Defense of Country," 5–40.

27. Light Townsend Cummins, "Luis de Unzaga y Amezaga, Colonial
    Governor, 1770–1777," in *The Louisiana Governors: From Iberville to Edwards*,
    ed. Joseph G. Dawson III, 52–56 (Baton Rouge: Louisiana State University
    Press, 1990); Gilbert C. Din, *Louisiana in 1776: A Memoria of Francisco
    Bouligny* (New Orleans: Louisiana Collection Series, 1977). Julia Carpenter
    Frederick, in "Luis de Unzaga and Bourbon Reform in Spanish Louisiana,
    1770–1776" (Ph.D. diss., Louisiana State University, 2000), has recently
    argued that Unzaga regulated the volume of clandestine trade. See also
    Robin Fabel, *The Economy of British West Florida* (Tuscaloosa: University
    of Alabama Press, 1988), 75–109; and Margaret Fisher Dalrymple, *The
    Merchant of Manchac: The Letterbooks of John Fitzpatrick, 1768–1790*
    (Baton Rouge: Louisiana State University Press, 1978).

28. John G. Clark, *New Orleans, 1718–1812: An Economic History* (Baton Rouge:
    Louisiana State University Press, 1970), 222–24; Gilbert C. Din, *Spaniards,
    Planters, and Slaves: The Spanish Regulation of Slavery, 1763–1803* (College
    Station: Texas A&M University Press, 1999), 73, 80.

29. Clark, *New Orleans*, 224–38; a book and two articles by Arthur P. Whitaker,
    *Documents Relating to the Commercial Policy of Spain in the Floridas, with
    Incidental Reference to Louisiana* (Deland: Florida State Historical Society,
    1931); "The Commerce of Louisiana and the Floridas at the End of the
    Eighteenth Century," *Hispanic American Historical Review* 8, 2 (1928):
    190–203; and "Reed and Forde, Merchant Adventurers of Philadelphia:
    Their Trade with Spanish New Orleans," *Pennsylvania Magazine of History
    and Biography* 61 (1937): 237–62; John Walton Caughey, *Bernardo de Gálvez
    in Louisiana, 1776–1783* (Berkeley: University of California Press, 1934);
    Carolyn Fick, *The Making of Haiti: The Saint-Domingue Revolution from
    Below* (Knoxville: University of Tennessee Press, 1990); David P. Geggus,
    A Turbulent Time: The French Revolution and the Greater Caribbean
    (Bloomington: Indiana University Press, 1997).

30. Gayarré, *History of Louisiana*, 2: 325–55. Although errors abound in Ernest
    R. Liljegren, "Jacobinism in Spanish Louisiana, 1792–1797," *Louisiana
    Historical Quarterly* 21, 1 (1939): 47–96, especially on Natchitoches, he has
    a reasonably accurate description of revolutionary activities in New Orleans.
    On strife in Natchitoches, see Gilbert C. Din, "Father Jean Delvaux and the
    Natchitoches Revolt of 1795," *Louisiana History* 40, 1 (1999): 5–30. See also
    Cyril L. R. James, *The Black Jacobins: Toussaint Louverture and the San
    Domingo Revolt* (2nd ed.; New York: Dial Press, 1963).

31. Laura Foner, in "The Free People of Color in Louisiana and St. Domingue:
    A Comparative Portrait of Two Three-Caste Slave Societies," *Journal of
    Social History* 3, 4 (summer 1970): 406–30, argues implausibly that planters
    encouraged their slaves to revolt. Gwendolyn Midlo Hall, in *Africans in*

Colonial Louisiana: The Development of Afro-Creole Culture in the Eighteenth Century (Baton Rouge: Louisiana State University Press, 1992), 373–74, asserts that lower-class whites supported a 1795 slave conspiracy but presents no evidence. For a different view, see Din, *Spaniards, Planters, and Slaves*, 205–8, 218–19; and Gilbert C. Din, "Carondelet, the Cabildo, and Slaves: Louisiana in 1795," *Louisiana History* 38, 1 (1997): 5–28.

32. Din, *Spaniards, Planters, and Slaves*, 122–24, 134; Diego de Gardoqui to the governor of Louisiana, Aranjuez, 24 January 1793, PC 184A, AGI. On the heterogeneity of Louisiana slaves, see Peter Caron, "'Of a nation which the others do not understand': Bambara Slaves and African Ethnicity in Colonial Louisiana, 1718–1760," *Slavery and Abolition* 18 (1997): 98–121; and Thomas N. Ingersoll, "The Slave Trade and Ethnic Diversity of Louisiana's Slave Community," *Louisiana History* 37, 2 (1996): 23–62. The New Orleans cabildo always needed the governor's approval to act.

33. Din, *Spaniards, Planters, and Slaves*, 155–76, 296–304; Juan José Andreu Ocariz, *Movimientos rebeldes de los esclavos negros de Luisiana* (Zaragoza, Spain: Cagisa, 1977), 117–77. Hall, in *Africans*, 376–80, argues that repression followed discovery of the 1795 slave conspiracy.

34. Din, *Spaniards, Planters, and Slaves*, 3–34, 127–29; Mathé Allain, "Slave Policies in French Louisiana," *Louisiana History* 21, 2 (1980): 127–38; Carl A. Brasseaux, "The Administration of Slave Regulations in French Louisiana, 1724–1766," *Louisiana History* 21, 2 (1980): 139–58; Louis Sala-Molins, *Le Code Noir, ou le Calvaire de Canaan; Records of the States of the United States of America: Louisiana, 1678–1810* (Paris: Presses Universitaires de France, 1987); two articles by Hans W. Baade, "The *Gens de Couleur* of Louisiana: Comparative Slave Law in Microcosm," *Cardozo Law Review* 18, 2 (1996): 535–86; and "The Bifurcated Romanist Tradition of Slavery in Louisiana," *Tulane Law Review* 70, 5 (1996): 1481–99.

35. Din, *Spaniards, Planters, and Slaves*, 91, 136–38; two articles by Thomas N. Ingersoll, "Free Blacks in a Slave Society: New Orleans, 1718–1812," *William and Mary Quarterly*, 3d ser., 48, 2 (1991): 172–200, and "Slave Codes and Judicial Practice in New Orleans, 1718–1807," *Law and History Review* 13, 1 (1995): 23–62. See also Gilbert C. Din, "Slavery in the Florida Parishes Under the Spanish Regime, 1779–1803," in *A Fierce and Fractious Frontier: The Curious Development of Louisiana's Florida Parishes, 1699–2000*, ed. Samuel C. Hyde Jr., 60–90 (Baton Rouge: Louisiana State University Press, 2004).

36. Din, *Spaniards, Planters, and Slaves*, 76, 126–29; Kimberly S. Hanger, *Bounded Lives, Bounded Places: Free Black Society in Colonial New Orleans, 1769–1803* (Durham, N.C.: Duke University Press, 1997), 17–54; Roderick A. McDonald, "Independent Economic Production by Slaves

on Antebellum Louisiana Sugar Plantations," in *Cultivation and Culture: Labor and the Shaping of Slave Life in the Americas*, ed. Ira Berlin and Philip D. Morgan, 275–99 (Charlottesville: University Press of Virginia, 1993). On coartación, see Hubert H. S. Aimes, "Coartación: A Spanish Institution for the Advancement of Slaves into Freedmen," *Yale Review*, old ser., 17 (1908–1909): 412–31; and Hans W. Baade, "The Law of Slavery in Spanish *Luisiana*, 1769–1803," in *Louisiana's Legal Heritage*, ed. Edward F. Haas, 43–86 (Pensacola: Perdido Bay Press, 1983).

37. Gilbert C. Din, "*Cimarrones* and the San Malo Band in Spanish Louisiana," *Louisiana History* 21, 3 (1980): 237–62; Din and Harkins, *New Orleans Cabildo*, 156–69. See also Gerald W. Mullin, *Flight and Rebellion: Slave Resistance in Eighteenth-Century Virginia* (New York: Oxford University Press, 1972), and John Hope Franklin and Loren Schweninger, *Runaway Slaves: Rebels on the Plantation* (New York: Oxford University Press, 1999).

38. Din, *Spaniards, Planters, and Slaves*, 133–93; Stephen Webre, "The Problem of Slavery in Spanish Louisiana, 1769–1803," *Louisiana History* 25, 2 (1982): 117–35.

39. Din, *Spaniards, Planters, and Slaves*, 70–88. See also Baade, "Law of Slavery in Spanish *Luisiana*," 43–86; and Gilbert C. Din, "Bernardo de Gálvez: A Reexamination of His Governorship," in *The Spanish Presence in Louisiana, 1763–1803*, ed. Gilbert C. Din, vol. 2 of *The Louisiana Purchase Bicentennial Series in Louisiana History*, gen. ed. Glenn R. Conrad, 77–93 (Lafayette: Center for Louisiana Studies, University of Southwestern Louisiana, 1996).

40. Din, *Spaniards, Planters, and Slaves*, 75–79, 205–8; and Din, "Bernardo de Gálvez," 77–93. On Spanish slave laws surviving into the American era, see Judith Kelleher Schafer, *Slavery, the Civil Law, and the Supreme Court of Louisiana* (Baton Rouge: Louisiana State University Press, 1994). On Nicolás María Vidal berating masters for abusing their slaves, see Vidal to the Cabildo, New Orleans, 21 October 1800, in Ronald R. Morazán, "Letters, Petitions, and Decrees of the Cabildo of New Orleans, 1800–1803," 2 vols. (Ph.D. diss., Louisiana State University, 1972), 1: 203.

41. Hanger, *Bounded Lives, Bounded Places*, 17–54. See also Donald E. Everett, "Free People of Color in Colonial Louisiana," *Louisiana History* 7, 1 (1966): 21–50; Virginia Meacham Gould, "The Free Creoles of Color of the Antebellum Gulf Ports of Mobile and Pensacola: A Struggle for the Middle Ground," in *Creoles of Color of the Gulf South*, ed. James H. Dormon, 28–50 (Knoxville: University of Tennessee Press, 1996); Thomas N. Ingersoll, *Mammon and Manon in Early New Orleans: The First Slave Society in the Deep South, 1718–1819* (Knoxville: University of Tennessee Press, 1999); and Gary B. Mills, *The Forgotten People: Cane River's Creoles of Color* (Baton Rouge: Louisiana State University Press, 1987). See also several articles

by Kimberly S. Hanger, "Conflicting Loyalties: The French Revolution and Free People of Color in Spanish New Orleans," *Louisiana History* 34, 1 (1993): 5–33; "Patronage, Property, and Persistence: The Emergence of a Free Black Elite in Spanish New Orleans," *Slavery and Abolition* 17, 1 (1996): 44–64; and "'Almost All Have Callings': Free Blacks at Work in Spanish New Orleans," *Colonial Latin American Historical Review* 3, 2 (1994): 141–64.

42. Two works by Gilbert C. Din, "Early Spanish Colonization Efforts in Louisiana," *Louisiana Studies* 11, 1 (1972): 31–49; and *The Canary Islanders of Louisiana* (Baton Rouge: Louisiana State University Press, 1988), 12–83.

43. Carl A. Brasseaux, *The Founding of New Acadia: The Beginnings of Acadian Life in Louisiana, 1765–1803* (Baton Rouge: Louisiana State University Press, 1987), 73–166; Fernando Solano Costa, "La emigración acadiana a la Luisiana española (1783–1785)," *Cuadernos de historia Jerónimo Zurita* 2, 7 (1954): 82–125; and Oscar William Winzerling, *Acadian Odyssey* (Baton Rouge: Louisiana State University Press, 1955).

44. Arthur Preston Whitaker, "James Wilkinson's First Descent to New Orleans in 1787," *Hispanic American Historical Review* 7, 1 (1928): 82–97; two articles by Gilbert C. Din, "The Immigration Policy of Governor Esteban Miró in Spanish Louisiana," *Southwestern Historical Quarterly* 73, 2 (1969): 155–75; and "Spain's Immigration Policy in Louisiana and the American Penetration, 1792–1803," *Southwestern Historical Quarterly* 76, 3 (1973): 255–76. See also James Ripley Jacobs, *Tarnished Warrior: Major-General James Wilkinson* (New York: Macmillan Company, 1938); Arthur Preston Whitaker, *Spanish American Frontier, 1783–1795: The Westward Movement and the Spanish Retreat in the Mississippi Valley* (1927; repr., Gloucester, Mass.: Peter Smith, 1962), *passim*; and Juan Navarro Latorre and Francisco Solano Costa, *¿Conspiración española? 1787–1789: Contribución al estudio de las primeras relaciones históricas entre España y los Estados Unidos de Norteamérica* (Zaragoza: Institución Fernando el Católico, 1949).

45. See a book and two articles by Jack D. L. Holmes, *Gayoso: The Life and Times of a Spanish Governor on the Mississippi, 1789–1799* (Baton Rouge: Louisiana State University Press, 1965), 33–135; "Irish Priests in Spanish Natchez," *Journal of Mississippi History* 29 (1967): 169–80, and "Father Francis Lennan and His Activities in Spanish Louisiana and West Florida," *Louisiana Studies* 5 (1966): 255–65; Gilbert C. Din, "The Irish Mission to West Florida," *Louisiana History* 12, 4 (1971): 315–34; Michael J. Curley, *Church and State in the Spanish Floridas* (Washington, D.C.: Catholic University of America Press., 1940).

46. Din, "Spain's Immigration Policy," 255–76; Holmes, *Gayoso*, 180–99.

47. On districts in Spanish Louisiana, see E. Russ Williams, *Filhiol and the
    Founding of Spanish Poste d'Ouachita: The Ouachita Valley in Colonial Louisiana,
    1783–1804* (Monroe, La.: published privately, 1982); Carmen González
    López-Briones, "Spain in the Mississippi Valley: Spanish Arkansas,
    1762–1803" (Ph.D. diss., Purdue University, 1983); Carl J. Ekberg, *Colonial
    Ste. Genevieve: An Adventure on the Mississippi Frontier* (Gerald, Mo.: Patrice
    Press, 1985); and Morris S. Arnold, *Colonial Arkansas, 1686–1804: A Social
    and Cultural History* (Fayetteville: University of Arkansas Press, 1991). See
    also by Arnold, *Unequal Laws unto a Savage Race: European Legal Traditions in
    Arkansas, 1686–1836* (Fayetteville: University of Arkansas Press, 1985).

48. Din, "Father Jean Delvaux," 5–30.

49. Gilbert C. Din and Abraham P. Nasatir, *The Imperial Osages: Spanish-Indian
    Diplomacy in the Mississippi Valley* (Norman: University of Oklahoma Press,
    1983); W. David Baird, *The Osage People* (Phoenix: Indian Tribal Series,
    1972). See also Willard H. Rollings, *The Osage: An Ethnohistorical Study
    of Hegemony on the Prairie-Plains* (Columbia: University of Missouri Press,
    1992); and Carl H. Chapman, "The Indomitable Osages in Spanish Illinois
    (Upper Louisiana), 1763–1804," in *The Spanish in the Mississippi Valley,
    1762–1804*, ed. John Francis McDermott, 272–84 (Urbana: University of
    Illinois Press, 1974); Morris S. Arnold, *The Rumble of a Distant Drum: The
    Quapaw and Old World Newcomers, 1673–1804* (Fayetteville: University of
    Arkansas Press, 2000).

50. Douglas Hilt, "Manuel Godoy, Prince of Peace," *History Today* 21
    (December 1971): 833–41; Alexander DeConde, *This Affair of Louisiana*
    (New York: Charles Scribner's Sons, 1976), 60–72; Samuel Flagg Bemis,
    Pinckney's Treaty: America's Advantage from Europe's Distress, 1783–1800
    (rev. ed.; New Haven, Conn.: Yale University Press, 1960); Raymond A.
    Young, "Pinckney's Treaty—A New Perspective," *Hispanic American
    Historical Review* 43, 4 (1963): 526–35; Arthur P. Whitaker, "New Light on
    the Treaty of San Lorenzo: An Essay in Historical Criticism," *Mississippi
    Valley Historical Review* 15, 4 (1929): 435–54; Arthur Preston Whitaker,
    The Mississippi Question, 1795–1803: A Study in Trade, Politics, and Diplomacy
    (repr., Gloucester, Mass.: Peter Smith, 1962), 183–86.

51. Gayarré, *History of Louisiana*, 3: 620. See also DeConde, *This Affair
    of Louisiana*, 196–208; Arthur Preston Whitaker, "The Retrocession of
    Louisiana in Spanish Policy," *American Historical Review* 39, 3 (1934):
    454–76.

CHAPTER FOUR

"They Conceal a Malice Most Refined"

Controlling Social and Ethnic Mobility in Late Colonial New Mexico

Ross Frank

Gauging the processes of social control at work in the northern provinces is not an easy process, but in New Mexico a report written in 1794 by Governor don Fernando de la Concha represents an unusual opportunity to view the internal thinking of colonial officials in the context of contemporary events. In this document Governor Concha transmitted his "instructions" to his successor, Lt. Col. don Fernando Chacón, "so that he may adopt [for New Mexico] that which appears suitable for the good, tranquility, and encouragement of the same Province."[1] The instructions have three sections, concerning: (1) understanding relations between the province and the non-Pueblo "Barbarous Nations"; (2) the conduct of the inhabitants of the province; and (3) managing the presidial company headquartered in Santa Fe.

The focus here falls on the second section, which provides a remarkable discussion of the forces at work within the province. The section begins:

Nothing is so difficult as knowing man, and only by constantly observing his conduct closely, adjusted on occasion, may one form some idea of his character. In general, the character that I have been able to form from experience of the inhabitants of the Province of New Mexico (with the exception of the Pueblo Indians) is not very advantageous. Under the simulated appearance of ignorance or rusticity, they conceal a malice most refined.[2]

The character assigned to New Mexico's *vecino* population, the unflattering comparison to the Puebloans, and the very language used by the governor to describe the problems that he identified, all signaled to Concha's successor that the underlying issue lay precisely in how to use the available tools for social control to greatest effect.

Governor Concha wrote the letter to his successor in the midst of a decade that represented a point of social, economic, and cultural departure for the province of New Mexico.[3] A rapidly growing vecino[4] population, peace and alliance with the Comanches, Utes, and Navajos, and expanding agricultural production and trade with Nueva Vizcaya and Sonora, led to a quickening economy, and an increasingly self-confident and assertive citizenry. Social and economic relations with the Pueblo Indians (*indios de pueblo*) suffered as a result, as vecinos came to define their own identity in contrast to the characteristics of their Pueblo neighbors.

Assessments disparaging of the settler population in relation to the Pueblo Indians did not begin in the 1790s. The secretary and archivist to Spanish officials in Mexico City concerned with the north, Fray Juan Agustín de Morfí, wrote in 1778 of the tendency of vecinos to spread out their houses along the banks of the Río Grande, ignoring their vulnerability to attack from Apache and Comanche raiders.[5] In contrast to the Pueblo Indians, "this example teaches nothing to the Spaniards, who should be conducting themselves with more propriety and self-discipline than the Indians, [but who] are not ashamed to prove themselves ruder than the pagans [unbaptized non-Pueblo Indians]."

The difference between Morfí and Concha's descriptions lies in the way in which the consequence of vecino behavior becomes not just a source of self-inflicted danger, but the willful disruption of the colonial state's ability to manage the consequences of economic and social change. Concha's instruction to Chacón places the governors and their subordinates squarely in opposition to the natural tendencies of the non-Indian populace of the province. In the process of setting out the situation that the new governor must confront over the course of his report, Concha reveals a striking contradiction between the state's role in encouraging and supporting the economic development and integration of New Mexico into the larger northern Mexican economy, and the aspirations for social mobility that accompanied vecinos who benefited from the pursuit of new commercial opportunities. In contrast, the Pueblo Indians receive praise, in part because they are more effectively subjected to the social controls created by the colonial structure: economic coercion or marginalization, and oversight and surveillance by provincial officials and Franciscan missionaries.

Governor Concha explained New Mexican vecino "malice" as the product of both circumstance and environment. "It is a very rare person," he writes, "in whom there does not run the vices of robbery and falsehood at the same time. The dispersion of the establishments, the poor education that results from this, and the proximity and dealings with the Barbarous Nations in which they find themselves immersed . . . is the origin that preserves and makes those vices propagate more every day." At the same time Concha delineated his view of the bounds of his authority to eliminate either the "vices" or their root causes. Ultimately, he recognizes that "these one cannot cut out except for under a new constitution, and in this way effect a complete variation in the actual system that exists. This great work is not in the power of the Governor, and it is also necessary to take care to reduce the harms in whatever ways that are possible: to which end I will expound on the methods dictated by prudence, reason, equity, and the practice of about seven years during which I have governed the province."[6] The governor defined his function as a contest over the containment of vecino excesses using the considerable, but ultimately limited, techniques of social control at his disposal.

Malicious Vecinos

Opportunistic economic behavior by vecinos in response to new and renewed markets lay at the center of Governor Concha's concerns. After decades of military campaigns and defense against raids from Comanche, Apache, Ute, and Navajo bands, Governor Juan Bautista de Anza concluded a series of treaties beginning in 1786 that established a system of alliances. Unlike the situation described in Texas by Juliana Barr (see chapter 7), the peace and system of alliances entered into by New Mexican officials held for much of the next generation, and allowed them to attempt to manage Spanish–Plains Indian–Pueblo relations.

As Concha explained to his successor, although the Comanches, Utes, and Jicarilla Apaches each had relationships with Spanish authorities, the latter two still hated the Comanche for having driven them out of their lands to the north of the province. Before the Comanche-Spanish alliance, Ute and Jicarilla raiding parties could attack Comanche encampments and exchange their spoils at trade fairs within New Mexico. The province welcomed this commerce, but in order to appear impartial Concha attempted to enforce a policy of interdicting and returning stolen animals crossing through New Mexico. The governor admitted that this policy had not been entirely successful. It had been thwarted, he said, "by the citizenry of the frontiers who, for the immediate advantage of buying a horse cheaply, or having taken some part in the robberies with impunity, habitually refuse to enforce the edicts."[7] Concha warned the incoming governor to take vigorous action in this matter "to keep in check an abuse that may be very prejudicial to this province." On one hand, the governor feared the consequences for the alliance system if goods seized from Comanches appeared at trade fairs in the hands of Utes and Apaches, which placed the provincial government in the way of vecino commercial interests. On the other hand, the determined actions of vecinos to take advantage of lower prices on the spoils of distant raids compromised the position of the governor as a creditable arbitrator among allied nations.

Another consistently disregarded regulation prohibited soldiers from trading or selling their mounts. During the 1770s the combination of incessant Comanche and Apache raids on New Mexican horse herds and periodic drought often left the soldiers of the Santa Fe presidio without enough animals to pursue their enemies effectively. As New Mexican herds recovered in peacetime, vecinos began to sell surplus horses in a vigorous market that developed within the province, among their Indian allies, and as far away as Sonora and Chihuahua. The sellers included soldiers, whose dealings in horses took place due to the "acquiescence of the sergeants and corporals." Apparently, soldiers sold horses from the presidio herd and replaced them with animals purchased elsewhere. Although soldiers had to provide six mounts for their use at their own expense, regulations prohibited them from selling their horses.[8] According to Concha, the ability of the soldiers to sustain this commerce depended on "the liaisons that these individuals have with the rest of the citizenry, [and] prevents the top officials from acquiring the necessary knowledge to work with vigor on this matter."[9] Concha recommended that proven buyers receive punishment and that soldiers found selling their horses lose their commissions.

The two examples above indicate how Spanish officials sought to control vecino participation in new opportunities created by late colonial economic expansion. In another arena, actions taken by provincial officials as a defensive necessity, to assert control over dispersed settlements during the 1770s, became an issue of the proper social behavior for a Spanish citizenry two decades later. Concha secured approval from the Commandant General of the Interior Provinces in 1789 to prohibit the rebuilding, repair, or resettling of any of buildings outside of the regular form desired for the Villa of Santa Fe. Again, the governor urged his successor to maintain constant vigilance. "The inhabitants are lazy," he explained. "They love the distance that provides them independence, and although they know the advantages that result from the union [of the houses], they affect ignorance of them in order to adopt the liberty and the freedom that the *vecinos* see and note in the Barbarous Indians."[10]

Vecinos acted maliciously in other ways as well. They aggressively renewed and prosecuted already settled complaints and lawsuits at each change in the provincial administration. Concha counseled,

> in order to understand what is current in this material, it is necessary to announce that all of the points of similar nature remain determined, in writing or verbally, in the general visitation that your predecessors have conducted, in which act the parties had been generally advised that those who do not remain satisfied, and consider themselves aggrieved, may always present themselves to the *Audiencia* of the district and produce the reasons that they have in their appeal. In consequence, no one has to understand or mix themselves in these affairs if it is not in order to facilitate them, and to draw attention to what they must do when they must make their appeals.[11]

A review of lawsuits that survive in New Mexico's colonial archives provides ample justification for Concha's concern about the constant revival of issues. Not surprisingly, cases involving land and water generally figured among the worst offenders.[12] Many of these issues arose toward the end of the eighteenth century and involved aggressive vecino farmers and merchants who responded to the renewed opportunities for overland trade with Nueva Vizcaya and Sonora by expanding their enterprises at the expense of their Pueblo neighbors.[13] In response, the governor recommended a conservative approach ("all of the points of similar nature remain determined") that had the effect of appearing to discount vecino economic aspirations when they hurt Pueblo interests. Further, Concha undermined vecino petitions of all kinds by describing complaints as subterfuges for other agendas, supported by perjured testimony.

> In order to make a determination in the matters and cases
> that occur, after proceeding to take the necessary accounts, the
> Governor does not have any other expedient but to value his
> own prudence, sound judgment, and good sense. This is what
> your predecessors have valued due to the lack of a lawyer with
> whom to consult. But today one must understand that never, or
> only rarely, is the first one who makes the demands in the right,
> and that he can find with the greatest facility, and without any
> gratification, whatever false witnesses that he needs.[14]

Tools for Social Control

Faced with citizen subjects whom he considered obstinate, untrustworthy, and even malicious, Concha continued the development of strategies for molding vecino social and economic behavior begun by Governor Anza before him. In his 1794 report to Governor Chacón, Concha laid out the available tools for social control and discussed some of their limitations. To the governor's eye, New Mexican society in the 1790s suffered from not having a clear hierarchy from which local leadership and governance might spring. "In no other country," he wrote, "is the renewal of the *alcaldes may- ores* [district magistrate] more difficult than in New Mexico due to the impossibility of finding a replacement. There are so few subjects that know how to write and to give a report, and much less undertake a charge of such importance, that few or none can be used." Not only did New Mexico lack educated elites who could perform the most rudimentary functions required of a local official, but "one must add that the same fortunes that rein in the Province disposes the souls of the *naturales* [natives] to obey with

*Gov. Concha had difficulty maintaining leaders in the 90s region

violence and repugnance any particular person that a short time before had no advantage at all over them."[15]

The lack of natural elites that the governor decried reflected the state of the social and economic transition associated with New Mexico's particular demographic history. The size of the vecino population had only surpassed that of the Pueblos in the generation before Concha's report, perhaps during the late 1770s. Concha's remarks refer to a transformation underway in the *casta* system, which served as a mechanism to socially differentiate classes on the basis of ethnic mixture. José Cuello describes and analyzes the system in his essay in this volume as it functioned in colonial Saltillo. By the 1790s in New Mexico, changing racial hierarchies made it difficult to rely upon the upper echelon of the castas as a source for a local elite, yet economic development had not yet identified an elite based upon wealth or another set of social indicators.

Although Franciscan missionaries and New Mexican officials used an arsenal of ethnic-racial designations to mark degrees of Spanish, Pueblo, Plains Indian, and African mixture, almost two centuries of cohabitation, punctuated by the 1680 Pueblo Revolt, the subsequent Spanish reoccupation, episodic violence with nonsedentary Indian groups, and eventual alliance, rendered such terms increasingly ambiguous and inconsistent. The terms *color quebrado*, *lobo*, *coyote*, *mulato*, *genízaro*, and *casta* used in New Mexican official documents did not bear a demonstrable relationship to the daily lives of individuals at the time Concha wrote his report. As in Sonora, Nueva Vizcaya, and other borderland provinces with a long history of settlement, the process of *mestizaje* reconfigured the vecino populations in terms of local demographic, economic, and social realities.

In response to this demographic shift, by the 1790s most descriptions of the settled New Mexican population used only two categories—"*Indios*" and "*vecinos y castas*"—to ascribe individuals on the basis of cultural behavior and domicile. As José Cuello argues for colonial Saltillo, rather than signifying a breakdown in the racialized social order, these changes mark its adaptation and reconfiguration as a system of social control. In New Mexico, with the meaning and identification of specific categories in flux, colonial officials moved to support and reinforce the alcaldes mayores in office as a source of continuity and acquired authority. As Concha put it, "the continuation in the office and the invariable custom of obeying at all times even the same individual, over time arrives at a point where this person gains some ascendancy over the rest, and whose actions they view with respect and consideration."[16] Continuing the same set of local officials in office for as long as possible helped to bolster authority for social control within the non-Indian ethnoracial category.

As in every borderland province with a presidial force, the military organization also provided a source for personal prestige and social status within the settler community. In addition, Pueblo Indian auxiliaries fought alongside presidio soldiers and vecino militia beginning in the early eighteenth century, shortly after the reconquest of New Mexico.[17] Military service against Apache, Comanche, and other enemies allowed Pueblo warriors to maintain indigenous military traditions, while receiving recognition from presidio officers. Like the Ópata troops in Sonora and the African militia in Florida, described in this volume by Cynthia Radding and Jane Landers respectively, Pueblo participation in the defense of New Mexico signified a measure of incorporation within the Spanish colonial sphere.

When New Mexican governors felt the need to engineer a mechanism to mold a social hierarchy within the redefined casta system emerging in the late eighteenth century, the military system provided a logical mechanism to turn to. Governor Anza had first expanded the militia system as a means of identifying and qualifying local elites to assist in the administration of the province. Anza had formed three companies of vecinos, and appointed deserving individuals as sergeants and corporals, Concha said, "with the desire to make distinction and foment in some way competition among those inhabitants that with little differences are equal in fortune and birth."[18] Concha had created a fourth company, but he ultimately judged the program a failure. "Far from obtaining the advantages that we have proposed," he wrote,

> the result has been the establishment and equipping of some
> men that lower the character of all of the officials who they
> touch, they form parties and always stir up the province, and
> with their particular ideas they accommodate themselves.
> Adding to this evil, that of getting out of contributing to the
> various tasks that keep the government occupied with what they
> need to practice, and [the harm done] to those who come to the
> rescue of the rest of the inhabitants that are not decorated with
> the character of an official.[19]

Concha suggested that Chacón move to abolish the vecino officers serving within the militia, if the commandant general concurred, and to place all militia companies within the regular command of the officers from the Santa Fe presidio. Vecinos had turned a potential tool for social control into an opening for discord.

The initiative that Concha described represented part of a strategy coordinated by successive governors for shaping New Mexican society that emerged from traditional, long naturalized colonial conceptions of the proper relationships between race, culture, and power applied to the particular context of the northern provinces. At critical junctures in his report, Concha makes explicit connections between vecino behavior and that of the "barbarous nations." The vecino vices of robbery and falsehood he assigns to structural causes: the dispersed nature of settlements and poor education. The catalyst that set the vecino's "malicious" behavior in motion, however, lay in "the proximity and dealings with the Barbarous Nations in which they find themselves immersed."[20] Vecinos leveled "repeated unfounded representations" against alcaldes mayores. "The lack of obedience," and "willfulness" of the citizenry became amplified by "the desire to live without subjection and in complete liberty, in imitation of the *Indios Barbaros* that they see in their proximity." Opposition to the regularization of the Villa of Santa Fe represented not just stubbornness or an unwillingness to undertake the considerable task of moving portions of the settlement. The impulse to obstruct the well-considered plans of colonial officials proceeded from an almost transformative urge "to adopt the liberty and the freedom that the vecinos see and note in the Barbarous Indians."[21] Concha's language represents one of the supports for a discursive structure that defined the boundaries for proper vecino behavior in relation to specific and reified cultural traits of the various "barbarous" non-Pueblo groups.

Language describing the Pueblo Indians supplied the other support for the structure emerging to provide social control in New Mexico. In his report, Concha systematically contrasted unsatisfactory vecino behavior with exemplary Pueblo Indian conduct. In the process, he exempted the Puebloans from his attribution of "malice most refined." While vecinos constantly renew old complaints and lawsuits, "it does not happen like this with the Pueblo Indians who proceed in this matter diametrically opposed to that of the citizenry. Always one encounters in them the truth, one can persuade them easily with reason, and never does one find in them, nor do they contribute to, any robbery."[22] In the case of the campaigns against the enemy Indians, those who participated generally received munitions distributed by the presidial officers. According to Concha, "the Pueblo Indians never ask for anything else, due to the advantages that they enjoy, but the *vecinos*, overbearing and of evil conduct, make trouble asking for horses and supplies."[23]

The significance of the position articulated by the governor goes beyond the trope that civilized *gente de razón* should not act like untamed, gentile Indians, and least of all be put to shame by the exemplary behavior of Pueblo Indians, only recently neophytes themselves. In the absence of usable definitions for late colonial citizenship based on blood, the presence of these two categories of Indian defined between them—and in contrast—the qualities of *vecinidad* in New Mexico, justified the actions taken by Bourbon officials to exert social control over the unruly vecino population, and suggested the tools that might build an effective system for implementation.

In one arena the Puebloans did not behave in an exemplary fashion, but Concha still used them to make his point. "Despite these good qualities," he continued, the Pueblos

> instigate demands for the removal of their Ministers of the
> Doctrine, or the Justices [alcaldes mayores] who govern them.
> They generally have no other object for this pretense than
> to oblige the missionaries who seek that specific destination,
> joining together with the *vecindario* (citizenry) annexed to the
> administration of the same *pueblos* [within the same *visita* of the
> missionary], to which end, one or another [party] implies and
> alleges a number of deeds against the missionaries in possession
> that generally turn out to be false.

Pueblo behavior performed an important anchoring function in the 1790s precisely because Puebloans lived under a relatively effective system of social control that had begun to coalesce as vecino social and economic aspirations had emerged. Regulations in New Mexico restricted the movement of Pueblo inhabitants without a permit signed by the alcalde mayor of the appropriate jurisdiction.[24] In addition to regulated passage through the province, the governor, the alcaldes mayores, and vecino merchants used the *repartimiento de efectos* (forced distribution of goods on credit) to extract goods from the Pueblos in demand by provincial and export markets. Although during the eighteenth century the practice ebbed and flowed throughout

New Spain, in New Mexico the economic opportunities of the 1790s unleashed this form of economic coercion on the Pueblos with particular vigor.
Concha explained to Chacón that,

> the only way that one can collect horses cheaply and of good
> quality is to order the commissioner [paymaster] to have
> supplies delivered from the presidio store of the kind that
> the Pueblo Indians use and with these tour all of the districts.
> In these [pueblos] there is much breeding of horses, and in
> that of Taos and Pecos there is a considerable portion that the
> natives barter from the Comanche nation.[25]

In addition to limited mobility and involuntary participation in a
vecino system of exchange, the third tool in the New Mexican system of
control over Pueblo life involved the power to officially create and erase
individual Pueblo Indian identity. In his discussion about what steps his
successor could take to fix the problem of the failed experiment to establish social difference within the vecino militia, Concha cautioned that whatever method he chose, decisions about which vecinos and Indians fought
on campaigns

> must be done with the utmost equity; the former by first name
> and last name, and the latter by number. In order to achieve
> this without confusion, and not to leave it to the *alcaldes mayores*
> arbitrarily, the new governor must immediately make ready for
> the introduction of a general census circulated to all of the men
> in these jurisdictions, with the expression of ages and disposition
> for war, by which means to obtain the power to form the lists of
> those that they take.[26]

By its very nature the taking of a colonial census defined vecinos in contrast to Pueblo Indians and those deemed not a part of the province, and
this process became more of an exercise in ethnic engineering as the eighteenth century came to a close.[27]

The case of Antonio Beitia illustrates the ways in which lived practice
and the colonial pretensions of control over Pueblo identity often clashed.[28]
In 1784 Governor Anza banished Beitia from Santa Clara Pueblo for seditious acts against the provincial government. The commandant general

confirmed Anza's action, and Beitia appeared subsequently as a vecino of the
Plaza de San Rafael neighboring the pueblo in the general census carried out
during 1789–1790. No doubt Santa Clara did not consider Beitia to have lost
his Pueblo ethnicity so suddenly and completely. Beitia reappears as a central figure in a series of meetings among Tewa Pueblos in 1793, prompting
a massive investigation of forty-three Tewa leaders by Alcalde Mayor Manuel
García de la Mora and Governor Concha. Concha sentenced Beitia to a year
of hard labor in chains, and a fine of 20 pesos in order to emphasize Beitia's
transgression into the affairs of his erstwhile pueblo.

The other area of governance discussed by the governor concerned
relations with the Franciscan missionaries who made up the Custody of
Saint Paul. The Franciscans had jurisdiction over the Pueblo missions and
many of the vecino parishioners, since diocesan priests only served in a few
of the larger New Mexico towns during the last decades of the colonial
period. Not surprisingly, Concha's depiction of the religious personnel
proved as unflattering as his view of vecinos:

> No affair in that place entails so many difficulties as checking
> the bad habits which govern the priests of the *custodia*. The
> greater part of them live in concubinage. Interest directs
> their maxims. They have many ways of insinuating malice
> to upset or destroy the good measures prescribed by the
> Governor, always directed toward checking their excesses.
> They have an absolute sway over the inhabitants. It is
> impossible to realize how far their effrontery and boldness
> goes with which they control every kind of affair, nor yet
> the facility with which they upset the same inhabitants,
> always meditating upon their own particular ends. In a
> word, their influence upon every one is such that the
> general expression used in the country is "If the Father
> says it is so, there can be no doubt."[29]

Once again, Concha's actions focus on controlling the unwanted effects
of "insinuating malice" and incessant meddling in the affairs properly left
to secular government. The previous mention of the conspiracies between
missionaries and vecinos that led to Pueblo petitions for the missionary's
transfer leave no doubt that Concha worried primarily about religious
influence among non-Indian communities.

The antidote proposed by the governor mirrored his advice relating to repeated complaints, petitions, and lawsuits:

That the injuries may be less (supposing it impossible to eradicate the vices) I am of the opinion the methods which during my administration have produced good results must be followed. These have been to ignore and to take no part in the disputes and strife that originate among them. Never yield to their annoying petitions to improve their offices. Oppose with firmness the actions that they constantly take to destroy good order, and keep on harmonious relations with their prelate, if this person is less vigilant. Add to these means that of intimidating them by means of threats that they may be removed from the Province as prejudicial persons provided they do not improve their behavior. In order to effect this measure if the circumstances require it, it is necessary to go along in accord with the prelate, as the law provides, and above all that the superior government may sustain the measure to the end that the Governor does not find himself exposed nor his honor questioned.[30]

A strong, steady hand and an understanding with the Custodian of the Franciscan Order in New Mexico could keep dangerous local missionaries in check.

When writing these paragraphs to Chacón, Concha alluded to an incident that began during August of the previous year when don Antonio Guerrero, lieutenant of the presidio in Santa Fe, unceremoniously arrested fray Severo Paterno in his mission at Santa Clara Pueblo.[31] Patero journeyed first to Santa Fe, then to El Paso, and finally arrived in Chihuahua, all under an armed guard. Patero appealed to no avail to the custodian fray Cayetano Bernal, the Commandant General of the Interior Provinces, and the Bishop of Durango, arguing that he had done nothing to merit his arrest and possessed ecclesiastical immunity. Patero contended that he had been ejected from New Mexico because he had "compelled, incited, and influenced some New Mexican *Vecinos* so that they would present to the Commandant General complaints against the above-mentioned Governor Concha." The case demonstrates both the persuasiveness of tools for social control in the hands of colonial officials, and the complex alliance formed between vecinos and local Franciscan missionaries as a result of the reconfiguration of the New Mexican economy.[32]

Concha had warned "It is extremely difficult to indicate in detail the incidents that can occur with the religious, . . . but watching them under the aspect that I have indicated, managing them with tact, firmness, understanding, and prudence, and resorting to opportunities to check them in your just duty, you will attain without doubt the appreciable object of quietude and tranquility within the interior of the Province," and Governor Chacón took care to follow his advice. In July of 1798 Chacón ordered Custodian fray Francisco Hocio to expel fray Isidro Cadelo from his post at Jémez Pueblo mission and escort him from the province.[33] Cadelo had already suffered imprisonment and removal to Chihuahua in chains from his first New Mexican assignment in December 1793. In this instance, the governor and custodian charged Cadelo with encouraging seditious meetings within Jémez Pueblo and challenging the authority of Alcalde Mayor Antonio Armenta. According to Cadelo, representatives of the Pueblo, Nereo Sánchez and Lázaro Sola, had accused Armenta of extorting goods from pueblo inhabitants in return for protecting their orchards and farmland from expropriation by vecinos. Found guilty of leading the seditious meeting at Jémez, Chacón sentenced Lázaro Sola to labor in chains for three years at the *obraje* (textile workshop) at the penal hacienda at Encinillas, Chihuahua.[34] Chacón wrote to the Audiendia of Guadalajara, in whose jurisdiction the case fell, that "because of this Father's energetic, restless, and seditious character, I am of the belief that he should not be permitted to return to introduce himself into this province [New Mexico], where the religious officials have a particular ascendance over the citizenry, the results of which have given and will give the government much to do; not to keep this in check, especially in these matters that could disturb the public tranquility, would mean the irredeemable total extinction of the province."[35] Although the Audiencia ultimately restored Cadelo to his position at Jémez, constant controversy limited his effectiveness in disturbing the "quietude and tranquility" of the province.

As these events serve to illustrate, by the 1790s colonial officials in New Mexico had developed and refined an array of effective tools for the social control of the province's inhabitants. In his 1794 report, Governor Concha identifies a trio of arenas in which to exercise social control: freedom of movement and association, unrestrained commerce, and expression of ethnic and cultural self-identity. He outlines the tools potentially available to the next governor, and of which subsequent heads of the colonial regime took advantage. Within each category of control, the methods used to control the vecino population worked in ways different and yet analogous to their use by the colonial regime to govern the Rio Grande Pueblos. The restraint of vecino movement among Comanches and Utes and the rebuilding of vecino settlements in regular form, the cessation of unlicensed economic activity, and the development of a social hierarchy, all occurred in order to maintain peace with allied Indian nations and perfect the general well being of the province. In every instance the ethnic-cultural behavior of the "barbarous" and the Pueblo nations justified and enabled the ability of the agents of Bourbon New Spain to envision a project of social control.

Conclusion

In New Mexico, the economic and social changes unleashed during the late eighteenth century allowed vecinos to extend their activities outside of the areas covered by time-honored provincial techniques of social control. In doing so they exposed colonial contradictions between the desire for social ordering—and a struggle between existing social hierarchies and emerging innovations—and the liberating and opportunistic reactions of the vecinos to economic transformation.[36] In contrast to the provincial attempts to control or reorder society expressed by Concha, the actual vecino responses to expanded economic opportunity inscribed their now dominant patterns of commerce and power in a class and casta system by the second quarter of the nineteenth century. While not the vision of a social order imagined by late eighteenth-century governors like Concha and Chacón, the development of class distinctions as a part of the commercial transformation of the province did provide a kind of resolution for the dilemma they had faced. By the end of colonial rule in New Mexico, those that Concha identified as possessing "a malice most refined" had become the architects of the new social order.

Along with the other chapters in this volume, this one on social control in late colonial New Mexico interrogates the conventional portrayal of the Spanish northern frontier as more inclusive of indigenous peoples. In comparison to the English frontier, the broad outlines of the hierarchy of inclusiveness in 1790s New Mexico appear more similar than different. Vecinos, like other settlers, despite all of their shortcomings formed the core of colonial citizenship. From Governor Concha's point of view, the

"Barbarous Nations" occupying his attention in New Mexico had no more right to claim citizenship as an organic part of colonial society than did Iroquois, Shawnee, or Seminole to contemporaneous American officials. Pueblo Indians existed within a zone of colonial inclusion in a manner similar to that of "praying towns" or "civilizing" nations in relation to the English colonies that became the United States.

Yet these similarities in structure mask vastly different uses of categories of ethnic difference to create tools of colonial social control. Counterpoised with the "pagan" and "barbarous" Indians, who nonetheless served as valuable allies and trading partners, Spanish officials in New Mexico contrasted unfavorable vecino behavior with that of the Puebloans, creating two discursive and subject categories of Indian difference that helped to define and discipline vecinos. More inclusive? Yes, but the process of constructing difference represented no less of a tool for social control on the New Mexican frontier of New Spain.

NOTES

1. Fernando de la Concha to Fernando Chacón, Chihuahua, 28 June 1794, Historia 41:11 327R–352R, Archivo General de la Nación, Mexico City (hereafter cited as Concha).

2. Ibid, 336R–336V.

3. Ross Frank, *From Settler to Citizen: New Mexican Economic Development and the Creation of Vecino Society, 1750–1820* (Berkeley: University of California Press, 2000).

4. The Spanish word *vecino* used here refers to the non-Indian settlers of New Mexico. The term, literally meaning "neighbor," took on a meaning that included a sense of belonging to the province as a citizen in late colonial New Mexican documents.

5. Fray Augustín de Morfí, "Account of Disorders, 1778" in *Coronado's Land: Essays on Daily Life in Colonial New Mexico*, ed. Marc Simmons, 130–32 (Albuquerque: University of New Mexico Press, 1991); and Marc Simmons, "Settlement Patterns in Colonial New Mexico," *Journal of the West* 8, 1 (1969): 7–21.

6. Concha, 337R.

7. Ibid., 349R.

8. Max L. Moorhead, *The Presidio: Bastion of the Spanish Borderlands* (Norman: University of Oklahoma Press, 1975), 44, 82–83, 191–93.

9. Concha, 350R.

10. Ibid., 347R.

11. Ibid., 342V.

12. See the Roybal–San Ildefonso Pueblo case in G. Emlen Hall, "The Pueblo Grant Labyrinth," in *Land, Water, and Culture: New Perspectives on Hispanic Land Grants*, ed. Charles L. Briggs and John R. Van Ness, 79–84 (Albuquerque: University of New Mexico Press, 1987); and the Taos example in Myra E. Jenkins, "Taos Pueblo and Its Neighbors," *New Mexico Historical Review* 41, 2 (1966): 85–114.

13. See Frank, *Settler to Citizen*, 201–5.

14. Concha, 342V–343R.

15. Ibid., 344V.

16. Ibid.

17. See Oakah L. Jones, "Pueblo Indian Auxiliaries in New Mexico, 1763–1821," *New Mexico Historical Review* 37, 2 (1962): 81–109; and *Pueblo Warriors and Spanish Conquest* (Norman: University of Oklahoma Press, 1966).

18. Concha, 337V.

19. Ibid., 338R.

20. Ibid., 336R–336V.

21. Ibid., 346V.

22. Ibid., 343V.

23. Ibid., 339R.

24. Pueblo Indian officials understood these restrictions very clearly. See the testimony of the Tewa leaders interrogated during the 1794 sedition trial in Frank, *Settler to Citizen*, 212–17.

25. Concha, 349R.

26. Ibid., 338R–V.

27. See Frank, *Settler to Citizen*, 177–80.

28. Ibid., 219.

29. Concha, 345V.

30. Ibid., 346R, V.

31. The documents for the action against Fray Patero are in Varios 51:132, 121 hojas, Archivo Catedral de Durango, Mexico.

32. See Ross Frank, "Making New Mexican Santos: Franciscan and Vecino Dominance in Late Colonial New Mexico," *New Mexico Historical Review* 75, 3 (2000): 369–96.

33. See Rick Hendricks, "The Exile and Return of Cadelo, Isidro, 1793–1810," *New Mexico Historical Review* 70, 2 (1995): 129–57, especially 133–40.

34. TW# 1427, 18 July 1798, Spanish Archives of New Mexico, Series II, 14:300, New Mexico State Records Center and Archives, Santa Fe.

35. Governor Fernando Chacón to Real Audiencia de Guadalajara, 3 October 1799 (copy courtesy of Charles Cutter), Civil-161-9-1765, 11R, Archivo Real de la Audiencia de Guadalajara.

36. Juan Pedro Viqueira Albán, Sonya Lipsett-Rivera, and Sergio Rivera Ayala, *Propriety and Permissiveness in Bourbon Mexico* (Wilmington, Del: Scholarly Resources, 1999), 213–15.

*imposition of
patriarchal
ideals*

CHAPTER FIVE

Subverting the Social Order

Gender, Power, and
Magic in Nueva Vizcaya

Susan M. Deeds

In May of 1691, a mulatta slave from Durango made a startling confession to a Jesuit priest in Parral, Chihuahua. For more than six years, Antonia de Soto had traversed much of New Spain's north central region (Nueva Vizcaya) while masquerading as a man. Her fantastic tale had all the elements of a swashbuckling adventure: travel, riches, derring-do, masculine prowess, murder, and mayhem. The story chronicles a thorough subversion of the social order that fleetingly freed Antonia not only from the legal bonds of slavery but also from the gendered bonds of patriarchy, in a frontier province.[1] Her narrative stands in stark contradiction to prescribed behaviors. Did the open spaces of this frontier afford her more freedom to deviate? It has been argued that in the urban mining center of Chihuahua in the eighteenth century, while there was some room for ethnic and class boundaries to be contested, the patriarchal system allowed little flexibility in regard to gender roles and female behavior. "Patriarchy furnished a relatively stable, non-negotiable set of governing principles even when all other rules came into question."[2]

In this chapter, I will look at the efficacy of church and state efforts to impose patriarchal ideals while more generally reinforcing the attempts of Spanish elites to keep indigenous and mixed-race peoples in their place in less settled areas of Nueva Vizcaya. For the purposes of this study, social control encompasses the theory developed by the Spanish state and the practice that evolved for enforcing conformity to idealized gender and ethnic roles and relationships in areas under its effective political dominion. Throughout New Spain this control was always tentative and dependent on the allegiance of local elites and brokers and their ability to coerce and co-opt lower status groups. "The Spanish state . . . excelled at leaving government to others, including the church, at knowing its own limitations and possibilities, and in philosophically accepting what it could get as long as basic control and allegiances remained."[3]

During the colonial period, the Spanish state exercised uneven jurisdiction over the vast expanses of Nueva Vizcaya, making its presence felt primarily in towns, mining centers, or *reales*, and to a lesser extent in missions. It never had much hold on the countryside. Separated by long distances, haciendas and urban areas stood vulnerable to hostile Indian groups throughout the colonial period. For this reason social control depended in part on limiting population movements across unsettled areas. To be sure, the Spanish Crown favored migrations when they were directed toward meeting the labor needs of Spanish mine owners and *hacendados*. But for the most part, free-flowing population movements were thought to encourage associations of peoples across spatial and ethnic lines in ways that were perceived to be subversive and destabilizing.[4] When this ethnic and cultural mixing was accompanied by gender transgressions, was it considered to be potentially even more threatening? Can Antonia's case shed light on this question?

Antonia's Story

After first confessing her story to Jesuit Father Tomás de Guadalajara, the twenty-year-old Antonia turned herself in to the Inquisition agent in Parral. Over the next two years, on several occasions in 1691 and 1692, she supplied further testimony about her activities during the previous six years. Her travels had taken her as far south as Veracruz and back again to the northern frontier. Her odyssey began when she escaped from her master (Francisco de Noriega) in the city of Durango, fleeing with a Tepehuan Indian worker named Matías de Rentería, also in his employ. They made their way first to Parral, a silver-mining town. There Antonia was aided by a mestiza woman nicknamed Juana Golpazos who gave her lily-like flowers called *cacomites* to conceal under her clothing over her breasts, which she claimed made her unrecognizable to the overseer who had been sent to fetch her back to Durango.

From Parral Antonia and Matías fled with their magical herbs and flowers to Cusihuiriachi, where a flood of immigrants had recently arrived to exploit newly discovered silver. On the way there, Matías introduced Antonia to a new magical spell, induced by peyote. In her mind-altering visions, Antonia witnessed the skillful maneuvers of Matías as he success-fully subdued a charging bull. In another state of trance they both learned to dance, taught by a beguiling woman who accompanied them on her gui-tar. As she recalled the dream state induced by the peyote mixture the two drank on Sundays, Antonia remembered also seeing many serpents, closely followed by an image of a very handsome man who appeared out of nowhere and promised her freedom "if she would be his." She took this black-garbed figure to be the devil.

In their travels Antonia and Matías spent several days in the Jesuit mis-sion of San Miguel de las Bocas (today Villa Ocampo in northern Durango), where Matías may have had Tepehuan kin. The presence of a mulatta slave in an Indian mission went unremarked, not surprising in this area of con-siderable Spanish and mixed-race inhabitants. The mission had been founded several decades earlier with both Tepehuan and Tarahumara con-verts, serving to produce corn and some wheat for the Parral market. By the 1660s it was surrounded by a dozen or so haciendas and ranches where many mission Indians supplied labor voluntarily or in *repartimiento*, the sys-tem of forced labor drafts that characterized mission areas in Nueva Vizcaya during the seventeenth and eighteenth centuries. A good deal of cultural and ethnic interchange accompanied their farming and herding activities as they worked alongside mestizos, mulattos, Nahuatl-speaking peoples from central Mexico, and other Indians. At the same time, dozens of Spanish *veci-nos* attended church at the mission, and a few Spaniards and mixed-race peo-ples resided there. Servants from nearby haciendas participated in the elaborate celebrations that had become a hallmark of San Miguel de las Bocas at Corpus Christi and Easter. At one point, Jesuit Father Nicolás de Zepeda counted 300 "vagrant *vecinos* in the area."[5] It was hardly surpris-ing, therefore, that a mulatta slave drew little attention in Las Bocas a few years later.

It was in this multicultural milieu that Antonia experienced a remark-able transformation, as she continued to experiment with flowering herbs and miraculous stones. She now, perhaps impulsively, made a pact with the devil. Her unholy bargain transformed her into a skilled horseman, bull-fighter, and gambler. She donned men's clothing and imagined a new, powerful life. One of the first signs of her newly acquired muscle was her ability to fight off an assault by her companion Matías, whom she nearly killed by beating him with a cattle prod. They apparently reconciled after this quarrel and set off once again, first spending some time in the unruly atmosphere of the new mining camps of Cusihuiriachi in western Chihuahua. In the next few years the two found work as *vaqueros* on cattle ranches in northern Durango. At one point Antonia hired on as a porter for a mule train that carried silver through Guanajuato to Veracruz, where it would be shipped to Spain. Returning with another muleteer, she passed through San Luis Potosí, eventually arriving back in the familiar territory of northern Durango.

Throughout these travels she continued to rub flowers and rosettes over her body and to use particular arrangements of magic stones and incantations to summon the devil. He usually appeared in the form of a white man in a black cape, but sometimes she could only hear him speaking to her, and once he materialized as a growling bear. Most often he came on horseback carrying a machete. In these encounters he spoke to her and empowered her to gamble, to break horses, and to fight bulls and even men. Her newly acquired skills proved effective beyond the defense of her person, at times leading her down a stormy path strewn with dead bodies. On one occasion in another mining camp of western Chihuahua, Coyachi, Antonia and three companions overpowered a mule train, killed three men, and made off with part of the silver shipment. When one of her accomplices snatched her silver-laden saddlebags, she pursued and killed him. Later, in the midst of a heated argument, she killed a coworker in Sinaloa. She had become more than just a man; now she was a violent bandit.

Eventually the harrowing experiences took their toll, at least on her conscience, and Antonia decided to give up her life as a swashbuckler. She made her confession to Father Tomás de Guadalajara in Parral, asking for forgiveness. A Jesuit missionary who had spent many years in the Tarahumara missions, Father Guadalajara told her that she would have to go before the Inquisition before he could give absolution. After hearing her testimony the Inquisition agent reported the incident to his superiors in Mexico City, asking how to proceed. Over the next two years Antonia supplied further testimony to various interrogators. During this time, she was returned to her master in Durango who lost no time in selling her to a military officer, the captain of the presidio of Tepehuanes. Perhaps this hacendado believed that a soldier could exercise more control over such a brazen troublemaker. Or, given her escapes and the trouble she had caused, he decided she was not worth the upkeep. Antonia's tale comes to an abrupt end for us when the Inquisition decided in July of 1693 that she was sufficiently repentant to be absolved under ecclesiastical jurisdiction. The Inquisition ordered her case to be transferred to a civil court, but I have not been able to find any records for such a case.

The Inquisition as Agent of Social Control

Before delving more deeply into Antonia's story, it is useful to consider the role of the Inquisition itself. As an institution for all of New Spain, it could be argued that it occupied the preeminent position as the proponent of social and religious conformity. Historians Solange Alberro and Noemí Quezada have suggested that it served the needs of a weak colonial state in the attempt to instill its values in a highly heterogeneous cultural and ethnic milieu.[6] From its initial primary function in Spain to target Jewish and Muslim apostates (converts to Christianity who continued their previous religious practices), it was transplanted to New Spain where apostasy and heresy cases were much fewer, involving mostly *conversos* (suspect Jewish converts to Christianity) and the occasional Protestant pirate. For a short time, it had jurisdiction over cases of Indian idolatry, but given the impracticality of dispatching these transgressions in a short period among neophytes, as well as the potential for widespread rebellion from indigenous peoples who greatly outnumbered Spaniards, the Crown decided to leave the task of correcting these "heathens" to bishops (who relied on local parish priests for information).

Of the thousands of cases investigated by New Spain's Holy Office, the great majority dealt with bigamy, blasphemy, sodomy, witchcraft, solicitation in the confessional, healing (*curanderismo*), misguided interpretations of the faith, and other similar offenses against the Catholic religion.[7] Although it would be difficult to argue that the Inquisition was a major enforcer of social control in the north, the cases that it did pursue there reflect its goals and suggest that its coercive messages did have some psychological impact. Its geographical reach was broad, but the cases from the far north are relatively few, reflecting both the sparseness of the population and the ability of nonconformists to escape detection in an area not completely incorporated by the state.

Policing the associations of lower status groups was not an easy task in the mountains and deserts of Nueva Vizcaya. Uncontrolled frontier expanses offered ample spaces for nonconformists to avoid oppressive conditions, providing what Gonzalo Aguirre Beltrán termed "zones of refuge."[8] Flight to inaccessible areas of the Sierra Madre Occidental proved to be the key factor in the ethnic persistence of some Indian groups like the Tarahumaras and the Tepehuanes. Somewhat paradoxically, their communities also sheltered mixed-race vagabonds from the Spanish world.

For most people who did resist, however, defiance of Spanish norms or protection from onerous demands was more covert and the relief all too fleeting. Nonetheless, there was no shortage of people who sought remedies. Diabolism, love magic, and other forms of *hechicería* (witchcraft) were practiced by women and men across class and ethnicity on the frontier, but a preponderance of petty witchcraft cases recorded by the Holy Office of the Inquisition in Mexico for the north concerns women. What can we learn from them about the extent and efficacy of church and state efforts to stem the subversion of patriarchal and racial ideals in frontier areas?[9]

Discovering Women on the Margins of Empire

Inquisition scholar Solange Alberro has examined cases from the early northern mining centers, especially Zacatecas, and concluded that they had a more radically irreverent and macho "frontier" character that she attributes to a more mobile, less cohesive, and feebly policed society than those of the much more populous areas of central and southern Mexico.[10] If macho violence and volatility are frontier hallmarks, how should we understand the significance of transgressions of prescribed female behavior? A number of historians have begun to incorporate gender into their analyses of cross-cultural contact and captivity on frontiers only partially incorporated by the state on the northern and southern edges of the Spanish empire.[11] Coincidentally, a few years ago a story that had only been known to a few scholars got a good deal of publicity when it was published in a book entitled *Lieutenant Nun: Memoirs of a Basque Transvestite in the New World*. This was the rather sensational title for the story of Catalina de Erauso, who as a young woman in 1600 fled from a convent in the Spanish Basque country to another frontier—remote areas of Peru and

Chile—where she gadded about as a soldier and adventurer, "brawling her way through mining towns of the Andean highlands."[12] She was a gambler, distinguished for fighting skills, who even killed her own brother in a duel. Catalina's thrilling story, which eventually reached the Pope, certainly seems to be a startling anomaly or exception to gender norms in the early modern Hispanic world.

In the last decade many textbook and conventional representations of colonial Latin American women have been shown to be stereotypical and misleading. A plethora of new studies demonstrates that women of all classes and ethnicities challenged the patriarchal order more frequently or in much more ingenious ways than we had previously thought.[13] Far fewer women's stories have been uncovered for Mexico's far north, however, owing in part to lower population density. Exceptions include Cheryl Martin's chapter on women, which describes a rigid patriarchal order in urban Chihuahua, and Cynthia Radding's work on the productive and reproductive contributions of indigenous women in Sonora. Another is James Sandos' article in this volume.[14]

We know the least about Indian women because they rarely appear in the documentary sources, authored only by Spanish men. Occasionally we find court cases in which Indian women were litigants or the accused. Elsewhere I have examined the story of Ysidora de Medina, a Tarahumara wife and mother who killed her abusive, alcoholic husband in 1806. This event took place in a former Jesuit mission community in southern Chihuahua whose inhabitants were overwhelmingly non-Indian by the end of the colonial period. Ysidora was tried without benefit of trained counsel or sympathetic witnesses and imprisoned for many years under penalty of death.[15] But this case of husband murder was so extraordinary that I could only speculate as to what it tells us about how the lives of Tarahumara women changed under Spanish rule and Catholic missions. Indian women seldom appear in court cases. Nor are Inquisition cases a rich source because Indians did not come under its jurisdiction. We frequently do find indigenous peoples in Inquisition cases as witnesses or sometimes supposed accomplices, but the information on them is more fragmentary than for non-Indians.

We are more likely to come upon non-Indian women in the archival documents for the north, especially in the eighteenth century, yet even here the record is thin for nonelite (or non-Spanish) women. Now and then, however, an exceptional story emerges in the records of the Inquisition in

Mexico City, as I discovered when I began to look for evidence of interethnic relationships between Indians in Nueva Vizcayan mission pueblos and
outsiders. The preponderance of Inquisition cases brought diverse groups
into contact around minor transgressions like love magic and healing. By
comparison, Antonia's adoption of male identity, induced largely through
witchcraft, certainly seems a more glaring sacrilege.

Antonia's Story as Female Agency

How did Antonia's gender change escape notice in Nueva Vizcaya? Like
Catalina de Erauso, the lieutenant nun, she traveled in the company of men
who never seemed to detect her lack of male anatomy. (This raises intriguing questions about features of everyday communal life—for example,
habits of bathing, eliminating waste, and sleeping.) How should we compare the motivations of these two women who decided that it would be
advantageous to behave like men? Both women seem to fit the generalized
modern-day definitions of either transvestite—"a person and especially a
male who adopts the dress and often the behavior typical of the opposite
sex especially for purposes of emotional or sexual gratification"—or trans-
gendered—"exhibiting the appearance and behavioral characteristics of the
opposite sex."[16] A recent interpretation from an extensive literary scholarship on Catalina de Erauso concludes that she was a lesbian, arguing that
lesbianism was viewed benignly in the seventeenth-century Spanish world
as long as there was no sign of genital contact or penetration.[17] In the case
of Antonia de Soto, we have little evidence as to her sexual orientation. Her
testimony provides two hints: one, she rebuffed the sexual overtures of
Matías; and two, the devil began to make love to her (*empezó a . . . hacerle
amores*) when he asked her if she wanted him to possess her. Can we infer
from this that her transgenderism was erotically inspired? What factors
motivated these women to dress as men and how did they escape detection
for so long?

There were plenty of models for donning men's garb for purposes of
combat and adventure. Stories of *doncellas guerreras*, or warrior maidens,
were popular in Europe, circulating in ballads and theatrical performances.
Scholars have noted numerous early modern examples of women who
dressed as men "for a variety of purposes, including both heterosexual and
same-sex romantic motives, patriotism, economic necessity, safety while
traveling, criminality, and the desire for freedom and adventure."[18] In these

stories, women might be depicted as evildoers or heroines, but in either case masquerading as a male virtually always afforded them power at least for a while. Nonetheless, they could not be masculine for too long without suffering an infelicitous end. It is likely that Catalina and Antonia had both been exposed to tales of swashbuckling women. Catalina's story itself became the subject of a Golden Age comedy by Juan Pérez de Montalbán, first performed in 1626.

In both Catalina's and Antonia's narratives, we find elements of the picaresque adventure story that customarily features a male rogue (a literary phenomenon that resulted from the preoccupations of Spain's minor nobility in the social and economic milieu of the seventeenth century). These tales chronicle a series of events over time and place—the protagonists are always moving on to the next encounter or job. The accounts are replete with heroic feats, violence, trickery, gambling, and unrepentant criminal behavior. Both women traveled across vast territories and frontiers where conditions of social and political instability often prevailed. In Antonia's case the volatility of the northern frontier was at a peak in the 1680s. The Pueblo Indian rebellion of 1680 had ripple effects to the south in Nueva Vizcaya, where fears of further Indian hostilities prompted the creation of several presidios to guard the royal road and shipments of silver to Mexico City. Then, in 1690, Tarahumara Indians rebelled in their recently established western missions of the Sierra Madre Occidental, reacting in part to Spanish attempts to coerce them to work in the new silver mines at Cusihuiriachi.[19] Life for women could be especially precarious in the situation of constant warfare that prevailed in seventeenth-century Nueva Vizcaya. Toboso and other band groups on the eastern frontier of the *camino real* (royal road) were a part of a trading and raiding network in which the taking of captives provided means of subsistence, both for providing labor and reproductive assistance to sustain kin groups. Sometimes these captives, especially women and children, were incorporated into the bands; in other cases they were treated harshly as slaves.[20] Yet it was in these unpredictable circumstances that Antonia moved freely around the perilous countryside.

In this situation, it is not peculiar that Antonia (like Catalina) enjoyed the camaraderie of men as she gambled and caroused, and easily seemed to resort to violence. The weak presence of the Spanish state in areas where conquest was incomplete often served to generate volatility and brutality. In another similarity, both women were Christians, familiar with the teachings of the

Roman Catholic Church. Catalina even had an audience with the Pope. And in her confession and testimonies, Antonia repeatedly declared she was a pious Christian. Her understanding of the devil was based on church doctrine, and her physical descriptions of him indicate that she was familiar with demonic iconography and its phallic imagery. She had enough information to link her visions of serpents with the temptation of Eve.[21] Recent scholarship makes a strong case that black and mulatto slaves had considerable knowledge of Christianity even though their religious education was often neglected by their owners.[22]

It is from an ethnic perspective, however, that we can begin to probe the great divide between the two women's worlds. Antonia's interpretation of Catholic dogma was very different from Catalina's, and it derived from her place as a mulatta slave. She did not enjoy the privilege of being white in colonial society. Even in her "freedom," rather than command respect as a Spanish soldier/conquistador, she labored in lower status occupations available to mixed-race males. More telling, though, is that Antonia believed that she could exercise male prowess only through magic or subversion of the church's order, while Catalina developed her fighting skills naturally and within the bounds of a militant Catholic Church. This last difference is of particular interest.

Folk Cultures of Resistance

Scholars of the African experience in Mexico have noted the propensity of slaves to blaspheme for very practical reasons. If a slave renounced God and invoked the devil during a beating, the owner was theoretically compelled to stop the punishment and turn over the blasphemer to the Inquisition. This strategy could bring temporary relief from physical punishment and sometimes provided an opportunity for a slave to denounce his or her master for suspicious behaviors, thus pitting patriarchs against each other. These actions ran the risk of calling down even greater penalties on the blasphemer, but the fact that blasphemy was so commonplace indicates that it had the potential to alleviate desperate situations.[23] In our story, Antonia went one step further than denying the power of God, by actually embracing the devil to alleviate her oppression. She also engaged in other forms of witchcraft taught to her by a number of other marginal people she came into contact with. Blacks and mulattos throughout New Spain were frequently drawn into this world of syncretic magic.[24]

Here the folk practices of diverse racial groups often intersected and brought Indians, mestizos, mulattos, and Spaniards into close contact.[25] In this case, Antonia was introduced to magic by the Tepehuan Matías and the mestiza Juana Golpazos (a nickname suggesting she was a heavy-hitting tough). Antonia ingested peyote, the hallucinogenic effects of which could be powerful. Peyote, ground into powder and mixed with water, was commonly used in curing and love magic. She gave magic charms to other transients she met in her travels, among them an Apache Indian and a mulatto slave. The Inquisition asked her quite direct questions about these associations, revealing official concern about the ways in which a popular subculture could undermine royal authority. Colonial laws attempted to regulate travel, which was believed to promote social intercourse in rural areas, and to control the ethnically heterogeneous working classes of mining towns in the north.[26] While authorities sought to impose social controls on the lower echelons of society, Indian and mixed-race northern migrants comingled with immigrants from the south (e.g., muleteers, itinerant vendors, and artisans), and attempted to forge new social networks.

In the north, livestock ranches with their wide open spaces were a common site of diabolic activity, as Fernando Cervantes has argued.

> It is perhaps no accident that most of the cases of self-assertive diabolism should come from a group of people engaged primarily in herding and riding activities; for such groups would come to constitute what was in many ways a world apart in New Spain. Drawing on the marginal culture developed among mestizos, mulattos, and a number of social misfits who had not found their place among Spaniards or Indians, shepherds and cowherds gradually developed a lore that partook of Indian, African and Iberian magic and which spread throughout the more or less geographically defined region stretching to the southwest into Michoacán and to the north into Zacatecas and Nueva Vizcaya.[27]

[handwritten margin note: mobility + decentr. spaces allowed for transcultur. movement + interethnic mixing]

Antonia lived in this world of itinerant associations, of stories told and ballads sung around the campfire, and of meetings with the devil in remote places. Other scholars of the Inquisition have suggested that in areas of greater interethnic mixing and more mobile populations, witchcraft and pacts with the devil were more common.[28] Antonia's story is a vivid example of the

ineffectiveness of the Crown's attempts to limit geographic mobility and ethnic mixing, especially in less populated northern areas. Her case offers a
startling illustration of how the practical use of supernatural or divine power
could be perceived as destabilizing.

The Church's Power to Shame

At the time Antonia met up with the devil, she had already achieved a certain liberty by escaping from her duties as a slave. But her gender imposed
definite limitations on this so-called "freedom." The need to enhance her
capacity for self-protection became all the more apparent in her dealings
with her companion, Matías. The devil evoked by Antonia comes across to
us as the alter ego of a male patriarch or master in his compassionate (and
perhaps sexual?) side, but he offered more than comfort. He was the dis-
penser of the skills she needed to defend herself—skills that were the preserve of only men. She asked for the same macho skills that men sought
(through natural or supernatural means) in order to elevate their status—
to be skilled equestrians, bullfighters, and gamblers.[29] Although we might
see this today as the most hackneyed version of machismo, contemporaries
might have seen her actions as a kind of noble defiance (because it was masculine) that went beyond petty sorcery and trickery (perceived as weak or
effeminate recourses). The devil was the provider of expertise that could
be empowering; at the same time, it fostered or furthered violence, which
meant that Antonia lived in a day-to-day atmosphere of uncertainty and
fearful consequences.

Her testimony suggests that Antonia was very ambivalent about the
devil. She chose him as her champion in an impetuous moment of drug-
induced delusion. Above all, he was a masterful, if sinister, advocate for the
underprivileged. At first, she seems to have seen him as a trickster who
could be temporarily invoked and then ignored. As time went on she appears to have taken his power more seriously; she invoked him as a means
of appropriating his power, and he obligingly extricated her from many
perilous situations. At some point, however, this benign force (in the sense
that she could control its awesome power) began to pale in comparison to
her fear of God as the power most likely to inflict dreadful consequences
(a preoccupation that may have grown stronger as she matured).

The internal mechanisms of social control instilled by the moral admonitions regarding obedience to the church undermined and over time eroded

the satisfactions of her new status. Antonia had invoked the devil to transcend femininity and domesticity, alienating herself from the home and
becoming a violent itinerant adventurer. Ultimately, however, she could not
sustain this lifestyle. Perhaps she grew weary of it, but her need to confess
also suggests the strong influence on her psyche of Catholic prescriptions for
proper behavior. These could have come from the everyday coercion of her
life as a slave, from her owners, her overseer, or from the local priest. Spanish
Hapsburg officials were also effective at using religious spectacle and staged
performances to establish a quasi-religious state legitimacy. Self-disgust or
fear—the inability to reconcile her illicit activities with Catholic teachings—
seem to have motivated her choice (or was it her choice?) to turn herself in.
As one historian has noted, "the empire found or co-opted or created groups,
even among the oppressed, who accepted its legitimacy and found the imperial system, on balance to be more tolerable, given real risks and possibilities
than any imagined alternatives."[30] On the other hand, if Antonia felt that she
was about to be exposed, she may have realized that she would have a better
chance if she got a hearing that allowed her to assert her contrition. Self-confessions helped to diminish the punishment if it was clear that the sinner truly
wished to be reintegrated into the fold.[31] Colonial records indicate that slaves
were rarely punished for demonic complicity in Mexico.[32]

Love Magic

On the whole, we often find women denouncing themselves to the Inquisition, but most of these cases involve much less serious transgressions than
pacts with the devil—they incorporate a whole range of minor magical
practice. Even petty offenses could provoke self-guilt and shame in a society suffused with inquisitorial prescription. Resort to petty witchcraft was
common throughout colonial Spanish America, and this kind of magic
seems to have been most commonly practiced by women of lower social
status. We know of many cases that concerned sorcery for healing, love
magic, and protection from abusive relationships.[33] Most cases of
witchcraft involved domestic situations or aspirations, and the protagonists
could be men or women. Magic was employed for attracting marriage partners (or at least protection), for curbing abusive male behavior, or, in the
case of the practitioners, for earning a living.[34]

The earliest denunciations of love magic that I have found for Nueva
Vizcaya come from the early mining establishments and are directed

against both men and women. Although women were by far more likely to employ love magic in the later colonial period, in the early seventeenth century when fewer female Spaniards or *gente de razón* (non-Indians) were present in the north, men were likely to be more insecure about their ability to attract marriage or sexual partners. By employing a secret incantation, Bartolomé de Salas, a Spanish miner from the mining real of San Andrés in Topia, was purportedly able to attract "all the women he wanted." Here we have the sense that his denouncer, a muleteer, was envious of this rival in the competition for females. Invoking the power of the Holy Spirit, Bartolomé called on the devil to dispose particular women to do his sexual bidding.[35] In a different kind of recourse, women, both Spanish and mestiza, were more likely to use potions and powders to attract men.[36] These were concocted out of various substances of plant, animal, and human body origin, and they were often ingested in the ubiquitous cup of chocolate or in other foods. Herbs and plants varied locally, but the fauna employed tended to be the same as in other parts of Mexico (and Europe). For example, the documents cite worms, lizards, mucous from various birds, fish, and dried burro brains. Secretions and parts of the body were perhaps the most common ingredients in these concoctions: menstrual blood, water used to wash private parts, semen, excrement, hair, nails, teeth, and bones. Peyote was also employed to attract lovers or to make them impotent. These measures seem to have been universally known to mixed-race hacienda servants who lived in close quarters in varying states of subservience. Mulattos, mestizos, Apache captives, and other Indian workers lived in close contact, sharing their cures and antidotes for getting by on a daily basis.[37]

Father Calderón and the Consequences of Love Magic

Mining towns also facilitated this kind of interethnic, cross-cultural exchange of information. By 1721, the non-Indian population of Cusihuiriachi, where Antonia had spent some time in its rough-and-ready founding days, had swelled to over a thousand.[38] After its early bonanza, silver production had declined somewhat, leaving the fates of many Spanish and casta miners and petty entrepreneurs to chance. Cockfights, card playing, and other venues for gambling provided distractions and attracted other Spaniards from surrounding mines and haciendas who came to buy supplies from the Basque store owners who had entrenched themselves at the turn of the century. The Jesuit priest at the Tarahumara mission of San Francisco Borja to the south was one of its regular visitors. A *criollo* from Mexico City, Father Felipe de Calderón was in his thirties. Probably drawn there first to buy items not included in the mission supply shipments that came irregularly from Mexico City, he soon succumbed to other enticements that had unforeseen and unwelcome consequences. In a despairing attempt to overcome these, in April 1721 Father Calderón traveled southeast to Parral where he sought out the local agent of the Inquisition to make a denunciation.[39] The primary target of his list of charges was Cristina de Villanueva, the wife of José de Acuña, a Spanish petty trader down on his luck. Calderón alleged that he had been seduced by Cristina who had not only employed an arsenal of love magic tricks but also used her "diabolical arts" to make him ill. The sickness consisted of chronic intestinal ailments as well as sexual impotence.

How Calderón had initially become acquainted with Cristina, her husband, and her father, Juan Núñez de Villanueva, is not known to us, but sometime in 1720 the Jesuit had become a frequent visitor to their home. His troubles began when he accompanied Cristina on a visit to her friend María (known by her nickname La Chanes), who was married to Francisco Ramos. They spent the night there apparently continuing a sexual liaison, which had begun some time earlier at the instigation of Calderón. The next morning, back in her own home, Cristina offered him a cup of chocolate. In retrospect, he identified this moment with the onset of his physical problems.

Although he continued to have sexual relations with Cristina, Father Calderón began to experience intestinal problems, ejecting "worms, pieces of bone, hair, bristles, and other filth" from his body. As time went on, he came to connect incidents that had occurred in Cristina's home to his maladies. As he tried to extricate himself from the relationship with her, he realized that he was unable to have sex with anyone else—he was "*ligado*," or tied, in the parlance of the times. In the early weeks of 1721, Calderón was seemingly powerless to resist Cristina's attempts to seduce him in her own home, where she was allegedly abetted in her efforts by her husband and her father. Before the Jesuit became fully convinced that he had been bewitched (*maleficiado*), he accepted a number of cures offered by Cristina for the intestinal problems, but instead of getting better his health continued to deteriorate. These ineffectual remedies and still others he sought from other Indian and mixed-race *curanderos* ended up costing him several hundred pesos. Nor were visits to nearby parish priests efficacious in removing the spells he believed she had cast. After several months, Calderón went to the Inquisition with his bizarre tale of illness, witchcraft, sexual perversions, curanderismo, abuse of Christian images, and a pact with the devil.

According to the Jesuit, Cristina had a history of many premarital affairs with local residents through which she had perfected "the art of tying men," including the one she married. Calderón admitted that because of her ill repute (*común fama*), he had initially perceived her as an easy conquest. She had continued to sleep with other men after her marriage, apparently with the approval of her husband and father (who may have been soliciting clients for her). Her father was alleged to have taught her many practices of witchcraft and healing. Among these was the use of peyote and potions concocted from a variety of herbs and plants. "Tying" men was accomplished through bundles that contained her own pubic hair wrapped around chameleons. Judging from the evidence we have, it is likely that Cristina de Villanueva engaged in magical and healing practices as a means of procuring some extra income for her family.

The Gendering of Deviance

In Calderón's testimony we see several strategies for discrediting Cristina. He casts her as a prostitute, a witch, and a curandera. He claimed to have seen her sign a pact with the devil in blood, and he cited the presence in her home of many images and animal familiars associated with Satan. Furthermore, she had contact with unsavory women of inferior ethnicity. Her connections to two mulattas and four *indias*, including an Apache, a Sonoran, and a Nahuatl speaker, made her even more suspect since these Indian and mixed-race women were deemed to have a proclivity to use the occult. Father Calderón interwove references to these "shady associations" throughout his testimony to enhance a portrait of her as lascivious, depraved, and treacherous.[40] At the same time he also named a number of other prominent local Spaniards who had succumbed to her wiles and perhaps attempts at extortion. It is interesting that his characterization of the "temptress" and "witch" obviates any direct reference to Cristina as a mother, even though at least two children are mentioned obliquely in his charges.

Why would this Jesuit priest go to such lengths to discredit Cristina de Villanueva, especially when it meant publicly exposing his own lack of celibacy, a violation of his priestly vows?[41] For one thing, the violation of celibacy was commonplace in the Iberian world and was not considered to be particularly grievous unless it occurred as a result of solicitation in the confessional. As other scholars have pointed out, Catholic clergymen were in an anomalous position in a world where masculinity was heavily tied to sexual activity. This helps to explain why priestly liaisons were tolerated as long as they were relatively discreet.[42] In this case, Calderón's afflictions constituted a pathology that drove him to seek the intervention of the Inquisition. A modern observer might see these as psychosomatic illnesses that, for him, demanded an explanation. From his testimony it is difficult to ascertain which of his ailments was most bothersome, but he seems to have been most tormented by the state of being "tied" and dominated by a woman. There is also some evidence that the affair with Cristina had begun through solicitation in the confessional and that he hoped to preempt her denunciation of this sin or charges by a third party.

In the end, the Holy Office declined to pursue his accusations, perhaps because they were perceived as too difficult to substantiate or too destabilizing of priestly legitimacy or authority on a turbulent frontier. Also, the Jesuit's testimony implies that Inquisition officials might have been compromised in her "nefarious" network. This is suggested by another case forwarded to Mexico City from Cusihuiriachi in 1721 that brought charges against a mulatta, Antonia de la Fabela. She was alleged to have been employed by several aggrieved wives to induce illness or impotence in their wayward husbands or their lovers. The interesting thing about this case is that Antonia de la Fabela was a servant in the household of the Inquisition commissary, Agustín Sánchez de Cantillana. The testimonies in the case show that she had been engaged in these practices for more than 15 years, indicating that the inquisitorial agent either did not know what transpired under his nose or that he was unconcerned.[43]

Whatever the reasons for the dismissal of the case, Father Calderón's allegations provide clues as to local society's views of proper gender behavior. The testimony constructs Cristina de Villanueva as the nemesis of an ideal patriarchal order that placed women below men in a clear sexual hierarchy and that tried to circumscribe women's participation in the public sphere. Using love magic Cristina reversed the order within her own family and also in the lay/cleric relationship that idealized the paternal role of the priest.[44] Father Calderón clearly believed that she had power over him. Of course this is one of the reasons that the church condemned love magic—it took away free will. This was in all likelihood perceived as a greater sin when directed against men. The language employed by men and women when they talked about the use of love magic also reveals gender differences that accorded males exclusivity in domination. While men used verbs such as *alcanzar* (to take or obtain), women were more likely to choose *atraer* (to attract) or *aficionar* (to inspire a liking) to describe their actions.

Women most often engaged in these practices as a way to seek protection and security—we could construe them as classic "weapons of the weak" or a kind of mild subversion that was often tolerated in colonial society. The association of love magic with diabolical pacts was more threatening, but by the eighteenth century, ecclesiastical authorities were less concerned with the influence of the devil in New Spain.[45] So the Jesuit priest's allegations could have been perceived by the Inquisition authorities in Mexico City as a tempest in a teapot, even though he constructed a portrait of Cristina that made her out to be much more than a woman looking for security. In his mind, she was deliberately seeking power by controlling men's bodies.

Of course she did not achieve these goals all by herself. She had a network of accomplices who enabled her. Even the more transient Antonia seemed to have no trouble linking up with supporters. In these and other inquisitorial cases we are given intimate glimpses of social networks, most often interethnic, that furnish clues as to what people were actually thinking and disclose a coincidence of sympathies among groups arrayed in different mixes of class, ethnicity, and gender.[46] Historians who have studied relationships between lower caste groups in large urban areas have argued that the state was somewhat effective in the kind of divide-and-rule tactics that inhibited lower-class solidarity,[47] but I would argue that frontier conditions were more likely to encourage cross-cultural reliance. The cases I have examined reveal close associations between men and women from diverse indigenous groups and castas who occupied subordinate positions in an especially unpredictable world. It is interesting that Father Calderón placed great emphasis on a web of uncontrollable women. To be sure, this network straddled ethnic and class boundaries, but it downplayed the influence of males to the point of emasculating them.

Conclusions

In my book on ethnic persistence among indigenous groups of Nueva Vizcaya, I trace the processes of ethnic mixing and demonstrate that changing intersections of ethnicity, culture, class, and identity on this frontier were shaped largely by local, often distinctively frontier factors. When the state intervened it tended to mirror these processes rather than transform them.[48] I have already suggested that state social control was severely limited in the north where violence was endemic as a result of several factors. The first is characteristic of the Spanish empire as a whole: the coercion that local elites exercised in limited areas engendered violent responses in turn.[49] The other two are peculiar to the frontier: (1) the relative absence of effective coercive administrative mechanisms, and (2) continuous warfare with indigenous peoples.

In general I would argue that deviance was less clear-cut and less threatening in this milieu. The failure of the Inquisition to severely punish or even pursue aberrant behavior is one indicator. The Holy Office virtually ignored the cases of petty witchcraft that sought to manipulate gender relationships. The allegations presented in the cases and the inquisitorial questioning around them do tell us a good deal about both idealized and subverted patterns of gender relations. From them we get glimpses, rich in anecdotal lore, of the ways in which a very diverse body of frontier women in Nueva Vizcaya interacted and positioned themselves in a hierarchical, patriarchal order. They also suggest that royal authorities could be circumscribed in their efforts to control "wild," undisciplined women, especially outside of the more settled urban areas of the north like the mining center of Chihuahua. Female sexuality was not always subject to vigilant control.

In the two cases profiled in greatest detail in this article, we have women who deliberately subverted the patriarchal order. Their stories are not typical, but they do allow us to make some observations about the boundaries that theoretically delimited women's roles, as well as how ethnicity and gender intersected along this idealized behavioral map. In both cases we see the blurring of boundaries as these women inverted gender hierarchies and occupied liminal (or in-between) spaces. Both women jumped outside the norms of domesticity to assume some control over their material and affective circumstances. For Antonia, the leap was more radical and transformative, allowing her to transcend both legal subjugation and female submissiveness. Her ethnic oppression in slavery was a burden, but she did not believe it was as debilitating as her gender. For Antonia de Soto, the freedom to act on her own was clearly rooted in male stereotypes. Power derived from maleness in either of the two worlds she claimed to know—the Spaniards' or the devil's. In the end, her usurpation of diabolic supermale energy could not eradicate the seeds of Christian obedience that had germinated in her psyche.

Cristina de Villanueva did not have to stray quite so far to reverse the patriarchal order. In her woman's body, she alternated between seducing and emasculating a Jesuit priest, rendering this symbol of paternal celibacy both sexually and spiritually impotent. Her success (either as a breadwinner or as a temptress) was also dependent upon harnessing male power. In both cases, the women were supported in their activities through alliances and confidences that crossed ethnic lines. Resisting the confines of their established place in the class and gender hierarchy, they negotiated daily with subalterns (Indians, mulattos, mestizos, servants, cooks, cowboys, herdsmen, carters, and mineworkers) and elites (officials, priests, and landowners). In these activities they were not so different from other women who lived in the far north. We might have assumed that their more contemptuous or audacious boundary crossings would have wrought more serious consequences. But even their alleged pacts with the devil elicited either moderate or no response; there was no compelling urge to mete out exemplary punishments as a deterrent to others. Being "betwixt and between" in gendered terms seems not to have been terribly threatening in less settled areas where violence and abnormality were the rule. That would change in the eighteenth century as the non-Indian population grew and patriarchal repression supplanted the more gratuitous forms of violence that characterized a fractious frontier.

NOTES

1. Denunciación que contra si hizo Antonia de Soto, mulata esclava de Francisco de Noriega, vecino de la Ciudad de Durango de diferentes hechos con pacto con el demonio, 1691, Inquisición, vol. 525, exp. 48, fols. 500–520, Archivo General de la Nación, Mexico (hereafter cited as AGN). See Laura A. Lewis, *Hall of Mirrors: Power, Witchcraft and Caste in Colonial Mexico* (Durham, N.C.: Duke University Press, 2003), 167–72, for an analysis of this case that advances her arguments about domains of sanctioned and unsanctioned power in colonial Mexico, and especially the positioning of caste and gender in these realms.

2. Cheryl Martin, *Governance and Society in Colonial Mexico: Chihuahua in the Eighteenth Century* (Stanford: Stanford University Press, 1996), 183.

3. Susan M. Deeds, "Colonial Chihuahua: Peoples and Frontiers in Flux," in *New Views of Borderlands History*, ed. Robert H. Jackson, 21–40 (Albuquerque: University of New Mexico Press, 1998).

4. ibid.

5. Catálogo de los pueblos y partidos, . . . San Miguel de las Bocas, ca. 1650, Jesuitas, I-16, exp. 19, AGN; carta ánua, San Miguel de las Bocas, 1662, Misiones, vol. 26, fol. 160, AGN; Juan Ortiz Zapata *visita* report, *Documentos para la historia de México*, 21 vols. in 4 series (Mexico City: Imprenta J. R. Navarro, 1853–1857), 4, 3: 317; testimony of Juana de Aguilar, Parral, 9 March, 1686, Inquisición, vol. 1551, part 2, exp. 39, fols. 563–71, AGN; report of P. Francisco Xavier de Medrano, Las Bocas, ca. 1690, Archivo Histórico de Hacienda, Temporalidades., leg. 279, exp. 69, AGN.

6. See Solange Alberro, *Inquisición y sociedad en México, 1521–1700* (Mexico City: Fondo de Cultura Económica, 1988) and Noemí Quezada, "Cosmovisión, sexualidad e Inquisición," 2: 77–86, in *Inquisición novohispana*, ed. Noemí Quezada et al. (2 vols., Mexico City: Universidad Autónoma de México, 2000).

7. Henry Kamen, *The Spanish Inquisition* (rev. ed.; New Haven, Conn.: Yale University Press, 1998); Noemí Quezada, Martha Eugenia Rodríguez, and Marcela Suárez, eds., *Inquisición novohispana*, 2 vols. (Mexico City: Universidad Nacional Autónoma de México, Universidad Autónoma Metropolitana, 2000).

8. Gonzalo Aguirre Beltrán, *Regiones de refugio: El desarrollo de la comunidad y el proceso dominical en mestizo América* (Mexico City: Instituto Indigenista Interamericano, 1967); see also his *La población negra de México, estudio etnohistórico*, 2nd ed. (Mexico City: Fondo de Cultura Económica, 1972). For a slightly different take on "marginals," see Peter Stern, "Marginals and Acculturation in Frontier Society," in *New Views*, ed. Jackson, 157–88.

9. We should note that the study of patterns of racial exogamy in marriages would also shed light on the colonial state's ability to preserve racial purity among elites. Suggestive are the studies of Durango by Sherburne F. Cook and Woodrow Borah, *Essays in Population History* (Berkeley: University of California Press, 1971), vols. 1 and 2, which show such a high percentage of pardos; and the analysis of marriage patterns in urban areas by Michael Swann, *Tierra Adentro: Settlement and Society in Colonial Durango* (Boulder, Colo.: Westview Press, 1982).

10. Solange Alberro, *Inquisición y sociedad en México, 1521–1700* (Mexico City: Fondo de Cultura Económica, 1988), 379–408.

11. For example: Ramón Gutiérrez, *When Jesus Came, the Corn Mothers Went Away: Marriage, Sexuality and Power in New Mexico, 1500–1846* (Stanford: Stanford University Press, 1991); Susan Socolow, "Women of the Frontier, Buenos Aires, 1740–1810," in *Contested Ground: Comparative Frontiers in the Greater Southwest and the Río de la Plata*, Donna J. Guy and Thomas E. Sheridan, eds., 67–82, (Tucson: University of Arizona Press, 1998); and James Brooks, *Captives and Cousins: Slavery, Kinship, and Community in the Southwest Borderlands* (Chapel Hill: University of North Carolina Press, 2002).

12. Catalina de Erauso, *Lieutenant Nun: Memoirs of a Basque Transvestite in the New World*, trans. Michele Stepto and Gabriel Stepto (Boston: Beacon Press, 1996), xxvi.

13. Among these are several anthologies on women and domestic life edited by Pilar Gonzalbo and Cecilia Rabell for the Seminario de Mentalidades of the Instituto Nacional de Antropología e Historia in Mexico; Asunción Lavrin, ed. *Sexuality and Marriage in Colonial Latin America* (Lincoln: University of Nebraska Press, 1989); Steve Stern, *The Secret History of Gender: Women, Men and Power in Late Colonial Mexico* (Chapel Hill: University of North Carolina Press, 1995); Susan Schroeder, Stephanie Wood, and Robert Haskett, eds., *Indian Women of Colonial Mexico* (Norman: University of Oklahoma Press, 1997); Lyman Johnson and Sonya Lipsett-Rivera, eds., *The Faces of Honor: Sex, Shame, and Violence in Colonial Latin America* (Albuquerque: University of New Mexico Press, 1998); and Ann Twinam, *Public Lives, Private Secrets: Gender, Honor, Sexuality, and Illegitimacy in Colonial Spanish America* (Stanford: Stanford University Press, 1999). For a recent survey that incorporates this literature and has an extensive bibliography, see Susan Socolow, *The Women of Colonial Latin America* (New York: Cambridge University Press, 2000).

14. Martin, *Governance and Society in Colonial Mexico*, chap. 7; Cynthia Radding, *Wandering Peoples: Colonialism, Ethnic Spaces, and Ecological Frontiers in Northwestern Mexico, 1700–1850* (Durham, N.C.: Duke University Press, 1997). See also Antonia I. Castañeda, "Presidarias y pobladoras: Spanish-Mexican Women in Frontier Monterey, Alta California, 1770–1821" (Ph.D. diss.: Stanford University, 1990).

15. Susan M. Deeds, "Double Jeopardy: Indian Women in Jesuit Missions of Nueva Vizcaya," in *Indian Women of Early Mexico*, ed. Susan Schroeder et al., 255–72 (Norman: University of Oklahoma Press, 1997).

16. *Merriam-Webster's On-line Collegiate Dictionary*, 2002.

17. A review of the literature is found in Sherry Velasco, *The Lieutenant Nun: Transgenderism, Lesbian Desire and Catalina de Erauso* (Austin: University of Texas Press, 2000); on lesbianism, see chap. 1. See also Antonio Rubial, "Catalina de Erauso o el travestismo tolerado," *Historias* 43 (1999).

18. Velasco, *Lieutenant Nun*, 31–40; Julie Wheelwright, *Amazons and Military Maids: Women Who Dressed as Men in the Pursuit of Life, Liberty, and Happiness* (Boston: Pandor, 1989). On women tranvestites in Spanish Golden Age theater, see Rosa Spada Suárez, *El travestismo femenino en "Don Gil de las calzas verdes" de Tirso de Molina* (Mexico City: Instituto Nacional de Antropología e Historia, 1998), 27–60.

19. P. Tomás de Guadalajara to P. Prov. Bernardo Pardo, Parral, 4 December 1681, Provincia Mexicana, vol. 17, fol. 466, Archivum Romanum Societatis Jesu; autos sobre las invasiónes, . . . 1691–93, Provincias Internas, vol. 29, exp. 5, AGN.

20. P. Nicolás de Zepeda to P. Provincial, San Miguel de las Bocas, 18 April, 1645, AGN, Historia, vol. 19, fols. 136–66; causa criminal contra Andrés Paez e indios, . . . June 1660, reel 1660c fr. 1692–1724, Archivo de Hidalgo de Parral (hereafter cited as AHP).

21. African slaves had been brought to the north from the early days of the conquest. And from her designation as a mulatta, we can surmise that Antonia was acculturated.

22. Joan Cameron Bristol, "Negotiating Authority in New Spain: Blacks, Mulattos, and Religious Practice in the Seventeenth Century" (Ph.D. diss.: University of Pennsylvania, 2001).

23. Alberro, *Inquisición y sociedad*, 455–85; Fernando Cervantes, *The Devil in the New World: The Impact of Diabolism in New Spain* (New Haven, Conn.: Yale University Press, 1994), 78–80.

24. Bristol, "Negotiating Authority," chap. 3.

25. Deeds, "Colonial Chihuahua," 30–31.

26. Cheryl Martin, "Public Celebrations, Popular Culture, and Labor Discipline in Eighteenth-Century Chihuahua," in *Rituals of Rule, Rituals of Resistance: Public Celebrations and Popular Culture in Mexico*, ed. William H. Beezley, Cheryl E. Martin, and William E. French, 95–114 (Wilmington, Del.: Scholarly Resources, 1994).

27. Cervantes, *The Devil in the New World*, 90.

28. There is at least one earlier mention of cross-dressing women in the north in a tale that involves bullfighting and love magic: Testimonio c ontra María negra por usar hierbas, Cuencamé, 1 September, 1725, Inquisición, vol. 356, fols. 474–76, AGN. On witchcraft in peripheral areas, see Ruth Behar, "Sex and Sin, Witchcraft, and the Devil in Late Colonial Mexico," *American Ethnologist* 14, 1 (1987): 34–54; Alberro, *Inquisición y sociedad*, 283–408.

29. Noemí Quezada, "La brujería: Salud y enfermedad. Nuevas perspectivas teóricas," lecture presented at the Escuela Nacional de Antropología e Historia, Mexico City, 27 April 2001.

30. MacLeod, "Thoughts on the Pax Colonial," 131.

31. Behar, "Sex and Sin," 36–38; Elia Nathan Bravo, "La Inquisición como generadora y trasmisora de ideologías," and Marcela Suárez, "Sexualidad, Inquisición y herejía en la Nueva España de las Luces," in Noemí Quezada et al., eds., *Inquisición novohispana*, 1:273–86, and 2:13–24, respectively.

32. Cervantes, *The Devil in the New World*, 79; see also the cases involving slaves, 1611, Topia, Inquisición, vol 292, AGN.

33. For example: Ruth Behar, "Sexual Witchcraft, Colonialism, and Women's Power: Views from the Mexican Inquisition," in Lavrin, ed., *Sexuality and Marriage*, 178–206; Mary Elizabeth Perry and Anne J. Cruz, eds., *Cultural Encounters: The Impact of the Inquisition in Spain and the New World* (Berkeley: University of California Press, 1991); Martha Few, "Women, Religion, and Power: Gender and Resistance in Daily Life in Late Seventeenth-Century Guatemala," *Ethnohistory* 42 (1995), 627–38.

34. For a survey of love magic cases from the Mexican Inquisition, see Quezada, "Cosmovisión, sexualidad e Inquisición," in Quezada et al., *Inquisición novohispana*, 2:77–86.

35. Denunciation by Hernando de Alessa, San Andrés, 23 March 1627, Inquisición, vol. 560, exp. 2, fol. 374, AGN. To increase his chances of getting the devil's ear, Bartolomé called him by multiple names: Reb, Adon, Belial, Asmodeus, and Belsebu.

36. Denunciation by Ignacia de Brizuela of Ana de Salas, San Andrés, 27 March 1627, Inquisición, vol. 560, exp. 2, fol. 384, AGN; comments of P. Alberto Clerici, Zape, 3 June 1627, Inquisición, vol. 360, fol. 30, AGN.

37. Compare, for example, the inventory in Quezada, "La brujería," with the case against Bernabe, Parral, December 1680, Inquisición, vol. 661, exp. 22, fols. 570–95, AGN. See also: contra María negra, Cuencamé, 1626, Inquisición, vol. 356, fols. 474–75, AGN; contra Francisca de la Cerda y San Miguel, mestiza, Saltillo, January 1665, Inquisición, vol. 513, exp. 35, AGN; contra Mariana de la Fuente, Saltillo, 17 May 1668, Inquisición, vol. 518, exp. 33, AGN; contra Nicolás de Guzmán, mestizo, Parral, 9 September 1673, Inquisición, vol. 516, fols. 405–31, AGN; causa criminal . . . por indicios de hechicero, March 1703, reel 1703 fr. 973–82, AHP; and contra Bárbara de Mata por supersticiones, Saltillo, 18 August, 1741, Inquisición, vol. 912, exp. 27, AGN.

38. Peter Gerhard, *The North Frontier of New Spain*, rev. ed. (Norman: University of Oklahoma Press, 1993), 190.

39. Denuncia de Cristina de Villanueva, Parral, 16 July 1721, Inquisición, vol. 791, exp. 31, fols. 493–502, AGN.

40. Ibid., 497v–498. Similar tactics in the portrayal of women have been noted by other scholars; e.g. Behar, "Witchcraft, Colonialism, and Women's Powers," 194–99; María Elena Sánchez Ortega, "Sorcery and Eroticism in Love Magic," in *Cultural Encounters*, ed. Perry and Cruz, 59–60.

41. Calderón complained in his letter of 16 July, 1721, that regional Inquisition officials were notorious in violating the rules of secrecy that were supposed to guide their investigations, Inquisición, vol. 791, fol. 500, AGN.

42. Gutiérrez, *When Jesus Came*, 314; William B. Taylor, *Magistrates of the Sacred: Priests and Parishioners in Eighteenth-Century Mexico* (Stanford: Stanford University Press, 1996), 188.

43. Antonia de la Fabela de casta mulata por maléfica, Cusihuiriachi, October 1721, Inquisición, vol. 789, fols. 196–211, AGN.

44. I thank my former student, Scott Wolf, for this observation in his: "Sex, Sickness, Magic, and Power: The Case of Padre Felipe Calderón," unpublished ms.

45. Cervantes, *The Devil in the New World*.

46. Other scholars have called attention to the exchanges of magic and ritual that occur across the margins of different cultures; for example, Nancy Farriss, *Maya Society under Colonial Rule: The Collective Enterprise of Survival* (Princeton: Princeton University Press, 1984), 295, and Bristol, "Negotiating Authority in New Spain," 259–63.

47. R. Douglas Cope, *The Limits of Racial Domination: Plebeian Society in Colonial Mexico City, 1660–1720* (Madison: University of Wisconsin Press, 1994); Christopher Lutz, *Santiago de Guatemala, 1541–1773: City, Caste, and the Colonial Experience* (Norman: University of Oklahoma Press, 1994).

48. Susan M. Deeds, *Defiance and Deference in New Spain: Indians under Colonial Rule in Nueva Vizcaya* (Austin: University of Texas Press, 2003).

49. MacLeod, "Thoughts on the Pax Colonial," 139–42.

CHAPTER SIX

Social Control and Native Territoriality in Northeastern New Spain

CECILIA SHERIDAN
TRANSLATED BY NED F. BRIERLEY

As of the second half of the eighteenth century, the area that I define as northeastern New Spain was already a Spanish possession, even though its territorial limits were not yet fixed. In the periodic reports of frontier governors, there stand out among the descriptions of this immense territory and its Spanish settlements—*ranchos* (small mixed-farms), mines, haciendas, missions, presidios, and towns—the distances and dangers of moving from one place to another.[1] Like small oases in the middle of the desert, Spanish settlements were grouped in restricted spaces, generally protected by a presidio or flying company (groups of mounted soldiers that moved constantly among the settlements). The inhabitants of these settlements— both Hispanics and their Tlaxcaltecan allies—maintained at the ready weapons and mounts, in the manner of militia, to defend themselves from the constant attacks perpetrated by the natives, whom they considered "enemy savages" and "frontier Indians." In fact, from the earliest days of Spanish settlement in the region the daily life of settlers revolved around the threat of attack, for which the Crown granted them status as "frontier settlers," which afforded them tax and legal privileges.

Documentation regarding the various Spanish strategies for conquering the frontier makes reference to two cardinal issues: rebellion and war. The former describes the responses of native groups that, after having been subjected to Spanish control in missions, towns, or *encomiendas* (grants of Indian labor/tribute to specific Spaniards), confronted their oppressors. The latter applies to the frequent attacks perpetrated by "enemy" natives who were the subject of varying policies of containment and deliberate extermination. These categories reflect the attitudes of royal and ecclesiastical authorities, and not necessarily the actual control that officials claimed to have established. That is, we can encounter a rebelling indigenous group to which various "punishments" had been applied and, immediately afterward, find the same group in hostile confrontation with settlers and, later yet, discover them in strategic alliance with the same Spaniards who had previously subjected or punished them and with whom they had been at war.

It is possible, therefore, to infer a state of permanent tension on the northeastern frontier that takes various forms, some from the changes in native territorial organization and others from Spanish desires to incorporate territories and their native occupants. We may say with assurance that despite the various attempts by authorities and settlers to establish control over the Indians, the obstinate hunter-gatherers of the northeastern wilderness never were entirely subjugated. On the contrary, the tension between nonsedentary natives and Hispanic settlers increased in direct proportion to the advance of Spanish occupation and territorial control.

In the second half of the eighteenth century, viceregal authorities opted for offensive warfare (as opposed to the policy of defensive war that had persisted since the last third of the seventeenth century) as a formal strategy of conquest and occupation of the northern frontier. While a new policy for royal officials, offensive warfare had never been abandoned by regional authorities who since the sixteenth century had argued for it as the only means to "pacify" the so-called "enemy frontier." Experience acquired through time had demonstrated to them that the natives were "irreducible" and, therefore, that offensive warfare and extermination of hostiles were the most secure means to achieving control over the conquered territories, if not over its aboriginal inhabitants.

In the long and complex process of conquest in northeastern New Spain, the control of native Indians was basically attempted by three means: 1) military conquest sustained by the use of presidial forces in the defense of Spanish settlements and punishment of the unsubmissive; 2) religious conversion through missionary activity aimed at reducing paganism; and 3) Spanish colonization, which can be characterized as the civilian expression of the process of conquest.[2] This last means, which we may measure by the persistence of civil settlements in zones considered hostile frontiers, is perhaps the most enduring achievement of Spanish expansion. For that reason the maxim "populate in order to use" became one of the most important principles of royal officials in making policy for northern New Spain. In the process, the fundamental objectives that nourished the first century of conquest—conversion of pagans to the Christian faith and providing for their adoption of Spanish ways of life—passed in the eighteenth century to a lesser plane, subordinated to the goal of achieving absolute control of territories considered to be under Spanish dominion.

To seize, consolidate, and control what they considered a "wilderness" region were justifiable actions from the perspective of the Spaniards who came to northern New Spain between the sixteenth and eighteenth centuries. Motivated by their desire to extend the territories of the Crown while at the same time seeking personal benefits, Spaniards developed various concepts of frontier in the practical context of seeking to control territories occupied by native peoples. To appreciate the historical process of this control, it is necessary to begin with a meaning of frontier that will permit us to understand its complexity within a context that includes both interaction and rivalry.

We begin, then, with the idea of the natives' territory as a continuous, diverse whole that was rationally utilized by its inhabitants. Territory in this sense is defined as a set of spaces—hunting, fishing, gathering, ritual, warring, exchange—in which a strategy of integrated management of the land is observed.[3] The alteration or physical transformation of those spaces (pollution, erosion, deforestation), produces a chain reaction of discontinuities: deprivation of means of sustenance, elimination in diversity of economic activities, radical changes in social relationships, transformation of relations with the environment. These discontinuities are made evident in the reconfiguration of the social relationships between groups and individuals.[4]

Subjection and Control

In the 1795 report issued by Lt. Col. don Félix Calleja on the state of the northeastern frontier, a certain preoccupation with evaluating the efficacy of the missions in the provinces of Nuevo Santander and Nuevo León and improving their condition can be perceived. Unlike the observations of previous, ecclesiastical inspectors, the soldier's evaluation considers the missions a necessary means to containing the Indians and to preventing their dispersion, both within territories under Spanish control and territories yet to be controlled. Only by restricting Indian mobility did Calleja see Spanish colonization and the securing of the royal dominions possible. The settlers could then play the role of defenders of those lands—organized in the form of urban militias—saving the Crown the high costs of maintaining permanent garrisons for defense of settlements.[5]

"Enemy" Indians, that is to say, those natives who maintained themselves in constant confrontation with colonists, would have to be controlled by means of the deployment of military forces at strategic locations within controlled territories.[6] The location and objectives of the military detachments visualized by Calleja makes clear his goal of constructing distinct frontier zones of control, defined by the intensity and frequency of Indian attacks on established settlements. These settlements, composed of *peninsulares, criollos*, mestizos, blacks, and mulattoes, as well as "friendly" Indians (indigenous and migrant), were part of a clear colonization policy conceived in the middle of the century by don José de Escandón to divide the frontier into small war zones, the boundaries of which were determined by the threat posed by enemy Indians.

Prior to Calleja's report, and as a result of other reports that gave cause for the issuance of the Presidial Regulations of 1772, other functionaries had looked for ways to control native mobility. In 1772 Nueva Vizcaya governor José Carlos de Agüero sent an order to the province of Coahuila in which he instructed that "every Spaniard" who might encounter "enemy" Indians wandering without leave or permission should detain them and turn them over to the judge of the jurisdiction and, in case they resisted, he should "take their lives," giving notice to the authorities. Whoever did not comply, Agüero declared, "is a traitor to the king, and let punishment be meted out to him."[7] In other words, Indian "friends" were potential enemies and, therefore, subject to supervision and extreme care.

Among the enemy Indians who worried Calleja were those listed by the Count of Revilla Gigedo as having been reduced to mission life. They were the survivors of a contest for the area and its resources that had lasted more than two centuries. They were those who had achieved the control of spaces for group survival and who had exhibited characteristics distinct from those of the enemy Indians of the previous century. By the last decades of the colonial period, these "enemies" had altered their codes of social grouping, forms of leadership, purposes for alliances, consumption patterns, and other characteristics. Like their Spanish enemies, they had transformed their perception of the territories they inhabited. Group names surviving into the second half of the eighteenth century are those of groups that succeeded in imposing themselves on others as they searched for the necessary resources to maintain their independence.[8]

Identities and Territories

Although the historical literature regarding the Indians who inhabited northeastern New Spain is very much in the initial stages of development, useful analyses have been produced highlighting the role of natives in the complex process of conquest undertaken by Spaniards beginning in the second half of the sixteenth century. Recent studies recount the transformations of identity as the reorganization and redefinition of a preexisting indigenous diversity.

Investigating "nations," "factions," ethnic groups, or simply group names mentioned in the colonial documentation is, therefore, a problem into which it is necessary to delve deeply. Despite the multiple difficulties that the sources present for trying to understand native diversity in New Spain's northeast, it is undeniable that groups of individuals with diverse designations inhabited this region before the beginnings of conquest. Moreover, it is convenient to begin with an understanding that "taxonomies are an expression of reality."[9]

With this agenda I devoted myself to the task of searching for the names and definitions of groups identified by Spaniards throughout the colonial period, whether as a result of direct contact with them or from having learned of their existence through contacted groups. A temporal and spatial investigation was made of the groups mentioned that permitted, on the one hand, defining periods of survival associated with specific contexts and, on the other, studying the territorial mobility of each one of the groups in question.[10]

Causes for the disappearance or extinction of some of these groups were varied: warfare; mortality as a result of diseases; dispersion as a result of forced reduction (slavery, missions); *mestizaje*; assimilation of one group within another, leading to the disappearance of the original group's designation. This last factor, in combination with various processes of alliance and of a consequent "deterritorialization," represent a complex process of ethnogenesis (cultural reinvention) that explains when, how, and why at the close of the colonial period the so-called "enemies" (surviving reconfigured groups) persisted in keeping themselves autonomous and disinclined to accept a foreign presence.

In defining native territories, or spaces of control, we have mistakenly supposed that the variable of "mobility," an intrinsic characteristic of nonsedentary (or hunter-gatherer) societies, is static. A group's territory, however, is an imaginary map encompassing the group's perception of the scope of the space it ancestrally inhabited. It is the space it uses and controls; in it resides the group's security. It nevertheless permits redefinition in accordance with external factors such as climatic changes, the invasion of stronger groups, and transformation of the economic uses of the space. This last factor is definitive for group reproduction because it supposes that in the transformation of a specific territory it is necessary to include the gradual transformation of collateral territories and, therefore, the reduction of the survival spaces of a set of peripheral groups.

Reduction in the territory available to native groups forced them to employ new subsistence strategies. These strategies took a variety of forms, both old and new: interethnic alliances; temporary or permanent loss of original identity; reorganization of subsistence territory; appearance of new ethnic designations; and changes in consumption, both of food and of goods. It is a matter, then, of ethnogenesis.[11] Illustrative, in this respect, is the declaration of four Cocoyome women who were taken prisoner in 1715 after an attack on Hacienda La Zarca in the present-day Mexican state of Durango. The women acknowledged that their "nation" maintained alliances with the Acoclame, Chisa, and Zizinble nations, with whom they were accustomed to gathering once a year "in the dry season":

> that they also get together and assemble in different locations
> to carry out thefts and killings ... that every year the four
> nations have the custom of assembling to barter, exchanging
> with each other the things that they have, and that then they
> discuss what they must do in everything that matters to
> them ... that she knows that they come to assemble in the
> locations where it seems appropriate for them to carry out
> the damages and hostilities to which they are accustomed,
> and that afterwards they return to their settlements.[12]

missions didn't estab. social control,
although they did invoke *technolog. influence*
& cultural change

Reconstitution of native subsistence spaces is manifested in the radical transformation of the said territories, as much by the introduction of new technologies in the exploitation of environmental niches as by reorganization of native groups in the face of the transformation of their subsistence spaces and in response to the Spanish invasion of their territories. We know that the introduction of the mission system, combined with the appearance of presidios and of Tlaxcaltecan colonizers[13] as allies of the Spanish government, did not achieve its principal goal of establishing social control over the natives of the northeast—reducing them to town life and "civilizing" them. It did, however, fundamentally alter their subsistence and cultural patterns.

Conflict with Spaniards forced native groups to reorganize intergroup relations. On one level Spaniards took on the role of challenger for territory, requiring indigenous groups to form the same types of alliances among themselves that they had formed previously when challenged by other Indian groups. On another level, in the face of the Spaniards' establishment of settlements, war became a permanent pattern of behavior, requiring more extensive alliances than had previously been necessary. For these alliances a principal end was the expulsion of the colonists entirely, but other goals also became important. In particular, frequent acts of looting of goods such as livestock, grains, and white captives, combined with the burning of crops and buildings and the destruction of animals, can be seen as the expression of a new territoriality.[14]

change of kinship patterns

It is a matter, then, of territoriality that is independent of the control of specific territory. It is a strategy that relies on establishing new and more ample physical and cultural subsistence zones with temporary boundaries, in accordance with the activity that interests the allied groups at a given moment. It is a process of opportunity in which the inclusion of other native groups willing to subject themselves to new leadership is fundamental to sustaining both resistance to invasion and establishing the limits of a new territoriality. These alliances, however, change constantly as an expression of the very dynamic of redefinition of the native territoriality, which depends on numerous circumstances, such as negotiation of peace treaties, alliance of natives with Spaniards, congregation of groups in missions, and renewed enmity between groups.[15]

fluidity of relations

For the weakest native groups, survival often meant choosing between subjecting themselves to the control of their stronger "allies" or to that of the Spaniards. Thus, on some occasions weak groups sought refuge within the mission environment. On other occasions groups injured by an unfavorable alliance sought the same protection on a temporary basis. Groups that permanently lost their subsistence territories also sought refuge in the missions, where they left their women and children while the men sought new pacts with other groups. Many groups did not completely relinquish the use of their lost territory, since at specific times (bison hunting and/or prickly pear gathering), which could last for three to five months, alliances were temporarily suspended and missions abandoned. In times of drought, however, when agricultural fields were in crisis, cattle scarce, and foraging insufficient, many groups took refuge in the missions for as long as two or three years, with sporadic departures to reaffirm alliances or to exchange goods and women. As a result, they avoided falling under the complete social control of both Spaniards and more powerful tribesmen.

The strongest groups, that is to say, those that succeeded in establishing broad (from three to fifteen or more groups) and long-lasting alliances, seldom settled in missions or became subject to service on Spanish properties. Their range was so wide that they could be found distributed along the northern frontier from Sonora to Texas and Tamaulipas, without ceasing to maintain certain "niches" of temporary refuge that the Spanish identified as the "territory" of this or that nation. The principal characteristic of these alliances is that the strongest constituent groups did not lose their names on establishing the alliance: in other words, they maintained their original group identity and retained autonomy of action. The groups that kept their own names generally were represented by particular leaders, resulting in the emergence of a dynamic of constant negotiation among leaders for status and control within the alliance. For the majority of groups that entered the alliance by accepting superior leadership, loss of their original name was an immediate consequence, along with surrender of autonomy.

Not all alliances resulted in a stronger group establishing control over one or more weaker ones. New groups were "born" in the process of deterritorialization when two or more existing groups united in a new one, the name of which derived from the activities that fostered the alliance. For example, there is mention of the group called "those who intercept carts," which was dedicated to raiding along the roadways. In these assaults they obtained trade goods and food that they used in the establishment, maintenance, or renewal of alliances. This type of alliance was generally formed temporarily under the direction of one or two leaders who remained in charge for the time that the alliance lasted.

The types of alliances just described are, therefore, not static or permanent. Discord among alliance members could lead to a group's withdrawal from the coalition, even though its membership might otherwise be stable. The dissenting group might then join other groups and transform itself into the enemy of the previous alliance, or even attach itself to the Spaniards as "friendly Indians" to support attacks on enemy nations.[16] In any case, we agree with anthropologist Guillaume Boccara that the collective entities "are not reduced to a single cultural inheritance, but instead are constructed as a system for distancing and differentiating themselves in relation to other significant entities in a determined historical and social context."[17]

In those cases in which groups that came under the control of colonists, principally in the form of *encomienda* or *congrega*, their original territory was also altered in an important way. In those cases, however, the transformation was not voluntary, but imposed by the specific actions of *encomenderos*. Only with difficulty could the natives remove themselves from the encomenderos' control, since the position of the encomendero was protected and maintained by the government as a means of controlling the new territory to be exploited.

Once within the encomienda system, the members of the subject Indian groups came under all sorts of control mechanisms. They were subject to removal from their place of origin by violent means. On occasion they were destined for dispersion when they were introduced into the slave market as individuals, or "pieces," for sale. They responded by attempting to make themselves "invisible" to the encomenderos to whom they had been assigned, by forming temporary alliances to resist the invaders, or by taking refuge in nearby missions, both of which subjected them to other controls. The important thing is that they did not lose their original designations, which to a certain extent were maintained by the encomenderos themselves as the only practical way of identifying the groups that had been assigned to them.

Alliances and Changes in Native Territoriality: The Toboso Case

The group called Toboso maintained a continuous presence throughout the colonial period, so that it is an important case study for analyzing the process of native deterritorialization. The eighteenth-century chronicler fray Agustín Morfi mentions this group as an enemy of a number of other nations as far back as 1598, principally of the groups that dwelt in the vicinity of Lake

Parras, which were known generically as Laguneros.[18] A contemporary historian, Salvador Álvarez, locates them earlier: in 1563 he places them in the Conchos Valley, and in 1567 in the mining camps of San Juan and Santa Bárbara, in Nueva Vizcaya, and some years afterward he finds them sharing the *reducción* of Atotonilco with the Conchos group. It is precisely in this town that Álvarez "fixes" them, that is, he places them in a permanent settlement. His hypothesis seems contradictory to that of historian William Griffen, who in his study of population movements in north-central Mexico argues for the mobility of the Toboso group throughout the northern territory.[19] Álvarez asks how the Tobosos could "appear and disappear with so much facility" in the documentation referred to by Griffen, and considers it unfeasible that they should be located in places so far removed from where they were originally contacted by Spaniards: "just let us think of the 600 kilometers that separate the Florido River basin from Nuevo León." He also asserts that in periods of war the group did not diminish in size, but on the contrary it multiplied: "the Tobosos were always there . . . [and] neither did they extend their territory." The argument, in essence, is rooted in the term Toboso itself. That is, Álvarez supposes that what was transformed in time was "the very definition of the term Toboso," which was influenced by changes in "local Spanish society."[20]

Griffen is interested in two basic questions regarding the Tobosos: mobility and changes in territoriality. He places them in 1590 in the area of La Laguna (Parras and San Pedro), a zone in which the Jesuits had established themselves that year, and he follows them until the second quarter of the eighteenth century, when he supposes them to be extinct. In fact, a Franciscan account of 1746 from the Colegio de Propaganda Fide de la Santa Cruz de Querétaro mentions the dangers involving the Apaches and the need to reduce them to a mission: "as to the enemies becoming worse hereby, they will be reborn as were the Tobosos, of whom only their name remained."[21] We have evidence, however, that at least until 1778 the documentation refers to the Toboso group as an active entity.

From my perspective, the Tobosos may be considered as one of the most belligerent groups in the long history of conquest and control in northeastern New Spain. Undoubtedly, it maintained an important and extensive territorial control sustained by permanent alliances that permitted them to grow in number and strength, especially after the last quarter of the seventeenth century. I do not doubt the permanent presence of the Tobosos in areas to which Álvarez refers; however, it seems evident that at the turn of the eighteenth century the group suffered a kind of internal breakup, which caused its dispersal throughout the length and breadth of the northern frontier. This fragmentation constitutes a good case for investigating a central problem in understanding colonial territorial organization. I refer to the transformation of native territoriality as substantiated in the emergence of new identities.

Among the strategies generated in response to the increase of the non-native population, the establishment of alliances oriented to the destruction and/or expulsion of the Spanish invaders reveals new forms of structuring territories of native activity. In the majority of alliances described in the documentation, one or two groups appear as leaders, both for the establishment of the alliance and for the realization of its proposed objectives. In this way, a broad group designated by one common name contains, within its structure, a number of groups that may or may not maintain their own names, depending on the activities to be carried out—assaults, peace negotiations, relocation of the allied group, and so forth.[22] Let us examine what occurs with the Toboso group and its alliances.

Following the Parral silver discoveries in 1631 the Hispanic population of the area grew rapidly, causing important alterations in the subsistence patterns of various hunter-gatherer groups in the region of Nueva Vizcaya located between the Florido and Conchos Rivers. In the 1640s area settlers suffered intense attacks from Salineros, Tobosos, and allied Indians, despite the fact that these groups had been congregated in the mission of Atotonilco since the first decade of the seventeenth century. They attacked an estate in the San Bartolomé Valley in 1644, and some months later, in March 1645, the town of San Francisco de los Conchos, where they killed the missionaries and Conchos governors who were congregated there.[23] After months of negotiations with the Toboso captains, in October 1645 the latter presented themselves before the Spanish authorities of Nueva Vizcaya to offer peace and accept being settled in a town. The Indians promised to return what had been stolen and to aid in punishing the rebels, "and that likewise they have to be obligated that if some other Indians, of whatever nations they may be, should come out from inland to do harm, . . . they have to set out against them as the occasion shall arise, going in company with the Spanish."[24]

The Toboso-led alliance of 1644–1645 was formed by, among others, groups that later participated in a broad alliance in 1687, among them the Cabezas, Chisos, and Gavilanes. Certainly the peace agreed to in 1645

creation of alliances

involved a part of the rebel Toboso group, constituted by some sixty persons, including men and women; however, it did not necessarily involve the Tobosos in their totality. The rebellions continued, and between 1650 and 1653 the Salineros, Tobosos, and Cabezas, with their "associates," continually attacked settlements and travelers in Nueva Vizcaya. The foregoing indicates that the Tobosos congregated in Atotonilco had not been settled harmoniously and permanently under the control of Hispanic settlers and that renegade Tobosos were involved in depredations, since in 1652 the congregated Tobosos abandoned the mission of Atotonilco and many never returned.

The Toboso alliances of 1687, in which several native groups gathered in the San Juan Valley of Nuevo León to form an alliance against the Spanish who had settled in their territories indicates the level of resistance that hunter-gatherer peoples could muster. This alliance was commanded by the Toboso and Cocoyome "petty captains" Dieguillo, Pedrote, Bartolo, and Santiago.[25] Building on this initial success, the Tobosos some months later called together another "copious assembly of people" on the margins of the Nazas River near Parras, in which they managed to cement an extensive alliance of at least thirty groups with the objective of "going out to the cart road to wait for droves of pack animals to pass, with the intention of attacking them, and that this is known because he has heard them say in their gatherings that it did not matter if they brought the said soldiers and guard because there would be no resisting such a number of people."[26]

By this time the Tobosos were considered by the Spanish as the most bellicose independent group in the northern frontier provinces. They had succeeded in controlling a broad territory in alliance with other groups, threatening the security of Nueva Vizcaya, Nuevo León, Coahuila, and some parts of Nueva Galicia. This mobility and the capacity for control of territory occupied by Spaniards had caused, from the point of view of Agustín de Echeverz y Subíza, the depopulation of zones previously under Spanish control "because they are not a people who only make war in their territory, but they also go out and cross 150 leagues of land settled by Spaniards."[27]

In response to the alliance of 1687 the Spanish government organized a campaign of offensive war against the rebellious Indians that lasted until 1693. The campaign was directed at the Toboso and Cocoyome Indians "because they are those who organize the other nations against the Spanish." Among the Indians the Spanish authorities utilized for the campaign, calling them "friends of the people," were 200 paid "friendly Indians," including

65 Conchos, 40 from Mamiquipa, 25 from San Pedro with their governor, 21 Tepehuanes, 16 Cabezas, and 10 Tobosos of Cuencamé. Moreover, among the Indians considered allies of the Spanish, the governor of Nueva Vizcaya, Isidro de Pardiñas, made use of don Juan Bautista, Toboso governor of the town of San Francisco de Conchos, and don Salvador Lorenzo, "a native of the said nation," so that they could function as interpreters in the interrogations of the apprehended rebellious Indians.[28] The war against the Tobosos, then, pitted "friendly" Indians of the same nation under Spanish control in missions or towns in Nueva Vizcaya, against their kinsmen who remained outside Spanish authority.

Subservience and Resistance: The Dilemma of the Cabeza Indians

Within the Indian alliances, groups remained capable of asserting their autonomy, although at a cost. The Cabeza Indians, led by don Pedrote and don Santiago, had "associated" with the Tobosos and their allies the Cocoyomes, and participated in the alliance of 1687, which was sealed by means of an exchange of women. Yet, one year later Toboso captain don Francisco Tecolote, leader of the alliance, expelled the Cabezas because they had gone to "discuss peace" in Parras, a settlement near their "lands." On breaking off their alliance with the Cabezas of El Pasaje, the Tobosos and Acoclames called together seven other groups to broaden the alliance. Again under the leadership of don Francisco Tecolote, "a great dance was held where they formed the confederation and league" which, among other objectives, sought to make an end of the Cabezas, who "had now become their enemies."[29] A group of eighty Cabezas then joined the Spaniards in the presidio of El Pasaje and the rest remained in the area of Parras under the command of don Pedrote, who subsequently rebelled again, stealing some pack mules and escaping toward the road to Cuatro Ciénegas, a settlement located in northwestern Coahuila, a distance of at least 400 kilometers.

At the same time the Tobosos and other groups assembled in the alliance, the Cabezas extended their active territory or, rather, they altered it so as to settle among Spaniards. According to an account of the nations, or *rancherías*, of Indians who dwelt at Lake Parras, the Cabeza Indians were registered in the records of the parish of Parras between the years 1605 and 1660, together with thirty other groups that are also mentioned, among them Tobosos, Mayos and Salineros.[30] In 1644, the Cabezas appear as a group "attached" to the Spaniards, working on the haciendas or in the

houses of the settlers of Parras. Around 1665 a group of Cabezas raided
in the vicinity of the villa of Saltillo. In 1675, during the expedition of don
Antonio Balcarcel Rivadeneira and fray Juan Larios to found new settlements and missions in the province of Coahuila, a group of fifteen Cabezas
was congregated in a mission following negotiations with Balcarcel. During
the negotiations they showed themselves distrustful "because of the fear
that they have of what is being done with them [in] the [province of]
Vizcaya, of deceptions . . . under cover of peace . . . killing them and locking
them up." They demanded, as a condition for their settlement, that their
women and children, who were found in Spanish hands in the mining camp
of Parral, be returned to them.[31]

The Cabezas were gathered into San Buenaventura de las Cuatro
Ciénegas, a mission founded in 1676 in which were also gathered "more
than a thousand Indians" of various other nations, including Tobosos and
Bausarigames.[32] In 1687 the latter were also found settled at the presidio
of El Pasaje in Nueva Vizcaya. Another group of Cabezas remained in
Parras, where they are found mentioned in parish registers from 1657 to
1722. Subsequently, in the war of 1687–1688 the Cabezas abandoned
Mission San Buenaventura and again allied themselves with the Tobosos
and Cocoyomes, as well as making separate alliances with other groups,
such as Mayos, Obayas, Pinanacas, and Teodocodamos.

In 1702, after twelve years of being "at peace" in the presidio of El
Pasaje, a Cabeza group, together with a group of Babosarigames, petitioned
for agricultural lands next to the presidio. They made the request "both
for their protection and that of their women and children, and so as to be
ready for the repeated forays and campaigns that present themselves
against the rebellious Tobosos; because all the time that they have been at
peace they have served as auxiliaries." Parral governor Juan Bautista de
Larrea, with the consent of the viceroy, granted them lands one league
(approximately 2.7 miles) from the presidio, settling them under the jurisdiction of two Jesuit friars. Although the grants were not legal because they
lacked royal approval, colonial officials considered them necessary to
prevent the two nations from absconding and becoming enemies anew.
To further cement the relationship, the viceroy made the Cabezas and
Babosarigames and their descendants "frontier militiamen," making them
exempt from tribute, *repartimiento*, "and other contributions paid by those
who are not that." As the viceroy reasoned, besides being warriors, these
Indians performed an ongoing service to the Crown by participating, "with

great knowledge, and traversing places and sierras in the nations of the Chichimecos," in campaigns against enemy Indians.[33]

Negotiating Territoriality and Identity

Leadership of the alliance established in 1687 resided in the Toboso, Cocoyome, and Gavilan groups. Representation of the alliance in the peace negotiations organized by Governor Pardiñas, as well as the establishment of new alliances that continued extending themselves according to how the war advanced, centered on the figure of Cocoyome governor don Lorenzo and Toboso captain Francisco Tecolote. To establish an alliance with the Chiso group, itself an ally of the Tatayolilas and Chichitames, the Cocoyomes and Tobosos traveled with the Gavilanes to "the land of the Chisos." There Captain Tecolote met Chiso captain don Felipe Tuerto, presenting him with a cape and a hat as a sign of friendship, thus sealing the alliance among the three nations. According to the terms of the agreement, don Felipe would participate on equal terms with the Toboso and Cocoyome captains only in *tlatoles* or war councils, without further involvement in negotiations with Spanish authorities or in decisions on the establishment of other alliances.

Cocoyome governor don Lorenzo, accompanied by the Indian Antonio, brother of Captain Tecolote, and by Juan Contreras, captain of the Acoclames and of the Hijos de las Piedras, Felipe el Tuerto, and the Indian Alonso of the Nonoxe nation, presented himself before Governor Pardiñas on 28 March, 1692. He indicated that "he was coming in the name of all the nations that followed him, despite the fact that their captains were coming for the same purpose," to ask for peace.[34] Don Lorenzo declared that those who followed him were ready to settle at the locations designated for them. He asked that the peace include the Tobosos congregated in the town of San Francisco de los Conchos, a request that indicates that even groups considered under Spanish control exercised a certain independence of action.

It is necessary to emphasize that in the negotiations the war leader Francisco Tecolote and the Cocoyome governor acted independently. Captain Tecolote urged the members of his alliance to make peace according to what Governor Lorenzo had negotiated. His allies refused, however, and split off. As the captain of the Gavilanes Felipe Tuerto described it: "The truth is that various ones have been on the lookout and seen that the

Cocoyomes do not want to come to render obedience; the Acoclames [and] Hijos de las Piedras have withdrawn to the old union that they have with the Chisos and their allies."[35] Don Felipe decided to make peace on his own account after recognizing that the "bloody war... in which he had lost the great part of his people, obliged him to do it, with the condition that his women and 'rabble' taken prisoner by the Spaniards in the mines of Nueva Vizcaya be returned to him."[36]

Although originally the Gavilanes were found in the parish registers of Parral, after making peace with the Spanish they are mentioned in chronicles relating to the missions of the Río Grande. For instance, we find a group of fourteen Gavilanes congregated in Mission San Francisco Solano in 1707.[37] In 1739 the governor of Nuevo León referred to the Tobosos and Gavilanes as living some fifty or sixty leagues away from Paraje de los Muertos, on the route to Saltillo, from which place they were in the habit of going to attack the settlements to the south in the province of Nueva Vizcaya, the western part of Nuevo León, and the province of Coahuila. He calculated that, on the whole, the group was composed of 90 or 100 individuals, the Gavilanes being the most numerous.[38]

Around September 1692 Governor Pardiñas carried out a series of consultations among the captains of the presidios of Nueva Vizcaya to assess the suitability of suspending peace negotiations. Pardiñas argued that "with the alliance they have made with the other enemy nations who today are invading this Kingdom and land outside it, I hold as unfruitful whatever efforts... whereby it is my feeling that it is indispensably suitable that war should be made on them continuously."[39] In the arguments presented, some presidio commanders favored war, but others favored peaceful congregation. The latter argued that settlement of the Indians, specifically of the Cocoyomes and Tobosos, was preferable "because their land is extensive, and in being scattered, their annihilation is difficult, since for their incursions it is easy for them to join together again... with the others from the interior, who follow them on all the occasions that present themselves."[40]

Of the thirty groups that appear as "allies" of the Tobosos during the seventeenth century and the first half of the eighteenth century, 50 percent were cited in the documentation solely to mention a specific alliance in a given year and are afterward not mentioned again. Of these, except for the Nonoxe, Baborimama, and Talcoyote groups, which are found as allies of at least two other groups, the rest did not establish an alliance with any other group. This permits us to suppose that they were weaker groups without leadership, which lost identity and territory on joining with the Tobosos. Of the allies of the Tobosos who maintained their identity after the alliance was established, 80 percent were registered under the mission system, be it in Parras, in Nueva Vizcaya, in one of the missions established in Coahuila from 1674 on, or in Nuevo León, as is the case with the Quechal or Gueyquesal group, of which a fragment was reduced in the mission of Gualeguas in 1677. The rest of the allies are registered as granted in encomienda in Nuevo León from 1666 to 1694.

Changes in the Territoriality of Encomienda Groups

Since the declaration of Francisco de Sosa, mayor of the villa of Nombre de Dios in the period of Viceroy Velasco in 1563, that "whoever may take a Chichimeca, no one shall take him away from him, because he will be his; the same if he takes two or three,"[41] the "right" to take Indians in war had superceded the New Laws of 1542 as a way to encourage settlement of frontier lands. Up to the time of the 1680 Pueblo Revolt encomiendas, along with slavery, had continued to flourish in an environment where reach of royal law was limited, labor scarce, and opportunities for the acquisition of social status limited. To each encomendero there were assigned one, two, and even three groups that were identified by the native name and its meaning in Spanish, as well as by the area in which they generally lived.[42] As royal pressure mounted to end the abuses of encomienda in the far north, the settlers of Nuevo León responded by renaming the practice *congrega* and continuing other coercive practices. In other words, there existed a tension between the type of social control that the Crown and its officials wished to see practiced with regard to the Indians and the system that had evolved among Spaniards living in frontier regions.

In 1709, the captain of the Alazapa Indians, a group located in the jurisdiction of San Pedro Boca de Leones, Nuevo León, expressed to Governor Luis de Pruneda the abuses committed by the Spaniards to whom they had been granted in encomienda: "acquired by the farmers and encomenderos of this kingdom, to whom at that time we were entrusted, and who . . . take us to their haciendas in order to force us to serve them, . . . was our motive for having left their service and requested a village in which to settle, all because of the considerable violence and wrongs they did to us."[43] During that period of time the region was exempted from the royal prohibition on the enslavement of Indians and to the restrictions on encomiendas.[44]

In 1714 Juan de Oliván Rebolledo, judge of the Audiencia of Guadalajara, discussed the abusive nature of the encomienda in a petition sent to the
Council of the Indies on the "lamentable state in which the Catholic and
heathen Indians bordering on the Kingdom of León find themselves." In
it he denounced the abuses of the *hacendados* and other property owners,
who were only interested that the Indians "may live in ignorance so as to be
able to make use of them more freely." He explained that as a result of

> a report that was made by the Most Illustrious Sr. Doctor Don
> Juan de Santiago de León Garabito to His Majesty, there came a
> decree that the *encomiendas* should be ended and that *congregas*
> would be made on the haciendas, but as this decree came after
> the Lord Bishop had died, only the name was changed to *con-
> grega* and the poor Indians remained in the same trouble as if
> they were still in *encomienda*, whereby they are more oppressed
> than slaves, because slaves are clothed and given all their food,
> but for these miserable ones, all their clothes consist of a small
> blanket and a doublet of coarse woolen cloth, and it is said that
> the most ordinary thing is for all the Indians to go completely
> naked; the days that they work they are given two ears of corn at
> night for dinner and lunch, and the food is a little cooked corn,
> for on the days that they do not work they look for sustenance
> from roots or things from the field: oh! necessity obliges them
> to steal for their sustenance.[45]

Not only were Indians placed in congregas, they continued to be sold as
slaves. For the judge, the only solution was that the congregas be prohibited and that the Indians be organized in towns, an order that had to originate in Spain because of the many interests that intervened in the
Audiencia of Mexico.

At about the same time as the Audiencia judge's petition, the interim
governor of Nuevo León, Francisco Barbadillo y Victoria, sent a report on
the state of the Indians in the province. He stated that the Indians settled
in towns came to some four thousand and that the petitions sent to the
viceroy by Spaniards lied in suggesting that the town of Nuestra Señora de
Guadalupe, located one and a half leagues from Monterrey, had no Indians,
since he calculated 1,100 of "many and various nations" in that town alone.
He disagreed with the proposal contained in the petitions that the Indians

should have their hair cut and should be given "muttonchops" or sideburns to distinguish the town Indians from the rebels, "because of the well-recognized value . . . that all the Indians generally have for their hair." He also argued against prohibiting their use of bow and arrow. Bows and arrows were indispensable to sustaining their families by hunting, Barbadillo maintained, since "the only thing that is given them each day is a ration of corn not sufficient to sustain their wives and children. With the bow and arrow they can go out to kill deer, javelinas, and many other animals so as to eat meat," besides serving them as defensive weapons in the face of attacks by warlike Indians. He also expressed disapproval for the attempted prohibition against letting them go out to eat prickly pears in season and against the use of the horse, because so many prohibitions would put at risk the stability of the Indians, who became difficult to domesticate once they rebelled.[46]

First as encomenderos and later with the title of protectors of Indians, the Spaniards made Indian hunting expeditions toward the Río Grande, or Bravo, and Tamaulipas, passing through the province of Coahuila. The expeditions were authorized by the governor and generally were made in the season of intense agricultural work or when there was work in the mines. In April 1651 Governor Martín de Zavala granted a "license" to Juliana Quintanilla "so that her sons and other persons may go out in pursuit of her Indians toward Boca de Leones, to bring them back for the wheat harvest."[47] In August of the same year, the governor ordered Sgt. Maj. Francisco García de Sepúlveda to campaign into the "land of the Alazapas to bring them to the silver-smelting works of Valle de las Salinas and farms of the district of Monterrey," which had been idled because the Indians did not show up to work in them.[48]

Among the groups subjected to encomienda, the Alazapas "survived" from 1636, when the "Guatae" ranchería was conceded in encomienda to the farmer Pedro Camacho, to 1778. That year the Alazapas could be found congregated in the settlement of Boca de Leones, Nuevo León, although in 1779 they are mentioned as being at war with the settlers of the province. Throughout the eighteenth century the Alazapas remained beyond mission control, except on rare occasions, because they were controlled by encomenderos. This control came about following a series of disputes between missionaries and encomenderos during the seventeenth century over control of the Indians. In 1684 Coahuila governor Alonso de León accused the Franciscans of bad administration of the missions for renting out their Indian charges and depriving the natives of their daily wages, besides abusing Indian women whom they took to their monastery cells from the rancherías. For his part, in 1697 the archbishop of Guadala-jara expressed to the king his concern over treatment of the Indians of Nuevo León: "I am very saddened by the practice that has developed in the Kingdom of León, which they call *encomiendas*, [in which] the governor gives permission for settlers to go to heathen lands and bring back [Indians] for their service." The Indians, he said, were treated like slaves and were not receiving the doctrine, prompting them to live "like beasts in the mountains and woods."[49]

The Alazapa group was congregated in Mission San Bernardino de la Candela in 1696. Two years later they are found at Mission San Antonio Galindo de Moctezuma, in the valley of El Cándamo, located ten leagues to the north of Monclova in the same province of Coahuila. At this latter mission, Alazapas and Zenizos were said to be

> servants of the settlers of the city of Monterrey, but because of
> the mistreatment that their masters gave them, they had with-
> drawn many days ago to the jurisdiction of Monclova, toward
> the wilderness, with some of those of their nation, [where] they
> had made friends and united with the Apinamis, Exmalquios and
> Zenizos, and that these nations were heathen and had desires of
> knowing the Spaniards and having communication with them.[50]

However, Mission San Antonio Galindo had a brief life, because the Spaniards who had settled in its vicinity tried to avail themselves of the con-gregated Indians for labor on their haciendas, and soon the mission was totally depopulated.[51] A half-century later, in a 1746 report of the Francis-can College of the Holy Province of Xalisco, the Alazapas are mentioned as among the converted nations in the missions of its jurisdiction, which also included Tobosos, Manos Prietas, Cocoyomes, Quetzales, and Cabezas.[52] Nevertheless, the Alazapas were not congregated in missions in a consistent manner, a situation that is repeated in the majority of the cases of the groups granted in encomienda in Nuevo León.

According to what Ladrón de Guevara reported in 1739, the method for maintaining them under the control in encomienda was very simple, since it was not a question of Indians who practiced war: "being so few in number, of such little courage, and so lacking in the art of war, they pre-sent few obstacles to being subdued and settled in that region . . . all that is required being knowledge of the life and customs of these heathens . . . along with the necessary astuteness to quickly understand their movements and intentions."[53] He notes, however, that the Indians under encomienda were very mistrustful about their territories, causing opposition among them. This characteristic, common to the majority of the groups that lived in New Spain's northeast, could be turned to profit by the encomenderos by setting the natives "free" in the seasons when one did not require agricultural labor, since it was always possible to locate them anew in their places of "habitation."

The "mortal enemy," a figure of speech applied by Spaniards in reference to the attacks of independent Indians on the towns and missions of settled Indians, constituted a form of "punishment" exercised by groups that remained free against groups that in some manner depended on, or found themselves subject to, some type of Spanish control. The frequent attacks on the missions, for example, besides providing goods to the attacking groups, were oriented toward punishing the Indians who had let themselves be dominated. It was not necessarily an ideological question. On the contrary, it was instead a practical matter, since the Indians under Spanish control, whether in missions or in the service of Spaniards, were generally employed against "enemy" Indians. In this way the subject groups were transformed into enemies of the rebellious Indians. For example, in 1656, in the face of the fear provoked by a "great council" of Indians, a Name Indian described the Alazapas as being of two classes: the "untamed" and the "friends" of the Spaniards. The former, allied with the Vaxares group "and other nations," attempted "to strike the hacienda and kill the Alazapas and everyone they may find and the Spaniards, and carry off whatever is there."[54]

Among Alazapa groups in encomienda or otherwise under Spanish control, only two "uprisings" are recorded. The first, in 1645, involved an alliance of Aguatas, Guaracatas, Icuaras, and possibly other groups. Although at present I have not been able to locate specific information in this regard, it is quite probable that the said alliance was related to the uprising of the Tobosos and Salineros described above, since they were located in Nuevo Almadén (later Monclova), a mining camp bordering the Bolsón de Mapimí, from where the uprising against the settlements of Nueva Vizcaya originated. Similarly, in 1686 the Queroamas and Alazapas rebelled in the vicinity of the mining camp of Santiago de las Sabinas, in Nuevo León.[55]

We may conclude that unlike the groups organized through constant alliances from the seventeenth century to the first third of the eighteenth century, the groups controlled under encomienda maintained their original group designations. They did so in spite of a process of deterritorialization exacerbated, on the one hand, by the introduction and consolidation of permanent agricultural settlements in their territory, and on the other by the pressure exerted by the "mortal enemy."[56]

Deterritorialization of the groups controlled under the encomienda system did not mean their extinction, however. In the mid-eighteenth century, as the Spanish occupation of northeastern New Spain accelerated, the Alazapas created a new form of territoriality that was expressed in the mobility of the group eastward. In Nuevo Santander they benefited from the slow process of conquest in that region, and from its new range in Nuevo León, it carried out surprise attacks on agricultural settlements for decades.

Conclusions

The Spanish frontier expanded by way of the establishment of settlements with fixed boundaries, creating islands of settlement scattered throughout the northeastern territory. It is not a question of physical frontiers, however, but of human frontiers that manifested themselves as sedentary settlements, as spaces defensible from the "other," marking the limits of their own territoriality. The "Indian frontier," the "Chichimeca frontier," the "infidel frontier," the "lands of the enemies," the "frontier Indians," were all necessary figures of speech to set them in opposition to the frontiers of the king and his frontier settlers. The names and categories employed in this confrontation describe, throughout the colonial period, the conquerors' indispensable need to express for themselves the limits of the achieved and the possible.

The natives experienced new forms of territoriality. Expanding the uses and possibilities of territory beyond the limits imposed in the creation of frontiers alien to their own subsistence spaces, they maintained control of their territories through the use of mobility and of knowledge of the space, weapons unknown to the invaders. In the process they transformed themselves into displaced peoples, enemies of a territory controlled by external forces.

Those who tried to contain the Spaniards were not always the same groups, nor did they always control the same territories. The Tobosos settled in the town of Atotonilco were a congregated group, while the Tobosos allied to the Gavilanes were an enemy group of the Tobosos of Atotonilco. Likewise, the Alazapas were both friends and enemies of the Spaniards, occasionally at one and the same time. They also were a commodity for the Spanish settlers of Nuevo León and, occasionally, Indians subject to mission discipline. Therefore, to ignore the social reorganization of territory as a response to invasion of native lands would be the same as to deny the ethnic diversity of New Spain's northeast. It would be erroneous to reduce this diversity to the dichotomy "agricultural natives/nomadic natives" and to employ that dichotomy as the measure of the successes or failures of the social control attempted by the Spanish in these territories.

It is also useful to emphasize that the period in which the greatest diversity of native group designations is registered in the colonial documentation coincides with the apogee of the encomienda or congrega on the one hand, and the increase in hostilities against new Spanish settlements on the other—that is to say, nearly a century (1625–1715) in which discontinuities became patent in the transformation and appearance of new territorialities.

After the second third of the eighteenth century, the number of designations is reduced, with some exceptions, to the mention of the "enemies" or, as a consequence of the taking of territories in the area of the Tejas Indians, the explicit mention of the Comanche, Apache, Lipan, and their "allied" Indians. As the Count of Revilla Gigedo accurately indicated in 1793, after listing the names of the groups existing at that time in the province of Coahuila,

> be these names true or mangled, according to the intelligence, caprices, or willfulness of those who occupied themselves in the country's pacification, or of the founders of the missions, it seems more credible that the said Indians were small factions, or branches, of some nation whose generic name it has not been possible to learn. Yet this matters little, and much less when the greater number of these peoples have already disappeared, joining the Apaches, or the Borrados Indians of the coast of the colony of Nuevo Santander, or perishing in the epidemics of smallpox and other illnesses experienced at different times.[57]

NOTES

1. See, for example, Testimonio de los autos de visita de esta provincia de San Francisco de Coahuila, Nueva Extremadura, hecha por Don Francisco de Barrios y Jauregui, 1760–1762, Fondo Colonial, c.6, e.35, 43 ff., Archivo General del Estado de Coahuila (hereafter cited as AGC).

2. With regard to the results of missionary control, see Cecilia Sheridan, *El suave yugo del evangelio: Las misiones franciscanas de Río Grande en el periodo colonial* (Mexico: Universidad Autónoma de Coahuila; Centro de Estudios Sociales y Humanísticos, A.C.; Instituto Coahuilense de Cultura, 1999).

3. Clarita Müler-Plantenberg, "Los indígenas y sus territorios. Choque cultural—recuperación de cultura y estudios de impactos ambientales y sociales. El caso de la Cuenca Amazónica," in Hans-Joachim Köning, ed., *El indio como sujeto y objeto de la historia latinoamericana: Pasado y presente* (Frankfurt/Main: Vervuert; Madrid: Iberoamericana, 1998), 121–36.

4. On the impact of human interaction on the frontier environment, Frederick R. Gelhbach, *Mountain Islands and Desert Seas: A Natural History of the U.S.-Mexican Borderlands* (College Station: Texas A&M University Press, 1993). See also Cynthia Radding, "Nomads and Villagers of Northeastern Mexico and Eastern Bolivia," X Meeting of Mexican Historians, Dallas–Ft. Worth, 21 November 1999, in which she asserts that "cultural ecology deepens our understanding of anthropogenic landscapes and divergent concepts of territoriality."

5. Informes del theniente coronel D. Felix Calleja, comisionado en las P. Internas, sobre misiones y milicias de la colonia de Nuevo Santander y Nuevo Reino de León, Secretaría de Guerra, 7027, exp.1, 1798 fol. 1–13, Archivo General de Indias, Seville (hereafter cited as AGI).

6. Ibid.

7. Orden de don Carlos de Agüero, 1 June 1772, Presidencia Municipal, c.28/1, e.41, Archivo Municipal de Saltillo, México (hereafter cited as AMS).

8. Kristine L. Jones compares the behavior of native groups in northern New Spain with hunter-gatherer groups of Paraguay and Chile from the perspective of a resistance strategy she terms "fierce guerrilla," which results in the emergence of "raiding economies." "Comparative Raiding Economies," in *Contested Ground: Comparative Frontiers on the Northern and Southern Edges of the Spanish Empire*, ed. Donna J. Guy and Thomas E. Sheridan, 97–114 (Tucson: University of Arizona Press, 1998).

9. Guillaume Boccara, "El poder creador: Tipos de poder y estrategias de sujeción en la frontera sur de Chile en la época colonial," in *Anuario de Estudios Americanos* 56 (1999): 65–94.

10. Entries of more than 3,000 citations, which sustain the proposition, come from diverse sources such as chronicles, inspection tours, mission registers, military campaign reports, civil, ecclesiastical, and military petitions, certificates of primogeniture, itineraries, and criminal trials, as well as registers made by other historians in which the original source is explicitly documented.

11. Gary Clayton Anderson, *The Indian Southwest, 1580–1830: Ethnogenesis and Reinvention* (Norman: University of Oklahoma Press, 1999).

12. "Ataque a la hacienda de La Zarca, 1715," in *The Presidio and Militia on the Northern Frontier of New Spain*, vol. 2, part 2, *The Central Corridor and the Texas Corridor 1700–1765*, ed. D. Hadley et al., 70 (Tucson: University of Arizona Press, 1997).

13. Regarding Tlaxcaltecan colonization see David B. Adams, *Las colonias Tlaxcaltecas de Coahuila y Nuevo León en la Nueva España* (México: Archivo Municipal de Saltillo, 1991) and Cecilia Sheridan, "Indios Madrineros: Colonizadores tlaxcaltecas en el noreste novohispano," *Estudios de Historia Novohispana* 24 (2001): 15–51.

14. Countless documents refer to this objective. Here I cite the case of the "confederation and league" of Cocoyolomes with various other nations in 1692 because in the assembly that was carried out on the Nazas River Captain Tecolote invited those present to attack travelers and despoil the Spanish, "because I do not attempt anything except to die or to finish everything off." Autos hechos sobre las invasiones que hacen los indios rebeldes en este Reyno y los que se han actuado sobre la guerra ofensiva que se les hace. Guerra de Tobosos, Provincias Internas, Vol. 29, e.5, Archivo General de la Nación, Mexico (hereafter cited as AGN).

15. Cecilia Sheridan, *Anónimos y desterrados: La contienda por el "sitio que llaman de Quauyla," siglos XVI–XVIII* (Mexico: CIESAS, Miguel Angel Porrúa, 2000), 149.

16. See Cecilia Sheridan, "'Indios amigos': Estrategias militares en la frontera noreste novohispana," in *Memorias del Primer Congreso Internacional sobre fuerzas militares en Iberoamérica, siglos XVIII–XIX* (Mexico: Universidad Veracruzana, forthcoming).

17. Guillaume Boccara, "Mundos nuevos en la frontera del Nuevo Mundo," in *E-Review: Nuevo Mundo, mundos nuevos,* UMR 8565 (2001).

18. Father Morfi's minutely detailed report, containing invaluable information, was sent to the Franciscans of the province of Jalisco in its original version Ms. (10/149), 1763, Archivo Franciscano del Fondo Reservado de la Universidad Autónoma de México, Mexico (hereafter cited as AF).

19. Salvador Álvarez, "Agricultores de paz y cazadores-recolectores de guerra: los tobosos de la cuenca del río Conchos en la Nueva Vizcaya," in *Nómadas y sedentarios en el Norte de México: Homenaje a Beatriz Braniff*, ed. Marie-Areti Hers et. al., 314 (Mexico: Universidad Autónoma de México, 2000).

20. Ibid. See also William B. Griffen, *Culture Change and Shifting Populations in Central Northern Mexico*, Anthropological Papers of the University of Arizona no. 13 (Tucson: University of Arizona Press, 1970) and *Indian Assimilation in the Franciscan Area of Nueva Vizcaya*, Anthropological Papers of the University of Arizona no. 33 (Tucson: University of Arizona Press, 1979).

21. Papeles pertenecientes a la reducción de los apaches, sus guerras, paces y diligencias en diversos tiempos, para fundar sus misiones, 1746, Archivo Histórico de la Provincia Franciscana de Michoacán, Mexico; Libro K, Leg 7, doc. 1, Inventario del Archivo del Colegio de Propaganda Fide de la Santa Cruz de Querétaro, Mexico.

22. Like the Toboso alliances, the Apache alliances present the same pattern. For example, in the general campaign against the Apache nation undertaken by the governor of the province of Texas in 1733, Don Antonio Bustillo y Zevallos, some Indians were taken prisoner who were interrogated about the Apache organization; they were asked what nations had organized under the name Apache, to which they responded "that with the name of Apaches, naming them by their own special names, there were thirty-six." See Autos sobre las providencias dadas por V. Exa. al Gobernador de la Provincia de Texas para la pacificación de los indios apaches y sus aliados, 1731–1734, Provincias Internas. Vol. 32 (2a. parte), Exp. 15, fol. 379v., AGN.

23. Griffen, *Culture Change and Shifting Populations*, 10, refers to this incident as the "first mayor rebellion" of the Indians of north-central Mexico.

24. Thomas H. Naylor and Charles W. Polzer, S.J., "Mid-Century Challenges and Realignment (1640–1660)," in *The Presidio and Militia on the Northern Frontier of New Spain*, vol. 1: 1570–1700 (Tucson: University of Arizona Press, 1986), 333.

25. Persecución de indios, October 1687, Donaciones, c.1, 4f, AMS.

26. Autos hechos sobre las invasiones que hacen los indios rebeldes en este Reyno y los que se han actuado sobre la guerra ofensiva que se les hace. Guerra de Tobosos, 1690–1693, Provincias Internas. Vol. 29, e.5, fols.110–395v., AGN.

27. Testimonio de autos y diligencias tocantes a los socorros, asistencias y continuación en el fomento de la provincia de Coahuila que hoy llaman la Nueva Extremadura. Vino con carta del Virrey Conde de Paredes de 9 de julio de 1681, Audiencia de México, 52, no. 29, e.2, fol. 237, AGI.

28. Ibid.

29. Ibid.

30. Relación de las naciones, 1786, Ms. 17/344, AF.

31. [Expediente de la entrada de Antonio Balcarcel y fray Juan Larios] 3 July 1675, Audiencia de México, 20, no. 6/2, fol. 448, AGI.

32. Testimonio de autos y diligencias tocantes a los socorros, asistencias y continuación en el fomento de la provincia de Coahuila que hoy llaman la Nueva Extremadura. Vino con carta del Virrey Conde de Paredes de 9 de julio de 1681, Audiencia de México, 52, no. 29, e.2, fols. 44–46, AGI.

33. Representación de diversos misioneros adscritos al presidio de Pasajes sobre las quejas presentadas por los indios babosariagamas y cabezas sobre carecer de tierras. Se acuerdan acuerdos del virrey conde de Galve y noticias sobre las campañas del marques de San Miguel de Aguayo, 1690–1703, Jesuitas, vol. I-14, exp. 331, fols. 1655–70, AGN.

34. Autos hechos sobre las invasiones que hacen los indios rebeldes, fols. 176v–177v.

35. Ibid., fol. 244.

36. Ibid., fol. 177.

37. Thomas N. Campbell, "Ethnohistoric Notes on Indian Groups Associated with Three Spanish Missions at Guerrero, Coahuila," in *Archaeology and History of the San Juan Bautista Mission Area, Coahuila and Texas*, Report no. 3, Center for Archeological Research, The University of Texas at San Antonio, (San Antonio, 1979), 14.

38. "Ladrón de Guevara's Report Concerning the Kingdom of Nuevo León (1739)," in *The Presidio and Militia on the Northern Frontier of New Spain*, ed. D. Hadley et al., 77–120.

39. Autos hechos sobre las invasiones que hacen los indios rebeldes, fols. 262–66.

40. Ibid., fol. 273.

41. Cited in Silvio Zavala, "Los esclavos en el Norte de México Siglo XVI," in *El Norte de México y el Sur de los Estados Unidos: Tercera Reunión de Mesa Redonda sobre Problemas Antropológicos de México y Centro América* (México: Sociedad Mexicana de Antropología, 1943), 88.

42. In March 1695 Governor Juan Pérez Merino gave permission to Miguel de León, a settler of the Pilón Valley, to add to his farm a settlement of Indians, "which he shall bring from inland, promising to declare its name and meaning," Monterrey, 13 March 1695, Ramo Civil, vol. 22, e.6, fol. 8, Archivo Municipal de Monterrey, México (hereafter cited as AMM).

43. Cited in Eugenio del Hoyo, *Historia del Nuevo Reino de León*, 1:437.

44. The treatment of natives as slaves occurred in other regions far from the centers of colonial power, such as in Florida, where the concept of the distribution and the "deposit of Indians" resulted in situations of forced labor outside of the laws in effect. See David J. Weber, *The Spanish Frontier in North America* (New Haven, Conn.: Yale University Press, 1992), 126–27.

45. La pacificación de los indios chichimecas del Reino de León, 1718–1724, Audiencia de Guadalajara, 166, AGI.

46. Ibid.

47. Licencia a Juliana Quintanilla, Villa de Cerralvo, 12 April 1651, Ramo Civil, vol. 8, e.28, fol. 20v., no. 33, AMM.

48. Orden al sargento mayor Fco. García de Sepúlveda, Villa de Cerralvo, 20 August 1651, Ramo Civil, vol. 8, e.28, fol. 22v., no. 36, AMM.

49. Eugenio del Hoyo, *Indios, frailes y encomenderos en el Nuevo Reino de León: Siglos XVII y XVIII* (Monterrey: Archivo General del Estado, n.d.), 139.

50. Fondo Colonial, c.1, e.8, 9f, AGC.

51. Cecilia Sheridan, *Anónimos y desterrados*, 156.

52. Ms. 5/101, AF.

53. "Ladrón de Guevara's Report," 77–120.

54. Fondo Presidencia Municipal, c.2, e.49, d.22, 2f, AMS.

55. Antonio López de Villegas, Solicitud de encomienda, Monterrey, 16 October 1698, Ramo Civil, vol. 26, e.4, fol. 41, AMM.

56. William B. Griffen, on the contrary, expresses the opinion that the groups near the Spanish settlements tended to disappear more rapidly than those that were located at a greater distance. *Culture Change and Shifting Populations*, 142.

57. Ibid., 60.

CHAPTER SEVEN

Beyond Their Control

Spaniards in Native Texas

JULIANA BARR

In the winter of 1764–1765, Antonio Treviño and other Spanish soldiers rode out from Presidio San Sabá, accompanying Lipan Apache men on a buffalo hunt. For several years Spanish officials in the province of Texas had been trying to maintain peace with Lipan Apaches, and part of this effort involved joint hunting parties as defense against the hostility of other natives. To Comanche and Wichita eyes, the joint Spanish-Apache venture was another in a growing number of signs of military and economic alliance between the two, and, more specifically, an alliance against themselves.[1] Lipans had been enemies of Comanches and Wichitas for a long time, and, by allying with Lipans, the Spaniards signaled their enmity for them as well. Moreover, the territories into which the hunting party rode were ones claimed by Comanches and Wichitas. Thus, the foray amounted to an act of trespass, if not act of war.

Not surprisingly, the party promptly came under attack by Wichita warriors from a Taovaya band. The outcome of the attack, however, was a surprise. During the skirmish, Antonio Treviño received four bullet wounds and two lance wounds yet still continued to fight the opposing force of forty-seven warriors, thus winning the attention of Taovaya chief Eiasiquiche. Eiasiquiche explained later that Treviño's demonstration of

valor and courage in defending himself against such odds had so impressed him that he ordered his warriors to spare Treviño's life and capture him in order to add him to the ranks of Taovaya warriors. Treviño's
feat assured him the respect of the chief and the welcome of the Taovaya
community with whom he lived for six months at one of their Red River
settlements. Yet what cemented the Taovaya men's goodwill for Treviño
was his identification as a soldier of the Los Adaes presidial force along
the Louisiana border rather than of Presidio San Sabá, to which he was
temporarily assigned. Wichitas apparently understood Spaniards to live
in bands similar to their own, and so differentiated those of eastern Texas
at Los Adaes, who maintained good relations with the Taovayas' Caddo
allies, from those at San Sabá (and by extension San Antonio), who gave
every appearance of alliance with their Apache enemies. Six months later
in the summer of 1765, "Despite the great and extreme love everyone
felt for him," Eiasiquiche chose to send Treviño back to his own people
as a gesture of good will. The Wichita chief made clear, however, that
this overture extended only to the Los Adaes Spaniards; peace was not
possible with those at San Sabá as long as they demonstrated alliance
with Apaches.[2]

Treviño's experience offers a telling perspective—a native perspective—on the political landscape of Texas. Spaniards in the region clearly
did not represent a conquering force or ruling power to Indian observers.
Nor did they merit Comanche and Wichita attention until they united with
Lipans. Spanish claims of imperial control clearly were not a reality in
much of the region they identified as the province of Texas. Instead, natives
had far more reason to identify different divisions of the area as Apachería,
Comanchería, Wichita, and Caddo territory. To bands of Lipan Apaches,
Comanches, Wichitas, and Caddos, Spaniards operated as just another
"band" like themselves in an equal, if not weaker position to struggle for
subsistence and survival in the region. In fact, the Spanish presence in
"Texas" often had little relevance to the region's predominant native political and economic relations.

The region that the Spaniards called Texas thus differed from many of
New Spain's frontiers because Indians not only retained control over much
of the province but also because they asserted control over Spaniards themselves. The region's eighteenth-century history is not one of Indian resistance, but of Indian dominance. To understand this world one should
imagine the region of present-day Texas divided into quadrants, three of

which were under native control with Apaches in the west, Caddos in the east, and Comanches and Wichitas in the north. The fourth, the Spanish quadrant of Texas, consisted of the south central areas of San Antonio de Béxar and La Bahía and the eastern area of Los Adaes-Nacogdoches.

In the Spanish-controlled region, mission-presidio complexes, where Franciscan missionaries sought to save Indian souls, served as the primary sites of Spanish-Indian interaction. By 1730, the area of southern rather than eastern Texas had emerged as the center of Spanish mission, settlement, and presidial development in the face of Hasinai Caddo indifference to the Spanish presence in their lands. Franciscans found a more promising mission field among Coahuiltecan and Karankawan peoples of southern and coastal Texas. Sadly, it was the severe disruption of native life-ways and cultural patterns in these regions that occasioned that promise. The intrusion of newly mounted Lipan Apaches from the northwest, and with them escalating raids and warfare, had been ongoing since the mid-seventeenth century. The advance of the Spanish frontier northward into Coahuila and Nuevo León over the same period had pushed Indians northward as well. They fled the forced labor of Spanish mines and ranches to seek sanctuary in the region of southern Texas, but European diseases often caught up to them even if they never had contact with Spaniards themselves. By the early eighteenth century southern Texas had become a refuge for an impressively diverse but ravaged congregation of both native and displaced Indians. Declining numbers in turn meant greater difficulty for survival. These, then, were people who might find attractive the food, shelter, and defense of the missions and so offered themselves to the missionaries' teachings and formed mission communities similar to the *común* described by Cynthia Radding (see chapter 8). Even still, many never sought the missions, others incorporated only periodic visits to the missions into their seasonal subsistence patterns, and permanent residents often kept Franciscans in negotiation over mission reforms they chose to resist.[3] Consequently, it can be maintained that the Spanish exercise of social control over the Indians living within their area of dominance was at best incomplete.

Outside of south Texas, powerful Indian nations dominated. Within this setting, Spaniards struggled to establish a presence among multiple native groups that had no need for mission salvation or welfare, no fear of Spanish military force, and no patience for the lack of Spanish markets or trade fairs (especially in comparison to those offered by the French in

Louisiana). Often, Indian groups like Comanches and Wichitas decided that if they could not trade for Spanish guns and horses, they would take them by force. Thus, for much of the eighteenth century Spaniards earned native attention only as targets for raids.[4] As a result, Spanish-Indian contact remained limited to a series of small-scale raids and attacks from which no stable structures of interchange developed. As groups fought for survival with few imperatives to be in contact much less to seek accommodation, disorder and violence, just as much as order and control, defined the power relations of the region.

Studies of frontier regions in Spanish America as "zones of constant conflict and negotiation over power" generally depict such regions as "boundaries beyond the sphere of routine action of centrally located violence-producing enterprises, although they may be within the range of isolated attacks."[5] From a Spanish perspective, the frontiers and borderlands of Spain's far northern provinces were just that—peripheries far from the imperial core. And, from this perspective, the question of social control in these peripheries was cast as measuring the extent or limit of New Spain's ability to exercise a "monopoly on violence" over Indian subjects or potential subjects far from its institutional core.[6] Yet in seeking to understand negotiations of power in Texas, it is essential to recognize that Texas was a core of *native* political economies, a core within which Spaniards were often the subjects or potential subjects of native institutions of social control. Spanish authorities encountered already existent and newly emerging native systems of trade, warfare, and alliance into which they had to seek entry. Control of the region's political economy (and with it the "monopoly on violence") rested in the collective (though not united) hands of Lipan Apaches, Caddos, Comanches, and Wichitas.

Because no one group controlled the entire region, social controls were not expressions of power by one dominant state within one clearly bounded society. Instead they were negotiations of power between separate societies and nations. The primary power relations were not European vs. Indian, but relations among multiple peoples. All competed in a region of intermingled native economies and polities, and Spaniards represented just another group of competitors. At stake in the contest were regional networks and markets that could be used to the advantage of individual groups in order to protect and, if possible, to expand their domestic political economies. Trade and economic well-being took precedence over territorial imperatives.

Competing Systems of Social Controls

So, what defined the social controls regulating relations in Texas? One cannot speak of a singular or united "Indian" group when studying European-native relations in Texas. Native modes of social control, broadly defined and distinctive within each group, prevailed. The vehicles of social control were not institutions like Spanish missions or presidios but were the relationships of alliance and diplomacy that, in themselves, constituted political-economic networks. Competing groups related to one another as allies or enemies, kin or strangers. Native groups expressed their political and economic alliances with one another in terms of kinship. Leading chiefs and warriors cast the bonds of military and trade alliances as "brotherhood" and the fictive kinship of male sodalities. Exchanges of women through captivity, adoption, and marriage provided further ties of both real and fictive kinship. In turn, such practices weighted political and economic cross-cultural interactions with gendered standards of honor associated with family, marriage, and social relations.

Just as notions of social rank and honor structured hierarchies within European and Indian societies, they also shaped power relationships between societies in Texas. The character of contact over the eighteenth century gave greater authority to certain kinds of masculinity associated with a military identity.[7] The constancy of raiding and warfare heightened concepts of militarized honor for Spanish and Indian men and colored the confrontations and negotiations between their societies.[8] Most studies of honor systems have analyzed systems *within* one society—demarcating the different ways in which categorizations of honor informed social hierarchies and the gender relations between and among the men and women of that society. Yet, in Texas the confrontations of honor were just as often *between* different societies, as challenges to a man's or a woman's honor sometimes came from outside his or her society. For Indian warriors, the Spaniards who challenged their political and economic power did so as "strangers" to kinship systems of familial relations and political-economic alliances—seen most clearly in ties of "brotherhood" among fellow Comanche, Wichita, and Caddo warriors and allies.

Euroamericans and Indians in this setting measured military, and thereby political and economic, power in terms of warrior numbers and ability. They also defined hostile actions as masculine endeavor, so the presence and involvement of Indian women in cross-cultural power relations assumed specific importance of its own. Relations with women offered the potential for expressing peace rather than hostility, and alliance rather than enmity. Yet the role of Indian women most often remained symbolic rather than active when it came to political and economic diplomacy. As the century progressed, coercive trafficking in native women through captivity, slavery, and intermarriage increasingly ratified political interpretations of femininity. This traffic always functioned unequally between Europeans and Indians, moreover, because the Spanish populations that interacted with native peoples remained predominantly male and few Euroamerican women became objects of political negotiation.

Plunged into this world of Indian politics, Spaniards found they could not assert control beyond the boundaries of south Texas and had trouble negotiating the native power relations outside those boundaries. Spaniards sometimes succeeded in selling themselves as better allies than enemies by following native men's diplomatic rituals, nomenclature, and gift-giving. Spanish policy stumbled, however, in the face of misunderstandings of native practices of intermarriage and captivity. Such stumblings in themselves cannot be blamed for the disorder and violence that so often characterized Spanish-Indian relations in Texas, yet without the force to conquer or the finances to trade, Spaniards needed to find other ways to form viable relationships with groups like Comanches, Apaches, Wichitas, and Caddos. They might have found them had they given greater attention or appreciation to the social controls guiding native political and economic diplomacy. Examination of three aspects of cross-cultural politics—intermarriage, male diplomatic ritual, and captive exchange—offers telling portraits of Spanish attempts to negotiate the complex waters of native political economies, and makes clear the mechanisms of social control at work in Texas.

Intermarriage

In the 1680s and 1690s Spain sought to establish a buffer region against French encroachments from Louisiana. The province of Texas, like Florida as depicted by Jane Landers (see chapter 2), was of crucial importance to Spanish goals of maintaining and defending New Spain's imperial boundaries against European competitors. Spanish expeditions went first to the Caddo Indians of the Hasinai Confederacy whose position along the present-day Texas-Louisiana border made them ideal potential allies against the French. Spanish missionaries and officials came in hopes of winning the Indians as Christian converts and military allies against a growing French presence in Louisiana. For Caddos the effects of a European presence in the Americas had reached them long before these new Spanish visitors arrived at the end of the seventeenth century. Drought, Old World diseases, and increasing warfare with the Osages to the east had already begun to reduce their numbers. These factors made independent agricultural communities more difficult to sustain and defend and encouraged the consolidation of Caddos into the confederacies that the Spaniards encountered in the 1680s. These circumstances also encouraged Caddo leaders to view the European newcomers as potential components to be incorporated into their already extensive trade networks.

It quickly became clear, however, that Caddo and Spanish ideas about the form their relationship might take diverged considerably. Both wanted the other as an ally, but Caddos sought to achieve that by making Spaniards into "kin" through marriage, while Spanish officers and missionaries envisioned Christian conversion as a means of Caddo "civilization" and subordination. Both failed in their design.

Intermarriage was well established among Caddos as a strategy for forming and solidifying political alliance. In the sixteenth and seventeenth centuries, marriage and family linkages had created three Caddo confederacies as well as unified villages and settlements in the face of war and disease.[9] These bonds were clear to European observers who arrived later in the eighteenth century. Bérnard de la Harpe noted that though the Caddo peoples lived in different villages, they nevertheless "formed together" a united nation.[10] Juan Agustín Morfi argued that shared friendships, relationships, and intermarriage had joined and made kin "under the general name Texas" remnants of the "Texas, Asinais, Nabedachos, Nacogdoches, Nacogdochitos, Nadocoges, Ahipitos, Cadogdachos, and Nasonis." They had also linked together bands of Caddos and of Wichitas.[11] To Caddos, therefore, intermarriage seemed a practical means of forming political ties and trade relations with Spaniards as well.

Nevertheless, Spaniards refused Caddo overtures. Why? Certainly, provincial Spanish officers did not have the financing necessary to set up extensive trade outposts, but the social ties pursued by Caddos would have come at little cost. Moreover, intermarriage with Indians was not uncommon in Spanish America. Such unions and the mestizo population that resulted from them have served as a key ingredient to portrayals of colonial Spanish America as a "zone of inclusion." Conversely, the absence of Spanish-Indian intermarriage in Texas marked Spanish *exclusion* from the region's native political economies. The explanation for this absence rests in Spanish (and Indian) determinations of acceptable behavior inside and outside the boundaries of society. In Spanish America, Spanish-Indian sexual relations and intermarriage took place within Spanish society. More specifically, it involved conquered Indian populations that were subject to the Spanish Church and State. Spaniards in Texas rejected Caddos, despite the political and economic costs of rejection, because these nations represented *indios bárbaros*, outsiders to Spanish society, religion, and authority. Intermarriage with Indians had never represented a tool of Spanish diplomacy with independent Indian nations. Rather, it took place only after Indians had been subordinated, and represented the incorporation of Indian peoples into Spanish society. The problem with extending such narrow views into the Texas borderlands, however, was that it insured Spanish exclusion from Caddo kinship systems and, thus, from economic and political networks that would have proved advantageous to Spanish imperial goals in Texas.

Spanish failure with the Caddos was made all the more obvious by French success in the same arena. When Caddos sought to make Frenchmen into military allies and trading partners through marriage, Frenchmen accepted the proposals. Frenchmen found they could solidify relationships with Indians through sexual and marital unions that became demonstrable acts of permanence and commitment within cross-cultural settings.[12] French settlers and traders in Louisiana by and large came from Canada rather than France and brought with them a social and cultural heritage marked by intimate associations with Indian peoples. Because French occupation of Louisiana was originally one of predominantly single male traders and agents who often lived among their native trading partners, the Frenchmen were in a position necessitating intermarriage if they were to have wives and families. Moreover, French settlement patterns made social and familial intermixing inevitable as they built their posts and establishments in or near native villages. French and native peoples consequently came together not only for trade but also for subsistence, family building, and daily life.[13]

By forming unions with Caddo women, French agents who sought to trade among Caddos did not simply ingratiate themselves with the native society. First, by taking part in bride-service customs, whether consciously or not, Frenchmen incorporated themselves into Caddo systems of male status and honor. In Caddo systems of bride service, marriage was a negotiation between a man and a woman's kin. Over the course of that negotiation, a man provided goods, such as horses or meat from the hunt, in order to demonstrate his ability to defend and provide for the woman's family. Services to the woman's family continued after marriage in order to maintain the relationship and the status the man held in the eyes of the woman's family and the community. Bridal goods thus served as symbols of the man's personal prowess. Second, having wives enabled the Frenchmen to participate in customary male exchanges of hospitality and gift-giving beyond those of the more formal diplomacy between nations. Marriage in a bride-service society was a key determinant of male rank. A married man, as opposed to a bachelor, had the benefit of a wife who fed and cared for their family, provided a home through her kin or by building shelters herself, and provided him with sexual services. A man thus achieved independence through marriage, since he was reliant upon no one else for these services. More importantly, marriage in bride-service societies allowed a man "to become a political actor—an initiator of relations through generosity," according to Jane Fishburne Collier, because "[a] man who has a wife and a hearth can offer hospitality to other men." Thus male status within a bride-service society rose through marriage.[14]

Because kinship was both a social and a political organizing principle for Caddos, Frenchmen ultimately realized profits, trade networks, political alliance, and population growth through their marriages and kin relationships. In turn, ties of settlement, marriage, and trade provided untold advantage to Frenchmen of western Louisiana as they competed with Spaniards in Texas for the loyalty of powerful Caddo allies. Spanish missionaries and officials alike watched helplessly as Frenchmen used marriage with Caddo women to cement relations with Caddo leaders. The commercial profit realized by the French from such unions was seen clearly. "They [the French] regard the Indians so highly that civilized persons marry the Indian women without incurring blame, for the French find their greatest glory in that which is most profitable to them," asserted Spanish governor Jacinto de Barrios y Jáuregui. "As a result, no Caudachos, Nacodoches, San Pedro, or Texas Indian is to be seen who does not wear his mirror, epaulets, and breech-clout—all French goods." In explaining Caddo devotion to the French, auditor Don Domingo Valcárcel wrote that the French "are making a silent conquest of the said nations with whom they fraternize to the stupid extreme of painting themselves and of living in the same licentiousness."[15]

While fearfully aware of the economic and political gains of French practices of settlement and intermarriage, few Spaniards sought life in the "wilds" or marriage with the Indian women there.[16] Spanish policy would not have condoned it, even if they had. Adding insult to injury, Spanish officials could not control the abusive and sometimes violent behavior of their soldiers. The earliest contacts with Hasinai Caddos in the 1690s ended in violence and tainted Spanish-Caddo relations for many years after. "Evidently some of [the men] thought they were to be made rulers of the Tejas," fray Damián Massanet wrote in 1691; he "hardly knew them for the same persons after we were in the village." The assertion of Spanish "rule" took the form of rape.[17] Massanet reported that Spanish soldiers entered Hasinai homes and attacked and raped any women they found, including the wife of one chief's brother. In response, Hasinai leaders made clear that further contact would be under strict regulation. No more did they seek unions with Spaniards. In fact, Spanish soldiers would not be welcome in Caddo lands without their own wives. In a letter to the viceroy, fray Francisco Casañas de Jesús María conveyed the message that "if the Spaniards want to live among them it must be under such conditions that no harm will be done their Indians by the Spaniards if they do come without their wives, but if the Spaniards bring their wives, the Indians will be satisfied."[18] Spanish rejection of Caddo diplomatic unions via intermarriage might have adhered to the social controls of Spanish society, but it lost them economic and diplomatic ground in an area of Texas where native social controls held greater sway.

Male Diplomatic Ritual

Sixty years later, Spaniards had another opportunity to ascertain Indian social controls in pursuit of peace, but the context of native social controls, and thus of European-Indian relations, had changed. From the 1710s through the 1760s, Caddo and French trading partners had incorporated Comanches and Wichitas into their lucrative exchange network. The political and economic ties among the Comanche, Wichita, Caddo, and French traders developed distant from realms of Spanish activity and observation. From 1758 onward, however, these ties commanded both Spanish and Lipan Apache attention. In the seventeenth century Lipan Apaches had entered Texas as conquerors, but by the mid-eighteenth century they were losing their military advantage in the region and suffering attrition rates of their own. These losses came at the hands of rival Comanches and Wichitas whose own advancement into the region pushed the Apaches ever southward. The power of the Comanche and Wichita military presence and these tribes' alliances with Caddos and the French momentarily led desperate Spaniards and Apaches to seek one another's aid against this united foe, as seen in the episode with which this essay began. The strength of the foe, however, just as quickly tore them apart when Spanish officials decided to abandon the Apaches in pursuit of peace and alliance with the more powerful Comanches and Wichitas.

In the 1770s the first Comanche and Wichita diplomatic contacts with Spaniards took place in the wake of the cession of Louisiana from French to Spanish control. The Spanish assumption of control in Louisiana in 1769 hampered economic and defensive capabilities of Comanches and Wichitas through the extension there of New Spain's prohibitions against trading guns to Indians. Moreover, Spanish officials in Louisiana moved quickly to outlaw the horse and slave trade with "hostile" nations to the west, thereby halting the eastward flow of horses and Apache captives from Texas that had proven so profitable for Comanche and Wichita warriors. As Gilbert Din attests (see chapter 3), Spanish officials in Louisiana focused their attention on issues of control internal to their newly acquired province, leaving Comanches and Wichitas to face a rocky road in seeking replacement for the loss of French trade. Though Comanche and Wichita warriors continued their raids on Spanish settlements to fulfill horse supply needs, the challenge of picking up the slack in arms and material goods formerly provided by Louisiana markets remained. Wichitas relied upon a few French traders who remained active either covertly or as operatives of the Spanish government, while Comanches turned to Spaniards in New Mexico. Nevertheless, necessity more and more turned Comanche and Wichita eyes to the Spaniards in Texas. At the same time, Spanish officials in Texas hoped to fill the void left by the French, though they offered political gifts and military promises in the place of commercial trade in their efforts to turn these powerful native groups from enemies into allies.

After years of contact only through raiding and counterattacks, Spaniards, Comanches, and Wichitas approached one another first for truce, then for alliance. In this hostile situation, turning truce into alliance meant diplomacy took its most powerful form in military commitments. Thus, pledges to fight against common enemies (primarily the Apaches) in joint campaigns dominated diplomatic discussions. Rituals and gifts that followed lent a further martial tone to negotiations, transforming all contractual communication into that of fellow warriors, now allied as comrades and brothers.

To forge bonds that could join rather than separate men on the battlefield, Comanches and Wichitas appealed to a language of military titles
and male kinship. Themes of warrior prestige found expression in titles of
"captain," "medal chief," and "*capitán grande*" as the Spanish and native men
sought to extend respect to those with whom they interacted. Such exchanges often took place with little shared understanding of the meanings
each group read into them. In this instance, however, ignorance worked to
everyone's benefit. Each could put his own interpretation on the exchange
and walk away pleased. At meetings in 1785, for instance, Comanche leaders appealed to obligations of kin when they referred to the Spanish governor as "our Father, the Capitán Grande" but made clear that their
relationship with the Spaniards would be one of "brothers."[19] The Spanish
representatives responded in kind and spoke of maintaining a "brotherly
peace under which neither one nor the other party will cause ourselves the
slightest harm."[20]

Though Spanish officials wistfully envisioned the role of "father" as
one of parental authority to discipline accompanied by the Indians' filial
responsibility to obey, Indian men had a different understanding of the
obligations they invoked by familial metaphors.[21] For instance, Wichita
and Caddo men simply may have transferred a form of address that had
worked with their French trading partners in Louisiana. But the French
relationship was a complex one. Patricia Galloway has suggested that the
French assertion of the title and role of "father" among the Choctaws
undercut the influence they sought, because the role of father in their
matrilineal kinship system carried little authority.[22] The Caddos and
Wichitas were also matrilineal societies, with the primary male authority
figure in the family the eldest maternal uncle rather than the father, so the
paternal role assumed by a Spanish governor did not come with much
power.[23] Perhaps, the absence of an assertion of predominance was the very
characteristic that made such French designations acceptable.

Even when designating the Spanish governor their "father," Caddo
and Wichita men never referred to themselves by the diminutive term
"children," in contrast to the expressions of Spanish officials. In a 1780 letter to Commandant General Bernardo de Gálvez, for instance, Taovaya
chief Qui Te Sain repeatedly addressed the commandant as "my father,"
but the only ones identified as his "child" and "children" were the Spanish
representative sent to the Taovaya village and the Spaniards of Texas
respectively.[24] It was not for rule, direction, or dominion that the Wichita

chief looked to the Spanish governor as "father" but for more practical needs of economic trade and military alliance—needs which firmly established Spaniards in a role of equal and reciprocal standing.

In that spirit, when metaphors of family bonds were used to express diplomatic ties, Comanche, Wichita, and Caddo men more often called upon a language of "brotherhood" particularly in signification of an alliance between soldiers and warriors. Among Wichita and Caddo warriors, "brother" already conveyed some element of a warrior bond. Various networks among Wichita men of the Taovaya, Tawakoni, Kichai, and Iscani bands found expression in terms of brotherhood.[25] Spanish observers similarly noted that men of the Nacogdoches, Hasinais, Nasonis, and other groups making up the Caddo Confederacies "treat one another as brothers and relatives," thus "they are always united in treaties of peace, or declaration of war."[26] Elsie Clews Parsons recorded that, among Caddos, "After a man had fought against the enemy together with another man the two might become friends, *tesha*, which was the same as brother."[27]

Comanche use of this terminology conveyed even more significance. At the individual level, Comanches recognized the closest types of relationships between men through an institution of formal friendship designated by the sibling terminology of "brothers." The bonds of such relationships almost always arose when men went off to war together and shared battlefield experiences that pledged them to one another. Ethnographers have argued that sodality groups and practices of male friendship among Comanche warriors often created stronger or more meaningful bonds than those of biological brotherhood. This terminology thus carried resonance for military bonds of camaraderie, but insured that the bonds were between men of equal standing.[28]

Gift exchange so prevalent in European-Indian encounters also proved to be charged with notions of war-related male honor and valor in Texas.[29] In an effort to end hostilities between Comanche warriors and Spanish forces, for instance, a Spanish representative sought to match native expectations by presenting Comanche leaders with a flag to signal peace, a blanket to cover the blood spilt between them, knives to straighten the crooked trail of their relations, and tobacco to be smoked by the young men "so that war may be at an end."[30] More often, gifts aimed to recognize the honor of individual men, and the acts of giving and receiving themselves, became contractual, sealing the relationship in the process. Military dress, adornment, and emblems predominated as gifts,

Often times miscommunication aided in the alliances

marking awareness that it was a compact among warriors and soldiers. In a public ceremony in 1772 meant to recognize a Spanish-Wichita alliance, chiefs from the Kichais, Tawakonis, Iscanis, Tayvayas, and Wichitas proper adorned Governor Ripperdá with feathers and wrapped him in buffalo skins according to custom and in ritual identification of him as an allied war chief. Though Ripperdá interpreted these gestures as ones of subordination on the part of Wichita men, Wichitas did not confer authority to him, but merely recognized Ripperdá as a leader with whom they shared a military, political, or economic alliance. Ripperdá symbolically became part of the dispersion of leadership within Wichita bands and the loosely constructed Wichita confederacy as a whole.[31]

In return, Spanish officers gave captain's uniforms, European flags, medals, and canes of office to Comanche, Caddo, and Wichita chiefs. Military hats, coats, smaller medals, and guns went to warriors and other secondary leaders.[32] In these negotiations, diplomatic gifts served as a peaceful analogy to the booty of raids or trophies of war. In fact, one Spanish official suggested that Comanche warriors be "given the equivalent of what they might obtain through pillage, theft, and the raids which they carry out when at war."[33] When a Comanche, Wichita, or Caddo warrior chose to wear or display the dress and decoration given him by a fellow soldier-diplomat, it marked him as the other man's ally.

The need to regularly renew relations of honor between Spanish and native male leaders meant regularly repeated ceremonial meetings and gift exchanges. In the 1780s and 1790s, Spanish presentation of gifts became institutionalized in annual ceremonies aimed at "permanently rooting" military alliances with these groups. Monthly logs and diaries of events maintained at Béxar and Nacogdoches through the 1810s recorded the regular arrivals of Indians (with their number and sex carefully noted) coming "in the practice of peace" and requiring customary presentations of gifts. In ritual return for native affirmations of peace, Spanish officials opened their stores for gifts of food and "necessities for their maintenance."[34] Spanish officials directed the diplomatic giving of gifts despite fears that it gave the Indians "cause for conceit or arrogance." Their greatest concern was sure knowledge that Indians viewed Spanish willingness to give presents as a sign of their weakness and need for native alliances.[35] Indeed, their gifts amounted to tributes offered to stop raids. Nevertheless, in this world of male ritual, security for the Spaniards came before pride, no matter how emasculating.

Captive Exchange

Security and peace might be achieved temporarily, but the limits of Spanish relationships with Comanches and Wichitas became clear in other interactions that, as with Caddos, involved an exchange of women. Spanish policy regarding the taking and exchanging of female Indian captives proved to run afoul of native law-ways. For much of the eighteenth century, bands of Caddos, Wichitas, and Comanches had found female captives whom they had taken from enemy groups to be as valuable as hides and horses in French markets. This captive trade offered the native groups guns and ammunition essential for hunting and defense. The trade also met the domestic and sexual needs of Frenchmen.[36] This slave trade added yet another dimension of exchange and intermarriage to the bonds tying Caddo, Comanche, Wichita, and French traders to one another. Thus, although the captive women involved in this trade network were themselves the products of war, the slave market they supplied helped to maintain peaceful alliances.

In contrast, Spanish involvement in native systems of captive-taking and exchange only rarely aided peace in Texas. Comanche and Wichita men looked to the Spaniards to replace the French as trading partners in their captive exchange, when the Indian slave trade in Louisiana was prohibited along with all French trading with Texas natives following the Louisiana cession. Despite Spanish trade prohibitions Comanche and Wichita warrior-diplomats still sought to turn female captives to economic use, but they sought profits from Spanish officials in Texas not through market exchange but from "ransom," or "redemption," payments. They soon found, however, that exchanges with Spanish officials came at a great cost.

Initially, Spanish officials assumed the role of broker as Comanche and Wichita captive trade shifted to Texas. In exchange for horses and material goods, Comanche and Wichita warrior-diplomats offered Spanish officials native women captured from enemy Indian groups, primarily Apache women. In turn, Spanish missionaries and officials returned these Apache women to their families or bands in exchange for promises of peace. Spaniards also offered Apaches the same option: officials would ransom Comanche and Wichita captives taken by Apaches in order to gain themselves an upper-hand in negotiations with those nations. For Spaniards, it quickly became a system not of trade, but of hostages given and taken within the politics of post-fight reparations and truce.

The experiences of two men, one Wichita and one Comanche, draw a compelling portrait of the role of captive exchange in the first diplomatic contacts between Spaniards and Comanches and Wichitas. Both stories took place in the year 1772. In February of that year, a detachment from the Béxar presidio returned to the town of San Antonio with an unexpected bonus for its commander: four Comanche captives, three women and one girl. The governor already had three other Comanche women, captured months before, who had been held so long in one of the San Antonio missions that all three had been baptized and two married off to mission neophytes. Because of their baptisms, these three women could not be returned to live among their people in apostasy, but the four new captives the governor decided to put to diplomatic use. He sent two of the women back to their chief with political gifts and messages of peace, but kept the other woman and little girl as hostages. The first act was to be a gesture of good will, and the second a measure of insurance.[37]

A month later citizens of San Antonio witnessed the arrival of people who had never before visited in peace. A Comanche party led by a woman rode into town carrying a cross and a white flag.[38] The woman leading the party was one of the female captives freed by the Spanish governor and was also the mother of the little girl still held hostage. Others in the party included the hostage girl's father, the husband of the other hostage woman held by the governor, and the brother of two of the Comanche women held in the missions. Altogether, they made up a tense party seeking lost family members. The group reunited with the governor's two female hostages, received more diplomatic gifts from the Spanish official, and, during their departure, sought profitable revenge for the women's captivity by making off with four hundred horses from the presidial herd. They also tried to liberate the three Comanche women held in the mission, but that escape Spanish soldiers stopped. In despair, one of the women from the mission tried to kill herself upon recapture. As for the Comanche rescue party, they too suffered an ill-fated end. A group of Apache warriors (themselves seeking to make points with Spanish officials) attacked the party as it fled the region, killed seven men, captured half of their horses and four of the women, and promptly turned them over to the Spaniards. The governor sent the women to imprisonment in Coahuila.[39]

The governor had not heard the last from Comanches regarding his captive policy, however, because later in the summer of 1772 Comanche warrior-diplomats came to San Antonio to retrieve the women sent to Coahuila. Initially, the governor attempted to shame the Comanche men by displaying the "false" white flag of truce carried earlier by the Comanche woman. It failed to silence the Comanche men. In fact, the husband of one woman hunkered down and prepared to wait out the governor in protest of his wife's captivity. Either the warrior made quite an impression upon the besieged governor or the governor recognized the need to make peace with the formidable Comanche bands, because he soon reported to the viceroy that he had advised the governor of Coahuila to insure that the Comanche woman was not baptized, so that indeed she could be returned to her husband.[40] Records fail to tell if and when she returned to her husband. If, in fact, she was redeemed, it did not buy the Spaniards peace for long, since hostilities continued unchecked.

The Texas governor also had the opportunity to advance Spanish diplomacy among the Wichitas, when Wichita delegations traveled to San Antonio to ratify a new treaty with the Spanish government in the summer of 1772. During their meetings, one of the principal chiefs told the Spanish governor that he had received word that his wife, who had been captured by Apaches a few months before, had been sold by the Apaches to a Spaniard in Coahuila. He pleaded with the governor to effect her return. "She is so much esteemed by him," the governor reported to the viceroy, "that he assures me that she is the only one he has ever had, or wishes to have until he dies, and, as she leaves him two little orphans, he begs for her as zealously as he considers her delivery difficult."[41]

The governor concluded that the strongest means had to be put to securing her, for if not, "all that we have attained and which is of so much importance would be lost." In other words, he was quite sure the success of the newly completed peace rested upon the captive woman's return. A month later the governor wrote again to the viceroy, but this time exulting that, in answer to his urgent requests, the governor of Coahuila had found and returned the chief's wife. She had been conveyed to San Antonio with a convoy of maize and was even then a guest in the Texas governor's home. More to the point, the Texas official again hoped "that she may be the key that shall open the way to our treaties." In March 1773 the governor again wrote to the viceroy to report that the happy husband was in the governor's home and wished authorization to continue on to visit the viceroy, presumably in thanks for the return of his wife. Good relations in this case had been secured, at least for the time being.[42]

In the spirit of making war to achieve peace, Spanish officials ordered even more Indian women to be taken captive in order to force peaceful diplomacy, determining that the best way to manipulate native groups was through their captive kinsmen, or more accurately, kinswomen. Sometimes Spanish officials went so far as to single out as political hostages the wives, daughters, sisters, and mothers of leading chiefs and warriors.

Spanish captive policy devastated Indian bands by targeting Indian women and children. Compared to Indian captive-taking, which took small numbers of individuals, Spaniards introduced a scale of captive-taking unimaginable to most Indian nations. Spanish forces aimed large-scale attacks on Apache and Comanche rancherías and took women and children captive in numbers in excess of fifty to one hundred people at a time. And, when diplomatic negotiations failed, many of those women and children ultimately fell victim to punitive policies that sent them to Mexican labor camps, prisons, or, in the case of young children, to missions for conversion. Many died in transit to Mexico. A majority never saw their homes again.[43]

To use captives, not commercially but politically, may have seemed a logical tactic to Spanish officials who could refer to long traditions of prisoner and hostage exchange in European warfare.[44] In Comanche and Wichita practice, however, captives were taken from enemies and traded to allies. Quite simply, capture was a hostile act of war, and trade was a commercial exchange. When Spanish forces attacked Comanche and Wichita rancherías, took captives, and then tried to force peace, they were trying to forge alliance through an act of enmity. It was nonsensical to native thinking. Even by Spanish standards, their captive policy was fundamentally unequal. Spanish diplomatic gestures were always made with other men's women. Captive "exchange" never represented a trade of Indian women for Spanish women. Although Spanish officials spent much time and rhetoric bemoaning the loss of Spanish women to Indian captivity, the charge remained primarily rhetorical. In eighteenth-century Texas it was Indian women who were most often subject to captivity, not Spanish women. Hence, Indian men were the ones faced with fears concerning the fate of their women in the hands of rival men.

Spanish captive diplomacy not only violated Comanche and Wichita definitions of the relations of alliance and enmity, it also resonated with social controls internal to Comanche and Wichita societies. Indeed, to the men of these nations, Spanish military and diplomatic policies that targeted their wives or female family members may have most resembled practices of "wife-stealing," which were defined in terms of male competition, challenges to honor, and attempts to humiliate. As E. Adamson Hoebel outlines for Comanches, "the competition for bravery ranking which was institutionalized in coup counting found its opportunity for expression within the tribe in the taking of women from their husbands." A husband then had to take action in response or suffer social disgrace, and the disgrace came in specifically male terms of being labeled a coward. Jane Fishburne Collier expands upon Hoebel's analysis to point out that in bride-service societies, which included Lipan Apaches and Wichitas as well as Comanches, "no other event can so dramatically affect [a man's] possibilities and relations with others" as the loss of a wife. With her loss, a man also lost home, shelter, and the provision of services that allowed him to offer other men hospitality. Moreover, people began to "question the husband's ability to keep what he claimed as his," which in turn led them to assume a lack of ability on his part that other men, particularly the man who stole his wife, possessed. Finally, the loss of reputation threatened a man's claim to the influence and privileges of a political actor of status.[45]

The negotiations following an act of wife-stealing occurred solely between men. Abram Kardiner argues that the competition among men, which served as a defining element of Comanche society, made women "constantly a pawn in the prestige struggles of the men." Male competition did not allow a man not to respond to the theft of his wife—to fail to do so amounted to cowardice. "Adultery and taking another's wife were direct attacks upon the prestige of the wife's husband," writes Hoebel, because "[b]oth acts were unmistakable challenges which could not be ignored by the man who would maintain enough face to make life livable." Thus, Hoebel argues, "the one outstanding factor around which the settlement of a dispute turned was not the question of the right or wrong of the situation, but rather the relative bravery in warfare of the two parties involved." Karl and Iva Osanai Schmitt similarly state that in Wichita conflicts over wife-stealing, "the affair was between two men."[46]

The taking of captives had analogies to the public nature of wife-stealing.[47] For instance, within Comanche society if a man outside the husband's kin or family unit was the guilty party, it became a public challenge to the man's honor and demanded public response (as opposed to transgressions that took place within the family and were considered a private matter with no public redress of male honor required). If wives could not be regained, warriors demanded compensation in the form of damage payments in goods, horses, clothing, and guns. The value of such an exchange lay not in the actual value of the articles but in the maintenance of prestige. If the maintenance of a reputation for bravery depended on seeking redress for the wife's loss in cross-cultural or intertribal situations, it is not surprising that the Spaniards encountered native men who came to San Antonio and refused to leave until they regained their wives or who exacted revenge by raids and warfare.

Despite treaties between Spaniards, Wichitas, and Comanches, raiding and hostility periodically continued to break the peace. Moreover, though nominal peace prevailed for much the colonial period after 1785, Spanish relations with Comanches, Wichitas, and Caddos remained little more than armed truce. That was the best they could do. In stark contrast to Ross Frank's portrait of neighboring New Mexico in the 1790s (see chapter 4), Spanish Texas came nowhere near attaining a stable political economy, much less regional dominion. Spanish failures to understand the native social controls guiding the political and economic relations of Indian nations in Texas cannot solely account for failures to conquer or failures to ally, but they do suggest missed opportunities to achieve some more sound form of interchange or to avoid misguided insult and hostility.

failed peace in Texas can be partly contributed to failed understanding of culture

Conclusions

In December 1819 Juan Antonio Padilla reported on the state of Spanish-Indian relations in Texas as Spanish rule in Mexico drew to a close. In his report he methodically assessed the position of major Indian nations in Texas vis-à-vis the Spanish government and the state's success or failure in converting or subduing them. His final estimation did not reflect well on the policies pursued by the Spaniards. Padilla began with Caddos and asserted that, though they were the most civilized of all the Indians in Texas as a result of their continuous trade with the French, they remained barbarous savages in the eyes of Spaniards as a result of their rejection of Christianity. Comanches, he continued, "cover the greater part of that vast region toward the north," "love their liberty so much that they will not bear servitude; and to have peace with them it is necessary to subdue them by arms. It is certain that they are not reducible to the Catholic religion." His reading of Apaches was similar. "It has not been possible to induce them to live in fixed habitations," Padilla reported of Apaches. "They love liberty and are greatly interested in their ideas of idolatry and heathen rites." Turning to Wichitas, he admitted that they receive the Spaniards hospitably and treat them kindly when at peace, but argued that trade with "foreigners" held their loyalty and provided them with arms and ammunition for their wars with the Spaniards. Finally, in an implicit reference to Coahuil-tecan and Karankawan bands of central and coastal Texas, Padilla related that the missions "are in a state of decadence" and "none of them have any Indian settlers, the principal object of their establishment." In sum, Padilla ominously concluded that the province of Texas remained "all under the domination of the barbarian."[48]

Though Padilla cast the province as one ruled by Indians, Spaniards still held the territory they had claimed in the first half of the century. They had not, however, attempted to move northward into Comanche and Wichita lands after the Indians' fierce response to the encroachments of the San Sabá presidio-mission complex in the 1750s and 1760s. Twice Spaniards had abandoned and then resettled Caddo regions of east Texas in steadily decreasing numbers. Lipan Apaches still challenged the Spaniards, despite a gradual retreat southward in response to Comanche and Wichita competitions. Caddo and Wichita trade networks remained oriented to the east and to commercial relations with French and newly arriving Anglo traders. Comanche groups had established more peaceful and thus profitable relationships with the Spaniards in New Mexico by the end of the century and pursued trade with them as well as the expanding number of Anglo-Americans in the Lower Plains. All groups, be they Spaniard or Indian, stood on relatively equal footing in their continued struggles to hold territory and to survive.

Spanish-Indian relations in eighteenth-century Texas were not strug-gles over social control but struggles over material and political resources. Except for the relations between a small number of Spanish Franciscans and Coahuiltecan and Karankawan Indians in the missions, neither Spaniards nor Indians intervened in the other's lives in terms of social practices. In Texas social controls and hierarchies of power remained within the realm of "international" politics and diplomacy. That is not to say that Spaniards drew no hierarchies among peoples, but those distinctions focused on cat-egorizing only the people within Spanish society. The Indians who were considered within Spanish society and thus included in these social orders were those who had been reduced and subdued by the Church and State. Indian nations that remained outside the purview of Spanish society and government—the native majority in Texas—were not incorporated into such categorizations. Just as Spaniards defined "indios bárbaros" as outside of the social or political classifications of Spanish society, Caddos, Comanches, Wichitas, and Apaches considered Spaniards "strangers" to the fictive and real kinship systems that constituted their political and economic networks. The negotiations of social control between separate societies and nations (or the failures thereof) insured that eighteenth-century Texas was a "zone of exclusion"—by mutual disagreement.

NOTES

1. Spanish officials in San Antonio recorded their first sight of Comanches when a Comanche war party pursued Lipan Apaches to the San Antonio area in 1743. From then on, hostilities grew apace, as Spaniards established peace with the Apaches and built missions for them north of San Antonio. The presidio-mission complex established for the Apaches fell under attack by a united force of Comanches, Wichitas, Caddos, and Tonkawas in 1758. Succeeding missions for the Apaches in the El Cañon region suffered similar attack until they stood completely deserted by 1767.

2. Father José de Calahorra y Saenz to Governor of Texas Don Angel de Martos y Navarrete, 16 July 1965, Statement of Father José de Calahorra y Saenz, 30 July 1765, Testimony of Antonio Treviño before Governor Angel de Martos y Navarrete, 13 July 1765, Béxar Archives, Center for American History, University of Texas at Austin (hereafter cited as BA); Juan Agustín Morfi, *Excerpts from the Memorias for the History of the Province of Texas: Being a Translation of those parts of the Memorias which particularly concern the various Indians of the Province of Texas*, trans. Frederick C. Chabot (San Antonio: Naylor Printing Co., 1932), 11–12. Having won the Wichita warriors' high regard by his valor, Treviño became an ideal emissary and diplomat to represent Spanish officials in their relations with the Taovayas and other Wichita bands. For Treviño's later service as mediator to the Wichitas, see various reports of Athanase de Mézières in *Athanase de Mézières and the Louisiana-Texas Frontier 1768–1780*, 2 vols., trans. Herbert Eugene Bolton (Cleveland: Arthur H. Clark Co., 1914), 2: 199, 205, 215, 322.

3. This myriad of native peoples—known only from European and archeological records since none of the groups survived past the early nineteenth century—was once categorized by scholars as one group, which they named "Coahuiltecan." Recent research, however, has shown that in fact they represented hundreds of small autonomous bands of at least seven different language groups—Coahuilteco, Karankawa, Comecrudo, Cotoname, Solano, Tonkawa, and Aranama. The other groups targeted by Spanish missionaries were the marine-adapted hunting and gathering Karankawas living along the Gulf coast between Galveston Bay and Corpus Christi Bay.

T. N. Campbell, *The Indians of Southern Texas and Northeastern Mexico: Selected Writings of Thomas Nolan Campbell* (Austin: Texas Archaeological Research Laboratory, University of Texas at Austin, 1988); T. N. Campbell and T. J. Campbell, *Indian Groups Associated with Spanish Missions of the San Antonio Missions National Historical Park*, Center for Archaeological Research Special Report No. 19 (San Antonio: University of Texas at San Antonio, 1985); W. W. Newcomb, Jr., "Historic Indians of Central Texas," *Bulletin of the Texas Archeological Society* 64 (1993): 1–63; W. W. Newcomb Jr., *The Indians of Texas: From Prehistoric to Modern Times* (Austin: University of Texas Press, 1961); Robert A. Ricklis, *The Karankawa Indians of Texas: An Ecological Study of Cultural Tradition and Change* (Austin: University of Texas Press, 1996).

4. It should be noted, however, that Spaniards in the area of Los Adaes and the East Texas missions did not fall prey to attack because they maintained peaceful relations with (and sometimes engaged in illicit trade with) neighboring Caddos and Frenchmen who were trading partners of the Comanches and Wichitas.

5. Donna J. Guy and Thomas E. Sheridan, "On Frontiers: The Northern and Southern Edges of the Spanish Empire in the Americas," in *Contested Ground: Comparative Frontiers on the Northern and Southern Edges of the Spanish Empire* (Tucson: University of Arizona Press, 1998), 4; Silvio R. D. Baretta and John Markoff, "Civilization and Barbarism: Cattle Frontiers in Latin America," *Comparative Studies in Society and History* 20 (1978), 587–620 (590 for quote).

6. Guy and Sheridan, "On Frontiers," 15. See also Jeremy Adelman and Stephen Aron, "From Borderlands to Borders: Empires, Nation-States, and the Peoples in between in North American History," *American Historical Review* 104, 3 (1999): 818–41, and the response of John R. Wunder and Pekka Hämäläinen, "Of Lethal Places and Lethal Essays," *American Historical Review* 104, 3 (1999): 1229–34.

7. Frank Raymond Secoy, *Changing Military Patterns on the Great Plains (17th Century through Early 19th Century)*, Monographs of the American Ethnological Society, vol. 21 (Locust Valley, N.Y.: J. J. Augustin Publisher, 1953); W. W. Newcomb, Jr., "A Re-examination of the Causes of Plains Warfare," *American Anthropologist* 52 (1950): 317–30; Thomas W. Kavanagh, *Comanche Political History: An Ethnohistorical Perspective, 1706–1875* (Lincoln: University of Nebraska Press, 1996); Cecile Elkins Carter, *Caddo Indians: Where We Come From* (Norman: University of Oklahoma Press, 1995).

8. Julian Pitt-Rivers defines honor as having two interrelated dimensions: (1) honor-virtue, which represents personal merit, and (2) honor-precedence, which represents social status and power. William Ian Miller makes clear

the relational and conflict-laden nature of honor, in that "honor is that disposition which makes one act to shame others who have shamed oneself, to humiliate others who have humiliated oneself." Julian Pitt-Rivers, "Honour and Social Status," in *Honour and Shame: The Values of Mediterranean Society*, ed. J. G. Peristiany (Chicago: University of Chicago Press, 1966); William Ian Miller, *Humiliation and Other Essays on Honor, Social Discomfort, and Violence* (Ithaca, N.Y.: Cornell University Press, 1993), 84.

9. Daniel A. Hickerson, "Historical Processes, Epidemic Disease, and the Formation of the Hasinai Confederacy," *Ethnohistory* 44, 1 (1997).

10. "Account of the Journey of Bénard de la Harpe: Discovery Made by Him of Several Nations Situated in the West," trans. Ralph A. Smith, *Southwestern Historical Quarterly* 62, 1–4 (1958–1959): 253–54.

11. Morfi, *Excerpts from the Memorias for the History of the Province of Texas*, 2–3, 4–5 (for quote), 7–9; Juan Agustín Morfi, *History of Texas, 1673–1779*, 2 volumes, trans. Carlos Eduardo Castañeda (Albuquerque: Quivira Society, 1935), 2: 79–92.

12. The historiography of French-Indian sexual relations and intermarriage includes Susan Sleeper-Smith, *Indian Women and French Men: Rethinking Cultural Encounter in the Western Great Lakes* (Amherst: University of Massachusetts Press, 2001); Jennifer S. H. Brown, *Strangers in Blood: Fur Trade Company Families in Indian Country* (Vancouver: University of British Columbia Press, 1980); Sylvia Van Kirk, *Many Tender Ties: Women in Fur Trade Society, 1670–1870* (Norman: University of Oklahoma Press, 1980); Jennifer Spear, "'They Need Wives': Métissage and the Regulation of Sexuality in French Louisiana, 1699–1730," in *Sex, Love, Race: Crossing Boundaries in North American History*, ed. Martha Hodes (New York: New York University Press, 1999).

13. Joseph Zitomersky, "The Form and Function of French-Native American Relations in Early Eighteenth-Century French Colonial Louisiana," *Proceedings of the Fifteenth Meeting of the French Colonial Historical Society, Martinique and Guadaloupe, May 1989*, ed. Patricia Galloway and Philip P. Boucher (New York: University Press of America, 1992).

14. John R. Swanton, *Source Material on the History and Ethnology of the Caddo Indians*, Bureau of American Ethnology Bulletin 132 (Washington, D.C.: Smithsonian Institution, 1942); Elsie Clews Parsons, *Notes on the Caddo*, Memoirs of the American Anthropological Association, 57 (1941); Jane Fishburne Collier, *Marriage and Inequality in Classless Societies* (Stanford: Stanford University Press, 1988), 22, 23 for quotes.

15. Governor Jacinto de Barrios y Jáuregui to Viceroy Conde de Revilla Gigedo, 8 November 1750 and 17 April 1753, in *Pichardo's Treatise in the*

Limits of Louisiana and Texas, trans. Charles Wilson Hackett, 4 vols. (Austin: University of Texas Press, 1931) 4: 16, 67; Auditor Don Domingo Valcárcel to Viceroy Conde de Revilla Gigedo, 25 September 1753, in *Pichardo's Treatise in the Limits of Louisiana and Texas*, 4: 98.

16. The notice given Miguel Jorge Menchaca who was reported living among the Comanches in the 1780s reflected his uniqueness. Commandant General Pedro de Nava spoke of a "class of wandering ones" who enjoyed "living among the barbarians in order to give free reign to their passions," and who needed to be prevented from doing so. In 1785, a Frenchman, Pedro [Pierre] Vial, and two unidentified others, Alfonso Rey and José Mariano Valdés, declaring that "they now knew the absurdity of what they had done in living for so many years among those savages," received official pardon, and rejoined Spanish society. Commandant General Felipe de Neve to Governor of Texas Domingo Cabello, 3 October 1783, BA; Commandant General Pedro de Nava to Manuel de Godoy, 3 November 1795, in Noel M. Loomis and Abraham P. Nasatir, *Pedro Vial and the Roads to Santa Fe* (Norman: University of Oklahoma Press, 1967): 171–72; Governor of Texas Don Domingo Cabello to Commandant General José Antonio Rengel, 17 February 1785, BA.

17. "Carta de Don Damián Massanet á Don Carlos de Sigüenza sobre el descubrimiento de la Bahía del Espiritu Santo," trans. Lilia Casís, *Quarterly of the Texas State Historical Association* 2, 4 (1899): 307–8; Father Damián Mazanet to Viceroy Conde de Galve, September 1690, in *The Presidio and Militia on the Northern Frontier of New Spain: A Documentary History*, vol. 2, part 2: *The Central Corridor and the Texas Corridor, 1700–1765*, ed. Diana Hadley, Thomas H. Naylor, and Mardith K. Schuetz-Miller (Tucson: University of Arizona Press, 1997), 336–37.

18. Father Francisco Casañas de Jesús María to the Viceroy, Aug. 15, 1691, in "Descriptions of the Texas or Asinai Indian, 1691–1722," trans. Mattie Austin Hatcher, *Southwestern Historical Quarterly* 30, 4(1927): 289.

19. "Replies given by the governor of the province of Texas to questions put to him by the lord commandant general of the Interior [Provinces] in an official letter of the 27th of January, 1786, concerning various circumstances of the Eastern Cumanche Indians, April 30, 1786," and Domingo Cabello to José Antonio Rengel, draft 20 February 1786, BA.

20. "Pedro Vial and Francisco Xavier de Chaves to Governor Domingo Cabello, Diary of their mission, 17 June to 29 September 1785," in "Inside the Comanchería, 1785: The Diary of Pedro Vial and Francisco Chaves," ed. Elizabeth A. H. John, trans. Adán Benavides, *Southwestern Historical Quarterly* 98, 1 (1994): 39–45.

21. Spanish officials referred to the governor's or king's affection for "his children," asked them to be "obedient sons," and couched their orders and directives as "fatherly" and the exhortations of a loving or true "father." Athanase de Mézières, for instance, wrote of the achievement of peace as the transformation of Indians into "children" of the king. *Athanase de Mézières and the Louisiana-Texas Frontier*, 2: 254, 275–76; 1: 206–20; 148–51; 209–10; Don Domingo Cabello appointment of Taboayaz chief, 14 February 1785, BA.

22. Patricia Galloway, "'The Chief Who Is Your Father': Choctaw and French Views of the Diplomatic Relation," in *Powhatan's Mantle: Indians in the Colonial Southeast*, ed. Peter H. Wood, Gregory A. Waselkov, and M. Thomas Hatley (Lincoln: University of Nebraska Press, 1989): 254–78.

23. George A. Dorsey, *The Mythology of the Wichita* (Washington, D.C.: Carnegie Institution of Washington, 1904); Karl Schmitt and Iva Osanai Schmitt, *Wichita Kinship, Past and Present* (Norman, Okla.: University Book Exchange, 1953); W. W. Newcomb Jr., *The People Called Wichita* (Phoenix: Indian Tribal Series, 1977).

24. Qui Te Sain, Chief of the Village of the Taovayas to Bernardo de Gálvez, 4 November 1780, in *Spain in the Mississippi Valley, 1765–1794*, 3 parts, ed. Lawrence Kinnaird (*Annual Report of the American Historical Association for the Year 1945*, vols. 2–4; Washington: U.S. Government Printing Office, 1946–49), 1: 392.

25. Pedro Vial and Francisco Xavier de Chaves to Governor Domingo Cabello, Diary of their mission, 17 June to 29 September 1785, in "Inside the Comanchería, 1785: The Diary of Pedro Vial and Francisco Chaves," 34, 46, 50.

26. Morfi, *Excerpts from the Memorias for the History of the Province of Texas*, 6.

27. Parsons, *Notes on the Caddo*, 28.

28. Thomas Gladwin, "Comanche Kin Behavior," *American Anthropologist* 50, 1 (1948): 80; E. Adamson Hoebel, "Comanche and H3kandika Shoshone Relationship Systems," *American Anthropologist*, new series, 41, 3 (1939): 448; Abram Kardiner, "Analysis of Comanche Culture," in *The Psychological Frontiers of Society* (New York: Columbia University Press, 1945, 1959), 81–100.

29. Cornelius J. Jaenen, "The Role of Presents in French-Amerindian Trade," in *Explorations in Canadian Economic History: Essays in Honour of Irene M. Spry*, ed. Duncan Cameron (Ottawa, Canada: University of Ottawa Press, 1985), 231–50; John C. Ewers, "Symbols of Chiefly Authority in Spanish Louisiana," in *The Spanish in the Mississippi Valley 1762–1804*, ed. John Francis McDermott (Urbana: University of Illinois Press, 1972).

30. J. Gaignard, Journal of an Expedition up the Red River, 1773–74, in *Athanase de Mézières and the Louisiana-Texas Frontier 1768–1780*, 2: 93–94.

31. Report of Athanase de Mézières, Captain of Infantry, to Colonel Barón de Ripperdá, 4 July 1772, Barón de Ripperdá to the Viceroy, 5 July 1772, in *Athanase de Mézières and the Louisiana-Texas Frontier*, 1: 299, 320–22.

32. Governor Domingo Cabello to Commandant General José Antonio Rengel, 25 November 1785; Commandant General José Antonio Rengel to Governor Domingo Cabello, 27 February 1786; "Report of the items which have been presented to three chiefs of the Comanche Nation," 25 September 1786, BA; J. Gaignard, Journal of an Expedition up the Red River, 1773–74, Athanase de Mézières to Bernardo de Gálvez, May 1779, and Athanase de Mézières to Teodoro de Croix, 5 September 1779, in *Athanase de Mézières and the Louisiana-Texas Frontier 1768–1780*, 2: 83–100, 250, 270.

33. Pedro Vial and Francisco Xavier de Chávez, "Diary of Trip from San Antonio to the Comanche Villages to Treat for Peace, 15 November 1785," in Kavanagh, *Comanche Political History*, 103.

34. Governor of Texas Domingo Cabello to the Governor of Louisiana, 20 September 1783, in *Spain in the Mississippi Valley*, 2: 80–85; Governor Domingo Cabello to Commandant General José Antonio Rengel, 9 December 1785, 24 December 1785, 10 January 1786, 24 January 1786, 20 February 1786, 24 April 1786, 30 July 1786, 31 August 1786, 25 September 1786, BA; Pedro de Nava to Viceroy Miguel José de Azanza, 23 July 1799, concerning the Spanish-Comanche Treaty of 1785 and their relations to 1799, in Odie Faulk, "Spanish-Comanche Relations and the Treaty of 1785," *Texana* 2 (1964): 44–53; Reports of Governor Rafael Martínez Pacheco, 31 March 1787, 3 September 1787, and 30 June 1789; Letters from Rafael Martínez Pacheco to Juan de Ugalde, 17 September 1787, 13 October 1788, 2 March 1789, and 17 August 1789, BA.

35. Bernardo de Gálvez, *Instructions for Governing the Interior Provinces of New Spain, 1786*, trans. Donald E. Worcester (Berkeley: Quivira Society, 1951), 64–78; Teodoro de Croix, General Report of 1781, October 30, 1781, in Alfred Barnaby Thomas, *Teodoro de Croix and the Northern Frontier of New Spain, 1776–1783* (Norman: University of Oklahoma Press, 1941), 97.

36. The minimal use of Indian slaves in the establishment of French plantation agriculture and French preference for enslaved African Americans as their labor force indicated that the *Indian* slave trade held importance only to French domestic and conjugal demands. Even as the importation of African-American slave laborers replaced Indian slaves and the importation of French women made unnecessary Indian concubinage and intermarriage

in most regions of Louisiana, Indian slave women, concubines, and wives remained fixtures of outpost settlements like Natchitoches, and helped to maintain a bond between the French, Caddo, and Wichita men throughout the eighteenth century. Nancy M. M. Surrey, *The Commerce of Louisiana during the French Régime, 1699–1763* (New York: Columbia University Press, 1916): 226–49; Daniel H. Usner, *Indians, Settlers, and Slaves in a Frontier Exchange Economy: The Lower Mississippi Valley before 1783* (Chapel Hill: University of North Carolina for the Institute of Early American History and Culture, 1992).

37. Viceroy Antonio María de Bucareli y Ursúa to Governor Juan María Ripperdá, 24 March and 28 April 1772, BA; Juan María Ripperdá to Governor of Louisiana Luis Unzaga y Amezaga, 26 May 1772, in *Athanase de Mézières and the Louisiana-Texas Frontier*, 1: 273.

38. Comanche leaders presumably had put a woman at the head of their delegation to insure that the Spaniards identified them as peaceful and allowed them entry to the town.

39. Viceroy Antonio María de Bucareli y Ursúa to Governor Juan María Ripperdá, 16 June 1772, BA; Juan María Ripperdá to Governor of Louisiana Luis Unzaga y Amezaga, 26 May 1772, in *Athanase de Mézières and the Louisiana-Texas Frontier*, 1: 273–74.

40. Juan María Ripperdá to Viceroy Antonio María de Bucareli y Ursúa, 5 July 1772, in *Athanase de Mézières and the Louisiana-Texas Frontier*, 1: 321–22.

41. Barón de Ripperdá to the Viceroy Antonio María de Bucareli y Ursúa, 5 July 1772; Barón de Ripperdá to the Viceroy Antonio María de Bucareli y Ursúa, 2 August 1772; and Barón de Ripperdá to Governor of Louisiana Luis Unzaga y Amezaga, 8 September 1772, in *Athanase de Mézières and the Louisiana-Texas Frontier*, 1: 322, 334–35, 348.

42. Ibid.; Barón de Ripperdá to Antonio María Bucareli y Ursúa, 30 March 1773, BA.

43. One could speculate that the nineteenth-century phenomenon of wide-scale adoption of captive Mexican women and children by Indian bands across Texas was in direct response to such depopulation in the eighteenth century.

44. James William Brodman, *Ransoming Captives in Crusader Spain: The Order of Merced on the Christian-Islamic Frontier* (Philadelphia: University of Pennsylvania Press, 1986).

45. E. Adamson Hoebel, *The Political Organization and Law-Ways of the Comanche Indians*, Memoirs of the American Anthropological Association, no. 54 (Menasha, Wisc.: American Anthropological Association, 1940), 49–65: 49; Collier, *Marriage and Inequality in Classless Societies*, 45–50.

Spaniards were to some limited degree aware of the law-ways regarding "wife-stealing" among the Comanches, but they did not take any lesson or significance from that knowledge regarding their own captive-taking. In 1788, Governor Rafael Martínez Pacheco recorded that three Comanche men and one woman had appeared in San Antonio, and that one of the men, the youngest brother of principal chief Guacuanquacis, was seeking sanctuary of a sort because "he had stolen the Indian woman" and "they are fearful that those of their nation might kill them, as they are used and accustomed to doing to those who steal their women." Rafael Martínez Pacheco to Commandant General Juan de Ugalde, 3 March 1788, BA.

46. Kardiner, "Analysis of Comanche Culture," 89; Hoebel, *The Political Organization and Law-Ways of the Comanche Indians*, 50, 54; Schmitt and Schmitt, *Wichita Kinship*, 30f.

47. The first-hand observations of Comanche society made by Felipe de Sandoval provide evidence of links between wife-stealing and captive-taking. Sandoval, a Spaniard who traveled through a Comanche settlement in the 1740s, associated female captivity with warriors' prerogative to polygyny, telling Spanish interrogators that Comanche warriors have "as many wives as possible, and they keep for themselves whatever [women] they seize from their enemies in war." Later he stated even more strongly that "they give full rein to their barbarity, the deity of their adoration being atrocity and the effusion of blood, and their first law being an abundance of women to increase their progeny. . . . [thus] They steal them [women] from other nations to augment their own." Because polygyny was reserved for warriors, Sandoval's observations substantiate the idea that captive women represented personal booty of warriors, and indicate that polygyny was an ideal means of incorporating captives into a community. Testimony of Felipe de Sandoval before Governor Tomás Vélez Cachupín, March 1 and March 8, 1750, in *Pichardo's Treatise on the Limits of Louisiana and Texas*, 3: 323, 329.

48. Juan Antonio Padilla, Report on the Barbarous Indians of the Province of Texas, December 27, 1819, in "Texas in 1820," trans. Mattie Austin Hatcher, *Southwestern Historical Quarterly* 23 (1919): 48–49, 54, 56, 57, 59, 60.

The Común, Local Governance, and Defiance in Colonial Sonora

Cynthia Radding

*All of these provinces are settled by reduced Indians who number
in the thousands, but the Pimas Altos and Bajos that still remain at
peace . . . if we do not speedily punish the old and new enemies, I fear
the domestic Indians of this province of Sonora, with the exception
of the Ópatas and Eudeves, will go the way of our enemies.*

—Captain Lorenzo Cancio, commander of the
Presidio of San Carlos de Buenavista,
to Viceroy Marqués de Croix, 1766[1]

The term social control *would seem odd to any eighteenth-century missionary,
alcalde mayor,* or indigenous governor who was transported in virtual time
to our world of transnational borders in the twenty-first century. Contemporary actors, whose words and deeds have filled the archival records on
which our histories are based, spoke purposefully about the territorial
defense of Sonora, a frontier province of northwestern New Spain, so distant geographically and politically from the viceregal centers of Mexico
City and Guadalajara. Indigenous leaders, invested with Hispanic offices,
Spanish administrators, religious clerics, and *vecinos* (settlers), tested and
adapted different strategies to ensure their own survival and to maintain

the colonial order.[2] Conscious of guarding shifting and porous boundaries between the settled colony and the forests and deserts dominated by hunter-gatherer nomadic bands, contemporaries defined defense in both military and social terms.

This chapter analyzes the concept of social control in terms of governance, violence, and the limits of a negotiated political order in the northwestern frontier of New Spain. It begins with the spatial and geographical contours of the Intendancy of Arizpe, covering the modern states of Sinaloa and Sonora (Mexico) and Arizona (United States), then follows with a description of the village councils and their political roles, and finally turns to gendered patterns of social control evidenced in marriage and household formation. The core question of this essay focuses on the tension inherent in institutions, like the village council, and their potential to both enforce social control and raise a concerted opposition to the colonial regime.

Defense was closely linked to *reducción,* a policy that was widely employed by officials of both the ecclesiastical and secular arms of the empire, but with specific meanings on the northern frontier of New Spain. Reducción meant, first and foremost, the spatial consolidation of indigenous settlements, by means of coercion and persuasion, to create nucleated villages that were susceptible to surveillance, taxation, and labor recruitment for colonial enterprises. Ideologically, reducción signified the observance of Christian ritual and adherence to the cultural norms of civilized Iberian life. To achieve both these ends the Crown subsidized missionary programs of evangelization and reducción, entrusted to the religious orders, whose labors followed the advancing mining frontier of northwestern New Spain.[3] Archaeological and architectural remains of these colonial endeavors bear witness to the partial success of Spanish policies of reducción, through the construction of village centers, churches and convents, and irrigation works. Indeed, most of the rural townships of today's Sonoran highlands trace their historical origins to colonial missions. Nevertheless, much of the social and cultural history of Sonoran mission communities bespeaks a central, ongoing tension between the parallel and opposing forces of nucleation and dispersion.[4] Indigenous communities came and went from consolidated mission pueblos to small, scattered *rancherías*.

Spanish military officers understood reducción as a means to curtail independent forays by indigenous warriors and recruit them as auxiliary troops for the presidios that marked a tenuous defensive line along the northern frontier and patrolled the wagon roads, along which precious cargoes of silver were transported to royal assay houses and treasuries in Parral, Zacatecas, and, finally, Mexico City. The correspondence exchanged among presidial commanders, provincial governors, and the commandant general of the Provincias Internas centered on the relentless warfare, both offensive and defensive, in which colonial forces were engaged against nomadic Indians and rebellious band members who left the settled life of the missions and turned to foraging and raiding. Spanish authorities in Sonora focused their primary efforts on subduing the Cunca´ac (Seris) of the desert coast extending along the Gulf of California and inland as far as the San Miguel valley, and the bands of Athapaskan warriors known as Apaches, that began hunting and raiding in the eastern and western foothills of the Sierra Madre Occidental during the seventeenth century. Hispanic and Indian agrarian villagers living in missions, presidios, and scattered ranches, whose livelihood depended on stored harvests and herds of livestock, developed to some degree a common cause against these nomadic raiders who carried off precious assets as well as human captives. Comanche and Apache raiding, so central a concern to Hispanic vecinos and Indian villagers in Sonora, Chihuahua, and New Mexico, was itself the product of historical forces emanating primarily from European invasions of North America. Likewise, Cunca´ac bands of the Sonoran desert coastal lands took their own place in the history of the province.[5] The present essay, however, focuses on "social control" from the point of view of the agricultural peoples of the Sonoran piedmont who formed the core population of the missions.

What, then, did "social control" mean to indigenous villagers under the colonial regime? Undoubtedly colonialism radically challenged the leadership of *caciques* (headmen) over the affiliated kin groups that Spaniards identified as nations. The conquest and all its ramifications—demographic, economic, and spiritual—violently curtailed the waning phase of long-distance trade networks on which the Sonoran chiefdoms had thrived during the fifteenth century; consequently, the slow recovery of village life among the survivors required serious regrouping and the adaptation of new strategies to define territorial and political boundaries.[6] Sonoran agricultural peoples reconstituted their communities, in part, through the missions. Spanish legal definitions of Indian pueblos provided indigenous leaders with an institutional framework to mount territorial defenses of agrarian resources—arable land and water—against rival communities and Hispanic herdsmen and planters. Equally significant, caciques found in the missions titles and public offices that reinstated their authority over indigenous commoners, as a labor force and as constituents of an ethnic polity. Sonoran village governors constructed the común as a concept that came to embody the community of people, the spatial demarcations of the villages they inhabited, and the productive resources of the land.[7]

For both Indians and Spaniards, reducción countered the prevailing pattern of spatial mobility. Colonial missions and frontier defense posts opened avenues for status distinctions among male *caciquil* leaders of Sonora. Furthermore, the commercial circuits that enveloped missions and mining centers renewed the flow of commodities to Sonoran pueblos, bringing them new kinds of textiles, tools, and religious emblems, and gave indigenous officers control over their distribution and the allocation of labor. Spanish officials enforced the terms of reducción under the legal formula of the "republic of Indians," with the intent of governing Indians in polity—*en policía.* Native leaders and the mass of commoners who lived in the missions developed over time a colonial political culture with new meanings for the exercise of authority and the confrontation of different agents and structures of power. Spanish and indigenous objectives met in the *cabildo*, the governing councils established in the missions. It is the purpose of this chapter to examine the council in both its social and political dimensions, thereby to show the multiple and at times contradictory ties between the native council and the común, on the one hand and, on the other, the colonial order that created it. The history of native councils and the communities they served is further complicated by the processes of racial and cultural hybridity set in motion by the settlement of Spanish vecinos in the province that produced new social roles and ethnic identities. While the central argument of this essay is that the council was both an instrument of social control and a vehicle for resistance, it is important to bear in mind that the lines of resistance did not cross a binary Spanish/Indian divide. Rather, the composition of putatively Indian communities was mixed and the lines of conflict were multidimensional, confusing and defying the juridical categories presupposed by the imperial distinction between the "republic of Indians" and the "republic of Spaniards."

Natural and Cultural Frontiers in Northwestern New Spain

Cultural and imperial borderlands intersected in the Sonoran Desert and the basin-and-range piedmont (*zona serrana*) that bordered the desert leading eastward to the Sierra Madre Occidental. Sonoran ecosystems

developed according to differences in topography, precipitation, and veg-
etation. Centuries of horticulture, gathering, and husbandry shaped human
landscapes in the deserts, grasslands, and forests that extended from the
Sea of Cortés to the mountains. Sonoran peoples had adapted Meso-
american farming practices, symbolized by the trilogy of maize, beans, and
squash, to the arid conditions of the Sonoran Desert and the piedmont
river valleys. Their systems of cultivation were centered on irrigated floodplain fields supplemented with ephimeral plantings in the arroyos and
swidden cultivation dependent on seasonal rainfall at higher elevations.
Cultivation and gathering were closely related in that Sonoran agriculturalists used both the wild and domesticated varieties of a number of species,
as is illustrated by indigenous knowledge of the teppary bean and the ama-
ranth grains and foliage.[8] In the river valleys of central Sonora, where the
mission system flourished among the Ópata, Eudeve, and Lower Pima villagers, native livelihood and mission economies depended on indigenous
agricultural technologies for soil and water management. The mission
regime added a number of European cultigens—principally wheat, chick-
peas, vegetables, and fruits—to indigenous horticulture and brought livestock to the Sonoran ecosystem.

   In northwestern Mexico, the Jesuit mission enterprise covered nearly
two centuries (1591–1767), initiated as the mining frontier expanded
northward from Zacatecas and Durango to Chihuahua and Sonora. While
the missionaries concentrated the populations of hundreds of scattered
rancherías into fixed pueblos, missions tended to follow precontact settlement patterns by placing the reducciones in existing villages. In the contiguous provinces of Sonora and Sinaloa, the Jesuit mission system at its
height comprised 103 villages, each with several hundred residents.[9]
During the first century of evangelization the Jesuits maintained the only
consistent line of authority over the Indian communities. After 1732, however, the provinces west of the Sierra Madre Occidental were placed in a
new governorship, bringing a distinct hierarchy of civilian governors that
intersected with indigenous polities. Jesuit tutelage of the Sonoran missions ceased abruptly in 1767, following the royal order to expel the Society
of Jesus from all Spanish dominions. Their administrative role in Sonora
was filled by Franciscan missionaries from the College of Querétaro and
the province of Jalisco and, in the neighboring provinces of Ostimuri and
Sinaloa, by clerical priests under the authority of the bishop of Durango
and, after 1779, the bishop of Sonora.[10]

Native Councils and Mission Communities

What, then, was the indigenous cabildo and how did it function in the colonial mission? It was the missionaries' intention to reproduce Hispanic institutions of local government in these frontier communities as an integral part of their evangelizing and civilizing mission. They did so, however, by modifying the standard make-up of the cabildo, as, for instance, those described by José Cuello for Saltillo and Gilbert Din for Spanish New Orleans (see chapters 9 and 3, respectively), to meet their needs for control. Indigenous officers of these councils, bearing titles of *alcaldes, fiscales, topiles*, and *gobernadores* modeled on Hispanic norms of municipal government and carrying canes of office as insignia of their authority, enforced law and order in the mission pueblos. Missionaries governed through the councils, in a form of indirect rule, and their presence was indispensable in implementing religious observance and work discipline; that is, for Christian indoctrination and the production of surpluses destined for circulation among the missions and for sale in colonial markets.

The councils established in the Sonoran missions adapted longstanding traditions of local governance from Iberia and Mesoamerica. Nahua, Mixtec, and Maya villagers of central and southeastern Mexico recognized different ranks of nobility and offices with both judicial and administrative functions from preconquest times. Colonial reducciones grouped several villages under the political jurisdiction of head towns, where indigenous cabildos were installed to collect tribute, complete labor drafts, and enforce Catholic observances. In some cases, as is documented for Cuernavaca, Nahuatl terms persisted well into the colonial period to describe council offices.[11] The outstanding features of indigenous cabildos that bear comparison with similar institutions established in the frontier missions are: (1) different offices were ranked in a definite hierarchy; (2) most of the offices were concerned with tribute collection; and (3) often the same office combined secular and religious responsibilities. Indians living in the northern missions were exempt from tribute payment; however, Indian males were subject to periodic labor drafts under the terms of *repartimiento*, and their recruitment fell to native governors and alcaldes.[12]

The governor was the most important officer of the indigenous cabildo in Sonora, with judicial and administrative responsibilities. Over time, native governors came to represent their pueblos in dealing with colonial authorities, and came to be viewed as the guardians of the común, the communal land and productive assets of their mission villages. Alcaldes, in

Iberia, were judges of the first instance. In the colonial missions their position in the councils was second to the governors and fulfilled both judicial and administrative roles. Governors and alcaldes gave testimony, defended the boundaries of village lands during property surveys, and signed written petitions and legal complaints. Within the pueblos these officers resolved internal disputes and meted out punishments to convicted offenders. *Alguaciles* and topiles were constables, with different but overlapping duties related to law and order. The alguacil, in Spain, was a lower ranked magistrate than an alcalde, or again, an administrative officer, who oversaw community resources—for example, an *"alguacil del campo"* safeguarded communal fields from damage. Topile, named in both ecclesiastical and civil documentation for colonial Sonora, is derived from the Nahuatl term *topilli* (pl. *topileque*), "one who bears a staff of office."[13] Both of these officers carried out the orders of the alcaldes and governors, enforced attendance at public meetings, and distributed tasks for fieldwork and maintenance of the churches and other mission buildings.

Three additional officers performed duties directly related to liturgical rites and Christian doctrine: collectively, they were called fiscales, implying their authority to oversee compliance with ecclesiastical norms and obligations. The first of these, called *mador*, was the missionary's direct assistant who served as ecclesiastical notary to keep the records of baptisms, marriages, and burials. The *temastianes* were in charge of teaching the catechism to children and adults up to the age of marriage, serving also as sacristans for the celebration of the Mass. Choirmasters occupied an important post in all the missions as directors of men and women singers and instrumentalists who accompanied the liturgy and other religious functions; counted among the few literate adults in the missions, choirmasters frequently served as council notaries.[14] Father Juan Nentvig noted that the Ópatas of his missions learned masses and chanted liturgies by heart, "for regularly the faculty of reading and writing does not go beyond the chapel master who, in his political functions, is the scribe." The deliberative aspects of the indigenous cabildos remain obscure, as I have not found any books of the "minutes" or official decisions of the councils for the Sonoran missions, such as have provided fecund material for studies of colonial Nahuatl used by the native councils in central Mexico.[15]

Ignaz Pfefferkorn, who lived among Piman and Ópata-Eudeve peoples, reported on the selection and duties of native councilmen, who collectively were called *justicias*, or magistrates.

Certain Indian magistrates were put at the head of each village. It was their duty to assist the missionary in fulfilling his office, to share with him the supervision and care of the Indians, and by vigilance, by the good reputation he enjoyed, and by good example to keep the other Indians in good order. In view of these responsibilities, Indians who were best fitted for the position and who seemed also to be true and pious Christians were appointed as magistrates.

In each village there were also one or two *mayoris*, or as the Spaniards say, *madores*, who supervised the grown children and also cared for the sick. This office was filled by Indians who from their reputations could be expected to be faithful, careful, and diligent.[16]

Father Juan Nentvig was even more explicit in his portrayal of the missionaries' supervisory role in the formation of the "senate or *cabildo* of these Indian republics." By royal provision issued by the Audiencia of Guadalajara in 1716, and reiterated thirty years later by the viceroy of New Spain, missionaries were to direct the Indians' election of their village governors and alcaldes and these, in turn, appointed the disciplinary officers (alguaciles and topiles) who enforced the Indians' attendance at mass, Christian doctrine, and work stints in the missions.[17]

The obligations incumbent on all mission Indians to attend catechism and liturgical ceremonies as well as to perform communal labor were enforced by moral suasion and by the threat of physical punishment by whipping or confinement to the stocks. Punishments were carried out by indigenous officers under orders from the missionaries or from the governors and magistrates. Abuses of physical punishment were often the source of bitter complaints; fear and resentment of physical punishment punctuated Indians' written protests, providing a recurring theme in their acts of resistance and open rebellion.[18] As we shall see below, whipping provoked a local uprising in one of the Ópata villages of Sonora that involved different Spanish and native authorities.

Certainly, from the missionaries' point of view, the council served as a vehicle for social control. The collaboration between missionaries and Indian officers, at times carefully orchestrated, was not merely theatrical staging. Pueblo governors and alcaldes were empowered by the missionaries' dependence on them to assign daily tasks in mission fields and workshops and to assure attendance at mass and catechism. More directly, and just as visibly, indigenous officers who held keys to the pueblos' granaries and warehouses played a central role in the semiannual distribution of food, clothing, and tools among families resident in the missions. Furthermore, the hierarchy of offices created through the council established a ranked order of privileges that defined concrete benefits in the form of additional rations of food and gifts and honored places to sit and stand in religious services. The elite status of privileged officeholders was underscored by the observation that literacy was reserved only for a few male council members, most often choirmasters and catechists.[19]

The solemnity of annual elections reinforced the council's authority and the elite status of its members. Mission commoners observed the day-to-day presence of village officers not so much as a sitting council, but as they moved through the pueblos, exhorting, visiting, distributing food and other gifts, and enforcing the rules for worship and work. The missionaries' candid statement that they appointed indigenous magistrates belies any appearance of village-based democratic elections. Nevertheless, the priests' words do not convey the different meanings their mission neophytes ascribed to public office or the ways in which they internalized the hierarchies established in the pueblos. We are left to ask how the Indians insinuated themselves into the selection process, how the missionaries were convinced of the relative virtues and fit of certain individuals to hold office. Specifically, the authority vested in native councils overlapped with native criteria of association and leadership based on kinship networks, ethnic alliances, and linguistic affiliations.

Sonoran missions combined families from different rancherías and dialectical groups, chiefly among the distinct bands of riverine and desert-dwelling Piman speakers. Social and ethnic inequalities were expressed in the ascendancy of certain groups over others and in the primacy of head villages (*cabeceras*) over smaller settlements called *visitas* in each of the mission districts. In central Sonora the Ópatas and Eudeves, village agriculturalists who held the best agrarian lands of the piedmont, provided the nuclear population of the missions and exercised dominion over more nomadic groups that entered and left the pueblos, notably the Jobas of the sierra and the Tohono o'odham of the desert plains.[20] These core populations, although not homogeneous, coalesced into ethnic polities through their control of mission councils, their identification with the villages, and their representation of these communities to Spanish officialdom and to colonial society.

Aspiring native leaders in Sonora had two principal avenues to elite status: elected offices in the missions and military rankings in the auxiliary troops that assumed a significant role in frontier defense. The Spanish presidial system, which expanded during the eighteenth century to contain the northern Mexican provinces in the face of widespread raiding by the Apaches from the Sierra Madre and Seris (Cunca´ac) from the Sonoran desert coast, depended on companies of indigenous soldiers who were salaried and organized under the command of their own captains. Furthermore, the General Command of the Interior Provinces, established in 1779, created a new hierarchy to which indigenous captains appealed for prestige and gifts to redistribute to their warriors. Ópata soldiers, in particular, were recruited for numerous punitive expeditions against Apache bands, traveling considerable distances from their home villages to Chihuahua and New Mexico. Three companies of Ópata and Pima soldiers manned presidial garrisons at Bavispe, Bacoachi, and San Ignacio.[21] As we shall see below, these two means of social and political ascendancy were not always compatible, but the dual presence of mission and presidio was central to the history of interethnic relations in the hybrid society of colonial Sonora.

Negotiation and Confrontation across Different Colonial Boundaries

According to colonial records conflicts erupted most frequently over the ownership and usufruct of land, the distribution of mission produce, and the competing fields of authority represented by the village councils and the military commands assigned to native presidial troops. The assertive action by one mission council, early in the eighteenth century, illustrates well the importance of arable land to native peasants and the political culture centered in the común. In 1716 Pima Indians of three small rancherías located within the mission district of Cumuripa in the middle Yaqui valley, Xecatacari, Oviachi, and Buena Vista, appealed to judicial authorities to reclaim land they and their forebears had occupied within the memory of six living witnesses before they were violently dispossessed by a Spanish rancher and militia captain, Antonio de Ancheta.[22] Two years before the Indians drew up their petition Ancheta had died, leaving the land "abandoned" and, by default, allowing the Pimas to repopulate Buena Vista and plant their crops anew. Diego Camorlinga, alcalde of Xecatacari, and the witnesses he brought before the Spanish magistrate constructed a history of occupancy, dispersion, and resettlement in the irrigable fields of Buena Vista. Their arguments rested on effective occupation of the land and the Indians' status as Christians desirous of living in polity, that is, in a settled pueblo. The petition was supported by a census showing 76 Christian households and 11 households of non-Christian adults (*gentiles*) with baptized children. Heading the list of Christian families were four council officers:

Diego Camorlinga, alcalde, married with five children
Lázaro, alguacil, married with one child
Sebastián, topil, married, with four children
Baltasar, topil, married, with one child

All the witnesses spoke in the Pima tongue, translated and transcribed by an interpreter. Their identity rested not so much on a particular ethnic origin, but rather on their status as *el común y naturales de Xecatacari*, commoners with a shared stake in a particular territory—the lands of Buena Vista. The común had material, political, and religious significance in the cultural production of community under the conditions created by colonialism. Camorlinga closed his successful petition with the following words: "We implore you to restore Buena Vista to us, the way we had it before it fell into Ancheta's hands, so that we may found a *pueblo* there for the good of our souls and the protection of our lands."[23]

The Pimas of Xecatacari appealed directly to the Spanish civil authorities, without evident intervention by their missionary. Sixty years later, native officers of the Mission of Opodepe in the San Miguel River valley addressed written petitions that reveal a more complex administrative matrix of competing interests among the Franciscan missionaries who had replaced the Jesuits as the spiritual guardians and administrative overseers of the pueblos, the governors and alcaldes mayores of the province, and presidial commanders.[24] Governors and cabildo members of individual villages were at times pitted against the captains-general who led troops of warriors and saw themselves aligned with the Spanish military hierarchy. These competing political actors operated in an economic environment of conflicting claims by missions, mines, presidios, and private estates on the productive resources of land, water, livestock, and human labor in Sonora.

In the summer of 1777 alcalde mayor Joaquín José de Rivera reported that Ambrosio and Diego, Ópata war captains of Nacameri, "representing themselves and all the individuals of that pueblo, and on behalf of the justices and the *común* of Opodepe," complained that their missionary fray

Antonio Martínez refused to supply them with grains from the mission's granaries when they were called to military campaigns and accused him of trafficking with mission produce for his own benefit. Rivera forwarded the Indians' request that fray Antonio be replaced with a missionary more to their liking to the Franciscan commissary fray Juan de Prestamero and to his own superior, Col. Juan Bautista de Anza, together with a more far-reaching complaint by the captain-general of the Ópata nation that missionaries and village justices of several pueblos refused to recognize his authority and supply his troops with the necessary supplies to carry out their military assignments. Fray Juan de Prestamero visited Opodepe and Nacameri, accompanied by three Spanish colonists, to observe conditions in the villages and question the Indian men and women living there concerning the gifts of food and clothing they received from their missionary and whether they were happy with him. On the basis of his own investigation Prestamero defended fray Antonio and dismissed the complaints raised by the Ópata captains as machinations by private ranchers in Nacameri who coveted mission lands. Furthermore, he retorted, if missionaries failed to supply presidial auxiliaries with food, it was because of shortages occasioned by the declining labor force and shrinking land base of the pueblos.

Political tensions increased as new social and economic conditions circumscribed indigenous communities by the late eighteenth century. Spanish and mixed-race colonists grew in number, equaling and even surpassing the native population of the province, and, with their expanding herds of livestock, encroached on mission lands. In 1790 colonial authorities began surveying communal lands in northeastern and central Sonora, the heartland of Ópata and Eudeve pueblos, ostensibly to assign individual plots of land to indigenous peasant families. Although aggressive privatization of village lands did not occur until the early republican era, in the 1830s, the mixture of private and communal holdings among both Indians and non-Indians in the arable valleys of the Sonoran piedmont complicated the identity of the ethnic polity—the común—that had been so closely tied to the land and to the mission community.[25]

Tensions erupted in a local tumult in the summer of 1790 in the Ópata pueblo of Bacerac, a mission head village that shared fertile land and stream flow for irrigation with the presidio of Bavispe, established four leagues downstream only nine years earlier with a company of Ópata troops.[26] On 9 July, 1790, a crowd of Ópatas had gathered in one of the mission fields where the wheat harvest was in progress. In the presence of the Spanish magistrate, *juez comisario* Juan Ignacio Gil Samaniego, the commanding officer of the presidio of Bavispe, the Ópata village governor José Antonio Mascorta, the Ópata captain general, and the Ópata troop leader of Bavispe, they witnessed the attempted punishment by whipping of one of their commoners accused of refusing to work and, furthermore, of offending the village governor. As the whipping began, Captain General Ignacio Noperi demanded to know, "what crime has this man committed for him to be punished so?" He then turned to the crowd, raised his cane of office, and called out: "My people, what are you waiting for? Why do you not free this man? In the name of the king, let him go!" Two Ópata soldiers rushed forward and untied the victim, Atanasio Zorrilla, and both the Spanish authorities and the Ópata village governor were forced to beat a hasty retreat.

The investigation carried out a month later revealed that rivalries had been simmering for several years among the different ranks of Ópata civilian and military officials, exacerbated by resentment over the intrusion of Spanish authorities in what the Indians considered to be an internal dispute. Trouble began in the local community when Zorrilla threatened the governor and alguacil of Bacerac, refusing to follow their orders, and Governor Mascorta appealed to juez comisario Gil Samaniego to discipline the unruly commoner through the mediation of his missionary fray George Loreto. When Captain General Noperi halted the punishment, he preempted the right to speak in the name of the king in full view of Ópata and Spanish civil and military authorities. Prior to the events of 9 July, Noperi had humiliated Governor Mascorta and his predecessor in public meetings of the Bacerac community and taken over the office of *juez de agua* in charge of distributing irrigation water, traditionally reserved for village councils. Following the confrontation in the wheat field Gil Samaniego lodged an appeal with his superior, *teniente de alcalde mayor* Gregorio Ortiz Cortés,[27] and Noperi rode to the provincial capital of Arizpe to lay his case directly before Intendant Governor Enrique de Grimarest.

Moving our lens to a slightly more abstract angle of analysis, we learn from this incident that the growing power of the late colonial Bourbon state was refracted through a number of competing figures on the Sonoran frontier. Indigenous office holding was split between village councils and military captains general; the colonial order was divided between ecclesiastical and secular arms; the former, represented by missionaries and parish priests, was losing ground to the cadre of presidial officers, governors, and lieutenants who exercised increasingly more direct control over the mission villages. This fragmentary application of power compromised the Indians' defense of village autonomy and augmented political tensions at a time when private Spanish settlement was increasing and mission lands were threatened with secularization and partition. Within the indigenous world, exemplified in this case by the Ópata community of Bacerac, council offices and military rankings visibly constituted an elite of extended families, not unlike the *criollo* propertied elite that held civil magistracies and militia titles. Captain General Ignacio Noperi had received the title from his elder kinsmen Gerónimo Noperi and Juan Manuel Varela; all three were natives of Bacerac.[28]

Political Culture and Gender in Colonial Sonora

The contradictory roles of indigenous councils on the Sonoran frontier point to the complexity of colonial political cultures that developed in northern New Spain. Native council officers collaborated in maintaining the colonial order, willingly or not, by enforcing work discipline and productivity as well as attendance at religious instruction and services in the missions. Ópata and Pima captains and the indigenous warriors they led under the guise of presidial auxiliary troops more often than not held the first line of defense in military skirmishes with encampments of Apache horsemen, in the Sierra, or Seri bands, in the desert lowland plains. Yet, as we have seen, these same captains and village officers confronted colonial authorities, assuming the role of spokespersons for the común to demand the fulfillment of expectations regarding the integrity of indigenous territories and the distribution of the fruits of the Indians' labor.

A small masculine elite emerged from the ethnic polities that took shape under colonial rule. Governors, alcaldes, and subordinate officers, with their canes of office, enjoyed ascendancy and limited powers of command in the mission pueblos. Yet, within this elite rivalries grew between these civilian officers and the military captains general of the Ópata and Pima nations, as was illustrated by the Bacerac tumult of 1790. Residual ethnic differences among different communities of Pimas, Ópatas, Eudeves, and Jobas, originating in the preconquest mosaic of tribal divisions in Sonora, but altered and reworked through the reducciones, were further complicated by distinctions of status and ranking and incipient class differences based on wealth and access to public office. Spanish vecinos and Indian villagers, many of whom lived and worked as rural peasants, began to separate into a small privileged group of proprietors with the means to accumulate land and a majority of rancheros or village commoners who maintained a subsistence economy. Sonoran agrarian landscapes at the close of the colonial period presented a mixture of communal lands, middling livestock ranches, and large haciendas, with a growing sector of tenants and landless peons. Furthermore, the social and political structures established by the mission regime metamorphosed as increasing numbers of Hispanicized Indians, mestizos, and other racially mixed populations settled in the pueblos (through marriage) or squatted on mission lands. Conversely, the movement of mission Indians out of the pueblos, either to hunt and gather in the desert forests of the monte or to join the labor forces of mines and haciendas, blurred the social demarcations of this frontier province and compromised the authority of the cabildos.[29]

Gendered divisions and inequalities conditioned the lived experience of reducción, intersecting with the ethnic and class identities of colonial Sonora. The formal hierarchies of ranked offices established through the village councils and military service were reserved for men—whether Spanish or Indian. Literacy in the mission pueblos was the privilege of a small elite, most probably limited to men; members of both sexes, however, became accomplished musicians for the mass and special festivals. Behind the formal edifice of political offices, women contributed in fundamental ways to economic subsistence and cultural production in the missions. Women's work in agriculture, food processing, gathering, and cloth production sustained both the family economy of indigenous peasants and the surpluses that, in turn, supported mission commerce. Women and children, as well as men, performed seasonal tasks in the agrarian cycle, including planting, guarding the fields from birds and insects, and harvesting the crops. Women processed grains, seeds, fruits, and stalks from planted and gathered plants, thus preparing food for storage and consumption. Furthermore, women participated in the ceremonial life of the pueblos as producers and servers of fermented corn drinks. *Tesgüino*, in northwestern Mexico, enlivened village fiestas, brought together extended families from different rancherías, and—albeit to the missionaries' consternation— became a conduit to sources of spiritual power.[30]

Women appear in the histories of colonial Sonora, as in the other northern provinces of New Spain, as captives in the multiple narratives of frontier warfare. The chapters in this volume by Juliana Barr and Cecilia Sheridan attest to the violence of seizure and forced labor in northeastern

Mexico. Equally striking are the roles that some women carried out as traders and mediators among different cultures and ethnic settlements. Hispanic and village-dwelling indigenous women (and children) were vulnerable to raids by nomadic bands in search of servants, conjugal partners, and persons to ransom. Equally telling, Spanish punitive raids on Apache and Seri encampments returned with *piezas*—women and youths—to ransom or sell as servants in colonial settlements. In northwestern Sonora the intermittent skirmishes between Pima and Yuma-speaking tribal peoples of the lower Gila and Colorado Rivers brought *nijoras*, young captives, into the missions and Spanish towns of the province. Female captives crossed ethnic and spatial boundaries against their will, but those who survived became cultural and linguistic brokers even as their very existence depended on residual powers of adaptation.[31]

Indigenous women of Sonora did, however, seek mobility on their own terms. Women exercised a degree of choice in their sexual and marital partners, occasioned by their movement across villages, rancherías, and mining centers. The bishop's census of 1796 shows that Ópata women frequently took Spanish or mestizo spouses, often changing their own ethnic status in the process. Furthermore, Hispanic and mestiza women occasionally entered the missions as the wives of Indian men. In both cases, the ambiguity of their social identities complicated the governance of mission pueblos, especially in reference to competing claims to communal resources and the fulfillment of labor obligations.[32] These mixed marriages, together with the concurrent processes of social mobility largely fueled by the growing vecino population, spurred new alliances within the común and called into question the very definition of the indigenous polity.

Conclusions

How, then, would our eighteenth-century guides explain the political culture of the Sonoran pueblos, in particular, the web of relationships between the común and the council? Clearly, there were points of union and of separation between the small elite of officeholders and the mass of commoners. Village peasants labored on community tasks, such as the maintenance of irrigation weirs and canals and the harvesting of crops, in return for the defense of communal lands and the cultural integrity of the común. Their allegiance to the councils and their recruitment into auxiliary presidial troops was predicated on the reciprocal expectations of caciquil leadership and on the ceremonial investiture of the office as well as the possibility of ascending through the ranks to higher status. Women, no doubt, nurtured and sought the protection of the community; however, the evidence of their conjugal unions with non-Indians may have been a means of opting out of the patriarchal authority exercised by village governors who claimed to control their labor and to speak on behalf of the entire común.[33]

At the close of the eighteenth century, Capt. Lorenzo Cancio's words of a generation earlier echoed throughout the pueblos and presidios of the Sonoran piedmont, where political alliances shifted, "old" and "new" enemies were increasingly difficult to distinguish, and village governance was refracted across different poles of civilian and military authority. Even as commoners may have chaffed under the privileges of the cabildo and presidial officers, they knew how to set limits to their leaders' power to command. Physical mobility and the capacity to survive outside the agrarian village sustained meaningful resistance, even without resorting to open defiance. Without the común, indigenous captains and governors held empty titles; lacking a constituency, their authority was meaningless. Spanish imperial hegemony, social control, and the colonial indigenous community were contingent upon a political culture that required consensus among different strata of an increasingly complex frontier society, comprised of changing identities across class, ethnic, and gender lines.

NOTES

1. Provincias Internas 48, 1 fols. 27–36, Archivo General de la Nación, Mexico (hereafter cited as AGN).

2. *Vecino* signifies a Hispanic landholding resident of a given place with political rights to elect or be elected to the local *cabildo* (town council); however, in a more general sense, *vecinos* describes non-Indian residents of the Spanish-American colonies, both men and women, whose occupations could range from merchant to miner, landholder, artisan, and farmer or rancher of varying economic means. See Cynthia Radding, *Wandering Peoples: Colonialism, Ethnic Spaces, and Ecological Frontiers in Northwestern Mexico, 1700–1850* (Durham, N.C.: Duke University Press, 1997), 161–65, 362; Ross Frank, *From Settler to Citizen: New Mexican Economic Development and the Creation of Vecino Society, 1750–1820* (Berkeley: University of California Press, 2000), 1, 294.

3. In Nueva Vizcaya (Zacatecas, Durango, and Chihuahua) and Sonora the principal religious orders authorized to establish reducciones were the Jesuits (Society of Jesus) and the Franciscans, from the Colleges of San Fernando, Guadalupe of Zacatecas, and Santa Cruz of Querétaro as well as the Province of Jalisco.

4. Radding, *Wandering Peoples*, 10. Similar observations are made by Nancy Farriss, "Nucleation versus Dispersal: The Dynamics of Population Movement in Colonial Yucatán," *Hispanic American Historical Review* 58, 2 (1978): 187–216; Ramón Gutiérrez, *When Jesus Came, the Corn Mothers Went Away: Marriage, Sexuality, and Power in New Mexico, 1500–1846* (Stanford: Stanford University Press, 1991), xx–xxii, 22; John Kessell, *Kiva, Cross, and Crown: The Pecos Indians and New Mexico, 1540–1840* (Washington, D.C.: National Park Service, U.S. Dept. of the Interior, 1979), passim.

5. Thomas E. Sheridan, ed., *Empire of Sand: The Seri Indians and the Struggle for Spanish Sonora, 1645–1803* (Tucson: University of Arizona Press, 1999).

6. Carroll L. Riley, *The Frontier People: The Greater Southwest in the Protohistoric Period* (Albuquerque: University of New Mexico Press, 1987); William E. Doolittle, *Pre-Hispanic Occupance in the Valley of Sonora, Mexico: Archeological Confirmation of Early Spanish Reports* (Tucson: University of Arizona Press, 1988); Daniel Reff, *Disease, Depopulation, and Culture Change in Northwestern New Spain, 1518–1764* (Salt Lake City: University of Utah Press, 1991).

7. Radding, *Wandering Peoples*, 171–75, 358.

8. William E. Doolittle, "Aboriginal Agricultural Development in the Valley of Sonora, Mexico," *Geographical Review* 70, 3 (1980): 328–42; Gary Nabhan, *The Desert Smells Like Rain: A Naturalist in Papago Indian Country* (San Francisco: North Point Press, 1982); Gary Nabhan and Thomas E.Sheridan, "Living Fencerow of the Río San Miguel, Sonora, Mexico: Traditional Technology for Floodplain Management," *Human Ecology* 5, 2 (1977): 97–111.

9. Charles W. Polzer, *Rules and Precepts of the Jesuit Missions of Northern New Spain* (Tucson: University of Arizona Press, 1976), 1–58; Peter Gerhard, *The North Frontier of New Spain* (1982; rev. ed.; Norman: University of Oklahoma Press, 1993), 161–74.

10. Ignacio del Río, "El noroeste novohispano y la nueva política imperial española," in *Historia General de Sonora*, II (Hermosillo, Mexico: Gobierno del Estado de Sonora, 1985), 193–219.

11. Robert Haskell, *Indigenous Rulers*, 95–99. Haskell wisely counsels, however, that the Nahuatl terms do not necessarily translate in function from their pre-Hispanic referents to their colonial usages.

12. Robert West, *Sonora: Its Geographical Personality* (Austin: University of Texas Press, 1993), 62–66, appendix D; *Sellos* for obtaining Indians to work in Sonoran mines under the *repartimiento* system, 1684, 1714, Archivo Histórico de Hacienda, *Temporalidades* 325, exp. 87, AGN.

13. *Alguacil*, defined by the *Diccionario de la Lengua Española*, Real Academia Española, 19th ed., (Madrid, 1970), 61. Haskell, *Indigenous Rulers*, 98–99.

14. Juan Nentvig, *Descripción geográfica, natural y curiosa de la provincia de Sonora*, ed. Germán Viveros (Mexico City: Archivo General de la Nación, 1971), 164–65.

15. Charles Gibson, *Aztecs under Spanish Rule: A History of the Indians of the Valley of Mexico, 1519–1810* (Stanford: Stanford University Press, 1964); *Tlaxcala in the Sixteenth Century* (New Haven, Conn.: Yale University Press, 1952); Robert Haskett, *Indigenous Rulers: An Ethnohistory of Town Government in Colonial Cuernavaca* (Albuquerque: University of New Mexico Press, 1991); James Lockhart, *The Nahuas after the Conquest: A Social and Cultural History of the Indians of Central Mexico, Sixteenth through Eighteenth Centuries* (Stanford: Stanford University Press, 1992).

16. Ignaz Pfefferkorn, *Sonora: A Description of the Province*, trans. and ed. T. Treutlein (1795; Tucson: University of Arizona Press, 1989), 266–67ff.

17. Nentvig, *Descripción . . . de Sonora*, 165.

18. Bernd Hausberger, "La violencia en la conquista espiritual: Las misiones jesuitas de Sonora," *Jahrbuch für Geschichte von Staat, Wirtschaft und Gesellschaft Lateinomerikas* 30 (1991): 27–54.

19. Nentvig, *Descripción . . . de Sonora*, 165.

20. Radding, *Wandering Peoples*, 146–50.

21. Radding, *Wandering Peoples*, 256–63, 276–79; John L. Kessell, *Friars, Soldiers, and Reformers: Hispanic Arizona and the Sonora Mission Frontier, 1767–1856* (Tucson: University of Arizona Press, 1976), 137–38.

22. Los pimas de Xecatacari y Obiachi solicitan a Tomás de Esquibel, teniente de justicia mayor del Real de San Miguel Arcángel, de la Provincia de Sonora, para fundar un pueblo en Buenavista, Ramo Civil doc. 27-9-359, 26 Mayo de 1716, 15 fojas, Archivo de la Real Audiencia de Guadalajara, Biblioteca Pública del Estado de Jalisco, Mexico. Published in Radding, *Entre el desierto y la sierra: Las naciones o'odham y Tegüima de Sonora, 1530–1840* (Mexico: INI, CIESAS 1995), 139–53. In 1742, a presidio was established in Buena Vista. Captain Lorenzo Cancio, cited in the opening epigram for this chapter, was commander of this presidio in 1766.

23. Ibid., fol. 1; Radding, *Wandering Peoples*, 170–75.

24. Representación del Padre comisario de las misiones, fray Juan Prestamero, sobre quejas de los ópatas contra el padre ministro de Opodepe. Cuaderno 2, año de 1777, Fondo Franciscano 34/735, 1777, 19 fojas, Biblioteca Nacional, Mexico (hereafter cited as BN); [Correspondence among Manuel Grijalba, Ópata governor of the pueblo of Opodepe, Pedro Tueros, the commander of the Presidio of San Miguel de Horcasitas, and Brigadier Theodoro de Croix, first Commandant General of the Internal Provinces.], Fondo Franciscano 40/912, 1778–1779, 11 fojas, BN. Opodepe, the head village, and Nacameri, its *visita* are located northwest of the Presidio of Horcasitas.

25. On division of communal lands, see Fondo Franciscano 35/722, BN; Radding, *Wandering Peoples*, 188–93.

26. Radding, *Wandering Peoples*, 288–91; Fondo Franciscano 35/767, fols. 3–11, BN; "Conflicto entre autoridades indígenas ópatas y militares (1798–1790)," in Radding, *Entre el desierto y la sierra*, 179–83. The following episode is based on these documents. A league is approximately 4 kilometers (2.4 miles).

27. Gil Samaniego and Gregorio Ortiz Cortés were landowners in the fertile valley between Bacerac and Bavispe. The two families were related by marriage. As *teniente de alcalde mayor*, Ortiz Cortés functioned as the judicial authority for the Bavispe valley northeast of the provincial capital of Arizpe, in Sonora.

28. Fray Ángel Antonio Núñez Fundidor, *Carta Edificante, Bacerac en 1777: Carta edificante de Fray Angel Antonio Núñez Fundidor*, ed. Julio César Montané Martí (Hermosillo, Mexico: Contrapunto 14, 1999), 67; Archivo Histórico de Hacienda leg. 278, exp. 20, AGN.

29. Radding, *Wandering Peoples*, documents in detail the processes of social differentiation among both indigenous and Hispanic peasant populations of colonial Sonora in terms of property allocation and changing ethnic identities. See especially chaps. 5, 6, and 7 (pp. 142–245).

30. Edward H. Spicer, *The Yaquis: A Cultural History* (Tucson: University of Arizona Press, 1980), 59–113; Cynthia Radding, "Crosses, Caves, and *Matachinis*: Divergent Appropriations of Catholic Discourse in Northwestern New Spain," *The Americas* 55, 2 (1998): 177–201; Campbell Pennington, *The Pima Bajo of Central Sonora* (2 vols., Salt Lake City: University of Utah Press, 1979) 1:149–50.

31. *Nijoras*, in Sonora, were identified as a "tribe" in early colonial maps and documents, but the term referred to captives separated from their communities of origin. See H. Dobyns et al., "What Were Nixoras?" *Southwestern Journal of Anthropology* 16, 2 (1960): 230–68; Julio Montané, "De *nijoras* y 'españoles a medias,'" *XV Simposio de Historia de Sonora* (Hermosillo, Mexico: Universidad de Sonora, 1990). See also James F. Brooks, "'This Evil Extends Especially... to the Feminine Sex': Negotiating Captivity in the New Mexico Borderlands," *Feminist Studies* 22, 2 (1996): 279–309.

32. Radding, *Wandering Peoples*, 126–41, 161–65; Archivo del Sagrario Caja 22, Padrón de 1796, Archivo de la Mitra, Hermosillo; *Jesuitas* IV–10, exp. 231, fol. 266, AGN.

33. Florencia Mallon, *Peasant and Nation: The Making of Postcolonial Mexico and Peru* (Berkeley: University of California Press, 1995), 63–88.

Sistema de castas (social castes) was a porous racial classification system in colonial New Spain

"hierarchal ordering of racial groups according to their proportion of spanish blood"

CHAPTER NINE

Racialized Hierarchies of Power in Colonial Mexican Society

The *Sistema de Castas* as a Form of Social Control in Saltillo

José Cuello

The creation of racialized societies in unprecedented numbers and sizes is one of the most enduring and pervasive consequences of the West European colonization of the Americas.[1] In these societies racialized identities (coded by skin color and defined by collective stereotypes) played a major role in organizing human relations at all levels. All of the public and private inter-actions of the socially constructed "races" were governed by values, orga-nizational structures, and mechanisms of enforcement (both formal and informal) that systematically elevated one racial identity over all others.[2]

   The Spanish created one of the most complex racialized social structures in the Americas when they reinvented the indigenous city-states of Meso-america into the Euroamerican polity of New Spain. The European colonial enterprise achieved this by seizing physical control over large populations

I would like to thank my colleagues of the social control group for their collective assistance in shaping this essay, particularly Frank de la Teja and David Weber for their insightful editorial recommendations. I would also like to thank my colleague Jorge L. Chinea at Wayne State University for his thorough reading and suggestions.

evaluation of genetic qualities as inferior

from two other branches of the human family. The Spanish ideological paradigm justified the violent conquest of American Indians and the massive enslavement of Africans by devaluing their phenotypes and cultures as inferior and illegitimate. At a time when state-level societies were unequivocally hierarchical in organization, the colonial apparatus confined millions of non-European peoples and their descendants to the permanent role of laboring and tributary classes at the bottom of the new social pyramid.

The Spanish labeled the colonial order in New Spain the *sistema* (or *sociedad*) *de castas*, a system of racial castes. Each "race" was a complicated social construct centered in the indelible, but often blurred, badge of skin color. The chief method for separating the major classes in society evolved, by design and ad hoc adaptation, into a hierarchy of color-coded categories of citizenship. These were used to profile everyone in society with stereotypical social roles that reinforced the primacy of everything Spanish. Each social race was equipped with a wide and flexible range of legal and informal characteristics that defined its role, even contradicted it, within the boundaries of the system.[3] As we shall see, the caste system had areas of very sharp definition. Spanish identities always got the best positions. It also had areas of ambiguity. *Mestizaje* (miscegenation) blurred the racial boundaries, while economic roles and racial statuses could not be made to completely fit each other.

Elements of a Racialized Society

Three racialized groups—Iberians, Amerindians, and Africans—constituted the initial New World colonial order. The Spanish assigned themselves the prime social position on the ideological basis of descent from good Christian ancestors. This combination of biology and ascribed inherited religious merit was known as "purity of blood." The standard was used in Spain to discriminate against anyone of Jewish or Moorish descent and against Spaniards who did not possess noble bloodlines.[4] Similarly, the Europeans ascribed inferior positions on their racial hierarchy to the descendants of the heathen and heretic peoples of the Americas and Africa whom they brought into the colonial setting. The colonizers created a race of *indios* ("Indians") as they homogenized thousands of native groups and cultures into a racialized identity by arbitrarily attributing inferior genetic, moral, and cultural characteristics to them. In a parallel process of societal construction, they simplified the rich cultural diversity of Africans into the narrow, dehumanized category of *negros* ("blacks"), who filled the growing demand for plantation field workers and domestic servants in the Americas.[5]

The rise of three major intermediate groups buffered the parent races from each other in social status and further complicated the European-controlled social hierarchy. Two of the groups were composed of individuals of mixed racial descent: the mestizos (genetic combinations of Spanish and Indian) and mulattos (genetic combinations of Spanish and African). Individuals of more complex racial descent were generally assigned one of these two major identities, or that of one of the parent races, as part of the process of social group construction.

The logic of racialized colonization also reached into the dominant European group and created what might be called a pseudo-race. *Criollos*, or *españoles americanos* (Spaniards born in America), occupied a lower racial status than that enjoyed by *españoles europeos* (European Spaniards, also known as *peninsulares* and *gachupines*) who emigrated to the New World. It profited European Spaniards politically and socially to believe that the New World's natural and cultural environments produced American Spaniards who were inferior to those of the metropolis. Belief and policy were reinforced by the existence, from the first post-conquest generation, of biological mestizos who acquired social identities as criollos. They were the paternally legitimized children of the conquerors by Indian women. Peninsulares thus treated criollos as racial cousins whom they needed to control, both domestically and from abroad, along with the more inferior groups. The principle of racial domination and the principle of colonial domination thus reinforced each other even among elites, on whom, as Alfredo Jiménez points out in his chapter, the king depended to maintain social control over colonial society as a whole.[6]

All societies are based on varying combinations of *other-imposed* and *self-imposed* social controls. The first occurs when one group imposes its will on other groups through legal and informal mechanisms. The second occurs when subordinate groups adopt elite-prescribed behavior as the accepted norm. Colonial Spanish-American societies were usually initiated by conquest. Violent, *other-imposed* forms of social control characterized the early stages of their formations. Protracted conflictive relations between Spanish invaders and unassimilated, resisting natives, as Juliana Barr's example of the Texas frontier makes clear, functioned as forms of social control when they affected the internal working of one or both of the competing groups. The more physical forms of Spanish exploitation predominated until the subordinated populations became integrated into their ascribed social locations, and adopted the custom of negotiating their conditions within the limits of the hierarchical and inequitable system, as Cynthia Radding explains happened in colonial Sonora. In highly-integrated social systems such as the late-eighteenth-century Louisiana of Gilbert Din's chapter, the police and judicial systems enforced the legal and extra-legal conditions of subordinate groups. Saltillo experienced an evolution from the more violent forms of social control to the more routine combination of external and internalized forms of socialization over the course of two and a half centuries.[7]

The history of Saltillo, within the context of the larger colonial world, suggests the sistema de castas was a much more flexible and fluid system of social control than its portrayal in the historiography. The standard interpretation is that of an urban social structure that rose to maturity in the seventeenth century and gradually disintegrated by the end of the eighteenth century in the Mexican colony and elsewhere in Spanish America. Historians base their interpretation of decline on two observations. One is that countless mestizos, mulattos, and Indians were able to change their public racial identities at will as a result of miscegenation among members of the lower groups. The other is that the occupational structures of urban locations were not neatly segregated by race in the lower sectors of society. It is believed that the large numbers of criollos in the laboring sector and the penetration of non-Spaniards into the artisan sectors undermined the effectiveness of the sistema de castas as a system of racialized social control.[8] Researchers have hypothesized that the pressure of commercial capitalism undermined the sistema in favor of an economic class system in the late colonial cities of Oaxaca and Guadalajara.[9] A corollary of the thesis of decline is that widespread racial passing on the frontier prevented the sistema's full development in the colonial North. In fact, the great diversity of form in how the colonial system realized itself in the numerous cities and regions of the Spanish American empire raises the question of whether the sistema de castas even existed in many of the places whose history we study.[10]

The interpretation of core region decline and frontier debility of the sistema de castas arises from its mistaken association with the rigid structure of the Hindu caste system of India. Accordingly, impermeable boundaries should have prevented social and occupational mobility among the races. The sistema de castas, however, is best understood as the result of a

racial principle that ordered the hierarchy of major social groups in interaction with the principles of gender, socioeconomic status, and political citizenship.[11] The ideology of Spanish racial and cultural superiority organized
Spanish relations with other groups. It shaped the strategies for incorporating external groups into colonial society. It directed the creation of the
colonial social structures and the subsequent adjustments that were necessary to maintain them.[12]

The racialized core principle of the system thus allowed the Spanish
to create colonial social structures in diverse environments. Both the colonizers and the colonized shaped the system in each location. The Crown
and colonial elites worked diligently to tighten the system of unequal citizenship through the requirement of racial purity ("purity of blood") for
all social positions of importance; and through their control of elite inter-
racial and interclass marriages.[13] Nonelite groups negotiated their identities and roles in the social order—or their exclusion from it—through
different combinations of political, economic, and cultural strengths and
weaknesses at all levels of colonial life over the course of three centuries.
Scholars have shown that the sistema de castas in any given place was
shaped by a number of factors. The major ones included gender ratios, the
presence or absence of one or more of the socially constructed races, the
need to fill essential occupational niches, the effectiveness of colonial laws,
the highly varied positions taken by the Church and clergy, and the strategies of adaptation and resistance by subaltern (socially subordinate) groups.
Parts of the standard tool kit of racial categories and mechanisms of implementation were often modified, replaced, or discarded—like interchange-
able modules or custom-made parts—as warranted by the specific social
ecologies.[14] Yet, the organizing racial principle created comparable patterns of culture across the regional variations of Spanish colonial society.
The spatial, temporal, and contextual fluidity of the sistema de castas thus
reinforced, rather than subverted, the racialized inequality that served as
the foundation for the European-dominated colonial social structure. The
perceived weakness of the sistema de castas in the Spanish settlements on
the northern rim of empire and its comparative strength in more central
locations were, in reality, manifestations of the highly successful adaptation of the same organizing principle to different environments.[15]

Saltillo's colonial history may be divided into four periods. These include
the local conquest and founding generations (1577–1625), seventeenth-
century depression (1625–1650s), recovery, growth, and crystallization

(1650s–1760s), followed by the era of Bourbon Reforms and imperial crisis (1760s–1821). Each period was characterized by different combinations of social control as changing combinations of peninsular and criollo elites sought to impose their hegemony on the rest of the groups, including poor criollos, who composed the local society. The following is a brief account of the types of social controls that characterized each of Saltillo's evolutionary stages.[16]

Local Conquest and Founding Generations (1577–1625)

Violent *other-imposed* forms of social control characterized the first three decades of Saltillo's history. The European invasion of Coahuila, Nuevo León, and Texas established patterns for the long-term forced exploitation of the tens of thousands of hunter-gatherers who inhabited northeastern New Spain.[17] The Spanish invaders did not recognize the property rights of the nomadic bands to their own land and labor because the *chichimecas* (the generic Aztec name for the nomads) were not sedentary agriculturalists. The regional conquerors and their descendants treated the indigenous population as an exploitable resource like land, water, and silver. They thus enslaved the natives as enemies of the Spanish state in "just war" for export to the mining centers. Within the region, the founders of the new Spanish order forced chichimecas into servitude as labor tributaries through the conquest institution of *encomienda*. This legal device reduced the Indians to political, economic, cultural, and spiritual wards of meritorious conquerors and colonizers. Since the nomads could not pay tribute in kind or in coin, the Spaniards treated the Northeast as a vast reserve of human labor for their economic activities. This was a contrast to the central Mexican model of encomienda imposed on agricultural communities whose labor tribute was taken over by the royal government even before Saltillo was founded.[18] Like other components of the racialized system of colonial exploitation, encomienda was a highly flexible mechanism of control.

The violent crucible of foundation created an incipient social structure in Saltillo held together by physical force. A small group of *encomendero-labradores* (farmers with encomiendas), who received grants of both Indian tributaries and land with water, occupied the top of the nascent social hierarchy. A roughly equal number of propertyless Spanish employees and craftsmen in the service of the elite formed the next highest group. *Castas* (mestizos, mulattos, and negros) were so few in number that they were not yet significant as a social group. Below the two Spanish economic group-ings was the much larger population of chichimeca migratory workers that formed the laboring base of the social pyramid. Conquest society was far from integrated, but the ideology of Spanish superiority and the effective social control of the native peoples were firmly established. The dominant Spanish social identity was constructed on the basis of racio-réligious "purity of blood" and the social honor that the regional conquerors achieved for themselves and their descendants through their military service to God and king. The Indian social identity became defined by servitude, legal minority, the inherited stain of recent heathenism, and the inferiority attributed to nomadic cultures by state-level civilizations.[19]

The adaptability of the racially constructed character of Spanish colo-nialism is clearly illustrated by the Tlaxcaltecan pueblo of San Esteban, estab-lished in 1591 adjacent to Saltillo to secure the Spanish settlement. It was organized as a separate social order, a *república de indios*, in the manner of its central Mexican counterparts. The Tlaxcaltecan republic was modified by two factors that distinguished it from most subordinate Indian communities. San Esteban's *vecinos* earned the status of equals to españoles as a reward for their military role in colonizing the northern frontier. As first-class citizens, they could bear arms and ride horses. They were exempted from the tribute obligation of other Indians. The constructed Tlaxcaltecan identity included a "purity of blood" equivalent to that of Spaniards. In the eighteenth century, at least two Tlaxcaltecans from San Esteban obtained legal certifications that they descended from old Christian families untainted by Moorish or Jewish blood so that they could enter religious orders.[20]

Equality with Spaniards, however, was limited by an equal-but-separate condition. Tlaxcaltecans were prevented from functioning politically, eco-nomically, or socially as Spaniards outside the boundaries of their closed cor-porate community. Rather, the preservation of their privileged Indian status required them to concentrate on preventing members of other races from taking up residence and citizenship within San Esteban. They thus preserved their status through a jealously guarded distinct political citizenship, resi-dential segregation, and racial endogamy. The Tlaxcaltecans deftly added to the construction of their racial purity by glossing over the genetic and cul-tural absorption of the large group of chichimecas that had been assigned to them for acculturation. Cynthia Radding's chapter more amply illustrates the kinds of privileges that Indian communities could obtain within the sys-tem by providing some type of service to the Crown.[21]

Seventeenth-Century Depression (1625–1650s)

Saltillo suffered a crisis of capital and credit from the mid-1620s to the mid-1650s that exposed the conflictive potential in the colonial relationship between the peninsular *alcaldes mayores* and American-born encomendero-labradores. The alcaldes mayores were merchants who bought their positions as chief executive officers in the locality from the governors of Nueva Vizcaya. The peninsulares effectively "Indianized" the criollos by advancing merchandise to the farmers in anticipation of the harvest through a system of credit akin to the *repartimiento* (distribution) of merchandise used by their counterparts to exploit Indian communities in central Mexico. After the provincial governor suspended Saltillo's *cabildo* (town council) in 1627 to weaken the farmers' resistance, the alcaldes mayores dominated Saltillo's one-person government and small commercial market until almost the end of the seventeenth century. Their major competitors in the exercise of local power were the parish priests, whose spiritual authority was complemented by their ability to extract religious fees from Saltillo's citizens and engage in commercial agriculture.[22] The systemic economic and social control to which Saltillo's Spanish farmers were subjected eroded their capacity to exercise their own form of social control over the hunter-gatherers. The farmers' inability to fully utilize the land or labor that they acquired from the chichimecas contributed to the decline of encomienda and to the rise of wage labor and debt peonage in the next period of Saltillo's history.[23]

Despite their poverty, Saltillo's criollo farmers continued the conquest-engendered practice of *other-imposed* violence in order to extract labor from the indigenous population. Militias of armed farmers provoked resistance from indigenous groups and accelerated the transformation of the hunter-gatherers into resident farm workers and domestic servants. The native labor pool outside of colonial society dried up over the course of the seventeenth century as a result of labor exploitation and war. The process of territorial reconstruction, analyzed by Cecilia Sheridan in her chapter, made it more difficult to enslave natives who lived farther and farther away and who responded with violence of their own against Spanish society. In 1668, 1695, and 1711, Saltillo's vecinos complained to the local authorities that Indian males were luring female servants away from their homes with promises of marriage. In the last two complaints, the vecinos stated that the servants had either been captured in war or had been raised in their homes from childhood. The dual process of absorption and annihilation caused Indians with identities as hunter-gatherers to disappear in the late seventeenth and early eighteenth centuries. The creation of a generic "Indian" population that was integrated into colonial society in Saltillo produced a permanent and sedentary multiracial labor force and resulted in a shift to less violent forms of social control. In the self-reproducing logic of the racialized colonial system, the local criollo elites added to their social prestige and status by earning military commissions for the violent "pacification" of the natives.[24]

Recovery, Growth, and Crystallization (1650s–1760s)

Saltillo experienced a period of economic recovery and population growth from the 1650s to the 1760s, as part of a colony-wide pattern. Saltillo's farmers found a more diversified market for their staples, and economic expansion brought about the growth of its population, which reached a plateau of 11,000 persons for the whole valley in the 1760s. The economic recovery and demographic expansion produced a process of socioeconomic involution that resulted in the crystallization of a mature multiclass social structure ordered by the sistema de castas.[25] The merchants and alcaldes mayores continued to battle the labradores over payment of goods and cash advanced against the wheat harvests. However, the cabildo reemerged as a countervailing authority at the end of the seventeenth century. The power of the alcades mayores to abuse the consumers of Saltillo was further weakened by the population's ability to support a larger number of merchants.[26]

[margin note: population growth]

[margin note: emergence of central authority]

For the criollo farmers it mattered little that they had many creditors instead of one. They, and their dependent artisans and workers, were subject to economic and political controls that translated into social controls. Every aspect of their lives was structured by Saltillo's condition as an internal colony. Miguel Ramos Arizpe, the father of Mexican federalism, represented Saltillo and the Northeast to the Spanish Cortes (parliament) of 1812. He characterized the inhabitants of the Northeast as subject to an economic slavery in which they had to export the very necessities of life in order to pay for overpriced manufactured imports. The annual trade fair at Saltillo was a scandalous theater where northeasterners went to pay the tribute of their shameful economic servitude.[27]

Saltillo's criollo farmers were also caught between the complementary forces of local demographic growth and Spanish inheritance laws. The majority grew increasingly poorer through the subdivision of the land among ever-larger numbers of family heirs. Saltillo's haciendas evolved into hamlets of small farmers akin to the rural populations of *rancheros* (small farmers) that emerged in regions to the south like Morelos, the Bajío, Tlaxcala, Puebla, and Guadalajara. On a colony-wide level, the rancheros constituted a multilayered rural middle sector between the Spanish owners of large estates and the Indian peasant communities. In Saltillo the labradores saw themselves obligated to work the land more intensively with family members. They lived in a state of perpetual indebtedness against the temporary economic relief promised by each harvest. Only a few individuals defied the predominant trend and built new haciendas from the pieces of subdivided units.[28]

Bourbon Reforms and Imperial Crisis (1760s–1821)

The last period of Saltillo's historical evolution, from the 1760s to independence, saw the pattern of global prosperity and farmer impoverishment modified by the intrusion of imperial forces, while the social structure became more complex.[29] Metropolitan transatlantic controls were tightened to increase economic revenues for the Crown and provide greater political and economic opportunities for peninsular immigrants in New Spain. Saltillo felt the impact of the reformist climate across the colony. From the 1760s onward, peninsulares gained dominance in the cabildo, asserted renewed control of commerce, and moved into land ownership. The so-called Bourbon Reforms amounted to a recolonization of Mexico, adding new layers of peninsular bureaucratic control at the regional and local levels. Criollos lost representation at the upper levels of government. The enforcement of "racial purity" and status equality was tightened in elite marriages. The reforms and the crisis of empire that followed Napoleon's seizure of the Spanish Crown in 1808 taxed away the vitality of the local and regional economies. The consequent wars for Mexican independence created instability in the town's government, as most of the peninsular members of the town council fled their posts for several years.[30] The losses suffered by Saltillo led its inhabitants to break their ties with the empire. On July 19, 1821, the cabildos of Saltillo and San Esteban joined to declare their support for Mexican independence.[31] The criollo subcaste thus gained its freedom from the higher peninsular caste and its ideology of racial purity, which had deprived the criollos of control of their own homeland.

The Multiple Dimensions of Spanish Racial Ideology

We now turn from the long view of Saltillo's colonial development to look for social control in a more horizontal examination of the racialized hierarchies of power. The mature society of eighteenth-century colonial Mexico was not a one-dimensional structure in which the different races were simply stacked upon each other. The Spanish elites who set the norms of colonial Mexican society classified the population in a number of bipartite and tripartite divisions that reinforced the racial structure. The most fundamental basis of division defined race in religious terms. Only Spaniards in the New World could claim religious and spiritual purity through descent from family ancestors who possessed uncontaminated bloodlines. A second two-part division separated the *gente de razón* (the Old World races possessing full human reason) from the (New World) Indians who were considered moral, intellectual, and legal minors. This division was formalized by the establishment of parallel legal systems to segregate the Indians from the other races in the colony. The indigenous communities were constituted into the república de indios, a system of territorial reservations in which the Indians governed their own communities under the supervision of royal officials and clerics. The rest of the Spanish colonial world constituted the *república de españoles*. This was a world of Europeans and the Europeanized who needed no special wardship to protect them. A third two-part division distinguished the nontributary populations (Spaniards and mestizos) from the tributary groups (Indians, free mulattos, and free negros) and slaves (African-descent and some Indians).

The colonizers reshuffled the classifications by grouping the mestizos, mulattos, and the shrinking number of negros into the larger classification of castas. This created a tripartite social order of Spaniards (racially superior, adult status), castas (racially inferior, adult status), and Indians (racially inferior, minor status). The castas were further subdivided into the *castas limpias* (clean castes), or *castas buenas* (good castes), composed of *castizos* and mestizos and the *raza mala* (bad race) of African descent. Within the convolutions of Spanish racial ideology, Indians were credited with a purity of blood that Africans were denied. Thus, Spanish-Indian genetic combinations were superior to Spanish-African or Indian-African combinations.[32]

Apart from the racialized peninsular-criollo division, the Spanish expanded a preexisting internal socioeconomic differentiation to include other racial groups and reinforce the racialized social order. The Spanish colonial elite distinguished itself, the *gente decente* (decent society) from the *plebe* (the general populace). This second group included not only castas and Indians, but also commoner Spaniards without major economic resources or high social status. The elite sector viewed criollo commoners as little better than the inferior races and as a corrupting influence on the Indians. The colonial elite did not think solely in terms of economic groups, but wealth was an important requirement for membership in the gente decente. Since not all Spaniards could be elites, the Spanish group was itself stratified into a class-like structure. The other races were also internally differentiated according to economic, political, and social conditions within the stunting racial ceilings set by the effectiveness of the colonial system in different regions.

An individual's socially defined race was constructed by one's physical appearance and its interwoven relationships with forms of social valuation and positioning that included birthplace, legitimacy of birth, family descent and reputation, personal honor, wealth, occupation, level of education, political prestige, marriage, and dress. Spaniards used the term *calidad* to sum up a person's total combination of biological and sociocultural worth. Race and calidad were ideologically synonymous. The idealized Spaniard was the prototype for a member of the gente decente: Old Christian, legitimate, pure blood, honorable, law-abiding, rich, noble, and unsullied by manual labor. The stereotypical casta, on the other hand, was the prototype for the dregs of the plebian masses: New Christian, illegitimate, contaminated of blood, disreputable, criminal, poor, and a manual worker.[33]

The boundaries of color and prestige were weakest at the lowest level of the social structure. Poor Spaniards still had the color of their skin, the legal system of racial discrimination, and stronger networks with more privileged Spaniards to give them an edge over the castas and Indians. They enjoyed an advantage in the competition for jobs, housing, spouses, and other resources. Yet, poor Spaniards represented the soft underbelly of Spanish racism. They were more likely to fall into exogamous marriages with castas and Indians. It was also easier for members of the two latter groups to acquire identities as poor Spaniards than identities as elites or middle-sector Spaniards. Without documented purity of blood, wealth, high-level occupations, literacy, and honorable marital alliances, neither poor Spaniards nor castas and Indians masquerading as Spaniards could pose a threat to the system of white Spanish privilege. Upward advancement in the social hierarchy was blocked by an interlocking complex of power and privilege that could only be unlocked by a number of codes that were inaccessible to the common person. The slight-of-body-and-race deception was beyond reach for the great majority of castas and Indians. Families of racially mixed backgrounds that had children with the "right" phenotypes might be able to place them in higher racial categories. However, the fortunate winners of the racial phenotype roulette found that acquiring an artificial Spanish identity, beyond a superficial color-of-the-skin valuation, carried the high price of disowning one's family and its thick web of social relations.

A small number of castas, who were too dark-skinned to pass as Spanish whites, still managed to acquire levels of wealth beyond their racial norms. They found their path to social and political advancement blocked by Spanish law and prejudice, or slightly facilitated by local tolerance. It was the great- *dishonor* est insult for a Spaniard to be called a mulatto, and it was the greatest stain on a Spanish family's honor for a member to marry a mulatto, both in Saltillo and in the rest of the colony. For those who carried the badge of dishonor in their skin, the reminders of their ascribed inferiority were constant.[34] Opportunities for castas to move upward improved in the simplified and fluid structures of conquests and frontier zones where Spaniards themselves often lacked the full complement of inherited and earned merits required of elites in more central locations. The fluidity of racial identities on the rim of the empire, however, should not obscure the power of the constructed Spanish identity in organizing colonial society in locations like Texas, New Mexico, and California. People of color affirmed that power every time they claimed the privileges of first-class, white Spanish citizenship.[35]

The Crystallization of Saltillo's Racial Structure

The power of the Spanish racial identity and its privileged position can be illustrated by dividing Saltillo's social structure of the early eighteenth century into four economic sectors for analytical purposes. A handful of prosperous merchants and labradores monopolized the top of the hierarchy. Most were members of local criollo families that managed to combine landownership, commercial farming, and trade to accumulate sizable personal and family fortunes. They were joined by peninsulares who established mercantile networks in the Northeast and married into local elite families. Together, they monopolized the town's political and religious structures. The more prominent peninsulares bought the office of alcalde mayor but did not buy land until after 1760. Small-time criollo landowners and petty merchants formed an upper middle sector. Criollos with very small amounts of property in land, water, and livestock, together with artisans, made up a third economic sector. Criollos, who only had their personal labor with which to sustain themselves, joined the growing laboring sector. The great majority of castas and the socially constructed colonial Indians earned their livelihood as members of this group.[36] The widespread distribution of criollos across the various levels of economic activities in Saltillo was not unusual for a Spanish town in colonial Mexico.[37] What was important was Spanish control of all of the power positions in society, the two top economic levels, and most of the third.

The parish priests of Saltillo left us their vision of the intersection of the racial and economic hierarchies in the baptismal and marriage records they kept in the first half of the eighteenth century.[38] The priests combined economic reality with a compatible dose of stereotyping when they identified members of the different racial groups as being in the service of (*del servicio de*) other persons. Spaniards were the only ones ever identified as employers and they were almost never identified as employees. Mestizos and *coyotes* (a local equivalent of mestizos) were identified as servants only with a rare frequency that places them closer to the Spaniards than to the other racial groups. *Mulatos libres* and *lobos* (mixed African and Indian descent) were identified much more frequently than mestizos as servants. Indians were identified as being in *del servicio de* more than any other group except mulatto and negro slaves.[39] The baptismal records indicate that Indians were born into the service of their parents' employers, thus acquiring a slave-like status. The local clergy's view of the racial and occupational identities of their parishioners reflected the distinction drawn by the colonial elite between the castas limpias (españoles, mestizos, and coyotes) and the *mala raza* of African descent. The categories also reflected the difference between the nontributary and tributary (and slave) populations; and the status of Indians as inferior to all others in the economic hierarchy, except black slaves.

The emergence of self-conscious local and regional elite groups in Saltillo and the Northeast reflected the colonial difference between the gente decente and the plebe.[40] Elite families in Saltillo subjected themselves to a form of social control when they followed a general colonial pattern by intermarrying with other elite families in the Northeast to preserve their positions as the local equivalent of the colonial gente decente. Families and clans arose throughout the Northeast whose members made extraordinary efforts to maintain their "purity of blood" and social honor by securing dispensations from the bishops of Guadalajara to marry their cousins in the third, fourth, and fifth degrees. In the years from 1653 to 1779, Spanish couples from the Northeast obtained at least 1,100 dispensations to avoid the dishonorable alternative of marrying mulattos, negros, and Indians. The criollo elite also absorbed through marriage the stream of foreign-born male peninsulares who established commercial circuits in the region, thus monopolizing the only unquestioned external source of "racial purity" and genetic regeneration.[41]

Elite families consolidated their power by raising their own priests. Saltillo's elite and middling families shared a cultural imperative with criollos in other regions of the colony when they sent their sons to Guadalajara and Mexico City for training as secular priests and friars. At least nine clerics returned to serve the community during the period 1650–1725.[42] The seminary college of San José in Guadalajara had 950 students between 1699 and 1800 whose places of origin are known. Forty came from Saltillo. Only Guadalajara with 136 students and Aguascalientes with 62 had more pupils than Saltillo.[43] Several local families also established *capellanías* (chaplaincies yielding an annual income of 5 percent on the principal) for the support of their cleric children. Saltillo's elite criollo families thus controlled the moral order and ritual life of the community as well as the economic and political structures.

At the other extreme of the social structure, the condition of African-descent slaves revealed another dimension of how race was socially constructed in Saltillo. Slave women were particularly vulnerable to the sexual abuses of their Spanish male owners. Because their children inherited their mothers' slave status, the result was an increasingly lighter-skinned population of slaves over the course of the eighteenth century. In their investigation of bills of sale for slaves in Saltillo, Carlos Manuel Valdés and Ildefonso Dávila found 120 slaves identified by skin color or racial composition. Only thirteen were recognized as negros. Ninety-three were identified as racially mixed. Fourteen were identified as *blancos* (whites).[44] Some were described as having clear eyes and straight hair. The "white" slaves, however, could not be socially constructed as Spaniards without exposing the contradiction that their condition as legal chattel posed to the racial system. In the very specific case of enslaved females, Saltillo's Spaniards thus applied their own version of the descent rule that assigns anyone with a single drop of African blood to the racial category of "black" in the

United States.[45] White slavery, as an exception to the social norm of colonial society, existed because the sistema de castas allowed for many legal and informal deviations from the dominant fiction in the exercise of social control of other human beings for profit, power, and prestige.

Racialized Hierarchies of Power in the Late Eighteenth Century

The censuses of 1777, 1785–1786, and 1791–1793 further reveal the racial values and structure of Saltillo's local society. The racialized system of social control reduced the degree of ambiguity among the constructed races by dispensing with the more complex permutations for which there was little public social utility. The census-takers classified the heads of household into four dominant racial categories, as would be expected for a colonial Mexican society. Two were primary racial groups, the españoles (54 percent) and the Indians (16 percent). By this time, the negros—the pure African parent category—had all but disappeared and did not register even as a single percent of the population. The other two dominant groups were mixed-race identities, the coyotes/mestizos (13 percent), and the mulattos (14 percent). Castizos and lobos—members of the tertiary racial categories—also did not register one percent of the householders separately.[46]

The patterns of racial endogamy (intramarriage) and exogamy (intermarriage) of the householders and their spouses in the census of 1777 suggest the extent to which persons born into the tertiary racial groups (castizos, *moriscos*, lobos) were reconstituted into members of the secondary (mestizos, mulattos) and primary groups (españoles, Indians). Only nine exogamous español-Indian marriages would have engendered children in a secondary racial group. Almost all of the 26 percent of the total married exogamous population bore children whose identities should have been recorded in the censuses as members of the tertiary racial groups of castizos, moriscos, and lobos. Their absence in the censuses means that individuals born as castizos acquired identities as españoles or coyotes/mestizos. Persons born as moriscos acquired identities as españoles or mulattos. Persons born as entresalvos acquired identities as mestizos or Indians. Persons born as lobos acquired identities as mulattos or Indians. The routine process of collapsing racial identities was a major factor in the formation of the four large racial groupings in Saltillo.

Since the endogamous unions among coyotes and mulattos were also producing racially mixed children, their addition to the exogamous marriages raises the proportion of the married population parenting castas to a very substantial 41 percent. If racial hybrids had been strictly identified and labeled with their appropriate racial identities, the tertiary and more complex racial combinations would have been much larger than the numbers they registered in the censuses. Instead, their racial identities were routinely and systematically reconstructed to absorb them into the parent groups. "Racial passing" was built into the sistema de castas as a normal process in the maintenance of socially defined group differences. Douglas Cope documents a similar pattern of consolidation, rather than proliferation, of racial categories in the parish records of Mexico City.[47] Social control of the subordinate races worked more effectively with a minimum number of racial identities.

The almost complete predominance of the four major groupings at the adult level suggests that the routine changes in identities from tertiary to secondary and to primary groups may have been accomplished prior to the achievement of householder status. Scholars have long suspected that the ritual junctures of baptism and marriage were used to formalize racial identities that were routinely in flux on an informal basis. Baptism was the ritual ceremony that fixed an individual's name, gender, and racial identity, thereby setting in place powerful parameters that determined one's social status and triggered the controls to keep each person in a social position, whether high or low. Robert McCaa concludes that marriage was an occasion for spouses to reduce the differences in their racial identities, but not necessarily in an upward direction.[48] The census-taking process itself was undoubtedly one of the formal mechanisms for concentrating and crystallizing racial identities.

The censuses suggest that racial identities in Saltillo were generally very stable among adults. In the three censuses taken between 1777 and 1793, it is possible to identify only 160 individuals who changed racial identity at least once. They represented 14 percent of the average number of 1,152 householders per census with known racial identities. The changes in identity occurred in more than one direction. If free mulattos are placed above Indians in the racial hierarchy, then 54 percent of the movement in racial identity was downward and 43 percent was upward, with 3 percent horizontal. If free mulattos and Indians are considered to have been socially equal, downward movement still constituted 43 percent of the change in racial identity, while 34 percent was upward and 23 percent was horizontal. The patterns of movement reinforce the interpretations of scholars that changes in racial identity represented a more complex phenomenon than the one-dimensional attempt by individuals to climb the racio-economic ladder. McCaa uses the term "racial drift" and Seed uses the term "racial variability" to avoid the implication suggested by the term "racial passing."[49] The fluctuations in racial identity in Saltillo may reflect little more than the normal ambiguity that characterized the boundaries among the artificially constructed racial groups in society. The social fiction of clear racial lines and identities required by the colonial system of racialized social control needed the power of state-sanctioned ritual to fully actualize itself.

Constructed identities, nevertheless, had real power in organizing society. The patterns of endogamy and exogamy of the major calidades reveal the importance of race in the selection of marital partners. The population of married español householders was a fortress of endogamy at 89 percent, with only 11 percent marrying members of other groups. The other groups had much lower endogamy levels. The Indians, the other primary racial group, held second position at 66 percent. The two mixed races—the coyotes and the mulattos—had the lowest levels of endogamy at 42 percent and 55 percent, respectively. The percentages confirm that españoles were much more concerned with preserving their racial status than the other groups. Coyotes and mulattos were already racially mixed, so their motivation to maintain a racial purity was much weaker. Coyotes even preferred marriages to members of other groups than to persons with their own racial identity. The relatively high endogamy rate of Saltillo's laboring Indians (who did not have communities, land, or cultures to protect) can be read not as an indicator of preference, but as an indicator of limited options. Saltillo's pattern of marital preferences adhered to a general pattern throughout the colonial world.[50]

The power of the español racial identity in ordering colonial Mexican society in Saltillo is confirmed in the patterns of spousal selection of each racial group. The españoles clearly expressed their view of the racial hierarchy by marrying twice as many coyotes as mulattos and three times as many mulattos as Indians. Only eleven out of 100 españoles married downward in the racial hierarchy. Only one out of every 100 españoles married an Indian. This order of preference was mirrored in the ability of the castas and Indians to find español marital partners. Coyotes married españoles 25 percent of the time, mulattos married españoles 12 percent of the time, and Indians married españoles only 4 percent of the time. The importance of the español racial identity in ordering the hierarchy is also pointedly illustrated by taking it out of the equation. Once the question of access to español spouses is removed, each of the other three groups—coyotes, mulattos, and Indians—chose partners from the other non-español groups very evenly when marrying outside of their own racial categories.

The occupational structure closely mirrored the racial hierarchy derived from patterns of endogamy and exogamy in the censuses as well as from other records. The españoles had a complete monopoly of the merchant occupation and almost a complete monopoly of the landholding and renter farming occupation of the labradores. Españoles also accounted for 68 percent of the positions in the skilled category and only 14 to 16 percent of those in the unskilled workers category. The distance between the españoles and the other three groups in the occupational structure was comparable to the gap that existed in español choices of marital partners. The castas and Indians had no one in the merchant occupational niche and made up only 2 to 4 percent each of the labrador group. Coyote and mulatto participation in the skilled occupations was equal at 15 percent each, while the Indian participation was minimal. Peninsulares and criollos held all positions of civil and religious authority.

The terms *don* and *doña* were used in colonial Mexican society to indicate social respect and deference attained by an individual through personal achievement and inherited family merit. Their widespread use in colonial Saltillo essentially divided the population into two large upper and lower groupings of honorific status. Among the 1,082 male householders with known racial identities, 311 or 29 percent were identified as dons, differentiating them from a larger non-don group of 771 individuals. The preferential position held in society by individuals with español racial identities is revealed by their almost total monopoly of the title. Among 311 male householders with the title of don, 306 or 98.4 percent of them were españoles. The other five individuals consisted of four coyotes and one mulatto in clear reflection of the racial hierarchy. The 306 españoles represented slightly more than half (50.6 percent) of the total of 605 español householders identified in the census of 1777. All 28 of the europeos possessed the title. The four don coyotes represented only 3 percent of the 139 coyote householders. The one mulatto represented 0.6 percent of the 164 mulatto householders in the sample. Not one of the 174 Indians (not including the residents of San Esteban de Tlaxcala) achieved the status. Spanish monopoly of the social honor crossed the gender line to include the female population. All 73 doñas with known race were españolas. The pattern held firm among the wives of the householders. Of the 188 wives who were identified as doñas, all were españolas, except for a lone coyota. The español monopoly of the don/doña status was a pattern Saltillo shared with Guadalajara at the end of the colonial period.[51]

Conclusion

A vigorous system of racialized social control operated in Saltillo, as it did in the rest of colonial Mexico, even on the northern frontiers. The central dynamic of the system was the privileged value assigned to the social identity of español. This value shaped identity formation and structured personal and group relations. The sistema de castas in Saltillo produced a social structure in which racial identity keyed differential access to the resources that defined social roles. The patterns in property ownership, occupation, racial endogamy and exogamy, social status assignations (don/doña), and political office reveal a well-defined hierarchy of privilege and preference among four major racialized groups.

The system worked for several reasons. It successfully maintained the absolute primacy of the Spanish identity in the power centers of society. Even the regional criollo elite, with its carefully documented and protected "purity of blood," had to acknowledge the ascribed racial superiority of European Spaniards. Large numbers of "Indians" and "Africans" were subordinated through different combinations of violence and socialization to form the bulk of the laboring population. A major characteristic of the system was a flexibility that accommodated the realities of racial miscegenation, racial drift or variability, and overlapping economic conditions among the major social groups. It did not matter that the mixed races complicated the structure of society, far beyond the bipolar white-black model of other American societies, as long as an elite Spanish identity was a prerequisite for holding power. The systematic suppression of tertiary and more complex racial identities is a further testament to the effectiveness of the colonial system of social control in channeling members of society to different racialized stations and roles in society.

The dynamics of the social order in Saltillo challenges the thesis— drawn from the study of other locations in the colony—that the sistema de castas was disintegrating at the end of the colonial period. It contradicts the view that the use of race as a form of social control was weakening.[52] There were real geographic differences in the shape and effectiveness of the sistema de castas throughout the colony. However, the adaptability and fluidity of the system has been misread as a pattern of disintegration. The Saltillo model also runs counter to the view that changes in racial identity from casta to Spanish were more frequent throughout the North than in the center of the colony. Although this may have been true in other locations like Texas, New Mexico, and California, Saltillo was two hundred years old in 1777 and possessed a mature social structure by central Mexican standards. Its history illustrates the diversity of Spanish colonial society on the northern frontier. It also underscores the capacity of the colonial system of racialized social control for adapting itself to a great variety of social ecologies.

NOTES

1. Eric R. Wolf, *Europe and the People without History* (Berkeley: University of California Press, 1982); Peter Wade, *Race and Ethnicity in Latin America* (London: Pluto Press, 1997).

2. Sociologist Eduardo Bonilla-Silva, *White Supremacy and Racism in the Post Civil Rights Era* (Boulder, Colo.: Lynne Rienner Publishers, 2001) provides a theoretical "framework" for the study of racialized social structures.

3. See Douglas Cope, *The Limits of Racial Domination: Plebeian Society in Colonial Mexico City, 1660–1720* (Madison: University of Wisconsin Press, 1994), 9–26, for the rise of the *sistema de castas*.

4. Mark A. Burkholder, "Honor and Honors in Colonial Spanish America," in *Sex, Shame, and Violence: The Faces of Honor in Colonial Latin America*, ed. Lyman L. Johnson and Sonya Lipsett-Rivera, 18–44 (Albuquerque: University of New Mexico Press, 1998).

5. For Africans in the Americas, see Gonzalo Aguirre Beltrán, *La población negra de México, estudio etnohistórico*, 3d ed. rev. (Mexico City: Fondo de Cultura Económica, 1989); David Eltis, "Europeans and the Rise and Fall of African Slavery in the Americas: An Interpretation," *The American Historical Review* 98, 5 (1993): 1399–1423; Douglas Richmond, "The Legacy of African Slavery in Colonial Mexico, 1519–1810," *Journal of Popular Culture* 35, 2 (2001): 1–16.

6. D. A. Brading, *The First America: The Spanish Monarchy, Creole Patriots, and the Liberal State, 1492–1867* (Cambridge: Cambridge University Press, 1991; first paperback edition, New York, 1993).

7. For a basic definition of social control, see David Jary and Julia Jary, *The HarperCollins Dictionary of Sociology* (New York: Harper-Collins, 1991), 449.

8. Magnus Mörner, *Race Mixture in the History of Latin America* (Boston: Little, Brown and Company, 1967), 53–73, first postulated the rise and decline of the sociedad de castas. For a summary of a generation-old debate on the relative importance of race and class to the sistema de castas, see Rodney D. Anderson, "Race and Social Stratification: A Comparison of Working-Class Spaniards, Indians and Castas in Guadalajara, Mexico in 1821," *Hispanic American Historical Review* 68, 2 (1988): 209–43. Cope, *The Limits of Racial Domination*, 7, affirms the idea of late colonial decline.

9. John K. Chance and William B. Taylor, "Estate and Class in a Colonial City: Oaxaca in 1792," *Comparative Studies in Society and History* 19, 4 (1977): 454–89; Anderson, "Race and Social Stratification," 219, 241–42.

10. The frontier corollary is not fully crystallized in the literature, but is suggested by the emphasis on the ability of racially mixed individuals to gain identities as Spaniards. See the essays in Robert H. Jackson, ed., *New Views of Borderlands History* (Albuquerque: University of New Mexico Press, 1998).

11. Bonilla-Silva, *White Supremacy*, 38–39, 47, 58, 85, 98, refers to the "ideological ensemble" and "interlocking hierarchies" of race, gender, and economics that shape and reinforce each other within the context of societies "structured in dominance."

12. The "centrality of Spanishness" was a subset of the "centrality of whiteness." For the latter, see Bonilla-Silva, *White Supremacy*, 37, 41–47, 55, 62–80, 197.

13. See the seminal study by Verena Martínez-Alier, *Marriage, Class and Colour in Nineteenth-Century Cuba: A Study of Racial Attitudes and Sexual Values in a Slave Society* (Ann Arbor: University of Michigan Press, 1974). Also see Patricia Seed, *To Love, Honor and Obey in Colonial Mexico: Conflicts Over Marriage Choice, 1574–1821* (Stanford: Stanford University Press, 1988). For New Mexico, see Ramón A. Gutiérrez, *When Jesus Came, the Corn Mothers Went Away: Marriage, Sexuality and Power in New Mexico, 1500–1846* (Stanford: Stanford University Press, 1991), 176–297.

14. Bonilla-Silva, *White Supremacy*, 41–47, makes this adaptability a central feature of his model. For examples, see Stuart B. Schwartz, "Spaniards, *Pardos*, and the Missing Mestizos: Identities and Racial Categories in the Early Hispanic Caribbean," *New West Indian Guide* 70, 1–2 (1997): 5–19; and Bruce A. Castleman, "Social Climbers in a Colonial Mexican City: Individual Mobility within the *Sistema de Castas* in Orizaba, 1777–1791," *Colonial Latin American Review* 10, 2 (2001): 229–49. The (East) Indian caste system, contrary to popular belief, is highly flexible, creating and eliminating thousands of subcastes as necessary. See A. Jeff Tudisco,

Class and Caste in Village India (San Francisco: Field Educational
Publications, 1969), 6–10. The concept of "social ecology" is used by
Cynthia Radding, *Wandering Peoples: Colonialism, Ethnic Spaces, and
Ecological Frontiers in Northwestern Mexico, 1700–1850* (Durham, N.C.:
Duke University Press, 1997).

15. David J. Weber, *The Spanish Frontier in North America* (New Haven,
    Conn.: Yale University Press, 1992), 326–34, discusses the various factors
    that shaped the sistema de castas in various societies across the far northern
    frontier. Also see Jackson, ed., *New Views of Borderlands History*, 227; Jesús
    F. de la Teja, *San Antonio de Béxar: A Community on New Spain's Northern
    Frontier* (Albuquerque: University of New Mexico Press, 1995), 24–28;
    and Cheryl E. Martin, *Governance and Society in Colonial Mexico: Chihuahua
    in the Eighteenth Century* (Stanford: Stanford University Press, 1996), 1–9,
    184–200.

16. This section is a synthesis of my doctoral dissertation, "Saltillo in the
    Seventeenth Century: Local Society on the North Mexican Frontier,"
    (Ph.D. diss., University of California, Berkeley, 1981) and several articles
    I have published elsewhere. The most direct source is "Socioeconomic
    Involution in Colonial Saltillo, 1577–1821," *European Review of Latin
    American and Caribbean Studies* 49 (1990): 55–77. Two other key sources
    are "The Persistence of Indian Slavery and Encomienda in the Northeast
    of Colonial Mexico, 1577–1723," *The Journal of Social History* 21, 4
    (1988): 683–700; and "The Economic Impact of the Bourbon Reforms
    and the Late Colonial Crisis of Empire at the Local Level: The Case
    of Saltillo, 1777–1817," *The Americas* 44, 3 (1988): 301–23.

17. Carlos Manuel Valdés, *La gente del mezquite: Los nómadas del noreste en
    la colonia* (Mexico City: Centro de Investigaciones y Estudios Superiores
    en Antropología Social, 1995).

18. Cuello, "The Persistence of Indian Slavery and Encomienda." For the
    central Mexican model, see Charles Gibson, *Spain in America* (New
    York: Harper Torchbooks, 1966) and Lesley Byrd Simpson, *The
    Encomienda in New Spain*, rev. and enlarged ed. (Berkeley: University
    of California Press, 1966).

19. Cuello, "Saltillo in the Seventeenth Century," 135–159.

20. David B. Adams, *Las colonias Tlaxcaltecas de Coahuila y Nuevo León en la
    Nueva España: Un aspecto de la colonización del norte de México* (Saltillo,
    Mexico: Archivo Municipal de Saltillo, 1991). For the Tlaxcaltecan
    certifications, see Raul J. Guerra Jr., Nadine M. Vásquez, and Baldomero
    Vela Jr., *Index to the Marriage Records of the Diocese of Guadalajara, Provinces
    of Coahuila, Nuevo León, Nuevo Santander, and Texas, vol. I: 1653–1750*
    (Edinburg: Published privately by the authors, 1989), 139; and Mormon

Microfilm (MM), Órdenes, Reel o, 168, 680 (August 27, 1693). Photostatic copy provided by Nadine Vásquez.

21. Cuello, "Saltillo in the Seventeenth Century," 31–42, 74–102.

22. Ibid., 286–312.

23. Cuello, "The Persistence of Indian Slavery and Encomienda."

24. Ibid.

25. The concept has been used by Clifford Geertz, *Agricultural Involution: The Process of Ecological Change in Indonesia* (Berkeley: University of California Press, 1968).

26. Cuello, "Saltillo in the Seventeenth Century," 93–99, 212–26.

27. "Memoria presentada a las Cortes de Cádiz," in *Miguel Ramos Arizpe, Discursos, memorias, e informes*, ed. by Vito Alessio Robles, 44–55 (Mexico: Universidad Nacional Autónoma de México, 1942); Jesús F. de la Teja, "St. James at the Fair: Religious Ceremony, Civic Boosterism, and Commercial Development on the Colonial Mexican Frontier," *The Americas* 57, 3 (2001): 395–416.

28. D. A. Brading, *Haciendas and Ranchos in the Mexican Bajío: León, 1700–1860* (Cambridge: Cambridge University Press, 1978); Cheryl E. Martin, *Rural Society in Colonial Morelos* (Albuquerque: University of New Mexico Press, 1985); James D. Riley, "Status and Residence: The Labradores of Tlaxcala and the City of Puebla, 1680–1800," Paper read at the VII Conference of Mexican and United States Historians, Oaxaca, 22–26 October, 1985; Eric Van Young, "Sectores medios rurales en el México de los Borbones: El interior de Guadalajara en el siglo XVII," *Revista Latinoamericana de Historia Económica y Social* 8 (1986), 99–117. Sergio Antonio Corona Páez, "Formas de producción y de consumo en una hacienda neovizcaína: San Juan Bautista de los González, 1663–1666" (Master's thesis, Universidad Iberoamericana, Mexico, D.F., 1999) provides a portrait of one family's efforts to preserve its property, purity of blood, and descent status in Saltillo.

29. For a complementary study of this period, see Leslie S. Offutt, *Saltillo 1777–1810: Town and Region in the Mexican North* (Tucson: University of Arizona Press, 2001).

30. Cuello, "The Economic Impact of the Bourbon Reforms"; Martínez-Alier, *Marriage, Class and Colour in Nineteenth-Century Cuba*; Seed, *To Love, Honor and Obey in Colonial Mexico*.

31. Vito Alessio Robles, *Coahuila y Texas en la época colonial* (Mexico City: Porrúa, 1938), 664–65.

32. D. A. Brading, *Miners and Merchants in Bourbon Mexico, 1763–1810* (Cambridge: Cambridge University Press, 1971), 19–25; Beltrán,

La población negra de México, 265–76; Morner, *Race Mixture,* 44; Patrick J. Carroll, *Blacks in Colonial Veracruz: Race, Ethnicity, and Regional Development,* 2nd ed. (Austin: University of Texas Press, 1991), 128–29; and Cope, *The Limits of Racial Domination,* 177.

33. For a discussion of *calidad,* see Robert McCaa, "*Calidad, Clase,* and Marriage in Colonial Mexico: the Case of Parral, 1788–90," *Hispanic American Historical Review* 64, 3 (1984): 477–501. For the elemental components of the stereotypes see Martínez-Alier, *Marriage, Class and Colour in Nineteenth-Century Cuba,* 171; and Cope, *The Limits of Racial Domination,* 19. For the intertwining of various social determinants, see the essays in Johnson and Lipsett-Rivera, eds. *Sex, Shame and Violence.*

34. Cope, *The Limits of Racial Domination,* 106–124; Carroll, *Blacks in Colonial Veracruz,* 124–29. Presidencia Municipal, leg. 40, exp. 18, 25 January 1788, Archivo Municipal de Saltillo, Mexico (hereafter cited as AMS).

35. Weber, *The Spanish Frontier in North America,* 326–34; Gutiérrez, *When Jesus Came, the Corn Mothers Went Away.*

36. The four-level economic hierarchy is derived from the study of notarial records reflecting the economic life of Saltillo. See Cuello, "Socioeconomic Involution"; "Saltillo in the Seventeenth Century," 234–68.

37. John K. Chance, *Race and Class in Colonial Oaxaca* (Stanford: Stanford University Press, 1978), 164–72; Chance and Taylor, "Estate and Class," 454–89; D. A. Brading, "Grupos étnicos; clases y estructura ocupacional en Guanajuato (1792)," *Historia Mexicana* 21, 3 (1972): 460–80; Celia Wu, "The Population of the City of Querétaro in 1791," *Journal of Latin American Studies* 16, 2 (1984): 277–307; Castleman, "Social Climbers"; and Carroll, *Blacks in Colonial Veracruz,* 115–18.

38. Saltillo Baptisms (1684–1700, 1706–1723) and Saltillo Marriages, (1703–1757), reel 605,065, Mormon microfilm, Church of Jesus Christ, Latter Day Saints. Six sample years from the baptismal records: 1685–1686, 1702, 1710, 1714, and 1721. Two sets of samples from the marriage records: 1703 to 1706 and five sample years spaced out by decades from 1710 to 1750. Nadine Vásquez provided the transcriptions of the parish records.

39. The usage of racial labels in Saltillo generally adheres to the main definition of those terms in Thomas M. Stephens, *Dictionary of Latin American Racial and Ethnic Terminology* (Gainesville: University of Florida Press, 1989). A *castizo* was the offspring of a white and *mestizo* (p. 54), if "white" is read as *español.* A *coyote* (*mestizo*) was the offspring of a white and an Indian (pp. 84–85). A *trasalvo* (*entresalvo* in Saltillo) was the offspring of a mestizo and an Indian. A *morisco* was the offspring of a white and mulatto. A *lobo* was the offspring of a black and Indian (p. 141).

40. Brading, *Miners and Merchants*, 20–21, discusses the division.

41. Guerra et al., *Index to the Marriage Records*, vol. I: *1653–1750* (cited above) and vol. II: *1751–1779* (Austin: Published privately by the authors, 1997).

42. Presidencia Municipal, leg. 1, exp. 38, item 1, 17 February 1667; leg. 4, exp. 56, 8 November 1689; Inventarios y Testamentos, leg. 1, 1617–1708, Testament of Nicolás de Aguirre, 5 and 7 February 1694; Actas de Cabildo, leg. 1, libro 1, 1701–1726, fols. 251–59, 4–9 May 1714, all in AMS.

43. Carmen Castañeda, *La educación en Guadalajara durante la Colonia, 1552–1821* (Guadalajara: Colegio de Jalisco, 1984), 284–99.

44. Carlos Manuel Valdés and Ildefonso Dávila del Bosque, *Esclavos negros en Saltillo: Siglos XVII a XIX* (Saltillo: Ayuntamiento de Saltillo and Universidad Autónoma de Coahuila, 1989).

45. For the descent rule, see Marvin Harris, *Patterns of Race in the Americas* (New York: W. W. Norton, 1964), 79–94.

46. For the censuses, see Ramo General, leg. 31, exp. 2, 1777; leg. 42, exp. 1, 13 March 1786; leg. 43, exp. 1, 1791–1793, AMS. In the 1777 census of 72 persons who were identified as slaves who were not householders, only 4 were *negros* while 55 were mulattos and 13 did not have their race identified.

47. Cope, *The Limits of Racial Domination*, 71–73.

48. Mörner, *Race Mixture*, 66–69; Cope, *The Limits of Racial Domination*, 68–70; McCaa, "*Calidad, Clase*," 497–501.

49. Mörner, *Race Mixture*, 69; Cope, *The Limits of Racial Domination*, 74–79; McCaa, "*Calidad, Clase*," 497–99; Seed, "Social Dimensions of Race," 591.

50. Cope, *The Limits of Racial Domination*, 79; Chance and Taylor, "Estate and Class"; Robert McCaa, "Modeling Social Interaction: Marital Miscegenation in Colonial Spanish America," *Historical Methods* 15, 2 (1982): 45–65; and David Brading and Celia Wu, "Population Growth and Crisis: León, 1720–1860," *Journal of Latin American Studies* 5, 1 (1973): 1–36.

51. Anderson, "Race and Social Stratification," 234–36.

52. Castleman, "Social Climbers," 234, concludes that the use of a limited number of racial categories in the Orizaba census of 1791 "paradoxically subverted some of the goals of the *sistema de castas*."

CHAPTER TEN

Colonization and Control

The Case of Nuevo Santander

PATRICIA OSANTE
TRANSLATED BY NED F. BRIERLEY

In the initial northern colonization process, the strong attraction exercised by silver on colonial society generated an important spontaneous migration led by conquistadors and men from the important mining regions of northern Spain. Aside from the mining boom, other motives propelling Spanish expansion into the Gran Chichimeca included the desire of *españoles, criollos,* and mestizos to acquire generous amounts of land, the Church's desire to proselytize among the hunter-gatherers and semisedentary peoples of the north, and the Crown's own wish to secure the borders of its domain.

Tempering the expansionist impulse was a set of conditions that militated against a steady migratory flow into the Gran Chichimeca. Some settlers became disenchanted with the failure of wealth and power to immediately materialize. Many were disillusioned and justifiably terrorized by the constant attacks of the hunter-gatherer groups in defense of their usurped territory and personal freedom, as Cecilia Sheridan's chapter illustrates. Also, the invasion of Old World fauna and diseases into the region had a deleterious effect on the indigenous population, causing a labor scarcity that adversely affected the chances of success. The result of these circumstances was the prolongation of a frontier situation in the Mexican North for well over two centuries, with the

attendant periodic abandonment of settlements and need for colonial authorities to attempt various strategies to foster immigration.

Consequently, for the proper analysis of Spanish colonization in the
vast north it is necessary to keep in mind that it was a long process that
lasted more than two hundred years. It was a multiethnic phenomenon
determined in large measure by factors of an economic and defensive
nature. Immigrants came not only from Spain but also from the center, the
west, and even the south of New Spain, including captive and free Indians,
as well as slave and free blacks. This migration included the participation
of Spanish, mestizo, and mulatto vagrants, a particularly difficult group to
incorporate into the labor force.[1]

The character of the colonists was a product of the diversity of settlements as well as the circumstances of the "pacification" and colonization
event. In the sixteenth century many colonists were soldiers and the Indian
auxiliaries who accompanied their captains in the occupation of certain
strategic sites of the north. Aside from the mining rushes, throughout the
seventeenth century and into the eighteenth, as the mission system became
a principal tool of imperial expansion, missionaries and presidial soldiers
became important elements in the occupation of the nonmining frontier
among hunter-gatherers and semisedentary natives. Beginning in the second half of the eighteenth century, an important migration toward the
northeast portion of the frontier was carried out by hundreds of families
of principally criollo, mestizo, and African descent. This movement marked
the beginning of the end of the mission system, as it set in motion a distinctive colonizing enterprise with an impresarial character. In the multi-
tudinous migratory flow toward the Gulf of Mexico, one can appreciate
clearly the uneasiness of the royal government in applying a new pacifying
and colonizing policy that joined with the established desire of a reduced
group of proprietary nobles—landowners, military, and functionaries—to
exploit the pasturelands of the said territory.

In speaking of the occupation of the Seno Mexicano[2] we are faced with
a unique colonization phenomenon. While settlement of this remote and
inaccessible region was of paramount interest to the royal government, it
was made feasible only due to the participation of a small group of prominent colonials who accepted the challenge of testing new settlement methods. Consequently, the rational and limited pacification and colonization
of the Seno Mexicano was an occurrence without parallel in the colonial
world, since it was an institutional colonizing project developed by mid-

eighteenth-century Enlightened officials for the benefit of the Spanish empire, but which served the economic and political interests of private investors who, besides financing part of the enterprise, were charged with directing and controlling the destiny of the society settled in the lands of the Seno Mexicano.[3]

In this particular Spanish colonization program, as in the rest of the settlement of the northern provinces, including the founding of Upper California in 1769, fraud and deceit were indispensable tools for stimulating migration. Likewise, it is understandable that a diversity of persuasive and coercive methods was used to entice people and firmly establish them in the north. These practices were elaborated and adapted in accordance with the occasion and the circumstances proper to each one of the political-administrative entities whose establishment was attempted. Such was the case with the family colonization project under study here, the Colony of Nuevo Santander—the present state of Tamaulipas, Mexico. Indeed, in the Spanish expansionistic advance, the familiar colonization was one of the best forms used by the royal functionaries to establish certain towns in the northern border of New Spain. These they populated with sedentary natives, Spaniards, and some other *gentes de razón* (rational persons)—criollos, mestizos, and mulattos—who contributed to expand and consolidate the dominion of the Spanish empire in that territory.

In this type of colonization royal authorities applied various formulas. The first of them was that of transporting various groups of sedentary natives to compensate for the dramatic decline that the indigenous population suffered following the entrance of the Spanish into a new area. The most representative case of this policy was the spectacular introduction of Tlaxcaltecan families, from 1591 onward, to support the colonization from the Gran Tunal to Nuevo Reino de León (Nuevo León) and Coahuila.[4] Another of the forms utilized by the royal government to stimulate frontier occupation was rooted in the transport of families from the Iberian Peninsula or the Canary Islands, as would occur in Texas with the arrival of a group of Canary Island families in the first third of the eighteenth century.[5]

In both cases, to persuade the families to transport themselves to the remote north they were offered, besides the coveted title of nobility, "the king offered to resettle 200 families of Canary Islanders, providing them free transportation, livestock, tools, arms, land, their maintenance for a year, and the title of hidalgo."[6] Likewise Indians and colonists were provided with provisions for a year, while they adapted to the territory and

became self-sufficient. Although it is known that the results with the Tlaxcaltecans were generally very satisfactory, the same cannot be said in the
case of the Canary Islanders, of whom, despite the great assistance offered
by the royal government, there finally arrived in Texas after a long and tor-
tuous journey only fifty-five individuals in twelve families. For colonial
officials the poor results obtained from colonizing efforts based on families from the Canary Islands was in no way worth the hardships suffered by
the Islanders to reach Texas. Much less did it justify the investment of the
royal government in the said enterprise—approximately 800,000 pesos.[7]
Thus, Brigadier Pedro de Rivera, who at first had supported and even promoted colonization of the north with Spanish families, proposed to the
viceroy of New Spain that he should ask King Philip V to issue an order
prohibiting "the passage of more Canary Island families to New Spain."[8]

Despite the preceding efforts, far northeastern New Spain remained
sparsely settled, particularly the coastal plain and piedmont above Tampico.
By the 1740s viceregal officials were particularly concerned with the danger
in the Gulf of Mexico posed by Spain's European rivals. Royal authorities proposed to resolve the dual problems of defense and underpopulation in the
northeastern frontier, by applying a new family colonizing method employing the nonindigenous human resources that inhabited adjoining areas. In
other words, to create a new frontier settlement along the Seno Mexicano,
they planned the removal of settlers, especially families of whatever socio-legal
condition, from the adjoining provinces that had been colonized long before.

It was precisely during the founding of the colony in the Seno Mexicano that this new settlement model was put into practice. As I describe it
above, the project was both rational and limited: rational due to the fact
that it arose from the new political currents of the eighteenth century; limited in that fundamentally it served the interests of the impresarial group
charged with its execution. Besides being a singular event that was not
repeated again during the colonial period, it clearly illustrates the induce-
ments that were utilized to attract settler families and, alternatively, the
coercion that was exercised on them to subject them to the service of the
group in power. Linked to the interests and expectations of the project
leaders, the restrictive actions applied to the new settlers were planned not
only to impede the immigrants' abandonment of the territory that so "gen-
erously" had welcomed them, but also to avoid, at all costs, the objections
that the families might present before viceregal authorities against the
unrestrained power that the colony's authorities might exercise over them.

Family Colonization in Nuevo Santander

Settlement of the vast expanse of territory between the Tamesí-Panuco and Nueces Rivers began in 1748, after two and a half centuries of failed colonization attempts, both royal and private, employing this new model. The boundaries of the new political-administrative entity that had as its name "the Colony of Nuevo Santander" were determined to be approximately 1,040 miles from south to north and between 400 and 480 miles from east to west. The new colony bordered on the north parts of the provinces of Coahuila and Texas, on the west the Kingdom of Nuevo León and parts of Coahuila, Charcas, and Guadalcázar, on the south portions of Río Verde, Valles, and the province of Pánuco, and on the east a little more than 640 miles of the Gulf of Mexico coast.[9]

While it is true that colonizing the Gulf of Mexico—a territory characterized then as unknown and inhospitable—had much to do with the eagerness of the Spanish government to preserve it from French intrusion, as well as its desire to contain the constant attacks of hunter-gatherer groups that lived in that portion of the northern frontier, it is necessary to insist that what finally determined the foundation of Nuevo Santander were private interests. The colony, then, was a scheme of a group of functionaries and landowning nobles—military and civil—from central and northeastern New Spain dedicated to the raising of large and small livestock.[10] These men, desirous of satisfying their needs for expanding their zone of productive and commercial activities, and requiring effective defense, embraced the new policy of settlement that some high functionaries at the viceregal court had begun to promote in the 1740s.[11]

Among the measures of the colonial administration, assumed by the impresarial sector, was the promotion of settlement by Spanish families and other "rational people" from neighboring provinces. This policy provoked the opposition of the missionaries. In other northern provinces the friars had shown themselves to be vehemently opposed to the entry of non-indigenous family groups into the lands of the heathens, under the pretext, said the clergymen, of the bad example that these gave to the Indians. Nevertheless, for viceregal authorities it had been proved repeatedly, as Cecilia Sheridan amply illustrates in her chapter, that the isolation from Spanish society promoted by the religious orders had also not succeeded either in integrating the Indians into mainstream colonial society or even of bringing an end to the attacks of the unsubmissive Indians, much less securing Spanish control in that region.[12]

It fell to José de Escandón y Helguera, a Spanish military man with long years of service in New Spain, to apply the colonial government's new policy of settlement with families from other parts of New Spain. Escandón had become interested in colonizing the uncultivated Seno Mexicano as early as 1744. He obtained formal authority over the project four years later, after he convinced viceregal officials not only of his capacity to juggle the great play of institutional and private forces with stakes in the occupation and exploitation of the region, but also of the viability of the impresarial strategy that he planned to put into practice. They especially welcomed his offer of integrating the territory into New Spain with a minimal investment from the royal treasury.[13] Moreover, Escandón's plan of government was theoretically well adapted to the urgent need of the Spanish Crown to correct weaknesses of the mechanisms of control in its overseas possessions by means of a new administrative structure in accordance with the guidelines of reformist policy makers. For the internal and external defense of the Seno Mexicano, as well as for control of the population that would settle in the said territory, Escandón adopted colonizing precepts recommended by Enlightenment functionaries. He proposed a military form of government for the entire jurisdiction and replacement of the mission-presidio system with a large civil population, to the benefit of the Spanish Crown and of colonial society in general.[14]

In his colonizing proposal, the peninsular military man also included the viceregal officials' idea of introducing a large labor force, so that, besides putting an end to the uncertainty of being able to employ the labor of the territory's Indians, there would be avoided the immigrants' almost complete dependence on the work of the natives, as occurred in Florida and New Mexico. In the latter province, as David Weber correctly notes, the excessive demands and coercive actions that friars, soldiers, colonists, and government functionaries exercised upon the natives of the territory led the latter to rebellion, and with it the destruction, in only a matter of days, of what with so much effort and time had been constructed.[15]

The expectations of viceregal authorities were very different, however, from the realities of the emerging regional power. Escandón and the prominent investors knew that once the spiritual and material government of the Indians in the future Colony of Nuevo Santander was snatched away from the missionaries, both the exploitation of the territory and the integration of the Indians into civil life would become an important part of their privileges. The investors were looking to create mixed settlements of

Spaniards, *castas*, and Indians, protected by military units under the command of the captains of the settlements. Hence, the absence of established missionary groups in the area would expedite the settlement process.[16]

The Power of Persuasion

Based on his previous experience in family recruitment in Sierra Gorda, southwest of the area he was now proposing to colonize, Escandón elaborated, with the advice of the Marqués of Altamira, advisor for War and Treasury of the Royal Audiencia of Mexico, a plan to obtain the material and human resources that would permit him to carry out the simultaneous establishment of the first fourteen settlements. It consisted of two promotional packets. The first of them was designed to persuade men of means to invest in the enterprise, and the second to induce the hundreds of families that represented the bulk of the population of the new province to change their residence. The latter group would form the labor force that the former required for the development and consolidation of their private businesses in that territory.[17]

To prominent men disposed to invest in the project with sufficient capital to cover the transportation of settler families to found the new settlements, José de Escandón offered lands, tax exemptions, and privileges according to what was stipulated in the Laws of the Indies. However, the two *sitios* (8,600 acres) of large livestock and the twelve *caballerías* (1,260 acres) of farmland that, upon entry, were promised to investors greatly surpassed the limit imposed by Law 9, Title 5, Book 4, of the *Recopilación de leyes Indias*, which stipulated not conceding "more than five *peonies* (105 acres), nor more than three *caballerías* (315 acres)" to new settlers. The generous offer of grazing land would prove difficult to ignore for those important livestock raisers who, for some time, had been profiting from, or planning to profit from, pasture lands in the future Colony of Nuevo Santander.[18]

In order to awaken the interest of members of this group even more, Escandón assured them of an annual salary of between 500 and 800 pesos as military commanders of the *villas*. To the wealthy landowners and military men who would settle in the new towns and collaborate with him to institute military government in the province, he also promised noble titles, political authority, and direct participation in the commercial network that he planned to establish within the province and beyond.[19] In these offers the double benefit that both the province's future governor and the investors hoped to obtain from their participation in the pacification and colonization of the Seno Mexicano can clearly be appreciated. For the private investors, obviously, this was the legal possession and unrestricted exploitation of desired lands, and political and economic power over the villas that they might establish. For José de Escandón the benefits were no less tangible, but broader in being able to muster the human and material resources needed to pacify and colonize the territory while establishing the support and loyalty of a select group of collaborators to institute in Nuevo Santander his own program of organization. These goals were as much in accordance with regional private interests as with those of the Spanish empire.[20]

As for the families of settlers, Escandón concentrated his persuasive stratagem on the offer of "some one-time cost assistance, both so that they may be able to transport themselves conveniently, and for the provision of supplies that they need the first year," but above all with the promise of granting them in property two sitios of small-stock land and six caballerías of land with "sufficient water," so that they may settle themselves in them, "making fields for planting and livestock raising." Of course, he also advertised that they would enjoy royal protection, as well as tax exemptions and privileges for a period of ten years. To console the soldiers of the military units that would defend the villas, Escandón offered an annual salary of 250 pesos to sergeants and 225 to soldiers, besides "giving them their own land to build their dwelling huts" and conceding to them the military *fuero* (code of privileges and exemptions). The colonel spoke also of compensating them with land as the territory was pacified, in accordance with the services that they might lend in the attainment of the enterprise.[21]

The propaganda campaign that Escandón employed had the hoped-for effect, since between 1748 and 1749, 540 civilian and military families had transported themselves to the territory. Seven years later 1,475 families were registered on the settler rolls, a total of approximately 6,350 persons.[22] On the face of it, the numbers reflect the triumph of Escandón's strategy of persuasion and the support offered by the prominent landowners and officials. As I see it, however, the key to the response of the hundreds of settler families to Escandón's call was rooted in the fact that the colonel had centered his attention on the great number of "inconvenienced families that reside or roam loose on haciendas, bearing various costs and labors that the owners were imposing on them, and [that] if they had not come here they would have gone to other provinces," to flee the "slavery in which they were living, made tenants of the owners of the haciendas, aspiring to free themselves from the one and from the other."[23] So the possibility of making themselves owners of a little more than 4,400 acres must have represented, for the impoverished inhabitants of the provinces adjacent to the territory of the Seno Mexicano, a more than sufficient incentive for them to change their residence.

Another matter that must have influenced, in a substantial way, the viability of such a spectacular massive settlement of the "Escandonian" villas, was the system of civil recruitment that was set in motion long before the foundation of Nuevo Santander. It is known that from 1746 on, José de Escandón initiated his propagandistic labor to entice as many of the families of the adjacent provinces as possible, under the premise that in the future colony there would have to be admitted all persons who might so desire, including those who were accused in other entities of grave offenses such as robbery and violent crimes, promising them protection and liberation from the penalties that they would be subject to in the places where they had committed their offenses. Later, Escandón proceeded to the recruitment of families with the assistance of military officials whom he commissioned to occupy themselves with transporting the settlers from the places in which they themselves lived. To facilitate the recruitment of families, he named as his agent, or representative, a settler of Linares, Nuevo León, named Roque de la Barrera, to whom he gave more than 40,000 pesos to contract in advance with the families that might be disposed to emigrate and to give those charged with bringing them to Nuevo Santander the promised cost assistance.[24]

The Rigors of Coercion

If the history of Nuevo Santander makes plain the success of Escandón's persuasive strategies in attracting the thousands of persons he needed to set in motion the colonizing work in the territory of the Seno Mexicano, it also brings to view the coercive methods that this military leader and his principal subordinates, backed by some high colonial officials, employed from the beginning to achieve the foundation and development of the colony. In the documents of the period there exists sufficient information to permit one to speak of the policy of intimidation applied from 1747 onward by the viceregal administration so that Escandón might successfully effectuate the reconnaissance expedition of the Seno Mexicano and conclude at least the first phase of colonizing Nuevo Santander.

In effect, the colonel was granted a "viceregal order which subjected to his authority the governments and the settlers of the provinces close to the Seno Mexicano," such as San Luis Potosí, Guadalcázar, Coahuila, Nuevo León, Texas, Valles, Tampico Viejo, and Pánuco, "and it obliged them, furthermore, to lend him material and human assistance during the three or four months that the expedition might last." Later, the resolution of the General Council of War and Treasury was issued, which, among other things, committed the governors and other officials of the region to lend assistance in all that José de Escandón might demand for the founding of the villas and the sustenance of their respective settlers, with the warning that severe "corporal and pecuniary punishments" would be applied to every person, no matter his rank or position, who might obstruct the said enterprise in any manner.[25]

The administration imposed by Escandón in Nuevo Santander reproduced the highly hierarchized structure existing in the other governments of the northern provinces, which accorded with the interests of the impresarial groups settled throughout the length and breadth of the north. For the rich stockmen and military men of high rank who made greater investments in the Nuevo Santander enterprise, the governor extended the power of their captaincies to zones very far from the villas that they had founded and granted them proprietary titles to a great number of large and small livestock estates, almost always exceeding the two sitios of large stock and the twelve caballerías of land originally promised.

A case illustrative of Escandón's policy of the use of the land in exercising persuasive control over investors is that of José Vázquez Borrego. This rich Coahuila landowner, after founding the Dolores estate in 1750 on the north side of the Rio Grande, in the present state of Texas, was granted 50 sitios of small stock. Three years later, in 1753, at his petition he was granted 25 more sitios of large stock, in total more than five leagues (approximately 13.5 miles) along the banks of the Rio Grande. Likewise, among other emoluments Vázquez Borrego received the commission of commanding captain of the north-central zone of Nuevo Santander.[26]

As for the small landowners and military men who only with great difficulty managed to cover the costs of the transport of settlers, or those who even required the aid of the royal treasury to establish a settlement, Escandón treated them differently and exercised a more coercive control over them—albeit veiled. He refused to give them the property titles that he had promised them for the lands that they enjoyed de facto, in order, as the colonel asserted, to assure the permanence of these men and their families in Nuevo Santander. An example of this practice is the situation suffered by Tomás Sánchez de la Barrera y de la Garza, who in his position as founder and captain of the villa of Laredo requested for himself, in 1754, fifteen sitios of large stock as compensation for all his effort and expenses in the construction of the settlement.[27] Sánchez de la Barrera was granted the right to unofficially occupy the sitios that he requested. However, in 1757, more than two years after the villa was established, he lamented before royal inspector José Tienda de Cuervo that he still did not have "any designated term nor any formality made in this matter nor in any other," because up until then Escandón had not appeared in Laredo.

Nevertheless, it must be said that Sánchez de la Barrera and those among the other military leaders of the villas having fewer resources, along with some stockmen who found themselves in similar circumstances, received enormous benefits because of their participation. Even lacking proper title, they exploited great expanses of land without payment of sales taxes and tithes during more than twenty years. A number of them gained these benefits simply for having facilitated the settling of certain locations or for having received credit for settlement, although some sites had been occupied or been under regular use long before the founding of the province.[28]

The mechanisms of control applied against the bulk of society established in Nuevo Santander—that is, settlers, soldiers, missionaries, and Indians—were characterized, in general, by their severity. One very important measure was that of delaying ad nauseam the assignment of specific tracts as promised to the settler families and to the soldiers of the villa garrisons, without even granting them the caballerías and peonías of land to which they were entitled by law as settlers, forcing on them in this way to carry on a protracted communal use of pastures and crop lands. In fact, José Tienda de Cuervo, in the report that he submitted to the viceregal court after his visit to Nuevo Santander in 1757, indicated that in none of the villas founded in the province had there been given even unofficial possession of lands to the settlers. Due to "this lack of provision, there results a recognized hardship to the community, because the wealthier ones avail themselves of the greater part [of the land] and the poor do not have the due convenience of the enjoyment thereof."[29]

Although it is true that this delaying policy served Escandón as a coercive tool to prevent the immigrants from absenting themselves from or abandoning Nuevo Santander, it also served as a lure for others. The possible ownership of land, he hoped, would continue functioning as a strong magnet to attract to the territory more settler families of scarce resources. The practice was basically one more artifice on Escandón's part to concentrate power in a few prominent men, since in Nuevo Santander land ownership and high-ranking military position were what guaranteed membership in the elite that was quickly forming in the province.

Neither the recommendations of Tienda de Cuervo nor the constant petitions and complaints of the settlers were of any avail to move Escandón to proceed with the distribution of land. Families of settlers who arrived in Nuevo Santander with some farm tools together with the few possessions they were able to acquire, thanks to the subsidy they had received from the royal government, did not experience an increase in their property, but saw their assets diminish little by little because of the difficult economic situation in which they found themselves. Their small herds turned into sources of subsistence, because the settlers lived on the meat and milk their animals produced. Likewise, the offspring of their cattle and mares were exchanged for corn before they were a year old, so that building up profitable herds became a long and arduous process.[30]

Few also were the soldiers who managed to provide themselves with a small plot during the Escandón era (1748–1766). In Güemes a sergeant and four soldiers received 30 sitios of large stock at a place known as Mesas Prietas. Yet, at Horcasitas a group of 66 soldiers had to divide two sitios of large stock among themselves. The insignificant amount of land granted to these latter colonists confirms the preferred policy of the governor of denying the majority of the settlers and soldiers the favor of receiving at least the caballerías and peonías that by law—independently of his original offer—belonged to them given their position as founders. The poverty into which the salaried soldiers fell, along with those men-at-arms who served on the haciendas under temporary contract, often for "10 pesos per month and three *almudes* [approximately 4 bushels] of rations each week," is an irrefutable fact. Apart from lower ranking officers, who made do by exploiting small farms, the majority of soldiers came to form part of the hacienda labor force, the properties of higher ranking officials and stockmen of more renown.[31]

It was also by way of the evasion of the required distribution of land that the Escandón government would attempt, together with the use of arms, to subject the Indians of the territory to its designs. Escandón began by subjecting the Franciscan missionaries of the Colegio de Guadalupe de

Zacatecas, charged with the evangelization of the natives, to military authority. Although it is true that since the beginning of the occupation of the Seno Mexicano, royal authorities had sought to suppress the old mission-presidio system and prevent the Franciscans from gaining in Nuevo Santander a power similar to that which the missionaries in the north retained, especially the Jesuits in the northwest, they did not completely discard the utility, albeit subordinated, of churchmen within the new colonizing model.[32]

However, the new policy of giving primacy to the establishment of civil settlements unleashed an open and tenacious struggle between churchmen and military over the exploitation of the land and control of the natives. In the long run, the Franciscans were virtually despoiled of the administration of the indigenous communities and their resources. The ministers, frankly annoyed by the treatment to which the captains of the villas subjected them, but especially by the antimission policy practiced by the governor, complained to the viceregal government concerning Escandón's breach of agreement in denying them legal possession of the land in the few places where it had been possible to establish missions, because of "some private interests" intervening therein.[33]

In fact, the Escandón government could not formally avoid the evangelization and reduction of area Indians, because of stipulations in colonial law. Since the late sixteenth century, colonial expansion had been linked— at least theoretically—to the spread of the gospel. So, in order to legitimize the enterprise and establish his privileges as a colonizer, José de Escandón found it indispensable to employ missionaries, who, furthermore, also proved useful to him in inspiring confidence among the new settlers and preventing them from deserting on the pretext that they lacked access to the holy sacraments that they required. Therefore, with consummate adroitness, he adapted to the interests of the province's elite the policy of founding missions for the aid of the Spanish communities only when it promised to gather a good number of natives capable of being utilized as a free labor force on the livestock estates of the prominent men of the territory, but without granting the possession of the lands to the Franciscans in the name of the Indians.[34] Consequently, according to Tienda de Cuervo's report of 1757, only twelve out of the 24 villas existing in the province had come to have approximately 1,926 congregated Indians, while in the remaining twelve, there were no reduced Indians. Moreover, of these twelve, "seven did not have a site assigned for a mission, and in five of them there was not even a missionary."

In fact, in only three mission centers—Aguayo, San Fernando, and Altamira—could the Franciscans utilize the natives in commercial activities like the cultivation of corn, beans, and other vegetables, the grinding of sugar, salt extraction, and the production of dried fish; and they could even trade in products made by the Indians.

Escandón's control over the missionaries extended well beyond their relationship with the natives. An important part of the control that the military government exercised over the churchmen consisted of depriving them of the right of payment for parochial services rendered to the settlers. The churchmen were to be content with the stipend assigned by the colonial government for their maintenance and the sustenance of the few missions that came to be built in Nuevo Santander.[35]

Together with the missions under the guardianship of the civil establishments, another means of subverting the rights of the Indians to receive from among the best lands in the process, was the system of dual settlements inhabited by Hispanics and Indians. Escandón viewed this as a quick means to incorporating the natives into the social and productive life of Nuevo Santander, for the benefit of the select group of prominent men of the province. It was also an easy way to separate the Indians from the land, to cite the Franciscans, who reported that "one Spaniard alone" had more land "than many towns of Indians together," as a result of the way the natives were despoiled of their lands in order that they be given to wealthy persons.[36] In the same manner, the settlers, when they had the opportunity, made use of the natives, surreptitiously or with the authorization of their superiors, for their business and their domestic needs. Even the few Indians under the guardianship of the Franciscans were exploited by the Hispanic population. Frequently, they were taken out of the missions by the military for use as Indian auxiliaries during military campaigns against the hostile Indians of the territory.

Despite their power over the missions and those Indians who had been congregated in Hispanic settlements, the prominent men of Nuevo Santander could not exercise complete control over the indigenous population of the region; much less freely exploit the working strength of the natives. As Cecilia Sheridan points out in her chapter, the permanent opposition of some Indian groups toward sedentary life, but above all toward Spanish control, made them a hindrance to peaceful exploitation of the territory and a disruptive element with regard to the more peaceful indigenous populations in the territory. Consequently, the governor and the captains of the villas of

Nuevo Santander, by common agreement with the high officials of the colonial government, opted for compulsory subjugation and extermination through death or exile of those groups that resisted Spanish control.[37]

In contrast to what Cynthia Radding proposes in her chapter regarding the Sonoran town council as an important instrument of social control in northwestern New Spain, in Nuevo Santander another clearly coercive means for subjecting the local society to an exclusively military regime was precisely not permitting town councils to be established in the province. The pretext for this policy was the provincial government's effort to protect newcomers from the well-known power cartels that under the auspices of the councils had been created in the various administrative units of the viceroyalty. Hence, it would be the military authority that would be charged with resolving all matters, including those of a civil character, and which, consequently, would deny the settlers the right of electing their local judges and of naming their councilmen.[38]

Along with exclusion from public matters, the greater part of the settlers was also subject to the tyranny of the province's prominent men. Besides ending up as their servants in their houses and haciendas, and lacking lawyers or scribes to formalize their complaints, it proved impossible for them to defend themselves from constant abuses. At one point there even circulated in the viceregal court a series of rumors that Escandón himself had threatened the settlers with hanging or exile if they dared to denounce the excesses that he had committed during his long term of management in Nuevo Santander. Even though we must take this last report with certain reservations, it intimates the degree of authoritarianism that the military leader could well have exercised.[39]

Likewise, ample documentation exists to affirm that the liberty of the settler families to live in the villa or other place that would best accommodate them was subordinate to the interests of the group in power. The settlers were obliged to settle in whatever places they had been transferred to by their captains, and it was unacceptable for them to change residence from one villa to another, even within the province, without the prior permission of the local authority. It is almost unnecessary to say that the petitioner obtained approval only with difficulty, due to the fact that his change signified the loss, for the military head of the villa, of the labor of one or more persons.[40] Settlers could not evade the obligation of collaborating with the captains in the construction of public works or in lending assistance to the military government "to attract the apostate Indians or to pursue the rebels in long and debilitating military campaigns, without receiving salary or any food ration in return."[41] These severe measures, together with others, such as sentencing minor criminal offenders to serve as soldiers in the military units or as servants or assistants to the missionaries, were purposely conceived to keep the families in the places that were most convenient for the governing group of Nuevo Santander, without recourse to higher authorities.[42]

Control over the soldiers stationed in the principal settlements was exercised by local authorities through a variety of practices that kept the men subservient to the interests of their officers and other prominent members of the communities. The aforementioned postponement in the distribution of lands, the application of severe punishments, and the form of salary payment established in Nuevo Santander all contributed to keeping soldiers under heel. Under this last practice, the governor authorized the captains of the villas, "under the category of collection and conveyance costs," to lower by a third the wages of the corporals and soldiers, and likewise he permitted the remaining two-thirds to be regularly satisfied with "goods and merchandise," so that besides being obliged to buy their provisions at very elevated prices, they often had to accept goods they neither needed nor found useful. The matter of in-kind salaries in Nuevo Santander—a pernicious practice characteristic of all the northern provinces—is even more revealing if one takes into account that Escandón, in his colonizing plan of 1747, explicitly stated that each corporal and soldier would be given his wages "in cash and in his own hand," so that he could buy whatever he needed "at his pleasure," in order that the abuses that the troops suffered in the other frontier jurisdictions would not be repeated.[43]

With all that has been pointed out thus far, it is not at all surprising that during his term of management as military head of Nuevo Santander, José de Escandón concentrated power in his own person and that he shared it only with his most faithful and supportive captains of the villas. It is also not surprising that in order to carry out the enterprise and to satisfy the immediate goal of the royal government and of the private investors, many of the persuasive and coercive means utilized by the military authority of the province were not only legalized by viceregal authorities, but that some of them had legal support in existing colonial legislation, as was the case with the arbitrary distribution of land carried out by Escandón.

On the one hand is the support offered by the advisor for War and Treasury of the Audiencia of Mexico, Domingo Valcárcel. This important official on repeated occasions declared that the distribution of land should not be so free, but rather "proportional and corresponding to the number of settlers," as a way of defending the governor against the accusations made by both the missionaries and the settlers regarding the excessive concessions of lands that he occasionally made to his principal subordinates. Valcárcel came to accept, and even to justify, the said policy with the argument that the limit imposed by Law 9, Title 5, Book 4 of the *Recopilación de leyes de Indias*, proved impractical in a territory that was still to be pacified and that for that very reason the value of the land was extremely low.[44]

As to the legal support that the colonel obtained from colonial legislation itself so as to control and distribute the lands at his discretion, he availed himself of the advantages presented by Law 1, Title 12, Book 4. The law in part states that the governor of a new province may distribute houses, plots, lands, caballerías, and peonías in the places and towns that he might believe pertinent, "making a distinction among nobles and laborers, and those who might be of lesser rank and merit, and that he might augment and improve them, in attention to the quality of their services."[45] In the same manner, in order to obstruct the distribution of mission lands and to control the Indians of the territory, Escandón relied on a resolution issued by the members of the General Council of War and Treasury, which since 1748 had been charged with ratifying his nomination as military head of the enterprise, that "since the Indians, even the less barbarous, are only impressed by what comes to them by sight and, because of their natural inconstancy and unruly appetite toward their barbarity, they require the contiguous settlement of Spaniards, respect for whom will contain, tame, and protect them."[46]

The same policy of establishing missions under the protection of the villas, because it was the most rapid and effective method of reducing and controlling the Indians, was repeatedly confirmed by the Marqués de Altamira, Valcárcel's predecessor. In defense of Escandón's delays in establishing some missions, the Audiencia's advisor undertook to disqualify the Franciscans in some of his judgments, pointing out that the failure of the missions was in no way due to the premeditated actions of the governor. He maintained that it was, instead, a result of the Indians not having responded to the desires of the missionaries in their task of spreading Christianity, "so that the distress is born of the intent, in part, not having corresponded to the practice." On the contrary, many Indians showed themselves friendly and prepared for the doctrine, thanks "to the settlers and under the shelter thereof."[47]

In short, it is clear how the personal, patriarchal, and patronage-granting power exercised by José de Escandón permitted the investors in the enterprise to enjoy highly advantageous conditions. Under his auspices they were able to gain control—legally or extralegally—of the best lands, with ample water rights, and exploit the settlers and Indians so as to obtain the labor force that they needed for the development, consolidation, and prosperity of the villas under their charge as well as their private estates. Of course, the enormous benefits that the governing group of the province obtained as recompense for the services rendered to Escandón contrasted glaringly with the sad reality of the missionaries and the Indians, as well as with the miserable existence of the settler families—civil and military— who had migrated to that territory to escape precisely the kind of tyranny to which they fell victim, and in search of a better life than the one they had in their provinces of origin.

Conclusions

During two and a half centuries, the royal government insisted upon the movement of families—peninsular, colonial, and sedentary Indians—to the northern frontier of New Spain, and attempted to stimulate, and even to compel, outsiders to settle in those lands. Royal settlement policy was based on the necessity to grow the social sector that promised to consolidate the Spanish dominion in that region. While this policy depended on the displacement of "rational people," it also sought to integrate the native hunter-gatherer communities into the Spanish productive system, through the process of military subjugation or by the missionaries in charge of the evangelization of natives who lived in the territory.

The Crown's desires, royal prompting, and support were not enough to make settlement viable; above all, it was necessary that there should exist favorable regional conditions. And that was precisely what occurred in the first migratory impulse toward the north-central region with the foundation of Zacatecas and of other mining centers around it, which attracted a significant mass of Spanish, criollo, mestizo, and mulatto settlers, as well as sedentary Indians from the central parts of New Spain. Manifestly these immigrants—impresarios, miners, free and captive Indians and blacks, and even vagrants—were moved, in essence, by a double purpose: to make their fortune in silver and to possess, in property, important portions of northern lands.

Although the success of this first expansionist advance would be reflected in the later foundation of other more northerly provinces, what impeded the quick and complete occupation of New Spain's northern frontier was precisely the scarcity of nonindigenous settlers, despite the existence of various colonizing initiatives, private and governmental. For example, Texas, founded in the 1710s, remained under extremely impoverished conditions throughout the eighteenth century; and the plan to settle Canary Islander families in the province during the 1730s ended in utter failure. Certainly the distance, the lack of easy communication with the center of the viceroyalty, and the absence of mineral resources brought about the almost complete abandonment of the province by colonial authorities and endangered Spanish control of the region. In other words, no amount of overt social control could bring about the successful occupation of frontier territory in the absence of basic attractions.

It was toward the middle of the eighteenth century, in the lands of the Seno Mexicano, that once more the political and regional conditions appeared highly favorable for attempting a new colonizing project. This one would be sustained, in part, by a series of political acts of persuasion and coercion aimed at attracting and dominating the hundreds of settler families required to establish the first fourteen Spanish settlements that formed the basis of the Colony of Nuevo Santander.

To understand the meaning and scope of this colonizing process, however, it is necessary to remember some of its most important aspects. In the first place, it is necessary to keep in mind that it was a matter of a massive colonization by families, which from its magnitude and importance may well be classified as unique in the history of New Spain. In seven years 1,331 civilian and 144 military families were transported to the new province, with an approximate number of 6,350 persons. If we think about that colonial north, unpopulated in its greater part by Spaniards and other gente de razón, the number of immigrants is astonishing. Moreover, in preparing a general balance sheet for the period between 1748 and 1764, the royal treasury expended in establishing or reorganizing the province's 24 settlements, including the annual pay of missionaries and soldiers, approximately 800,000 pesos, an amount similar to that spent on the unfortunate relocation of the Canary Islander families to Texas.

These figures are a clear indicator of the great significance that the coincidence of royal and private interests had in the settlement process in Nuevo Santander. On the one hand, the royal government's colonization effort was fortified by the capital injected into the enterprise by investors from central and northeastern New Spain. On the other hand, the investors were able to attain their pecuniary and power goals thanks to the support received from royal authorities, who instituted various policies and abetted certain tactics employed by the dominant local group, to attract and retain the large number of newcomers whose permanent settlement was necessary to the creation of the Colony of Nuevo Santander. Only through the exploitation of this workforce could the province achieve consolidation and economic stability as a province of the viceroyalty of New Spain.

Moreover, the vigor of the program of Spanish settlement in the Seno Mexicano was in large measure tied to the beginning of the process of "liquidation" of the mission regime which, together with the presidio, had up to that time functioned as a pacifying and "civilizing" instrument among the independent groups of Gran Chichimeca. Since land ownership was the principal motive for both the prominent men and the common settlers who lived in the surrounding provinces, government support for the suppression of Indian property rights was a precondition for settlement. It would not have been possible, without the legal and, at times, even extralegal possession of land that otherwise would have been used in establishing missions and Indian settlements, to realize the colonists' hopes of acquiring generous grants of land endowed with the water necessary to make their private businesses prosper, especially the raising of livestock.

During this essay, we have seen how Nuevo Santander society—that is to say, the civilian newcomers, military, churchmen, and natives who inhabited the territory—proved seriously affected by governmental policy carried out by a select group of prominent men directed by José de Escandón. It is a fact that the most unprotected settler families had to wait nearly twenty years to enjoy their small properties, despite the fact that such ownership represented the principal offer with which they had been persuaded to settle in Nuevo Santander. For their part the missionaries lost control of not only the lands that would have made up the domain of the missions, but the indigenous communities themselves. The friars ended by subordinating themselves to the military authority of the province, to the detriment of the prerogatives and privileges that the religious orders had enjoyed in undertaking missionary labors during the greater part of the colonial regime. Lastly, the rare groups of natives that accepted Spanish domination and were integrated into the Spanish colonial system continued succumbing little by little, due to abuses and illnesses, until they finally disappeared, while the hunter-gatherers who resisted the Spanish presence and control were literally exterminated.

The superficial success of the colonization project initiated and led by Escandón under the auspices of the colonial government, masked the fundamental failure of the "modernization" efforts of Enlightenment reformers in New Spain. Above all, the reformers failed to alter power relations in northeastern New Spain, much less enjoy, as they had hoped, the benefits obtained with the new colonizing project. In effect, the landed elite, which made up the prominent men of Nuevo Santander, proved to be the only true beneficiaries. Even when in 1766, at the outset of the political, economic, and social modernization effort known as the Bourbon Reforms, a political crisis overtook the Escandón regime, culminating in the governor's destitution and the disassembling of the power group of the province, the ineffectiveness of the mechanisms of political and economic control imposed by the royal and viceregal government in northeastern New Spanish was obvious. The crisis signaled, in a prophetic manner, the end of the colonial regime in Spanish America.

NOTES

1. Philip W. Powell, *La Guerra Chichimeca (1550–1600)* (Mexico City: Fondo de Cultura Económica, 1977), 27, 29–30, 145–46.

2. Although *Seno Mexicano* generally refers to the Gulf of Mexico, during the colonial period it also signified the coastal strip between the Nueces and Pánuco Rivers.

3. See Patricia Osante, *Orígenes del Nuevo Santander, 1748–1772* (Mexico: Universidad Nacional Autónoma de México, Universidad Autónoma de Tamaulipas, Instituto de Investigaciones Históricas, 1997).

4. Vito Alessio Robles, *Coahuila y Texas en la época colonial*, 2d ed. (Mexico: Porrúa, 1978), 121, 124, 125, 134, 136.

5. Mexico 616 and 291, and Guadalajara 178, Archivo General de Indias, Seville (hereafter cited as AGI).

6. David J. Weber, *The Spanish Frontier in North America* (New Haven, Conn.: Yale University Press, 1992), 192.

7. Ibid., 193–94.

8. Virginia González Claverán, "Una migración canaria a Texas en el siglo XVIII," in *Historia Mexicana* 37, 2 (1987): 194. Despite the advice, a new initiative to transport fifty peninsular families took place in 1777; in this case Catalonians were sent to Sonora under the supervision of Juan Pujol, sergeant of the Free Company of Volunteers of Catalonia. The result of this enterprise was much worse than that obtained in Texas with the Canary Islander families, since as of 1781 only six men and one woman from the Spanish Mediterranean coast had reached Sonora, Archivo Franciscano (hereafter AF), caja 34/737, fols. 1–49 and 34/738, fols. 10v–11; Biblioteca Nacional, Mexico (hereafter cited as BN).

9. Vicente de Santa María, *Relación histórica de la Colonia del Nuevo Santander*, intro. and ed. Ernesto de la Torre Villar (Mexico City: Universidad Nacional Autónoma de México, Instituto de Investigaciones Bibliográficas, 1973), 194.

10. *Ganado mayor*, or large stock, refers to bovine and equine livestock; *ganado menor*, or small stock, refers to ovine and caprid livestock.

11. Patricia Osante, *Orígenes del Nuevo Santander*, 176–84.

12. Dictamen del marqués de Altamira sobre reajuste de misiones en el Nuevo Reino de León y Coahuila . . . México, 27 de mayo de 1747, AF, caja 5/102, BN.

13. Copia impresa de lo resuelto por la Junta General de Guerra y Hacienda . . . México, mayo de 1748, AF, rollo 16, caja 44, exp. 1005, fol. 7v; rollo 17, caja 45, exp. 1032, apéndice, fol. 1v, microfilm, Instituto Nacional de Antropología e Historia (hereafter INAH).

14. "Dictamen del marqués de Altamira sobre poblamiento en Nueva Vizcaya . . . México, 23 de diciembre de 1749," Guadalajara, 191, AGI; José de Escandón y Helguera, *1747, Informe de Escandón para reconocer, pacificar y poblar la costa del Seno Mexicano* (Ciudad Victoria, Mexico: Consejo Estatal para la Cultura y las Artes de Tamaulipas, 1998).

15. Weber, *The Spanish Frontier*, 122–23.

16. Osante, *Orígenes del Nuevo Santander*, 116–18.

17. Civil, v. 1981, exp. 5, fols. 37–38; Historia, v. 522, fol. 133, both in Archivo General de la Nación, Mexico (hereafter cited as AGN).

18. Escandón, *1747, Informe de Escandón*, 57–58.

19. Tierras, v. 3519, exp. 7, fol. 13; Provincias Internas, v. 178, fols. 305–6, v. 248, exp. 5, fol. 58v, both in AGN.

20. Osante, *Orígenes del Nuevo Santander*, 135.

21. Agustín López de la Cámara Alta, *Descripción general de la Nueva Colonia de Santander*, comp. and ed. Gabriel Saldívar (Mexico: Archivo de la Historia de Tamaulipas, 1946), 151, 157; Escandón, *1747, Informe de Escandón*, 57–58.

22. Tierras, v. 2734; Provincias Internas (hereafter cited as PI), v. 172 and 178; both in AGN; *Estado general de las fundaciones hechas por don José de Escandón en la Colonia del Nuevo Santander, costa del Seno Mexicano*, 2 vols. (Mexico: Secretaría de Gobernación, Publicaciones del Archivo General de la Nación, 1930); AF, rollo 16, caja 44, exp. 1005, fol. 1, INAH.

23. Declaración del capitán de la villa de Hoyos, Domingo de Unzaga, a Tienda de Cuervo...Hoyos, 7 de mayo de 1757, en *Estado general de las fundaciones hechas por don José de Escandón*, 1: 105.

24. Parecer del auditor de Guerra y Hacienda, Domingo Valcárcel, sobre el cargo decimoctavo en contra de Escandón...México, 1766, PI, v. 178, fols. 110–14, 268–70v; Consulta del coronel José de Escandón al superior gobierno sobre el estado general de las fundaciones...Querétaro, 13 de junio de 1749, PI, v. 173, exp. 8, fol. 279v, both in AGN.

25. Respuesta del auditor de Guerra y Hacienda, el marqués de Altamira, a la consulta hecha por el gobernador del Nuevo Reino de León, Vicente Bueno de la Borbolla, al virrey, primer conde de Revilla Gigedo...México, 24 de septiembre de 1749, PI, v. 173, exp. 8, fol. 288; PI, v. 248, exp. 5, fol. 80, both in AGN; Santa María, *Relación histórica de la Colonia del Nuevo Santander*, 187–88.

26. The quantity of land officially granted to Vázquez Borrego exceeded by more than a league the territory assigned in that province by the royal government for the establishment of a *villa*, the dimensions of which ordinarily occupied a square of four leagues in each cardinal direction, as stipulated in the royal ordinances of 1573. Likewise, Domingo de Unzaga Ibarrola and Francisco de Barberena were among the men clearly favored by Colonel Escandón, who, besides being granted the captaincy of two villas or settlements—as occurred for Unzaga with the command of Hoyos and the encampment of Borbón, or in the case of Barberena who commanded the villas of Santa Bárbara y Altamira, assisted in this last by a lieutenant of justice named by himself—were placed in charge of the three flying squadrons that were occupied with the security of the territory in three enormous and important subregions of Nuevo Santander. Concesiones hechas por José de Escandón a José Sánchez Borrego...Santander, 16 de febrero de 1753, PI, v. 172, exp. 9, fols. 162–69, AGN; "Informe de José Tienda de Cuervo al superior gobierno,..." in *Estado general de las fundaciones*, 2: 229; Tierras, v. 3519, exp. 7, fol. 5v; PI, v. 172, exp. 9, fol. 168; exp. 14, fol. 234, and v. 178, fol. 138, all in AGN.

27. Parecer del fiscal, el marqués de Aranda, sobre la fundación de
    Laredo...México, 25 de mayo de 1756, Tierras, v. 3519, exp. 7,
    fols. 9–10; Carta de José de Escandón al virrey, primer conde de Revilla
    Gigedo...Santander, 12 de noviembre de 1754, PI, v. 172, exp. 14,
    fols. 254–54v, both in AGN.

28. "Declaración de Tomás Sánchez a José Tienda de Cuervo...Laredo,
    22 de julio de 1757," in *Estado general de las Fundaciones*, 1: 444; Tierras,
    v. 3519, exp. 7, fols. 10–19v, AGN.

29. "Informe de José Tienda de Cuervo," in *Estado general de las fundaciones*,
    1: 81.

30. Informe privado de fray José Joaquín García a José de Gálvez...México,
    Colegio de San Fernando, 15 de enero de 1766, PI, v. 248, exp. 5, fol. 58v,
    AGN.

31. José Hermenegildo Sánchez García, *Crónica del Nuevo Santander*, prologue
    Candelario Reyes Flores (Mexico: Consejo Nacional para la Cultura y las
    Artes, 1990), 219, 226–28; "Consulta de José de Escandón al superior
    gobierno...Querétaro, 13 de junio de 1749," PI, v. 173, exp. 8, fol. 279v;
    v. 172, fols. 21–23, and v. 248, exp. 2, fols. 18, 19, AGN; *Estado general
    de las fundaciones*, vols. 1 and 2.

32. Parecer del auditor de Guerra y Hacienda, el marqués de Altamira, sobre
    el gobierno de indios, AF, caja 44/1010, fol. 7v; Carta de José de Escandón
    al comisario general del Colegio de Guadalupe de Zacatecas, fray Juan
    Antonio de Abasolo...Querétaro, 12 de febrero de 1750, AF, caja 44/1006,
    fol. 6; Expediente que el superior gobierno formó en virtud de la consulta
    de Escandón acerca de las funciones de los misioneros en el Nuevo
    Santander...Nuevo Santander, 17 de marzo de 1749, AF, caja 44/1012,
    fols. 1–11, all in BN.

33. Representación hecha por el padre guardián y el discretorio del Colegio
    de Guadalupe de Zacatecas al virrey, primer conde de Revilla Gigedo...
    Zacatecas, 12 de septiembre de 1752, AF, rollo 16, caja 44, exp. 1009,
    fol. 5, INAH.

34. Expediente que el superior gobierno formó en virtud de la consulta de
    Escandón acerca de las funciones de los misioneros en el Nuevo
    Santander...Nuevo Santander, 17 de marzo de 1749, AF, caja 44/1012,
    fols. 1–11, BN; Informe privado de fray José Joaquín García, PI, v. 248,
    exp. 5, AGN.

35. "Informe de Tienda de Cuervo," in *Estado general de las fundaciones*,
    vols. 1 and 2.

36. In this case the churchmen were making an allusion to the estate of San Juan, located in the vicinity of the villa of Soto la Marina, property of José de Escandón. Besides this estate, the governor possessed in Nuevo Santander other rural properties in San Fernando and Santillana, named El Verde and Buenavista. PI, v. 248, exp. 11, fols. 229–78, AGN. Representación hecha por el padre guardián y el discretorio del Colegio de Guadalupe de Zacatecas, al virrey, primer conde de Revilla Gigedo... Zacatecas, 12 de septiembre de 1752, AF, rollo 16, caja 44, exp. 1009, fol. 5, INAH.

37. Testimonio de José de Escandón al virrey, primer conde de Revilla Gigedo... 21 de septiembre de 1750, PI, v. 172, fol. 287, and exp. 17, fol. 316, AGN.

38. Diligencias practicadas sobre la censura que promovió un misionero... Villa de Santander, 3 de abril de 1772, PI, v. 140, exp. 8, fol. 111, AGN; Sánchez García, *Crónica del Nuevo Santander*, 27–28.

39. PI, v. 173, exp. 6, fols. 205, 211, 213, 217v, AGN.

40. Osante, *Orígenes del Nuevo Santander*, 216–20.

41. López de la Cámara Alta, *Descripción general*, 151, 157.

42. Escandón, *Estado general de las fundaciones*, 1: 26–27, 2: 111; AF, rollo 17, caja 45, exp. 1003, fols. 22–23v, INAH; Santa María, *Relación histórica de la Colonia del Nuevo Santander*, 78, 91.

43. Escandón, 1747, *Informe de Escandón para reconocer, pacificar y poblar la costa del Seno Mexicano*, 57–60; Fiel compendio del proyecto que planteó José de Escandón en consulta, después de la inspección del Seno Mexicano... elaborado por el auditor de Guerra y Hacienda, Domingo Valcárcel... México, 1773, PI, v. 178, fol. 176v, AGN.

44. Parecer del auditor de Guerra y Hacienda, Domingo Valcárcel, sobre la fundación de Laredo... México, 1756, Tierras, v. 3519, exp. 7, fol. 13, AGN.

45. Parecer del auditor de Guerra y Hacienda, Domingo Valcárcel, sobre los agostaderos de las misiones de las Californias en el Nuevo Santander... México, 5 de mayo de 1757, PI, v. 140, exp. 6, fol. 259, AGN.

46. Copia impresa de lo resuelto por la Junta General de Guerra y Hacienda... México, mayo de 1748, AF, rollo 16, caja 44, exp. 1005, fol. 3v, INAH.

47. Parecer del auditor de Guerra y Hacienda, el marqués de Altamira, sobre el gobierno de los indios... México, 18 de octubre de 1752, AF, caja 44/1010, fol. 7v, and caja 44/1009, fols. 11v–13, BN.

CHAPTER ELEVEN

Social Control within Missionary Frontier Society

Alta California, 1769–1821

JAMES A. SANDOS

Issues of social control affected all levels of Spanish society in what proved to be Spain's last colony in North America. Both Crown and Cross agreed that Indians as prospective new members of this society would need to be disciplined. But the Crown and the Cross also recognized the need to control Spain's military and clerical elites as well as Alta California's soldiers and settlers of mixed blood. Into an area containing perhaps 60,000 Indians at contact in 1769, Spanish colonizers introduced a new population of 150. By 1820 the white and mixed-blood population counted only 3,400, while the Indian people, declining largely from European diseases inadvertently introduced, numbered less than 22,000. During that time the Franciscans founded twenty missions to congregate and convert the Indians. In the process they occupied a coastal strip that began at San Diego in the south and extended seven hundred miles north to San Rafael. Wherever possible, Franciscans sought flatland with a good water source to allow irrigated farming. Mission influence extended inland in a meandering pattern to the ridge of the coastal range in the north and center, and in the south to the base of the mountains, distances varying between 50 and 150 miles.[1]

In the seventeenth century, missionaries led the effort to extend Spain's dominion over new peoples and territories in a policy largely based upon persuasion rather than military conquest. By the last third of the eighteenth century, however, especially under the impress of the Bourbon Reforms, the military became dominant in the campaign to subjugate Indians. The regulations of 1772 issued by Carlos III codified military superiority over the clergy in colonial frontier matters and remained in effect throughout the rest of Spanish rule.[2] Three years earlier in 1769, however, the Crown had resorted to the older, superseded policy when it chose to occupy Alta California. Lacking sufficient numbers of soldiers and settlers to effect conquest, the Crown gave the lead hand to Junípero Serra, first Father President of the missions, and the Franciscans. Serra, a Mallorcan missionary with twenty years experience preaching and administrating in New Spain, brought to his task a profound sense of religious determination reinforced by a personal piety that led him to asceticism. The Crown's abrupt and anomalous backward turn from the path of reform in this instance proved a continuous source of friction between the Sword and the Cross, especially with military officers who moved from province to province in the northern frontier, enjoyed their power and pride of place, and were reluctant or unwilling to subordinate their authority to the unique situation in Alta California. For this reason social control can be fruitfully examined by studying this society from the top down.

This chapter considers the state's efforts to control all components of California society. Soldiers and settlers, men and women, administrators and missionaries are examined along with the Indians they sought to colonize. Simply imposing legal constrictions did not achieve social control; the weak had weapons of their own. Moral precepts and psychological manipulation through the categories of gender and status influenced social behavior. I begin with two stories that illustrate the nature of social control in elites and conclude with an analysis of the state's efforts to control mission Indians—the key to the province's survival.

The Affair of Governor Pedro Fages

Sexual scandal in a colonial setting provides insights into issues of imperial social control that no other action can. Such a scandal almost by definition involves elites behaving badly since commoners were scarcely noticed in official correspondence. Elites transgress, or allegedly transgress, defined social conventions for personal gratification. They challenge prevailing gender roles, or make public generally privately tolerated but officially condemned gender behavior.

California offers a case that involved conflicts between a man and wife who were also, respectively, the colony's highest-ranking political official and social elites. Their personal difficulties led to friction between the civil and religious authorities who had the jurisdiction to sanction their behavior. It also raised questions concerning the obligations a wife owes her spouse, the priority of professional duty to the Crown versus marital obligations within the nuclear family, and the proper treatment of female Indians.

On Thursday morning, 3 February, 1785, in Monterey, capital of the sixteen-year-old colony of Alta California, doña Eulalia Callis de Fages confronted her husband, don Pedro Fages, the colony's governor, in his headquarters at the *casa real* (government hall). They had approached the administrative area of the casa from their separate apartments. Don Pedro later said that he was awakening a young Indian girl; doña Eulalia, however, claimed that she saw her husband *sobre* (on or upon) the Yuma Indian girl servant. *La gobernadora* had suspected her husband of seeking an alternative source of sexual gratification since she had denied him the marital bed for the last four months. Now she believed she had proof. In a fit of pique doña Eulalia fled don Pedro's headquarters and publicly denounced his infidelity before the local citizenry. She swore to have witnessed it with her own eyes and demanded a divorce.[3]

Failing to assure his wife of his innocence, don Pedro sought the counsel and assistance of the missionaries at nearby San Carlos. A priestly delegation headed by Father Matías Noriega came to Monterey to inquire into the matter and to persuade doña Eulalia to drop her allegations and to return to her husband. She replied that she would rather be in hell with the devil than in Alta California with her husband. Under priestly order she was removed to her own apartment in the casa real and denied visitors. Soon don Pedro had to travel south on imperial business and asked that his wife be moved to mission San Carlos in his absence. When Fr. Noriega sent a military officer to collect her, doña Eulalia resisted and locked herself in her room with her son and daughter. Don Pedro had to force the door and threaten to tie her before she agreed to go. Once there, nonetheless, she continued to protest, prompting Fr. Noriega to denounce her from the pulpit for spreading rumors and gossip and for failing to follow his directives and her husband's wishes that she return to her wifely role.

Both individuals were Catalán by birth but married in Mexico City. By all accounts the twenty-two-year-old bride was beautiful and from a good family. The fifty-year-old groom was a senior military officer who had held numerous important frontier posts, including that of commander of the presidios of Alta California in the 1770s, before he wed in June 1780. In early 1781 the couple traveled together to Sonora and to a ragged frontier outpost at Arizpe, an arduous overland journey under the best of conditions and one not made more bearable for doña Eulalia by her first pregnancy. For the next four years, in addition to Arizpe, doña Eulalia lived at other remote frontier locations in El Pitic, Loreto, Monterey, and San Francisco. She lived in each place for only a few months, was frequently separated from her husband, who then sent for her to join him. Her total travel time consumed nearly a year of this period, and for much of it she was pregnant. In Sonora she gave birth to a son, Pedrito, and four months after arriving in California, where her husband served as military governor of both Baja and Alta California, she gave birth to a daughter, María del Carmen. In between she had been pregnant in 1783 but miscarried en route from Loreto to Monterey. By the time of her daughter's birth, "doña Eulalia had been pregnant for a total of twenty months, approximately 40 percent of her married life and 64 percent of the time she had been with her husband."[4]

Doña Eulalia had endured frontier hardships throughout this period of her married life. Despite an enthusiastic greeting by local citizens in California, she found the place remote and uncomfortable. While pregnant with María del Carmen she prevailed upon her husband to move her from the dampness of San Francisco to the more salubrious climate of Santa Clara. Despite don Pedro's insistent request for hospitality for his wife, the missionaries evasively refused. The real reason was that these single men, devoted to missionary activity, did not want a white woman, especially a gobernadora, in their mission, fearing that somehow the mere presence of a pregnant white woman would cause scandal. Thus, an unhappy doña Eulalia gave birth to her daughter in San Francisco on 2 August, 1784. Shortly afterward she requested that don Pedro resign his governorship and that the family return to the more agreeable society and climate of Mexico City. After some weeks of pressing her desire, which was countered by his refusal, she denied him the marriage bed. Four months later she "discovered" his affair.

Doña Eulalia had played her gender role appropriately for the marriage up to the prescandal termination of coitus. Her husband, despite or because he was twenty-eight years her senior, had proven ardent at procreation. She had cooperated and together they had helped to people the empire. Of this activity the priests surely approved. Driven to take drastic action to remedy her situation, however, doña Eulalia used her sexual power to force her husband to accede to her wishes. When that failed she pursued a more public remedy, yet in doing so both husband and wife suffered loss of honor. Viewing gender as "*a historical, ideological process,*"[5] one in which historical actors, under certain circumstances, can exploit the ambiguity in their cultural definitions of man and woman to change their position in the context of the social relationships that bind them, offers an insight into doña Eulalia's behavior. She sought to reposition herself from wife and gobernadora to aggrieved woman, wife, and mother. To ascribe her motivation to haughtiness, whim, or postpartum depression, although the latter may well have reinforced her sense of desperation, is to miss the point. She sought a better life for herself and her surviving children, something she believed she could not have in California, or probably anywhere on the northern frontier. If her husband refused to leave, she would have to divorce him to escape. Divorce in this setting would mean permanent separation and spousal support, not dissolution of the union and freedom to remarry.

From her confinement at mission San Carlos, on 12 April, 1785, doña Eulalia wrote to her husband's superior, José Antonio Rengel, acting commandant general of the Interior Provinces, in Chihuahua City, seeking justice and imploring that she was "a woman and helpless." She sought his adjudication in her dispute with her husband because she believed that the priests favored don Pedro. As proof she noted that Fr. Noriega had taken testimony in the case from several people supportive of her husband, but had not asked for her testimony. The matter then had been sent forward to the bishop of Sonora who would render a judgment she felt would be against her, the offended party. Living in the mission was intolerable, she claimed, because the priests treated her like a prisoner, not a visitor, and forced her to fast for Lent despite the fact that she was ill and needed to eat. She pleaded with the commandant general to free her and to provide the funds necessary to relocate herself and her children to Mexico City. It took six months for her appeal to reach him and nearly another month for him to decide.

Commandant General Rengel endorsed the opinion of his legal advisor, or *asesor*, who accepted doña Eulalia's version of events. The asesor thought that the matter appropriately belonged to the jurisdiction of Antonio de los Reyes, the recently appointed bishop of Sonora. He nonetheless recommended that doña Eulalia be removed from San Carlos and sent to a home of respectable women in Sonora, that the Indian girl be treated likewise, and that one-third of don Pedro's salary be garnished by the treasury in Mexico City to pay doña Eulalia's expenses. Rengel so ordered and notified Bishop Reyes and the other parties involved. Thus, unbeknown to her, doña Eulalia had succeeded in getting the civil-military authority of the state to recognize, at least in part, her newly defined role.

Bishop Reyes, however, took umbrage at Rengel's behavior, for it seemed to the prelate that it made him dependent upon the military in a matter where the jurisdiction of the church was clear. The asesor had insulted him, usurped his prerogatives, and deserved a reprimand. Reyes demanded that Rengel take appropriate steps to restore respect for the bishop's office or he would be forced to bring the issue before the *audiencia* (high court) in Mexico City or before the king if necessary. Reyes may have had personal reasons to champion his churchly prerogatives that simultaneously helped his friend don Pedro. The governor had helped fund a trip Reyes had taken recently to Spain, and he had written Reyes three letters congratulating him on his appointment as bishop, on his safe return from Spain, and on his arrival in Sonora.[6] Even if those letters were mere flattery, Fages nonetheless enjoyed cordial relations with the bishop, something Father President of the Alta California missions, Junípero Serra, did not.[7]

Fages, whom Serra had succeeded in removing from his earlier post in 1774, returned to California with a more gracious demeanor toward the missionaries while still insisting on military values in determining colonial rule. The Serra-Fages rivalry reflected the ongoing tension between military/civil and religious authority in the colonial enterprise. If Fages could not get along with the Father President of the California missions, he nevertheless cultivated good relations with several of Serra's subordinates. Chief among them stood Francisco Palóu, Serra's second in command, who was also Serra's former student, religious companion, fellow apostolic missionary, confessor, and long-time friend. Palóu had received the Fages family at Mission San Francisco and had had four months to observe don Pedro very closely. After Serra's death, Palóu wrote to his superior that Fages "gave a fine example to those neophytes [newly baptized Indians] and soldiers. With his conduct and presence much was accomplished. May God reward him for it!"[8] Fages and the Catalán troops he commanded caused no scandal with Indian women, a major accomplishment in the friar's eyes.

but all had distinct agendas and the determination of who "won" in this instance depends solely upon when the investigation is closed.

Doña Eulalia used the "historical, ideological process" of gender to exploit patriarchy to remake herself. She negotiated her new status. To do so she had to embarrass herself, her husband, and the local clergy. She advanced her position at the expense of the Indian girl, a person of such low status that she was never asked to speak for the civil or clerical record. The only report of her is third hand, from doña Eulalia through don Pedro. Although doña Eulalia was inferior to her husband in the patriarchal order, she was still an elite woman, racially and socially superior to most colonials. Although dominated by patriarchy, domination she was able to alter, doña Eulalia as a colonial elite nevertheless dominated a social and political inferior, and manipulated this Indian subordinate to secure her advantage. Gender identification clearly has class, race, and educational boundaries that prevent any casual assumption of affinity between same-sex people based simply on biology. Doña Eulalia used social control to her advantage in this instance and challenged it in the case of her husband. Social control through definition of gender on the Alta California frontier was not clearly defined and could be successfully contested, at least by elites. Susan Deeds' essay shows how those at society's margins made their own successful challenges.

An Indigenous Challenge to Spanish Control

While don Pedro tried to cope with his marital crisis, the threat of an Indian uprising raised again the issues of colonial control over subject people. In October 1785, a plot by eight Kumi•vit (Gabrielino) villages to overthrow mission San Gabriel and expel the Spaniards was discovered by the corporal of the mission guard. When the Indians penetrated the mission compound to effect their plan, they were seized. Four ringleaders were identified, including Nicolás José, a mission neophyte, and three gentiles (unbaptized Indians). All three came from different villages. Two were men, one of whom Fages later accused of using warlock spells or charms against the neophytes; and a woman, Toypurina, known for her wisdom, had come unarmed to exhort the warriors to action. Toypurina, from Jachivit *ranchería* where her brother was headman, had been given beads by Nicolás José to invite people from the surrounding rancherías to join the plot.[13] Obviously a high status Kumi•vit woman as indicated by her personal reputation, her brother's position, and the neophyte's willingness to pay her in the currency of gentiles, Toypurina's special power indicated that she was also a shaman.

At the trial, over which Fages presided, Nicolás José complained that the priestly prohibition against native dances had particularly disturbed him because he wished to perform a mourning dance for his recently deceased son and could not do so. Nicolás José had been at the mission for about ten years and had been involved in an earlier plot against the priests. He had participated in both the worlds of the mission and of his Gabrielino culture and found himself in late 1785 forced to choose between them. He chose to try and restore his Indian world by ousting the Spanish.

Toypurina's interrogation revealed that she, a gentile (a non-Christian Indian), took offense at the presence of the priests and of all those at the mission because they occupied her tribal land. Toypurina resented not just the Spaniards, but also those Indians who had entered the mission and adopted its ways. Fages, at the sentencing, expressed disgust and amazement that warriors had allowed themselves to be dominated by this woman. Fages sentenced Nicolás José to perpetual banishment at the San Diego presidio, the southernmost military outpost; Fages exiled Toypurina to Monterey, the northernmost presidio.

Following the trial Toypurina made a series of choices crucial to her future. She accepted baptism, the outward sign of conversion, adopted the Christian name Regina Josefa, and married a presidio soldier, Manuel Montero, a Spaniard from Puebla.[14] She bore him four children and subsequently died, from European-introduced disease, ten years after the plot against San Gabriel.[15] Was Toypurina a victim of colonial domination or was she an insurgent resisting as far as she could the imposition of Christian European culture? Did Toypurina lose or gain in this experience, and what does her example, and that of Nicolás José, indicate about the social control of Indians?

Those who view Toypurina as a model of feminist resistance emphasize her behavior before and during her trial; those who view her case as the triumph of civilization over darkness through the vehicle of religion emphasize her life following baptism. There is at least one other perspective, however. The aftermath of the trial not only meant that Toypurina's plan and those of the others had failed, but also it meant that she had made enemies among the neophytes by her condemnation of them. Even if she could do so, which she could not, remaining in her homeland would be

personally dangerous. By accepting the outward sign of the Christian religion she could begin her life anew. Removal to a new land without enemies
offered survival and a fresh start. Marriage to a presidial soldier gave her
some status in the nascent Hispanic community. The mixed-blood marriage she entered, between herself as a native and the soldier as newcomer
and eventual settler, was a model highly desired by the priests but rarely
replicated. Hers was one of only two such marriages recorded at missions
San Carlos, Santa Clara, and San Juan Bautista in the decade following the
San Gabriel plot.[16]

In accepting the Spanish system she saved herself to live a life different from the one she had known. Superficially, she would seem to have
been conquered by colonial ideas of social control. For the priests, the
acceptance of baptism by a pagan Indian represented another body counted
in the "spiritual conquest" of the province. To the priests baptism signified
conversion, meaning that the pre-existing religious belief system of the
Indians had been expelled from their hearts and minds in favor of the one
truth taught by the missionary, yet everywhere they saw instances where
this had not been the case. Take, for example, Nicolás José, who had been
Christianized for a decade but still practiced his native religion. The priests
saw in his behavior not the failure of baptism to convert, but rather the failure of the Indian to live up to his newly adopted standards. Indians were
guilty of backsliding, and they fell into behavior that priests identified as
sin. The priestly calculation that baptism equaled conversion was an error.
Conversion was a process of some indeterminate length initiated by, rather
than completed by, baptism.[17]

For Toypurina, then, accepting baptism offered a way to begin the process that a social psychologist describes as "protective ingratiation." It is a
strategy by which a subordinate assumes the behavior the superior wants
in order to minimize or avoid further interference in the subordinate's
life.[18] If she converted at all, and Spanish language acquisition among a
host of other variables influenced that outcome, Toypurina doubtless had
not done so at the time of her baptism. Rather, by going along, she got
along with the system. Certainly the priests taught California Indians patriarchy, and her husband had been reared under its influence, but in the inti-
macy of her marriage patriarchy's impact upon Toypurina's life is
impossible to calculate. She had resisted as a gentile; in her Christian life
she may well have continued a less visible resistance. Despite appearances
to the contrary, there is no reason to think that the boundaries of social

control as applied to Indians and to Indian women had defeated her. She had negotiated another course of action. Such behavior by California Indians, and by Indians elsewhere, is often difficult to comprehend. As defined, Indians must defend "Indianness," usually some cultural essentialism, against the onslaught of externally induced cultural change; Indian failure to do so then becomes the secular equivalent of backsliding. Yet instances abound of Indians seemingly changing patterns in their lives in order to continue them, a pragmatic survival option that permitted them to closet the behavior of yesterday in favor of living tomorrow. Toypurina's case, one of thousands in California and the north Spanish frontier, illustrates the limits of social control. Behavior can be modified but it is more difficult to secure the assent of mind and heart.

Modeling the Virtuous Life as a Form of Social Control

Franciscans subjected themselves to social control. As priests they were expected to lead virtuous and celibate lives; as apostolic missionaries, they dedicated themselves to bringing their spiritual message to difficult areas and to work among potentially dangerous people. The Apostolic College of San Fernando in Mexico City sent 125 missionaries to Alta California in the Spanish era. Even for men accustomed to hardship, the physical and psychological challenges of work in California proved daunting. In that respect they may have shared doña Eulalia's response to the place. Although legally obligated to stay for ten years, fifty-seven served less than that while a near equal number, fifty-eight, died at their missions. In the words of one Franciscan historian, the preponderance of missionaries "might be classed as men of ordinary ability, zeal, learning and virtue." Compared to Franciscan behavior in New Mexico, where sexual dalliance was common,[19] California missionaries, influenced by Serra's stern orders and example, lived conspicuously celibate lives, as their treatment of doña Eulalia revealed. An examination of the fourteen missionaries who served at mission San Fernando is illustrative. Nine were classed as ordinary, two possessed superior virtue, one was a scholar, one an alcoholic, and one a womanizer. The alcoholic had been relieved at two previous missions before being sent from San Fernando to San Diego, where he eventually recovered his sobriety under the tutelage of the senior missionary.[20] Priests battled boredom, loneliness, and deprivation while trying to accomplish an enormous task. In contrast to the situations in Florida,

Texas, Nueva Vizcaya, and parts of Sonora, Spanish efforts met with seeming success in California.

What the missionaries so steadfastly attempted to practice themselves, they also expected of the colonial military on which they depended. After sentencing the plotters against mission San Gabriel, Fages turned his attention to prescribing a new code of conduct toward Indians. He addressed gentile presence in mission communities, while simultaneously reinforcing existing standards of behavior toward native peoples. Fages had been among those admonished by Governor Gaspar de Portolá in the founding of the colony in 1769, and Portolá himself followed strict orders from Inspector General José de Gálvez, to insure that "the soldiers and muleteers of his company observe a most exact discipline." The governor, Gálvez said, must make them understand "as an inviolable regulation the need for treating the Indians well and he shall punish them as for an irremissible crime any molestations or violence toward the native women for, besides being offenses against God which they would commit by such excesses, they could also endanger the success of the expedition."[21]

Fages and his professional Catalonian Volunteers took these admonitions to heart, as Palóu's description of them confirms. But the Catalonians, numbering about twenty-five, comprised only a small portion of the soldiers in California, a number that only exceeded two hundred late in the colonial era. The remaining soldiers were poorly trained conscripts and recruits and their behavior proved very difficult to control. Sexual abuse of Indian women, including rape, became a serious problem. Priests and officers protested against it, but disciplining soldiers with public floggings, banishment, or death became a serious problem for the military. Officers feared that such actions would make Spanish rule appear weak and encourage Indian resistance. Even incarceration, the customary punishment, could leave military posts more lightly staffed. In the 1790 enumeration, for example, two of the six soldiers assigned to mission San Gabriel were in prison for sexual crimes against or with Indian women. The control of soldiers, especially with women Indians, proved difficult for Spanish authority. But it would be incorrect to assert, as one historian has, that the Spanish condoned an informal policy of allowing the rape of Indian women in order to control Indian society.[22] As Gálvez had noted from the beginning of Spanish settlement, instead of conquering native society, Spanish rape of indigenous women would provoke native resistance and thwart imperial goals.

Creating the Spanish Indian

The Indian became the central object of social control. Mission Indians—neophytes—constituted the core of the colony. They were the work force upon which all else was built. To create that human base Franciscans sought to persuade hunter-gatherers to abandon coastal plains and forests to become sedentary farmers and pastoralists in a new life at the missions. Those remaining in their native state, the gentiles, offered an alternative to mission ways and a refuge for mission runaways. Consequently, tensions developed between neophytes and gentiles. Over time the gentile villages nearest the missions declined as their members succumbed either to disease or to priestly blandishments, and priests had to move further inland to find recruits.

Inside the mission compound priests had extraordinary power. By 1773, Serra had achieved a viceregal decree recognizing that baptized Indians and those being catechized were under the protection of the priests, meaning that Franciscans had the power over mission Indians of conservator to ward or patriarchal father to his children. Priests employed the immersion system of conversion by taking complete control of their wards' lives from cradle to grave. Serra knew and disapproved of the approach described by Patricia Osante in Nuevo Santander of missionizing Indians by having them live with colonizing families. In California Franciscans directed their charges in the ways of religion and work; two activities united by the European sense of time embodied in the sundial and translated into measured activity by the bell. Everything had its appropriate daily time—-breakfast, religious instruction, participation in the daily Mass, morning work, noontime prayer and meal, siesta, afternoon work, choir practice for some and catechism for others, dinner, evening activities, and bed. At bedtime unmarried Indian women over seven years of age were locked down in a single dormitory (*monjería*) under the supervision of an elderly Indian woman and released only at morning. At some missions the boys were also sequestered. Both practices derived from the Franciscan views that sex happened only at night and that Indian girls, like their European superiors, must save their chastity until marriage in order to bring honor to their husbands.

In the new Spanish material culture, which also incorporated some earlier Indian practices, Indian women ground corn, prepared meals, supervised children, wove woolen thread on looms, helped with grain threshing, and hauled wood and water. In religious culture women, like men, were to learn beyond the catechism in the daily experience of the Mass. At Mass women faced the right side of the altar, the Epistle side, where the statues for their edification, depictions of the virgin or female saints, supposedly reinforced notions of the Christian family with the female Indian as mother. Seeking to communicate to Indian women in a language of equivalents, priests placed before them statues of Mary as mother and nurturer, symbolizing both purity and forbearance that equated to Indian women's new roles, the images and significance of which they could contemplate while at prayer. Men faced the left side of the altar, the Gospel side, where through images of St. Joseph and some versions of the Christus they could contemplate their new roles as Christian husbands bound to provide and sacrifice for their families. Indians participated in the Mass as they prayed aloud, sang responses, and listened to or were part of Indian choirs joining together with Franciscan priests in the symbolic recreation of the Last Supper of Christ.

Priests organized their communities hierarchically, replicating part of Spanish society, so that Indians could learn their place in this complex order. In this hierarchy priests placed men in one of four groups according to occupation. First were the skilled artisans, consisting of masons, carpenters, blacksmiths, cobblers, weavers, and tanners. Second came stockmen and herdsmen, who were also tallow workers, hide cleaners, meat curers, butchers, and *vaqueros* (cowboys), as well as Indian auxiliaries used to return mission runaways. Third were the horticulturists, who tended gardens along with mission vineyards and orchards, planting, pruning, and collecting materials weekly if not daily. And fourth were the laborers and field hands, who made adobe tiles for building and cleared and plowed the fields, planted cereal crops, and harvested them. Children frequently weeded gardens and served the missionaries' table. When needed, everyone helped with harvest.

Within the mission compound friars created a new Indian elite group, the choir, the ability to join depending solely upon the ability to replicate European sound in song. There was, however, a catch. Unlike their missionary counterparts in Sonora who, as Cynthia Radding notes, used women as choristers, Franciscans in California chose only men. These all-male groups in Alta California eventually had their own uniforms to distinguish them from nonchoristers and they generally held better jobs, closer to the priests. They also learned Spanish well and formed an important bonding unit between priest and congregation.

The "greatest problem of the missionary," according to the second Father President of the missions, was "how to transform a savage race such as these [*sic*] into a society that is human, Christian, civil, and industrious. This can be accomplished," he continued, "only by 'denaturalizing' them."[23]

Franciscans undertook a challenging task in trying to transform the Indian gentile into a Christian and Spanish subject, a task that demanded of the Indian fundamental personal change.

To effect the division of labor and to instill correct behavior in Indians, priests employed several instruments of social control at their missions. The *escolta*, or mission guard, usually comprising six soldiers and their families, represented Spanish military power while also reinforcing the proper mode of family life. A *mayordomo* (overseer), a retired military man, and his family helped to oversee daily life. To punish the disobedient, priests had the power to have Indians flogged,[24] shackled in irons, or placed in wooden stocks. Those who carried out such orders and who assisted the mayordomo were Indian officials called *alcaldes*.

But the veiled threats of the soldiers or the routine use of punishments were only external corrective devices. In seeking to remake the Indian from within, the priests had other techniques. To persuade the Indian to accept personal responsibility for his behavior, the priest needed to replace the indigenous sense of shame with the Judeo-Christian concept of guilt. At the daily Mass all Indians recited the *Confiteor*, the public confession of sin. Once a year, each individual had to confess his sins before a priest and receive the Eucharist to maintain his religious standing within the church. In between, however, priests punished Indian behavior they regarded as sinful, usually with the lash. The public humiliation of sinners invoked a medieval practice designed to encourage proper behavior of the group by punishment of the individual miscreant. Since the mission community stood as a microcosmic equivalent of the entire earthly church, both united in the "Mystical Body of Christ," punishment required reconciliation. In this way sinners could be chastised and reintegrated into the religious community, free to do better but also to sin again. Thus, external and internal corrections were supposed to accomplish the Indians' conversion and pacification that Franciscans and Spanish authorities sought.

Contending Views of the Indian's Role in Spanish Society

The Franciscans' primary purpose in the missions was to mold good Christians. Their secondary aim was to mold a labor force to occupy the bottom social rung of the town each mission was to become. Secular interests valued the secondary goal above the Franciscan's primary objective, and nowhere was that conflict clearer than in the struggle over mission secularization or the cessation of priestly rule. Ordinarily, missions were to become pueblos or towns, a process that took about ten years. At that time the vast amount of land originally entrusted to the Franciscans—generally more than 22 square leagues, or about 100,000 acres[25]—was to be divided unequally. Franciscan holdings, serving as the parish for the new town, would be reduced to the church building, living quarters of the friars, and some adjacent land.[26] The Indians would be given small plots for subsistence around the former mission. The remaining land—about 97,000 acres—was to be given to the settlers and soldiers for whom the emancipated Indians would work.

By 1776, a trend toward improved harvests at all missions except San Diego indicated that the Franciscan system had overcome survival problems and was on its way to producing significant agricultural surplus and economic success.[27] Anticipating Indian emancipation, the governor of California in 1778 ordered Serra and the missionaries at older establishments to hold elections for Indian officials, an act preparatory for secularization. Indians needed experience in governing themselves, the secular reasoning went, and among those to be chosen the most important office would be alcalde. The governor himself or his designated representative would instruct these elected Indians in their new duties.

Serra complied outwardly with the governor's order but privately told his confreres to choose the officers for whom the Indians would vote. With this civil interference in their enterprise, Franciscans feared that Indians were being given mixed signals from the Crown, suggesting that the priests were no longer supreme. Alcaldes did begin to abuse their power almost at once, committing sin with greater abandon than their fellows, which was the Franciscan way to describe, albeit unknowingly, Indian reassertion of the prerogatives of native culture. Eventually, priests found a way to graft the office of alcalde onto indigenous social systems, but by the end of Spanish rule alcaldes had become increasingly restive. Under the Mexican regime they would launch major revolts against secular and religious authorities.[28] Yet despite the civil government's success in creating the Indian offices, Franciscans denied that their charges were morally prepared for pueblo life and no mission was secularized during the Spanish period.

What Franciscans regarded as the California Indians' predilection toward sinfulness was, in part, resistance to Spanish rule and Spanish ways, and this resistance Indians expressed in multiple forms. Even as some Indians sang in choir for the congregation, other Indians marked the church walls with graffiti. At mission San Miguel, for example, Indians inscribed graffiti just below the choir loft and opposite the pulpit. When discovered, priests ordered the walls whitewashed, but repeated graffiti merely brought new layers of whitewash. Indians engaged in work slowdowns, were tardy to Mass or inattentive during services, failed to learn Spanish, circulated rumors of uprisings or discontent, poisoned the friars' food, even plotted a missionary's death. Indian men with multiple wives, when forced to choose one upon entering the mission, frequently chose the youngest, instead of the first they had married as required by church law. The very multiplicity of wives offended the Franciscans and added to their workload in sorting out the "appropriate wife" for Christian remarriage. Indians with sufficiently large numbers entered the missions en masse, literally overwhelming the two resident missionaries' ability to handle their spiritual good fortune. With so many then to supervise, more than could reasonably be managed, there was more room for Indians to continue their traditional behavior clandestinely. Indians also resisted overtly by shooting arrows into cattle and horses and by attacking, on two occasions, the missions themselves.

Conclusions

The relatively peaceful negotiation of social control permitted mission establishments to become successful producing surplus harvests to feed presidios and pueblos, but within the context of a disturbing trend. Throughout the Spanish era, priests recognized that missionized Indians lived shorter lives than their gentile counterparts. Although the Franciscans could not accurately quantify the phenomenon, historical demography indicates that from 1771 to 1820 the mean annual birth rate stood at forty-one per thousand, the death rate at seventy-eight per thousand. Deaths exceeded births by thirty-seven per thousand.[29] Such numbers indicate a crisis state for a population, and priests knew well that without active gentile recruitment deeper into the interior the missions, no matter how prosperous in land, crops, and cattle, would fail.

From his headquarters at mission La Purísima, the fifth Father President, Mariano Payeras, wrote a pensive and disturbing letter to his superiors in Mexico City early in 1820. "Every thoughtful missionary," he began, "has noted that while gentiles procreate easily and are healthy and robust (though errant) in the wilds ...as soon as they commit themselves to a sociable and Christian life, they become extremely feeble, lose weight, get sick, and die. This plague affects the women particularly, especially those who have recently become pregnant." Payeras noted that earlier missionaries had believed that the children born in the missions would recover their natural health. "However," he continued, "the sad experience of fifty one years [since the beginning in 1769] has showed us all too well that we too have erred in our calculation. Having already seen two generations in the missions, we sadly observe that the mission native dies equally, and perhaps more so than the Indians of the sierra." Payeras saw a grim future and asked his superiors to take actions that "would free us for all time from undeserved reproach."[30] Payeras received no answer, his superiors doubtless beset by the vicissitudes of the civil war then convulsing New Spain. That turmoil would terminate Spanish rule within two years and render moot the success of Spanish imperial efforts at social control in Alta California. Ironically, the myth of Franciscan missionary success would be initiated late in the nineteenth century by an American Protestant woman, Helen Hunt Jackson, and gain momentum in the twentieth century in the quest to make Junípero Serra a saint.[31]

Social control had ironies when applied to all groups in Alta California and the traditional hierarchies, whether civil and clerical or those imposed upon the Indians, were far more complex than the traditional story makes them out to be. Spanish military and religious social control involved attempts to subordinate people regarded as inferior. Inferiority, in turn, was assumed to be inherent in such qualities as gender and/or race. Yet in Alta California Spanish colonization did not lead straightforwardly to social control; the "inferiors" contested it. Doña Eulalia successfully contested the patriarchy that in her estimation imposed unacceptable hardships upon herself and her children. Toypurina, the Indian rebel, remade herself through "protective ingratiation" to avoid death and to limit the colonizers' intrusions into her life. Other Indians pursued that strategy or resisted in behavior patterns that continued their cultures inside the missions. Franciscans misdiagnosed such Indian behavior as "sin" while they wrestled with and generally bested their own sinful tendencies. Elite soldiers did better at controlling themselves through internal governors than did their subordinates. No policy, however, official or unofficial, of raping Indian women was pursued.

On this frontier the social control of colonizer over colonized had been negotiated, not imposed. Perhaps that process of negotiation accounted for the ability of ex-mission Indians to endure. For the long-term history of California, former mission Indians adapted to and survived the American onslaught occasioned by the gold discovery in 1848, something that gentiles, less exposed to European contact, did not.

NOTES

1. Peter Gerhard, *The North Frontier of New Spain* (Princeton: Princeton University Press, 1982), 304–12; Sherburne F. Cook, *The Population of the California Indians, 1769–1970* (Berkeley: University of California Press, 1976), 20–43.

2. David J. Weber, *The Spanish Frontier in North America* (New Haven, Conn.: Yale University Press, 1992), 212–16.

3. The basic documents in this case are to be found in "Instancia de Doña Eulalia Callis, mujer de Don Pedro Fages, gobernador de Californias, sobre que se oiga en justicia y redima de la opresión que padece," Provincias Internas, Tomo 120, Expediente 3, Archivo General de la Nación, Mexico (hereafter cited as AGN), transcripts of which are in the Bancroft Library at the University of California, Berkeley. The best treatment of the matter, and with a different interpretation than mine, is Donald A. Nuttall, "The Fages Marital Crisis of 1785: Elaboration and Explanation," *Southern California Quarterly* 83 (2001): 1–22. See also Antonia Castañeda, "Engendering the History of Alta California, 1769–1848," in *Contested Eden: California before the Gold Rush*, ed. Ramón Gutiérrez and Richard Orsi (Berkeley: University of California Press, 1998), 230–59.

4. Nuttall, "The Fages Marital Crisis of 1785," 16.

5. Gail Bederman, *Manliness and Civilization: A Cultural History of Gender and Race in the United States, 1880–1917* (Chicago: University of Chicago Press, 1995), 7 (her emphasis).

6. Fray Francisco Palóu to fray Juan Sancho, Mission San Cárlos, 13 September 1784, in *Historical Memoirs of New California by Fray Francisco Palóu, O.F.M.*, ed. Herbert E. Bolton, 4: 362–73 (Berkeley: University of California Press, 1926).

7. Maynard F. Geiger, *The Life and Times of Junípero Serra, O.F.M., or The Man Who Never Turned Back (1713–1784)* , 2 vols. (Washington, D.C.: Academy of American Franciscan History, 1959), 2: 364–66.

8. Fray Francisco Palóu to fray Juan Sancho, Mission San Cárlos, 13 September 1784, in Bolton, *Historical Memoirs of New California*, 4: 371.

9. Geiger, *The Life and Times of Junípero Serra*, 2: 394–95. On apostolic missionaries see Maynard F. Geiger, trans. and annot., *Palóu's Life of Fray Junípero Serra* (Washington, D.C.: Academy of American Franciscan History, 1955), 328–29 n. 13, 14.

10. Pedro Fages to Fray Francisco Palóu, Mission San Gabriel, 2 January 1787, in Bolton, *Historical Memoirs of New California*, 4: 378–81.

11. Cheryl English Martin, *Governance and Society in Colonial Mexico: Chihuahua in the Eighteenth Century* (Stanford: Stanford University Press, 1996), 183.

12. To add further complexity and perhaps ambiguity to the crisis, Monsignor James Culleton, *Indians and Pioneers of Old Monterey* (Fresno: Academy of California Church History, 1950), 117, avows that "Doña Eulalia gave birth to a daughter May 14, 1786," but the child died eight days later. This event, in Culleton's view, explains doña Eulalia's change of heart toward her husband. It does more than that. If true, then doña Eulalia either reconciled with don Pedro earlier than heretofore documented or there was yet another scandal in this matter, one involving the gobernadora herself.

13. The core of the documentation for this case is found in the trial transcript in "Ynterrogatorio sobre la sublevación de San Gabriel, 10 octubre de 1785," Provincias Internas, Tomo 120, Expediente 3, AGN, microfilm, 31a–47b, Bancroft Library. Steven Hackel, in a paper on the uprising and Toypurina presented at the Western History Association annual meeting in Sacramento, California, October 1998, first called attention to the misperception of Toypurina presented forty years earlier by Thomas Workman Temple II in "Toypurina the Witch and the Indian Uprising at San Gabriel," *Masterkey* 32 (1958): 136–52. Temple had seen the documentation but probably considered it hastily since his goal was to write a dramatic and exciting recreation of the event. In his version Temple created the kind of courtroom speech for Toypurina completely at odds with Spanish legal practice but reminiscent of those seen on a popular television show of his era, *Perry Mason*.

14. William Marvin Mason, *The Census of 1790: A Demographic History of Colonial California* (Menlo Park: Ballena Press, 1998), 96, entry 41 wherein Montero is classified as "español."

15. Edward D. Castillo, "Gender Status Decline, Resistance, and Accommodation among Female Neophytes in the Missions of California: A San Gabriel Case Study," *American Indian Culture and Research Journal* 18, 1 (1994): 78–81.

16. Albert L. Hurtado, *Intimate Frontiers: Sex, Gender, and Culture in Old California* (Albuquerque: University of New Mexico Press, 1999), 25–26, table 2.1.

17. James A. Sandos, "Christianization among the Chumash: An Ethnohistoric Approach," *American Indian Quarterly* 15, 1 (1991): 65–89.

18. Edward Jones, *Ingratiation: A Social Psychological Analysis* (New York: Appleton-Century-Crofts, 1964), 47. "Protective ingratiation" also may apply to doña Eulalia's behavior.

19. Ramón A. Gutiérrez, *When Jesus Came, the Corn Mothers Went Away: Marriage, Sexuality, and Power in New Mexico, 1500–1846* (Stanford: Stanford University Press, 1991), 123–25, 313–15, describes instances of Franciscans fornicating with women and men.

20. Maynard F. Geiger, *Franciscan Missionaries in Hispanic California, 1769–1848* (San Marino: The Huntington Library, 1969), x–xi. I calculated Spanish era missionaries from Appendix II, 281–93. Doyce B. Nunis Jr., "The Franciscan Friars of Mission San Fernando, 1797–1847," in *Mission San Fernando Rey de España, 1797–1997: A Bicentennial Tribute*, ed. Doyce B. Nunis Jr., 217–48 (Los Angeles: Historical Society of Southern California, 1997).

21. Maynard F. Geiger, "Notes and Documents: Instructions Concerning the Occupation of California, 1769," *Southern California Quarterly* 47, 2 (1965): 212. For Fages' new regulations see William Marvin Mason, "Fages' Code of Conduct toward Indians, 1787," *Journal of California Anthropology* 2 (1975): 90–100.

22. Antonia Castañeda, "Sexual Violence in the Politics and Policies of Conquest: Amerindian Women and the Spanish Conquest of Alta California," in *Building with Our Hands: New Directions in Chicana Studies*, ed. Addela de la Torre and Beatríz M. Pesquera (Berkeley: University of California Press, 1993), 15–33.

23. "Refutation of Charges," Fermín Francisco de Lasuén, Mission Santa Clara, 16 June 1802, in *Writings of Fermín Francisco de Lasuén*, ed. and trans. Finbar Kenneally, 2: 202 (Washington, D.C.: Academy of American Franciscan History, 1965).

24. I disagree with apologists for the Franciscans who claim, as does Father Francis F. Guest, that "When a neophyte was whipped at a mission, he was, as a general rule, spanked rather than flogged." Guest's reasoning is historically faulty and he tortures the Spanish words *azotes* and the verb *azotear* into absurd meanings. See his "The California Missions Were Far from Faultless," *Southern California Quarterly* 76, 3 (1994): 255–307, quoted at 265.

25. Crane S. Miller and Richard S. Hyslop, *California: The Geography of Diversity* (Mountain View, Calif.: Mayfield Publishing Co., 1983), 146. Iris H. Engstrand, "California Ranchos: Their Hispanic Heritage," *Southern California Quarterly* 67, 3 (1985): 281–90.

26. At the time of the California Land Commission in the 1850s, the secularized holdings of the former missions ranged from a low of 6.5 acres at San Rafael to a high of 283 acres at Santa Barbara. Most were less than 35 acres. Crisóstomo Pérez, *Land Grants in Alta California* (Rancho Cordova, Calif.: Landmark Enterprises, 1996), 73–75.

27. David Hornbeck, "Early Mission Settlement," in *Some Reminiscences about Fray Junípero Serra*, ed. Francis J. Weber, 55–66 (Santa Barbara: Kimberly Press, 1985).

28. Stephen W. Hackel, "The Staff of Leadership: Indian Authority in the Missions of Alta California," *William and Mary Quarterly*, 3rd Series, 54, 2 (1997): 347–76.

29. My calculations are from Cook, *The Population of the California Indians, 1769–1970*, 107, table 13.

30. Mariano Payeras, mission La Purísima, to Reverend Father Guardian and Venerable *Discretorio* [body of counselors] of Our Apostolic College of San Fernando de México, 2 February 1820, in *Writings of Mariano Payeras*, trans. and ed. Donald Cutter, 225–28 (Santa Barbara: Bellerophon Books, 1995).

31. James A. Sandos, "Between Crucifix and Lance: Indian-White Relations in California, 1769–1848," in *Contested Eden: California before the Gold Rush*, ed. Ramón Gutiérrez and Richard Orsi (Berkeley: University of California Press, 1998), 221–22; James A. Sandos, "Junípero Serra's Canonization and the Historical Record," *American Historical Review* 93, 5 (1988): 1253–69.

Glossary

adelantado   The holder of a royal contract (*capitulación*) providing for the conquest of a certain area with mutual obligations and privileges for both the crown and the adelantado.

aficionar   To inspire a liking.

alcalde   In general, a civil official with judicial, executive, and legislative functions; elected Indian official at the missions; a *cabildo* officer.

alcalde de barrio   Justice of the peace.

alcalde mayor   Magistrate and judge, governor of an *alcaldía mayor*.

alcalde ordinario   Municipal magistrate; one of the two elected officials of a town council; *cabildo* judge who sat in cases of persons not protected by a *fuero* (legal privilege).

alcaldía mayor   Administrative division subordinate to a *gobierno*, ruled by an *alcalde mayor*.

alcanzar   To take or obtain.

alguacil   Sheriff or constable; elected official for mission governance.

alguacil mayor   Chief constable.

almud(es)   Dry measure normally used for grain, approximately 4 bushels. There are 12 almudes in a *fanega*, and 4 *cuartillos* in an almud. Also a measure of planted land (see *fanega de sembradura*).

arbitrio justicial   Judicial discretion.

arroyo   Brook or river bed with seasonal water flow.

asesor   Legal counsel to the commandant general of the Interior Provinces.

Athapaskan   Language group encompassing the dialects spoken by Apache groups.

atraer   To attract.

audiencia   Royal high court of appeal organized by region in Spanish America. Major cases could be appealed from it to the Council of the Indies (*Consejo de Indias*) in Spain. The viceroyalty of New Spain (*virreinato de Nueva España*) comprised the audiencias of Santo Domingo, Mexico, Guatemala, Guadalajara, and Manila. During most of the colonial period much of the north fell under the jurisdiction of the Real Audiencia of Guadalajara.

ayuntamiento   Municipal council of a town or city, same as *cabildo*.

bando de buen gobierno   Edict of good government (to regulate behavior).

barrera   Barrier.

blancos   Whites.

bozal   African-born slave: usually a recent arrival who could not yet speak Spanish and was not acculturated.

caballería   Unit of land for cultivation measuring about 315 acres.

cabecera   Head village of a mission district; principal settlement and administrative seat of a political jurisdiction.

cabildo   Municipal government, town council, or *ayuntamiento*.

cabildo abierto   Municipal forum open to the colonial elite of a town.

cabildo eclesiástico   Governing body of a diocese.

cacique (caciquil)   Local headman or chief.

cacomites   Lily-like flowers.

cajas reales   Treasury offices or branches of the *real hacienda*.

calidades   Racial categories of the system of castes (*sistema de castas*).

camino real   Royal highway; main road or highway.

capellanías   Chaplaincies generally producing an annual income of five percent on the principal.

capitán grande   Indigenous name of Spanish governor.

capitulación   Charter granted by the Crown to an *adelantado* for the conquest or colonization of a region.

casa de la contratación   House of trade established in Seville in 1503 and moved to Cádiz in the eighteenth century. Controlled traffic of passengers and merchandise between Spain and the New World and held responsibility for scientific and technical matters related to navigation. Functioned as a checkpoint, registry, and customs collecting agency for incoming and outgoing fleets.

casa real   Government building.

castas   Persons of mixed racial heritage.

castas buenas   Good castes.

castas limpias   Clean castes.

castizo   Product of a union between a mestizo and a Spaniard.

causa criminal   Criminal suit.

cédula   Edict; decree.

cédula real   Royal edict or decree.

Chichimeca   Hispanicized plural of Náhuatl *chichimícatl*; the hunter-gatherers of the arid plains and mountains north of Mesoamerica (*Gran Chichimeca*). Became the generic Aztec name for nomadic Indians, equivalent to *indios bárbaros* or wild Indians.

ciudad   City, a settlement with royally granted privileges superior to those of a *villa*, and always a *cabecera*.

clientela   Patronage network.

coartación   Spanish legal practice originating in Cuba that permitted slaves to purchase their freedom.

Cocoyome   Indigenous group in northern New Spain, in the present state of Durango.

code noir   Black code; French slave code.

code noir ou loi municipale   Failed 1778–1779 effort by planters on the New Orleans cabildo to impose a stringent slave code on the management of slaves in Spanish Louisiana.

color quebrado   Person of broken color or mixed background, in other words, not white (Spanish) or dark (Indian).

comandancia general   Military-political district under a *comandante general*. Carlos III created *La Comandancia General de las Provincias Internas del Norte de la Nueva España* in 1776.

comandante general   Royal appointee in charge of the military and administrative affairs of the northern frontier provinces collected into the Comandancia General de las Provincias Internas.

comisario de barrio   Neighborhood commissioner.

compadrazgo   God-parentage; social and spiritual fictive kinship established between *compadres*.

compadre   Godfather; a man who sponsors a person at baptism; in Mexico and the Southwest also a friend or close companion.

compañía volante   Special lightly armed cavalry units, literally flying companies, created in 1782 by Teodoro de Croix, first Commandante General of the Provincias Internas, to respond quickly to Indian raids over a greater territory than could regular presidial troops.

común   Mission communal land; also refers to commonwealth.

común fama   Reputation of ill repute.

confiteor   Public confession of sin.

congrega, congregación   Nuclear Indian settlement into which a dispersed population was moved, often forcibly, to facilitate administrative control as well as religious instruction and acculturation. Equivalent to *reducción*.

Consejo de Indias   Royal and Supreme Council of the Indies formally established in 1524 in the manner of other royal councils, such as the Council of Castile, to be competent to govern and administer the Indies; the highest agency in Spain for the administration of the Spanish overseas empire.

contador   Accountant; one of the four *oficiales reales*.

converso   Jewish person converted to Christianity (and therefore suspect).

corregidor   Magistrate and judge; governor of a *corregimiento*. In most cases the same as an *alcalde mayor*.

corregidor de indios   Official placed in charge of Indian towns paying tribute to the crown. In addition to the duties of a *corregidor* or *alcalde mayor*, the corregidor de indios was to protect and encourage Indian welfare.

corregimiento   District; within a province, governed by a *corregidor*.

coyote   Person of mixed blood with different regional meanings; referred to African-Indian unions in some areas, used synonymously with *zambo*; elsewhere described the product of Spanish or *casta* (*mestizo*) and Indian parents.

criollo   Creole; an American-born Spaniard; also called *español americano*.

cuera   Leather and cotton jacket worn by soldiers in their frontier war with the Indians.

Cunca'ac (Seri)   Nomadic bands of the Sonoran Gulf Coast.

cura   Priest; more specifically, *cura párroco*, priest in charge of a parish (see *curato, parroquia*).

curandero, curanderismo   Healer, often employing indigenous or syncretistic religious practices.

curato Parish or curacy.

custodia Franciscan or Jesuit jurisdiction for governing
    Indian missions.

derecho Customary right.

doctrina Indian congregation, more often called mission in its early years.
    Its minister, whether secular or regular, was a *cura doctrinero* until the
    congregation was organized as a parish (see *parroquia, curato*);
    congregation of Indians smaller than a mission.

doctrinero See *doctrina*.

doncella guerrera Warrior maiden.

encomendero Holder of an *encomienda*.

encomienda Grant of tribute assigned to a Spaniard from Indians living
    on a specified tract of land. In return for tribute (in goods or labor),
    the grantee (*encomendero*) had the responsibility to provide for the
    welfare of the Indians and their Christian religious instruction.

entrada An armed Spanish expedition into hostile territory.

equidad Justice.

escolta Escort; soldiers assigned as a mission guard.

español americano American-born Spaniard; criollo.

españoles Those of Spanish descent; meant non-Indian in a number
    of the northern provinces during the colonial period.

español peninsular/español europeo European-born Spaniard.

estancia Outlying settlement subordinate to a *pueblo*.

estancia de ganado Cattle ranch (see *ganado mayor, ganado menor*).

eudeve Highland villagers of central Sonora.

factor Royal factor; one of the four *oficiales reales*.

fanega Dry measure of approximately 2.6 bushels.

fanega de sembradura Land measure of approximately 8.8 acres.

fiscal Royal attorney appointed as a watchdog over bureaucratic
    departments. During the second half of the eighteenth century there
    was a fiscal presiding over civil and criminal matters, and in 1780 the
    Crown appointed a Fiscal de Real Hacienda; attorney for a city,
    municipality, or other organization; in indigenous and non-Indian
    villages, official with responsibility for the maintenance of
    community lands and irrigation ditches, or mission lands.

fuero   Legal privilege under Spanish law given to soldiers and clerics.

ganado mayor   Larger livestock such as cattle and horses.

ganado menor   Smaller livestock such as sheep and goats.

genízaro   Indians of nomadic tribes who, after ransom or capture, became incorporated into colonial society.

gente decente   Decent society.

gente de razón   Literally, the "people of reason"; Christians, as opposed to *gentiles* (gentiles), as the nomadic Indians were often called. In the northern provinces, the term normally included congregated or settled Indians.

gentiles   Literally gentiles; those Indians who had yet to accept Spanish dominion.

gobernador   Governor (see *gobierno*), the king's representative and administrator in a *reino* or *provincia*; also, indigenous official in a mission.

gobernadora   Governor's wife.

gobierno, gobernación   Political jurisdiction headed by a governor (*gobernador*) subordinate to the viceroy (*virrey*). *Gobiernos* are also called kingdoms (*reinos*) or provinces (*provincias*). Nuevo México and Texas were *gobiernos* or *provincias*.

habitant   Settler, usually French.

hacendado   Owner or holder of a *hacienda*.

hacienda   Landed property as an estate or ranch.

hechicería   Witchcraft.

hidalgo   Member of the minor nobility in Spain.

Indias, Las   The Indies; West Indies of the New World (America), to be distinguished from the East Indies which Columbus tried to reach by traversing the Atlantic Ocean.

indios bárbaros   Literally, the "barbarous Indians," as distinguished from those under the jurisdiction of a mission, or otherwise converted and settled.

indios de pueblo   Indians under the jurisdiction of a mission, or otherwise converted and settled, as distinguished from *indios barbaros* or *indios gentiles*.

inquisición   Tribunal of the Roman Catholic Church directed at the suppression of heresy. The Inquisition began in the thirteenth century and functioned in the Papal States and other European countries. The Spanish Inquisition, established in 1478 by Ferdinand and Isabella, was independent of the medieval Inquisition and was controlled by the King of Spain.

intendencia Intendancy; late colonial administrative division in New Spain headed by an *intendente*. This system was tried out in America, first in Cuba, and later on the mainland in Sonora and Sinaloa. In 1786 all Spanish America was divided into *intendencias* with the exception of certain frontier provinces ruled by military governors.

intendente Intendant; an official with administrative, judicial, financial, and military functions who governed an *intendencia*.

jobas Semi-nomadic natives of eastern Sonora.

juez comisario Spanish magistrate on a local level.

juez de agua Spanish officer in charge of irrigation water.

juez de residencia Judge investigating an official at the end of his term (see *residencia*).

justicia Elected official of Indian villages.

labrador Farmer.

Laguneros Indigenous group from the vicinity of Parras, Nueva Vizcaya.

ley Written law.

ligado Tied; used here euphemistically to mean impotent.

lobo Person of mixed blood with different regional meanings product of an African-Indian union; product of Pueblo and Plains Indian parents in New Mexico (sometimes used synonymously with *coyote*).

mador Indigenous religious official, assistant in mission district.

mala raza Bad race, normally referring to African descent.

maleficiado Bewitched person.

merced Royal grant, generally of land, office, or other state prerogative.

mestizaje Miscegenation; the process of racial mixing through intermarriage.

mestizo Person of mixed blood, generally the product of a Spanish-Indian union.

misión Congregation of Indians, neophytes in theory; in areas settled longer the term *doctrina* was more common.

monjería Dormitory for nuns; in Alta California a dormitory for locking up mission Indian women at night.

moreno Dark-skinned African.

morisco Muslim person converted to Christianity (and therefore suspect).

mulato Generally the product of an African-Spanish union.

natural   Native, indigenous; people who originally inhabited or were born in the area; unbaptized.

negro   Person of African descent.

obraje   Workshop, often for the production of textiles.

oficiales reales   Royal treasury officials: *tesorero, contador, factor, veedor.*

oidor   Judge of an *audiencia*; literally, "listener"; when reviewing the administration of their district they became *veedores*," those who see."

Ópata   Tegüima-speaking villagers of highland Sonora.

Ostimuri   Colonial administrative district within Sonora.

pardo   Synonymous with *mulato.*

parentela   Kinship network.

parroquia   Parish.

particular   Private citizen; nonroyal, nonecclesiastic officials.

patronato real   The privilege, reserved to the Spanish king, of nominating (in effect, appointing) bishops and other high church dignitaries. Viceroys and governors as vice-patron nominated the parish priests. The royal patronage was the body of rights and duties which the Spanish monarchs possessed over the Catholic Church in America and which derived from papal grants of the early years after the "discovery" of the Indies.

peninsular(es)   Spanish born; also called "*español peninsular*" and "*español europeo*" (see *criollo*).

peonía   Unit of land for cultivation measuring about .86 acres.

piezas   Indigenous women and youths seized by Spaniards during punitive raids.

plebe   Commoners; general populace.

presidial   Soldier belonging to a *presidio.*

presidio   Frontier military post or garrison.

provincia   Region or district; province or territorial jurisdiction of a religious order headed by a provincial (see *gobierno, gobernación*).

Provincias Internas   The administrative unit set up in 1776 in order to provide centralized military authority separate from the Viceroy. In 1777, the Provincias Internas included the Cailfornias, New Mexico, Texas, Coahuila, Nueva Viscaya, and Sonora.

provisión, real provisión   Royal decree (see *cédula*).

pueblo Small settlement inferior to a *ciudad* and a *villa* (*pueblo de españoles*); Indian settlement (*pueblo de indios*) which could be either a *cabecera* (center of Indian government and tribute collection) or a dependency (*sujeto*).

ranchería Ranch, agricultural compound inhabited by Spanish settlers; indigenous encampment or small settlement and/or sociopolitical unit of nomadic or seminomadic, hunter-gatherer Indians.

rancho Ranch, generally a small settlement subordinate to a *hacienda*.

real de minas Mining settlement or district organized as a *ciudad*, *villa*, or *pueblo* and usually the residence of an *alcalde mayor*, a *corregidor*, or neither.

real hacienda Royal treasury, exchequer.

Recopilación de leyes Indias Compilation of the laws of the Indies.

reducción Forcible relocation by Spanish missionaries or civil authorities of Indian villages into larger communities. Authorities used the reducción at various times in New Mexico, the Sonoran Pimería Alta, the Californias, and elsewhere in New Spain, in order to force religious conversion and cultural change toward Spanish norms (see *congregación*).

regidor Member of a municipal council.

reglamento Body of regulations or ordinances.

reino Kingdom (see *gobierno*, *gobernación*).

repartimiento Distribution; forced labor recruited from native villages and sent to Spanish estates and mines for stipulated periods of time.

repartimiento de efectos Forced distribution of trade goods to Indians on credit in exchange for Indian products found in many areas of colonial New Spain.

república de españoles Sphere of governance encompassing non-Indian settlements.

república de indios Sphere of governance encompassing the villages of indigenous populations constituted by Spanish officials.

residencia Investigation in situ (*juicio de residencia*) of an official at the end of his term.

sistema de castas System of racial castes.

sitio Unit of land for raising livestock; *sitio de ganado mayor* measured around 4,316 acres; *sitio de ganado menor* measured about 1,918 acres.

soldado de cuera Soldier serving in the northern provinces equipped with a leather and cotton jacket worn to protect himself against Indian arrows during an engagement (see *cuera*).

sujeto Subordinate settlement (see *pueblo*, *cabecera*).

sumaria   Fact-finding inquiry.

temastianes   Indigenous religious official that taught catechism.

tesgüino   Fermented maize drink.

tesha   Indigenous Caddoan word for good friends, like brothers.

tesorero   Royal treasurer; one of the four *oficiales reales*.

tlatoles   War councils.

Toboso   Indigenous group of Nueva Vizcaya, in northeastern New Spain.

topil   Native minor official for law and order.

vaquero   Herdsman; cowboy.

vecindario   Non-Indian citizenry.

vecino   Inhabitant of a *pueblo, villa, ciudad*, etc.; householder or resident of a
   community; citizen; neighbor.

veedor   Royal overseer; one of the four *oficiales reales*.

vida política   Civic life.

villa   Incorporated settlement with royally granted privileges inferior
   to those of a *ciudad* but superior to those of a *pueblo*. A villa always served
   as a *cabecera*.

virreinato   Viceroyalty, the largest territorial jurisdiction in Spanish America.
   There were two viceroyalties in the sixteenth century (Nueva España and
   Peru) and two added during the seventeenth century (Nueva Granada and
   Río de la Plata). See *virrey*.

virrey   Vice-king, with almost plenary powers, subject to control by
   the Council of the Indies (*Consejo de Indias*) (see *virreinato*).

visita   Formal inspection by a religious or civil official (*visitador*) of
   his jurisdiction; mission without a resident priest, administered
   to by a priest residing in another nearby parish.

visitador   Royal or ecclesiastical official designated for an inspection (*visita*)
   of an institution or a district.

zambo   Person of mixed blood, generally African-Indian, in some
   areas used synonymously with *coyote*.

zona serrana   Highlands area in the Sierra.

Abbreviations

AF   Archivo Franciscano del Fondo Reservado de la Universidad Autónoma de México, Mexico

AGC   Archivo General del Estado de Coahuila

AGI   Archivo General de Indias, Seville, Spain

AGN   Archivo General de la Nación, Mexico

AHP   Archivo de Hidalgo de Parral

AMM   Archivo Municipal de Monterrey, México

AMS   Archivo Municipal de Saltillo, México

BA   Béxar Archives, Center for American History, University of Texas at Austin

BN   Biblioteca Nacional, Mexico

CPR   Cathedral Parish Records, Diocese of St. Augustine Catholic Center, Jacksonville, Fla.

EFP   East Florida Papers

INAH   Instituto Nacional de Antropología e Historia

PC   Papeles procedentes de la isla de Cuba

PI   Provincias Internas

PKY   P. K. Yonge Library of Florida History, University of Florida, Gainesville

SD   Santo Domingo

Bibliography

1747: Informe de Escandón para reconocer, pacificar y poblar la costa del Seno Mexicano. Tamaulipas, México: Consejo Estatal para la Cultura y las Artes de Tamaulipas, 1998.

"Account of the Journey of Bénard de la Harpe: Discovery Made by Him of Several Nations Situated in the West." Translated by Ralph A. Smith, *Southwestern Historical Quarterly* 62, 1–4 (1958–1959): 75–86, 246–59, 371–85, 525–41.

Adams, David B. *Las colonias Tlaxcaltecas de Coahuila y Nuevo León en la Nueva España: Un aspecto de la colonización del norte de México.* Saltillo, Mexico: Archivo Municipal de Saltillo, 1991.

Adelman, Jeremy, and Stephen Aron. "From Borderlands to Borders: Empires, Nation-States, and the Peoples in between in North American History." *American Historical Review* 104, 3 (1999): 818–41.

Aguirre Beltrán, Gonzalo. *La población negra de México, estudio etnohistórico.* 2nd ed. Mexico City: Fondo de Cultura Económica, 1972.

———. *Regiones de refugio: El desarrollo de la comunidad y el proceso dominical en mestizo América.* Mexico: Instituto Indigenista Interamericano, 1967.

Aimes, Hubert H. S. "Coartación: A Spanish Institution for the Advancement of Slaves into Freedmen." *Yale Review*, old ser., 17 (1908–1909): 412–31.

Aiton, Arthur S. "The Diplomacy of the Louisiana Cession." *American Historical Review* 36, 4 (1931): 701–20.

———. "Spanish Colonial Reorganization under the Family Compact." *Hispanic American Historical Review* 12, 3 (1932): 269–80.

Alberro, Solange. *Inquisición y sociedad en México, 1521–1700.* Mexico City: Fondo de Cultura Económica, 1988.

Alessio Robles, Vito. *Coahuila y Texas en la época colonial.* Reprint, Mexico City: Porrúa, 1978.

Allain, Mathé. "French Emigration Policies: Louisiana, 1699–1715." In *Proceedings of the Fourth Meeting of the French Colonial Historical Society.* Washington, D.C.: University Press of America, 1979.

———. *"Not Worth a Straw": French Colonial Policy and the Early Years of Louisiana*. Lafayette: Center for Louisiana Studies, University of Southwestern Louisiana, 1988.

———. "Slave Policies in French Louisiana." *Louisiana History* 21, 2 (1980): 127–38.

Álvarez, Salvador. "Agricultores de paz y cazadores-recolectores de guerra: los tobosos de la cuenca del río Conchos en la Nueva Vizcaya." In *Nómadas y sedentarios en el Norte de México: Homenaje a Beatriz Braniff,* edited by Marie-Areti Hers et al. Mexico: Universidad Autónoma de México, 2000.

Anderson, Gary Clayton. *The Indian Southwest, 1580–1830: Ethnogenesis and Reinvention*. Norman: University of Oklahoma Press, 1999.

Anderson, Rodney D. "Race and Social Stratification: A Comparison of Working-Class Spaniards, Indians and Castas in Guadalajara, Mexico in 1821." *Hispanic American Historical Review* 68, 2 (1988): 209–43.

Andreu Ocariz, Juan José. *Movimientos rebeldes de los esclavos negros de Luisiana*. Zaragoza, Spain: Cagisa, 1977.

Archer, Christon I. *The Army in Bourbon Mexico, 1760–1810*. Albuquerque: University of New Mexico Press, 1977.

Arnold, Morris S. *Colonial Arkansas, 1686–1804: A Social and Cultural History*. Fayetteville: University of Arkansas Press, 1991.

———. *The Rumble of a Distant Drum: The Quapaw and Old World Newcomers, 1673–1804*. Fayetteville: University of Arkansas Press, 2000.

———. *Unequal Laws unto a Savage Race: European Legal Traditions in Arkansas, 1686–1836*. Fayetteville: University of Arkansas Press, 1985.

Athanase de Mézières and the Louisiana-Texas Frontier 1768–1780. Translated by Herbert Eugene Bolton. 2 vols. Cleveland: Arthur H. Clark Co., 1914.

Baade, Hans W. "The Bifurcated Romanist Tradition of Slavery in Louisiana." *Tulane Law Review* 70, 5 (1996): 1481–99.

———. "The *Gens de Couleur* of Louisiana: Comparative Slave Law in Microcosm." *Cardozo Law Review* 18, 2 (1996): 535–86.

———. "The Law of Slavery in Spanish *Luisiana*, 1769–1803." In *Louisiana's Legal Heritage*, edited by Edward F. Haas. Pensacola: Perdido Bay Press, 1983.

Baird, W. David. *The Osage People*. Phoenix: Indian Tribal Series, 1972.

Bakewell, Peter J. *Silver Mining and Society in Colonial Mexico: Zacatecas, 1546–1700*. Cambridge: Cambridge University Press, 1971.

Baretta, Silvio R. D., and John Markoff. "Civilization and Barbarism: Cattle Frontiers in Latin America," *Comparative Studies in Society and History* 20 (1978): 587–620.

Bederman, Gail. *Manliness and Civilization: A Cultural History of Gender and Race in the United States, 1880–1917*. Chicago: University of Chicago Press, 1995.

Beezley, William H., Cheryl English Martin, and William E. French, eds. *Rituals of Rule, Rituals of Resistance: Public Celebrations and Popular Culture in Mexico*. Wilmington, Del.: Scholarly Resources, 1994.

Behar, Ruth. "Sex and Sin, Witchcraft, and the Devil in Late Colonial Mexico." *American Ethnologist* 14, 1 (1987): 34–54.

———. "Sexual Witchcraft, Colonialism, and Women's Power: Views from the Mexican Inquisition." In *Sexuality and Marriage in Colonial Latin America*, edited by Asunción Lavrin. Lincoln: University of Nebraska Press, 1989.

Bemis, Samuel Flagg. *Pinckney's Treaty: America's Advantage from Europe's Distress, 1783–1800*. Revised edition. New Haven, Conn.: Yale University Press, 1960.

Berlin, Ira. *Many Thousands Gone: The First Two Centuries of Slavery in North America*. New Haven, Conn.: Yale University Press, 1998.

Bjork, David K. "Alexander O'Reilly and the Spanish Occupation of Louisiana, 1764–1770." In *New Spain and the Anglo-American West: Historical Contributions Presented to Herbert Eugene Bolton*. Edited by George P. Hammond. 2 vols. Reprint, New York: Kraus Reprint Co., 1969.

———. "The Establishment of Spanish Rule in Louisiana, 1762–1770." In *New Spain and the Anglo-American West: Historical Contributions Presented to Herbert Eugene Bolton*. Edited by George P. Hammond. 2 vols. Reprint, New York: Kraus Reprint Co., 1969.

Boccara, Guillaume. "El poder creador: Tipos de poder y estrategias de sujeción en la frontera sur de Chile en la época colonial," *Anuario de Estudios Americanos* 56 (1999): 65–94.

———. "Mundos nuevos en la frontera del Nuevo Mundo," *E-Review: Nuevo Mundo, mundos nuevos*, UMR 8565 (2001).

Bolton, Herbert Eugene, ed. *Historical Memoirs of New California by Fray Francisco Palóu, O.F.M.* 4 vols. Berkeley: University of California Press, 1926.

———. "The Mission as a Frontier Institution in the Spanish American Colonies." *American Historical Review* 23, 1 (1917): 42–61; reprinted in *Bolton and the Spanish Borderlands*, edited by John Francis Bannon. Norman: University of Oklahoma Press, 1964.

Bonilla-Silva, Eduardo. *White Supremacy and Racism in the Post Civil Rights Era.* Boulder, Colo.: Lynne Rienner Publishers, 2001.

Boyer, Richard. "Respect and Identity: Horizontal and Vertical Reference Points in Speech Acts." *The Americas* 54, 4 (1998): 491–509.

Brading, D. A. *The First America: The Spanish Monarchy, Creole Patriots, and the Liberal State, 1492–1867.* Cambridge: Cambridge University Press, 1991.

———. "Grupos étnicos; clases y estructura ocupacional en Guanajuato (1792)." *Historia Mexicana* 21, 3 (1972): 460–80.

———. *Haciendas and Ranchos in the Mexican Bajío: León, 1700–1860.* Cambridge: Cambridge University Press, 1978.

———. *Miners and Merchants in Bourbon Mexico, 1763–1810.* Cambridge: Cambridge University Press, 1971.

Brading, David, and Celia Wu, "Population Growth and Crisis: León, 1720–1860." *Journal of Latin American Studies* 5, 1 (1973): 1–36.

Brasseaux, Carl A. "The Administration of Slave Regulations in French Louisiana, 1724–1766." *Louisiana History* 21, 2 (1980): 139–58.

———. *Denis-Nicolas Foucault and the New Orleans Rebellion of 1768.* Ruston, La.: McGinty Publications, 1987.

———. *The Founding of New Acadia: The Beginnings of Acadian Life in Louisiana, 1765–1803.* Baton Rouge: Louisiana State University Press, 1987.

Bravo, Elia Nathan. "La Inquisición como generadora y trasmisora de ideologías." In *Inquisición novohispana*, edited by Noemí Quezada, Martha Eugenia Rodríguez, and Marcela Suárez. Mexico City: Universidad Nacional Autónoma de México, Universidad Autónoma Metropolitana, 2000.

Bristol, Joan Cameron. "Negotiating Authority in New Spain: Blacks, Mulattos, and Religious Practice in the Seventeenth Century." Ph.D. diss., University of Pennsylvania, 2001.

Brodman, James William. *Ransoming Captives in Crusader Spain: The Order of Merced on the Christian-Islamic Frontier.* Philadelphia: University of Pennsylvania Press, 1986.

Brooks, James F. *Captives and Cousins: Slavery, Kinship, and Community in the Southwest Borderlands.* Chapel Hill: University of North Carolina Press, 2002.

———. "'This Evil Extends Especially . . . to the Feminine Sex': Negotiating Captivity in the New Mexico Borderlands." *Feminist Studies* 22, 2 (1996): 279–309.

Brown, Jennifer S. H. *Strangers in Blood: Fur Trade Company Families in Indian Country*. Vancouver: University of British Columbia Press, 1980.

Burkholder, Mark A. "Honor and Honors in Colonial Spanish America." In *Sex, Shame and Violence: The Faces of Honor in Colonial Latin America*. Edited by Lyman L. Johnson and Sonya Lipsett-Rivera. Albuquerque: University of New Mexico Press, 1998.

Bushnell, Amy Turner. *Situado and Sabana: Spain's Support System for the Presidio and Mission Provinces of Florida*. Athens: University of Georgia Press, 1994.

Cáceres, Rina. *Rutas de la esclavitud en África y América Latina*. San José: Editorial de la Universidad de Costa Rica, 2001.

Campbell, Thomas N. "Ethnohistoric Notes on Indian Groups Associated with Three Spanish Missions at Guerrero, Coahuila." In *Archaeology and History of the San Juan Bautista Mission Area, Coahuila and Texas*, Report No. 3. San Antonio: University of Texas Center for Archeological Research, 1979.

———. *The Indians of Southern Texas and Northeastern Mexico: Selected Writings of Thomas Nolan Campbell*. Austin: University of Texas Archaeological Research Laboratory, 1988.

Campbell, T. N., and T. J. Campbell. *Indian Groups Associated with Spanish Missions of the San Antonio Missions National Historical Park*. Special Report No. 19. San Antonio: University of Texas Center for Archaeological Research, 1985.

Caron, Peter. "'Of a Nation Which the Others Do Not Understand': Bambara Slaves and African Ethnicity in Colonial Louisiana, 1718–1760." *Slavery and Abolition* 18 (1997): 98–121.

Carroll, Patrick J. *Blacks in Colonial Veracruz: Race, Ethnicity, and Regional Development*. 2nd ed. Austin: University of Texas Press, 2001.

"Carta de Don Damián Massanet á Don Carlos de Sigüenza sobre el descubrimiento de la Bahía del Espiritu Santo." Translated by Lilia Casís. *Quarterly of the Texas State Historical Association* 2, 4 (1899): 253–312.

Carter, Cecile Elkins. *Caddo Indians: Where We Come From*. Norman: University of Oklahoma Press, 1995.

Castañeda, Antonia I. "Engendering the History of Alta California, 1769–1848." In *Contested Eden: California before the Gold Rush*, edited by Ramón Gutiérrez and Richard Orsi. Berkeley: University of California Press, 1998.

———. "Presidarias y pobladoras: Spanish-Mexican Women in Frontier Monterey, Alta California, 1770–1821." Ph.D. dissertation, Stanford University, 1990.

————. "Sexual Violence in the Politics and Policies of Conquest: Amerindian Women and the Spanish Conquest of Alta California." In *Building with Our Hands: New Directions in Chicana Studies*. Edited by Addela de la Torre and Beatríz M. Pesquera. Berkeley: University of California Press, 1993.

Castañeda, Carmen. *La educación en Guadalajara durante la Colonia, 1552–1821*. Guadalajara: Colegio de Jalisco, 1984.

Castillo, Edward D. "Gender Status Decline, Resistance, and Accommodation among Female Neophytes in the Missions of California: A San Gabriel Case Study." *American Indian Culture and Research Journal* 18, 1 (1994): 67–93.

Castleman, Bruce A. "Social Climbers in a Colonial Mexican City: Individual Mobility within the *Sistema de Castas* in Orizaba, 1777–1791." *Colonial Latin American Review* 10, 2 (2001): 229–49.

Caughey, John Walton. *Bernardo de Gálvez in Louisiana, 1776–1783*. Berkeley: University of California Press, 1934.

Cervantes, Fernando. *The Devil in the New World: The Impact of Diabolism in New Spain*. New Haven, Conn.: Yale University Press, 1994.

Céspedes, Guillermo, *América Hispánica (1492–1898)*. Barcelona: Editorial Labor, 1983.

Chance, John K. *Race and Class in Colonial Oaxaca*. Stanford: Stanford University Press, 1978.

Chance, John K., and William B. Taylor. "Estate and Class in a Colonial City: Oaxaca in 1792." *Comparative Studies in Society and History* 19, 4 (1977): 454–89.

Chapman, Carl H. "The Indomitable Osages in Spanish Illinois (Upper Louisiana), 1763–1804." In *The Spanish in the Mississippi Valley, 1762–1804*, edited by John Francis McDermott. Urbana: University of Illinois Press, 1974.

Chevalier, François, *Land and Society in Colonial Mexico: The Great Hacienda*. Berkeley: University of California Press, 1963.

Clark, John G. *New Orleans, 1718–1812: An Economic History*. Baton Rouge: Louisiana State University Press, 1970.

————. "The Role of the City Government in the Economic Development of New Orleans: Cabildo and City Council, 1783–1812." In *The Spanish in the Mississippi Valley, 1762–1804*, edited by John Francis McDermott. Urbana: University of Illinois Press, 1974.

Clowse, Converse D. *Measuring Charleston's Overseas Commerce, 1717–1767: Statistics from the Port's Naval Lists*. Washington, D.C.: University Press of America, 1981.

Collier, Jane Fishburne. *Marriage and Inequality in Classless Societies*. Stanford: Stanford University Press, 1988.

Conrad, Glenn R. "*Emigration Forcée*: A French Attempt to Populate Louisiana, 1716–1720." In *Proceedings of the Fourth Meeting of the French Colonial Historical Society*. Washington, D.C.: University Press of America, 1979.

————, comp. *The First Families of Louisiana*. 2 vols. Baton Rouge: Claitor's Publishing Division, 1971.

————, ed. *The French Experience in Louisiana*. Vol. 1 of *The Louisiana Purchase Bicentennial Series in Louisiana History*, gen. ed. Glenn R. Conrad. Lafayette: University of Southwestern Louisiana Center for Louisiana Studies, 1995.

Cook, Sherburne F. *The Population of the California Indians, 1769–1970*. Berkeley: University of California Press, 1976.

Cook, Sherburne F., and Woodrow Borah. *Essays in Population History*. 3 vols. Berkeley: University of California Press, 1971.

Cope, R. Douglas. *The Limits of Racial Domination: Plebeian Society in Colonial Mexico City, 1660–1720*. Madison: University of Wisconsin Press, 1994.

Corona Páez, Sergio Antonio. "Formas de producción y de consumo en una hacienda neovizcaína: San Juan Bautista de los González, 1663–1666." Master's thesis, Universidad Iberoamericana, Mexico, D.F., 1999.

Cortés, Hernán, *Letters from Mexico*. Translated and edited by A. R. Pagden. New Haven, Conn.: Yale University Press, 1986.

Coser, Lewis, *The Functions of Social Conflict*. Glencoe, Ill.: The Free Press, 1956.

Crane, Verner W. *The Southern Frontier, 1670–1732*. New York: W. W. Norton, 1981.

Cuello, José. "The Economic Impact of the Bourbon Reforms and the Late Colonial Crisis of Empire at the Local Level: The Case of Saltillo, 1777–1817." *The Americas* 44, 3 (1988): 301–23.

————. *El norte, el noreste y Saltillo en la historia de México*. Saltillo, Mexico: Archivo Municipal de Saltillo, 1990.

————. "The Persistence of Indian Slavery and Encomienda in the Northeast of Colonial Mexico, 1577–1723." *The Journal of Social History* 21, 4 (1988): 683–700.

————. "Saltillo in the Seventeenth Century: Local Society on the North Mexican Frontier." Ph.D. diss., University of California, Berkeley, 1981.

————. "Socioeconomic Involution in Colonial Saltillo, 1577–1821." *European Review of Latin American and Caribbean Studies* 49 (1990): 55–77.

Culleton, James. *Indians and Pioneers of Old Monterey*. Fresno: Academy of California Church History, 1950.

Cummins, Light Townsend. "Luis de Unzaga y Amezaga, Colonial Governor, 1770–1777." In *The Louisiana Governors: From Iberville to Edwards*, edited by Joseph G. Dawson III. Baton Rouge: Louisiana State University Press, 1990.

Curley, Michael J. *Church and State in the Spanish Floridas*. Washington, D.C.: Catholic University of America Press, 1940.

Cutter, Charles R. *The Legal Culture of Northern New Spain, 1700–1810*. Albuquerque: University of New Mexico Press, 1995.

Cutter, Donald, trans. and ed. *Writings of Mariano Payeras*. Santa Barbara: Bellerophon Books, 1995.

Dalrymple, Margaret Fisher, ed. *The Merchant of Manchac: The Letterbooks of John Fitzpatrick. 1768–1790*. Baton Rouge: Louisiana State University Press, 1978.

Davis, Edwin Adams. *Louisiana: A Narrative History*. 3rd ed. Baton Rouge: Claitor's Publishing Division, 1971.

Deagan, Kathleen A. *Spanish St. Augustine: The Archaeology of a Colonial Creole Community*. New York: Academic Press, 1983.

Deans-Smith, Susan. "The Working Poor and the Eighteenth-Century Colonial State: Gender, Public Order, and Work Discipline." In *Rituals of Rule, Rituals of Resistance: Public Celebrations and Popular Culture in Mexico*, edited by William H. Beezley, Cheryl English Martin, and William E. French. Wilmington, Del.: Scholarly Resources, 1994.

DeConde, Alexander. *This Affair of Louisiana*. New York: Charles Scribner's Sons, 1976.

Deeds, Susan M. "Colonial Chihuahua: Peoples and Frontiers in Flux." In *New Views of Borderlands History*, edited by Robert H. Jackson. Albuquerque: University of New Mexico Press, 1998.

———. *Defiance and Deference in New Spain: Indians under Colonial Rule in Nueva Vizcaya*. Austin: University of Texas Press, 2003.

———. "Double Jeopardy: Indian Women in Jesuit Missions of Nueva Vizcaya." In *Indian Women of Early Mexico*, edited by Susan Schroeder, Stephanie Wood, and Robert Haskett. Norman: University of Oklahoma Press, 1997.

De la Teja, Jesús F. "St. James at the Fair: Religious Ceremony, Civic Boosterism, and Commercial Development on the Colonial Mexican Frontier." *The Americas* 57, 3 (2001): 395–416.

———. *San Antonio de Béxar: A Community on New Spain's Northern Frontier*. Albuquerque: University of New Mexico Press, 1995.

Del Río, Ignacio. "El noroeste novohispano y la nueva política imperial española." In *Historia General de Sonora*, II: *De la Conquista al Estado Libre y Soberano de Sonora*. Hermosillo, Mexico: Gobierno del Estado de Sonora, 1985.

"Descriptions of the Tejas or Asinai Indians, 1691–1722." Translated by Mattie Austin Hatcher. *Southwestern Historical Quarterly* 30, 3–4 (1927): 206–18, 283–304; 31, 1–2 (1927): 50–62, 150–80.

Din, Gilbert C. "Bernardo de Gálvez: A Reexamination of His Governorship." In *The Spanish Presence in Louisiana, 1763–1803*, edited by Gilbert C. Din. Vol. 2 of *The Louisiana Purchase Bicentennial Series in Louisiana History*, gen. ed. Glenn R. Conrad. Lafayette: Center for Louisiana Studies, University of Southwestern Louisiana, 1996.

———. *The Canary Islanders of Louisiana*. Baton Rouge: Louisiana State University Press, 1988.

———. "Carondelet, the Cabildo, and Slaves: Louisiana in 1795." *Louisiana History* 38, 1 (1997): 5–28.

———. "*Cimarrones* and the San Malo Band in Spanish Louisiana." *Louisiana History* 21, 3 (1980): 237–62.

———. "Early Spanish Colonization Efforts in Louisiana." *Louisiana Studies* 11, 1 (1972): 31–49.

———. "Father Jean Delvaux and the Natchitoches Revolt of 1795." *Louisiana History* 40, 1 (1999): 5–30.

———, ed. "The First Spanish Instructions for Arkansas Post, November 15, 1769." *Arkansas Historical Quarterly* 53, 3 (1994): 312–19.

———. "'For Defense of Country and the Glory of Arms': Army Officers in Spanish Louisiana, 1766–1803." *Louisiana History* 43, 1 (2002): 5–40.

———. "The Immigration Policy of Governor Esteban Miró in Spanish Louisiana." *Southwestern Historical Quarterly* 73, 2 (1969): 155–75.

———. "The Irish Mission to West Florida." *Louisiana History* 12, 4 (1971): 315–34.

———. *Louisiana in 1776: A Memoria of Francisco Bouligny*. New Orleans: Louisiana Collection Series, 1977.

———. "Protecting the 'Barrera': Spain's Defenses in Louisiana, 1763–1779." *Louisiana History* 18, 2 (1978): 183–211.

———. "Slavery in Louisiana's Florida Parishes under the Spanish Regime, 1779–1803." In *A Fierce and Fractious Frontier: The Curious Development of Louisiana's Florida Parishes, 1699–2000*, edited by Samuel C. Hyde Jr. Baton Rouge: Louisiana State University Press, 2004.

———. "Spain's Immigration Policy in Louisiana and the American Penetration, 1792–1803." *Southwestern Historical Quarterly* 76, 3 (1973): 255–76.

———. *Spaniards, Planters, and Slaves: The Spanish Regulation of Slavery in Louisiana, 1763–1803*. College Station: Texas A&M University Press, 1999.

Din, Gilbert C., and John E. Harkins. *The New Orleans Cabildo: Colonial Louisiana's First City Government, 1769–1803*. Baton Rouge: Louisiana State University Press, 1996.

Din, Gilbert C., and Abraham P. Nasatir. *The Imperial Osages: Spanish-Indian Diplomacy in the Mississippi Valley*. Norman: University of Oklahoma Press, 1983.

Dobyns, H., P. Ezell, A. Jones, and G. Ezell. "What Were Nixoras?" *Southwestern Journal of Anthropology* 16, 2 (1960): 230–68.

Documentos para la historia de México. 21 vols. in 4 series. Mexico City: Imprenta J. R. Navarro, 1853–1857.

Donnan, Elizabeth. *Documents Illustrative of the History of the Slave Trade to America*. Washington, D.C.: Carnegie Institution, 1930–1935.

Doolittle, William E. "Aboriginal Agricultural Development in the Valley of Sonora, Mexico." *Geographical Review* 70, 3 (1980): 328–42.

———. *Pre-Hispanic Occupance in the Valley of Sonora, Mexico: Archaeological Confirmation of Early Spanish Reports*. Tucson: University of Arizona Press, 1988.

Dorsey, George A. *The Mythology of the Wichita*. Washington D.C.: Carnegie Institution of Washington, 1904.

———. *Traditions of the Caddo*. Washington, D.C.: Carnegie Institution of Washington, 1905.

Easterby, J. H. *Journal of the Commons House of Assembly, May 18, 1741–July 10, 1742*. Columbia: Historical Commission of South Carolina, 1953.

Ekberg, Carl J. *Colonial Ste. Genevieve: An Adventure on the Mississippi Frontier*. Gerald, Mo.: Patrice Press, 1985.

Elliott, J. H. *Spain and Its World, 1500–1700*. New Haven, Conn.: Yale University Press, 1989.

Eltis, David. "Europeans and the Rise and Fall of African Slavery in the Americas: An Interpretation." *The American Historical Review* 98, 5 (1993): 1399–1423.

Engstrand, Iris H. "California Ranchos: Their Hispanic Heritage." *Southern California Quarterly* 67, 3 (1985): 281–90.

Erauso, Catalina de. *Lieutenant Nun: Memoirs of a Basque Transvestite in the New World.* Translated by Michel Stepto and Gabriel Stepto. Boston: Beacon Press, 1996.

Estado general de las fundaciones hechas por don José de Escandón en la Colonia del Nuevo Santander, costa del Seno Mexicano. 2 vols. Mexico: Secretaría de Gobernación, Publicaciones del Archivo General de la Nación, 1930.

Everett, Donald E. "Free People of Color in Colonial Louisiana." *Louisiana History* 7, 1 (1966): 21–50.

Ewers, John C. "Symbols of Chiefly Authority in Spanish Louisiana." In *The Spanish in the Mississippi Valley 1762–1804*, edited by John Francis McDermott. Urbana: University of Illinois Press, 1972.

Fabel, Robin. *The Economy of British West Florida.* Tuscaloosa: University of Alabama Press, 1988.

Farriss, Nancy. *Maya Society under Colonial Rule: The Collective Enterprise of Survival.* Princeton: Princeton University Press, 1984.

———. "Nucleation versus Dispersal: the Dynamics of Population Movement in Colonial Yucatán," *Hispanic American Historical Review* 58, 2 (1978): 187–216.

Faulk, Odie. "Spanish-Comanche Relations and the Treaty of 1785," *Texana* 2 (1964): 44–53.

Few, Martha. "Women, Religion, and Power: Gender and Resistance in Daily Life in Late Seventeenth-Century Guatemala." *Ethnohistory* 42 (1995): 627–38.

Fick, Carolyn. *The Making of Haiti: The Saint-Domingue Revolution from Below.* Knoxville: University of Tennessee Press, 1990.

Flint, Richard. *Great Cruelties Have Been Reported: The 1544 Investigation of the Coronado Expedition.* Dallas: Southern Methodist University Press, 2002.

Foner, Laura. "The Free People of Color in Louisiana and St. Domingue: A Comparative Portrait of Two Three-Caste Slave Societies." *Journal of Social History* 3, 4 (1970): 406–30.

Fortier, Alcée. *A History of Louisiana.* Edited by Jo Ann Carrigan. 2nd ed. 2 vols. Baton Rouge: Claitor's Book Store, 1966–1972.

Frank, Ross. *From Settler to Citizen: New Mexican Economic Development and the Creation of Vecino Society, 1750–1820.* Berkeley: University of California Press, 2000.

———. "Making New Mexican Santos: Franciscan and Vecino Dominance in Late Colonial New Mexico." *New Mexico Historical Review* 75, 3 (2000): 369–92.

Franklin, John Hope, and Loren Schweninger. *Runaway Slaves: Rebels on the Plantation*. New York: Oxford University Press, 1999.

Frederick, Julia Carpenter. "Luis de Unzaga and Bourbon Reform in Spanish Louisiana, 1770–1776." Ph.D. diss., Louisiana State University, 2000.

French, Benjamin Franklin, ed. *Historical Memoirs of Louisiana from the First Settlement of the Colony to the Departure of Governor O'Reilly in 1770: With Historical and Biographical Notes*. 5 vols. New York: Lamport, Blakeman and Law, 1853.

Gallay, Alan. *The Indian Slave Trade: The Rise of the English Empire in the American South*. New Haven, Conn.: Yale University Press, 2002.

Galloway, Patricia. "'The Chief Who Is Your Father': Choctaw and French Views of the Diplomatic Relation." In *Powhatan's Mantle: Indians in the Colonial Southeast*, edited by Peter H. Wood, Gregory A. Waselkov, and M. Thomas Hatley. Lincoln: University of Nebraska Press, 1989.

Gálvez, Bernardo de. *Instructions for Governing the Interior Provinces of New Spain, 1786*. Translated by Donald E. Worcester. Berkeley: Quivira Society, 1951.

Gaspar, David Barry, and David Patrick Geggus. *A Turbulent Time: The French Revolution and the Greater Caribbean*. Bloomington: Indiana University Press, 1997.

Gayarré, Charles. *History of Louisiana*. 3rd ed. 4 vols. Reprint, New York: Arno Press, 1972.

Geertz, Clifford. *Agricultural Involution: The Process of Ecological Change in Indonesia*. Berkeley: University of California Press, 1968.

Geiger, Maynard F. *Franciscan Missionaries in Hispanic California, 1769–1848*. San Marino: The Huntington Library, 1969.

———. *The Life and Times of Junípero Serra, O.F.M., or The Man Who Never Turned Back (1713–1784)*. 2 vols. Washington, D.C.: Academy of American Franciscan History, 1959.

Geiger, Maynard F., trans. and ed. "Notes and Documents: Instructions Concerning the Occupation of California, 1769." *Southern California Quarterly* 47, 2 (1965): 209–18.

———, trans. and annot. *Palóu's Life of Fray Junípero Serra*. Washington, D.C.: Academy of American Franciscan History, 1955.

Gelhbach, Frederick R. *Mountain Islands and Desert Seas: A Natural History of the U.S.-Mexican Borderlands*. College Station: Texas A&M University Press, 1993.

Gelo, Daniel J. "On a New Interpretation of Comanche Social Organization." *Current Anthropology* 28 5 (1987), 551–55.

Gerhard, Peter. *The North Frontier of New Spain*. Princeton: Princeton University Press, 1982 (revised edition, Norman: University of Oklahoma Press, 1993).

Gibson, Charles. *Aztecs under Spanish Rule: A History of the Indians of the Valley of Mexico, 1519–1810*. Stanford: Stanford University Press, 1964.

———. *Spain in America*. New York: Harper Torchbooks, 1966.

———. *Tlaxcala in the Sixteenth Century*. New Haven, Conn.: Yale University Press, 1952.

Giraud, Marcel. "German Emigration." Translated by Glenn R. Conrad. *Revue de Louisiane/Louisiana Review* 10 (1981): 143–57.

———. *Histoire de Louisiane Française*. Vol. 3, *L'Epoque de John Law, 1717–1720*. Paris: Presses Universitaires de France, 1966.

———. *Histoire de Louisiane Française*. Vol. 4, *La Louisiane àpres le système de Law*. Paris: Presses Universitaires de France, 1978.

———. *A History of French Louisiana*. Vol. 1, *The Reign of Louis XIV (1698–1715)*. Translated by Joseph C. Lambert. Baton Rouge: Louisiana State University Press, 1974.

———. *A History of French Louisiana*. Vol. 2, *Years of Transition, 1715–1717*. Translated by Brian Pearce. Baton Rouge: Louisiana State University Press, 1993.

———. *A History of French Louisiana*. Vol. 5, *The Company of the Indies, 1723–1731*. Translated by Brian Pierce. Baton Rouge: Louisiana State University Press, 1992.

Gladwin, Thomas. "Comanche Kin Behavior." *American Anthropologist* new series, 50, 1 pt. 1 (1948): 73–94.

Gold, Robert L. *Borderland Empires in Transition: The Triple Nation Transfer of Florida*. Carbondale: Southern Illinois University Press, 1969.

González Claverán, Virginia. "Una migración canaria a Texas en el siglo XVIII." *Historia Mexicana* 37, 2 (1987): 153–204.

González López-Briones, Carmen. "Spain in the Mississippi Valley: Spanish Arkansas, 1762–1803." Ph.D. diss., Purdue University, 1983.

Gould, Virginia Meacham. "The Free Creoles of Color of the Antebellum Gulf
    Ports of Mobile and Pensacola: A Struggle for the Middle Ground." In
    Creoles of Color of the Gulf South, edited by James H. Dormon. Knoxville:
    University of Tennessee Press, 1996.

Griffen, William B. *Culture Change and Shifting Population in Central Northern
    Mexico*. Anthropological Papers of the University of Arizona No. 13.
    Tucson: University of Arizona Press, 1970.

————. *Indian Assimilation on the Franciscan Area of Nueva Vizcaya*.
    Anthropological Papers of the University of Arizona No. 33. Tucson:
    University of Arizona Press, 1979.

Griffin, John W. *Narrative of a Voyage to the Spanish Main in the Ship "Two
    Friends."* Gainesville: University of Florida Press, 1978.

Griffin, Patricia C. *Mullet on the Beach: The Minorcans of Florida, 1768–1788*.
    Jacksonville: University of North Florida Press, 1991.

Griffith, William Joyce. *The Hasinai Indians of East Texas as Seen by Europeans,
    1687–1772*. Middle American Research Institute, Philological and
    Documentary Studies 2. New Orleans: Tulane University Press, 1954.

Guerra, Raul J., Jr., Nadine M. Vásquez, and Baldomero Vela Jr. *Index to the
    Marriage Records of the Diocese of Guadalajara, Provinces of Coahuila, Nuevo
    León, Nuevo Santander, and Texas, vol. I: 1653–1750*. Edinburg: Published
    privately by the authors, 1989, and *vol. II: 1751–1779*. Austin: Published
    privately by the authors, 1997.

Guest, Francis F. "The California Missions Were Far from Faultless." *Southern
    California Quarterly* 76, 3 (1994): 255–307.

Gutiérrez, Ramón A. *When Jesus Came, the Corn Mothers Went Away: Marriage,
    Sexuality, and Power in New Mexico, 1500–1846*. Stanford: Stanford
    University Press, 1991.

Guy, Donna J., and Thomas E. Sheridan, eds. *Contested Ground: Comparative
    Frontiers on the Northern and Southern Edges of the Spanish Empire*. Tucson:
    University of Arizona Press, 1998.

Hackel, Steven W. "The Staff of Leadership: Indian Authority in the Missions
    of Alta California." *William and Mary Quarterly*, 3rd series, 54, 2
    (April 1997): 347–76.

Hadley, Diana, Thomas H. Naylor, and Mardith K. Schuetz-Miller, eds. *The
    Presidio and Militia on the Northern Frontier of New Spain, vol. 2, pt. 2,
    The Central Corridor and the Texas Corridor 1700–1765*. Tucson: University
    of Arizona Press, 1997.

Hall, G. Emlen. "The Pueblo Grant Labyrinth." In *Land, Water, and Culture: New Perspectives on Hispanic Land Grants*, edited by Charles L. Briggs and John R. Van Ness. Albuquerque: University of New Mexico Press, 1987. 67–138.

Hall, Gwendolyn Midlo. *Africans in Colonial Louisiana: The Development of Afro-Creole Culture in the Eighteenth Century*. Baton Rouge: Louisiana State University Press, 1992.

———. *Social Control in Slave Plantation Societies: A Comparison of St. Domingue and Cuba*. Reprint, Baton Rouge: Louisiana State University Press, 1996.

Hanger, Kimberly S. "'Almost All Have Callings': Free Blacks at Work in Spanish New Orleans." *Colonial Latin American Historical Review* 3, 2 (1994): 141–64.

———. *Bounded Lives, Bounded Places: Free Black Society in Colonial New Orleans, 1769–1803*. Durham, N.C.: Duke University Press, 1997.

———. "Conflicting Loyalties: The French Revolution and Free People of Color in Spanish New Orleans." *Louisiana History* 34, 1 (1993): 5–33.

———. "'Desiring Total Tranquility' and Not Getting It: Conflict Involving Free Black Women in Spanish New Orleans." *The Americas* 54, 4 (1998): 541–56.

———. "Patronage, Property, and Persistence: The Emergence of a Free Black Elite in Spanish New Orleans." *Slavery and Abolition* 17, 1 (1996): 44–64.

Hann, John H. *Apalachee: The Land between the Rivers*. Gainesville: University Press of Florida, 1988.

———. *A History of the Timucuan Indians and Missions*. Gainesville: University Press of Florida, 1996.

———. *Missions to the Calusa*. Gainesville: University Press of Florida, 1991.

Hann, John H., and Bonnie G. McEwan. *The Apalachee Indians and Mission San Luis*. Gainesville: University Press of Florida, 1998.

Haring, C. H. *The Spanish Empire in America*. New York: Harcourt, Brace & World, 1947.

Harris, Marvin. *Patterns of Race in the Americas*. New York: W. W. Norton, 1964.

Haskett, Robert. *Indigenous Rulers: An Ethnohistory of Town Government in Colonial Cuernavaca*. Albuquerque: University of New Mexico Press, 1991.

Hatcher, Mattie Austin. "Texas in 1820." *Southwestern Historical Quarterly* 23, 1 (1919): 48–60.

Hausberger, Bernd. "La violencia en la conquista espiritual: las misiones jesuitas de Sonora." *Jahrbuch für Geschichte von Staat, Wirtschaft und Gesellschaft Lateinamerikas* 30 (1991): 27–54.

Hendricks, Rick. "The Exile and Return of Cadelo, Isidro, 1793–1810." *New Mexico Historical Review* 70, 2 (1995): 129–57.

Hennessy, Alistair. *The Frontier in Latin American History.* London: Edward Arnold, 1978.

Hickerson, Daniel A. "Historical Processes, Epidemic Disease, and the Formation of the Hasinai Confederacy." *Ethnohistory* 44, 1 (1997): 31–52.

———. "Trade, Mediation, and Political Status in the Hasinai Confederacy." *Research in Economic Anthropology* 17 (1996).

Higgins, Robert. "Charleston: Terminus and Entrepot of the Colonial Slave Trade." In *The African Diaspora: Interpretive Essays*, edited by Martin L. Kilson and Robert I. Rothberg. Cambridge, Mass.: Harvard University Press, 1976.

Hilt, Douglas. "Manuel Godoy, Prince of Peace." *History Today* 21 (1971): 833–41.

Hoebel, E. Adamson. "Comanche and H3kandika Shoshone Relationship Systems." *American Anthropologist*, new series, 41, 3 (1939): 440–57.

———. *The Political Organization and Law-Ways of the Comanche Indians.* Memoirs of the American Anthropological Association No. 54. Menasha, Wisc.: American Anthropological Association, 1940.

Hoffman, Paul E. *Florida's Frontier.* Bloomington: Indiana University Press, 2002.

Holmes, Jack D. L. "Father Francis Lennan and His Activities in Spanish Louisiana and West Florida." *Louisiana Studies* 5 (1966): 255–65.

———. *Gayoso: The Life and Times of a Spanish Governor on the Mississippi, 1789–1799.* Baton Rouge: Louisiana State University Press, 1965.

———. *Honor and Fidelity: The Louisiana Infantry Regiment and the Louisiana Militia Companies, 1766–1821.* Birmingham, Ala.: Louisiana Collection Series, 1965.

———. "Irish Priests in Spanish Natchez," *Journal of Mississippi History* 29 (1967): 169–80.

Hornbeck, David. "Early Mission Settlement." In *Some Reminiscences about Fray Junípero Serra*, edited by Francis J. Weber. Santa Barbara: Kimberly Press, 1985.

Houck, Louis, ed. *The Spanish Regime in Missouri*. 2 vols. in 1. Reprint, New York: Arno Press, 1971.

Hoyo, Eugenio del. *Indios, frailes y encomenderos en el Nuevo Reino de León: Siglos XVII y XVIII*. Monterrey: Archivo General del Estado, n.d.

Hurtado, Albert L. *Intimate Frontiers: Sex, Gender, and Culture in Old California*. Albuquerque: University of New Mexico Press, 1999.

Ingersoll, Thomas N. "Free Blacks in a Slave Society: New Orleans, 1718–1812." *William and Mary Quarterly*, 3rd series 48, 2 (1991): 172–200.

———. *Mammon and Manon in Early New Orleans: The First Slave Society in the Deep South, 1718–1819*. Knoxville: University of Tennessee Press, 1999.

———. "Slave Codes and Judicial Practice in New Orleans, 1718–1807," *Law and History Review* 13, 1 (1995): 23–62.

———. "The Slave Trade and Ethnic Diversity of Louisiana's Slave Community." *Louisiana History* 37, 2 (1996): 23–62.

"Inside the Comanchería, 1785: The Diary of Pedro Vial and Francisco Chaves." Edited by Elizabeth A. H. John. Translated by Adán Benavides. *Southwestern Historical Quarterly* 98, 1 (1994): 27–56.

Jackson, Harvey H. "The Darien Antislavery Petition of 1739 and the Georgia Plan." *William and Mary Quarterly*, 3rd series, 34 (1977): 618–19.

———. "Hugh Bryan and the Evangelical Movement in Colonial South Carolina." *William and Mary Quarterly*, 3rd series, 43, 4 (1986): 594–614.

Jackson, Robert H., ed. *New Views of Borderlands History*. Albuquerque: University of New Mexico Press, 1998.

Jacobs, James Ripley. *Tarnished Warrior: Major-General James Wilkinson*. New York: Macmillan Company, 1938.

Jaenen, Cornelius J. "The Role of Presents in French-Amerindian Trade." In *Explorations in Canadian Economic History: Essays in Honour of Irene M. Spry*, edited by Duncan Cameron. Ottawa, Canada: University of Ottawa Press, 1985.

James, Cyril L. R. *The Black Jacobins: Toussaint Louverture and the San Domingo Revolt*. 2nd ed. New York: Dial Press, 1963.

Jary, David, and Julia Jary. "Social Control." *The HarperCollins Dictionary of Sociology*. New York: Harper-Collins, 1991.

Jenkins, Myra E. "Taos Pueblo and Its Neighbors." *New Mexico Historical Review* 41, 2 (1966): 85–114.

Jiménez, Alfredo. "Don Juan de Oñate and the Founding of New Mexico: Possible Gains and Losses from Centennial Celebrations." *Colonial Latin American Historical Review* 7, 4 (1998): 381–412.

———. "El fenómeno de frontera y sus variables: Notas para una tipología." *Estudios Fronterizos* 40 (1997): 11–25.

———. "El juicio de residencia como fuente etnográfica: Francisco Briceño, gobernador de Guatemala (1565–1569)." *Revista Complutense de Historia de América* 23 (1997): 11–21.

———. "El Lejano Norte español: Cómo escapar del *American West* y de las *Spanish Borderlands*." *Colonial Latin American Historical Review* 5 (1996): 381–412.

———. "El Norte de Nueva España: Visiones *EMIC* de una sociedad de frontera." In *Actas del XI Congreso Internacional de AHILA*, edited by John Fisher. 4 vols. Liverpool: Asociación de Historiadores Latino-americanistas Europeos and Institute of Latin American Studies, University of Liverpool, 1997.

———. "Historia y antropología: Las fronteras de América del Norte." *Revista Española de Antropología Americana*, vol. extra. (2003): 99–113.

———. "La frontera en América: Observaciones críticas y sugerencias." In *Entre Puebla de los Angeles y Sevilla: estudios americanistas en homenaje al Dr. José Antonio Calderón Quijano*, edited by Justina Sarabia. Sevilla: Universidad de Sevilla and Escuela de Estudios Hispano-Americanos, 1997.

———. "La historia oral como fabricación del pasado: La frontera del Oeste o *American West*." *Anuario de Estudios Americanos* 58, 2 (2001): 737–55.

———. "Persistencia y crisis de la frontera en la historiografía norteamericana." In *VII Congreso Internacional de Historia de América*, edited by J. A. Armillas. 2 vols. Zaragoza: Diputación Provincial de Aragón, 1998.

John, Elizabeth A. H. *Storms Brewed in Other Men's Worlds: The Confrontation of Indians, Spanish, and French in the Southwest, 1540–1795*. College Station: Texas A&M University Press, 1975.

Johnson, Lyman, and Sonya Lipsett-Rivera. *The Faces of Honor: Sex, Shame and Violence in Colonial Latin America*. Albuquerque: University of New Mexico, Press, 1998.

Jones, Anne Goodwyn, and Susan V. Donaldson. *Haunted Bodies: Gender and Southern Texts*. Charlottesville: University of Virginia Press, 1997.

Jones, Edward. *Ingratiation: A Social Psychological Analysis*. New York: Appleton-Century-Crofts, 1964.

Jones, Kristine L. "Comparative Raiding Economies." In *Contested Ground: Comparative Frontiers on the Northern and Southern Edges of the Spanish Empire*, edited by Donna J. Guy and Thomas E. Sheridan. Tucson: University of Arizona Press, 1998.

Jones, Oakah L. *Los Paisanos: Spanish Settlers on the Northern Frontier of New Spain*. Norman: University of Oklahoma Press, 1979.

———. *Nueva Vizcaya: Heartland of the Spanish Frontier*. Albuquerque: University of New Mexico Press, 1988.

———. "Pueblo Indian Auxiliaries in New Mexico, 1763–1821." *New Mexico Historical Review* 37, 2 (1962): 81–109.

———. *Pueblo Warriors and Spanish Conquest*. Norman: University of Oklahoma Press, 1966.

Kamen, Henry. *The Spanish Inquisition*. Rev. ed. New Haven, Conn.: Yale University Press, 1998.

Kardiner, Abram. "Analysis of Comanche Culture." In *The Psychological Frontiers of Society*. New York: Columbia University Press, 1945, 1959.

Kavanagh, Thomas W. *Comanche Political History: An Ethnohistorical Perspective, 1706–1875*. Lincoln: University of Nebraska Press, 1996.

Kenneally, Finbar, trans. and ed. *Writings of Fermín Francisco de Lasuén*. 2 vols. Washington, D.C.: Academy of American Franciscan History, 1965.

Kessell, John L. *Friars, Soldiers, and Reformers: Hispanic Arizona and the Sonora Mission Frontier, 1767–1856*. Tucson: University of Arizona Press, 1976.

———. *Kiva, Cross, and Crown: The Pecos Indians and New Mexico, 1540–1840*. Washington, D.C.: National Park Service, U.S. Dept. of the Interior, 1979.

Kilson, Martin L., and Robert I. Rothberg. *The African Diaspora: Interpretive Essays*. Cambridge, Mass.: Harvard University Press, 1976.

Kinnaird, Lawrence, ed. *Spain in the Mississippi Valley, 1765–1794*. 3 Pts. Washington, D.C.: Government Printing Office, 1949.

Kuethe, Alan J. *Cuba, 1753–1815: Crown, Military, and Society*. Knoxville: University of Tennessee Press, 1986.

La Vere, David. *The Caddo Chiefdoms: Caddo Economies and Politics, 1700–1835*. Lincoln: University of Nebraska Press, 1998.

Landers, Jane. "African and African American Women and Their Pursuit of Rights through Eighteenth-Century Spanish Texts." In *Haunted Bodies: Gender and Southern Texts*, edited by Anne Goodwyn Jones and Susan V. Donaldson. Charlottesville: University of Virginia Press, 1997.

————. *Black Society in Spanish Florida*. Urbana: University of Illinois Press, 1999.

————. "*Cimarrón* Ethnicity and Cultural Adaptation in the Spanish Domains of the Circum-Caribbean, 1503–1763." In *Identity in the Shadow of Slavery*, edited by Paul E. Lovejoy. London: Continuum, 2000.

————. *Colonial Plantations and Economy in Florida*. Gainesville: University Press of Florida, 2000.

————. "Female Conflict and Its Resolution in Eighteenth-Century St. Augustine." *The Americas* 54, 4 (1998): 557–74.

————. "La cultura material de los cimarrones: Los casos de Ecuador, La Española, México y Colombia." In *Rutas de la esclavitud en África y América Latina*, edited by Rina Cáceres, 145–74. San José: Editorial de la Universidad de Costa Rica, 2001.

————. "Rebellion and Royalism in Spanish Florida: The French Revolution on Spain's Northern Colonial Frontier." In *A Turbulent Time: The French Revolution and the Greater Caribbean*, edited by David Barry Gaspar and David Patrick Geggus. Bloomington: Indiana University Press, 1997.

Lane, Kris. *Pillaging the Empire: Piracy in the Americas 1500–1750*. Armonk, N.Y.: M. E. Sharpe, 1998.

Lane, Mills. *General Oglethorpe's Georgia: Colonial Letters 1738–1743*. 2 vols. Savannah: Beehive Press, 1975.

Lavrin, Asunción, ed. *Sexuality and Marriage in Colonial Latin America*. Lincoln: University of Nebraska Press, 1989.

León-Portilla, Miguel, ed. *The Broken Spears: The Aztec Account of the Conquest of Mexico*. Rev. ed. Boston: Beacon Press, 1992.

"Letters of Manuel de Montiano: Siege of St. Agustine [*sic*]." *Collections of the Georgia Historical Society*. Vol. 7, pt. 1. Savannah: Georgia Historical Society, 1909.

Lewis, Laura A. *Hall of Mirrors: Power, Witchcraft and Caste in Colonial Mexico*. Durham, N.C.: Duke University Press, 2003.

Liljegren, Ernest R. "Jacobinism in Spanish Louisiana, 1792–1797." *Louisiana Historical Quarterly* 21, 1 (1939): 47–96.

Lipsett-Rivera, Sonya. "*De Obra y Palabra*: Patterns of Insult in Mexico, 1750–1856." *The Americas* 54, 4 (1998): 511–39.

Lockhart, James. *The Nahuas after the Conquest: A Social and Cultural History of the Indians of Central Mexico, Sixteenth through Eighteenth Centuries*. Stanford: Stanford University Press, 1992.

Lockhart, James, and Stuart B. Schwartz. *Early Latin America: A History of Colonial Spanish America and Brazil*. Cambridge: Cambridge University Press, 1983.

Loomis, Noel M., and Abraham P. Nasatir. *Pedro Vial and the Roads to Santa Fe*. Norman: University of Oklahoma Press, 1967.

López de la Cámara Alta, Agustín. *Descripción general de la Nueva Colonia de Santander*. Compiled and edited by Gabriel Saldívar. México: Archivo de la Historia de Tamaulipas, 1946.

Lovejoy, Paul E. *Identity in the Shadow of Slavery*. London: Continuum, 2000.

Lutz, Christopher. *Santiago de Guatemala, 1541–1773: City, Caste, and the Colonial Experience*. Norman: University of Oklahoma Press, 1994.

Lyon, Eugene W. *The Enterprise of Florida: Pedro Menéndez de Avilés and the Spanish Conquest of 1565–1568*. Gainesville: University Press of Florida, 1974.

———. *Louisiana in French Diplomacy, 1759–1804*. Reprint, Norman: University of Oklahoma Press, 1974.

MacLeod, Murdo J. "Some Thoughts on the Pax Colonial, Colonial Violence, and Perceptions of Both." In *Native Resistance and the Pax Colonial in New Spain*, edited by Susan Schroeder. Lincoln: University of Nebraska Press, 1998.

Mallon, Florencia. *Peasant and Nation: The Making of Postcolonial Mexico and Peru*. Berkeley: University of California Press, 1995.

Martin, Cheryl E. *Governance and Society in Colonial Mexico: Chihuahua in the Eighteenth Century*. Stanford: Stanford University Press, 1996.

———. "Public Celebrations, Popular Culture, and Labor Discipline in Eighteenth-Century Chihuahua." In *Rituals of Rule, Rituals of Resistance: Public Celebrations and Popular Culture in Mexico*, edited by William H. Beezley, Cheryl E. Martin, and William E. French. Wilmington, Del.: Scholarly Resources, 1994.

———. *Rural Society in Colonial Morelos*. Albuquerque: University of New Mexico Press, 1985.

Martínez-Alier, Verena. *Marriage, Class and Colour in Nineteenth-Century Cuba: A Study of Racial Attitudes and Sexual Values in a Slave Society*. Ann Arbor: University of Michigan Press, 1974.

Mason, William Marvin. *The Census of 1790: A Demographic History of Colonial California*. Menlo Park: Ballena Press, 1998.

———. "Fages' Code of Conduct toward Indians, 1787." *Journal of California Anthropology* 2 (1975): 90–100.

Matthews, Richard Ira. "The New Orleans Revolution of 1768: A Reappraisal." *Louisiana Studies* 4 (1965): 124–67.

Mauss, Marcel. *The Gift: The Form and Reason for Exchange in Archaic Societies.* Translated by W. D. Halls. Reprint, New York: W. W. Norton, 1954.

Mayer, John A. "Notes towards a Working Definition of Social Control in Historical Analysis." In *Social Control and the State*, edited by Stanley Cohen and Andrew Scull. New York: St. Martin's Press, 1983.

McAlister, Lyle N. "The Reorganization of the Army of New Spain, 1763–1766." *Hispanic American Historical Review* 33, 1 (1953): 1–32.

———. *Spain and Portugal in the New World, 1492–1700.* Minneapolis: University of Minnesota Press, 1994.

McCaa, Robert. "*Calidad, Clase,* and Marriage in Colonial Mexico: The Case of Parral, 1788–90." *Hispanic American Historical Review* 64, 3 (1984): 477–501.

———. "Modeling Social Interaction: Marital Miscegenation in Colonial Spanish America." *Historical Methods* 15, 2 (1982): 45–65.

McDonald, Roderick A. "Independent Economic Production by Slaves on Antebellum Louisiana Sugar Plantations." In *Cultivation and Culture: Labor and the Shaping of Slave Life in the Americas*, edited by Ira Berlin and Philip D. Morgan. Charlottesville: University Press of Virginia, 1993.

McEwan, Bonnie G. *Indians of the Greater Southeast: Historical Archaeology and Ethnohistory.* Gainesville: University Press of Florida, 2000.

———. *The Spanish Missions of La Florida.* Gainesville: University Press of Florida, 1993.

Micelle, Jerry A. "From Law Court to Local Government: Metamorphosis of the Superior Council of French Louisiana." *Louisiana History* 9, 1 (1968): 85–107.

Milanich, Jerald T. *Florida Indians and the Invasion from Europe.* Gainesville: University Press of Florida, 1995.

Milanich, Jerald T., and Charles Hudson. *Hernando de Soto and the Indians of Florida.* Gainesville: University Press of Florida, 1993.

Miller, Crane S., and Richard S. Hyslop. *California: The Geography of Diversity.* Mountain View, Calif.: Mayfield Publishing Co., 1983.

Miller, William Ian. *Humiliation and Other Essays on Honor, Social Discomfort, and Violence.* Ithaca, N.Y.: Cornell University Press, 1993.

Mills, Gary B. *The Forgotten People: Cane River's Creoles of Color.* Baton Rouge: Louisiana State University Press, 1987.

Montané, Julio. "De *nijoras* y 'españoles a medias.'" *XV Simposio de Historia de Sonora*. Hermosillo, Mexico: Universidad de Sonora, 1990.

Moore, John Preston. "Antonio de Ulloa: A Profile of the First Spanish Governor of Louisiana." *Louisiana History* 8, 2 (1967): 189–218.

———. *Revolt in Louisiana: The Spanish Occupation, 1766–1770*. Baton Rouge: Louisiana State University Press, 1976.

Moorhead, Max L. *The Presidio: Bastion of the Spanish Borderlands*. Norman: University of Oklahoma Press, 1975.

Morazán, Ronald R. "Letters, Petitions, and Decrees of the Cabildo of New Orleans, 1800–1803." 2 vols. Ph.D. diss., Louisiana State University, 1972.

Morfí, Fray Augustín de. "Account of Disorders, 1778." In *Coronado's Land: Essays on Daily Life in Colonial New Mexico*, edited by Marc Simmons. Albuquerque: University of New Mexico Press, 1991.

Morfi, Juan Agustín. *Excerpts from the Memorias for the History of the Province of Texas: Being a Translation of those parts of the Memorias that particularly concern the various Indians of the Province of Texas*. Translated by Frederick C. Chabot. San Antonio: Naylor Printing Co., 1932.

———. *History of Texas, 1673–1779*. Translated by Carlos Eduardo Castañeda. 2 vols. Albuquerque: Quivira Society, 1935.

Mörner, Magnus. *Race Mixture in the History of Latin America*. Boston: Little, Brown and Company, 1967.

Müler-Plantenberg, Clarita. "Los indígenas y sus territorios. Choque cultural— recuperación de cultura y estudios de impactos ambientales y sociales. El caso de la Cuenca Amazónica." In *El indio como sujeto y objeto de la historia latinoamericana. Pasado y presente*, edited by Hans-Joachim Köning. Frankfurt/Main: Vervuert; Madrid: Iberoamericana, 1998.

Mullin, Gerald W. *Flight and Rebellion: Slave Resistance in Eighteenth-Century Virginia*. New York: Oxford University Press, 1972.

Nabhan, Gary P. *The Desert Smells like Rain: A Naturalist in Papago Indian Country*. San Francisco: North Point Press, 1982.

Nabhan, Gary, and Thomas E. Sheridan. "Living Fencerow of the Río San Miguel, Sonora, Mexico: Traditional Technology for Floodplain Management." *Human Ecology* 5, 2 (1977): 97–111.

Navarro García, Luis. *Don José de Gálvez y la Comandancia General de las Provincias Internas del norte de Nueva España*. Sevilla: Escuela de Estudios Hispano-Americanos, 1964.

Navarro Latorre, Juan, and Francisco Solano Costa. *¿Conspiración española? 1787–1789: Contribución al estudio de las primeras relaciones históricas entre España y los Estados Unidos de Norteamérica.* Zaragoza: Institución Fernando el Católico, 1949.

Naylor, Thomas N., and Charles W. Polzer, eds. *The Presidio and Militia on the Northern Frontier of New Spain, 1570–1700.* Tucson: University of Arizona Press, 1986.

Nentvig, Juan. *Descripción geográfica, natural y curiosa de la provincia de Sonora.* Edited by Germán Viveros. Mexico City: Archivo General de la Nación, 1971.

Newcomb, W. W., Jr. "Historic Indians of Central Texas." *Bulletin of the Texas Archeological Society* 64 (1993): 1–63.

———. *The Indians of Texas: From Prehistoric to Modern Times.* Austin: University of Texas Press, 1961.

———. *The People Called Wichita.* Phoenix: Indian Tribal Series, 1977.

———. "A Re-examination of the Causes of Plains Warfare." *American Anthropologist,* new series, 52, 3 (1950): 317–30.

Núñez Fundidor, Fray Angel Antonio. *Bacerac en 1777: Carta edificante de Fray Angel Antonio Núñez Fundidor.* Edited by Julio César Montané Martí. Hermosillo, Mexico: Contrapunto 14, 1999.

Nunis, Doyce B., Jr. "The Franciscan Friars of Mission San Fernando, 1797–1847." In *Mission San Fernando Rey de España, 1797–1997: A Bicentennial Tribute,* edited by Doyce B. Nunis Jr. Los Angeles: Historical Society of Southern California, 1997.

Nuttall, Donald A. "The Fages Marital Crisis of 1785: Elaboration and Explanation." *Southern California Quarterly* 83, 1 (2001): 1–22.

Offutt, Leslie S. *Saltillo 1777–1810: Town and Region in the Mexican North.* Tucson: University of Arizona Press, 2001.

Osante, Patricia. *Orígenes del Nuevo Santander, 1748–1772.* México: Universidad Nacional Autónoma de México, Universidad Autónoma de Tamaulipas, 1997.

Padgett, James A., ed. "A Decree for Louisiana Issued by the Baron of Carondelet, June 1, 1795." *Louisiana Historical Quarterly* 20, 3 (1937): 590–605.

Parker, Susan R. "Men without God or King: Rural Settlers of East Florida, 1784–1790." *Florida Historical Quarterly* 64, 2 (1990): 135–55.

———. "Spanish St. Augustine's 'Urban' Indians." *El Escribano* 32 (1993): 1–15.

———. "Success through Diversification: Francis Philip Fatio's New Switzerland Plantation." In Jane G. Landers, *Colonial Plantations and Economy in Florida*. Gainesville: University Press of Florida, 2000.

Parson, Elsie Clews. *Notes on the Caddo*. Memoirs of the American Anthropological Association No. 57. Menasha, Wisc.: American Anthropological Association, 1941.

Pennington, Campbell. *The Pima Bajo of Central Sonora*. 2 vols. Salt Lake City: University of Utah Press, 1979.

Pérez, Crisóstomo N. *Land Grants in Alta California*. Rancho Cordova, Calif.: Landmark Enterprises, 1996.

Pérez González, María Luisa, "Royal Roads in the Old and the New World: The Camino de Oñate and Its Importance in the Spanish Settlement of New Mexico." *Colonial Latin American Historical Review* 7, 2 (1998): 191–218.

Perry, Mary Elizabeth, and Anne J. Cruz, eds. *Cultural Encounters: The Impact of the Inquisition in Spain and the New World*. Berkeley: University of California Press, 1991.

Pfefferkorn, Ignaz. *Sonora: A Description of the Province*. Edited by Bernard Fontana. Translated by Theodore E. Treutlein. 1795; Tucson: University of Arizona Press, 1989.

Pichardo's Treatise in the Limits of Louisiana and Texas. Translated by Charles Wilson Hackett. 4 vols. Austin: University of Texas Press, 1931.

Pitt-Rivers, Julian. "Honour and Social Status." In *Honour and Shame: The Values of Mediterranean Society*, edited by J. G. Peristiany. Chicago: University of Chicago Press, 1966.

Polzer, Charles W. *Rules and Precepts of the Jesuit Missions of Northwestern New Spain*. Tucson: University of Arizona Press, 1976.

Powell, Philip W. *La Guerra Chichimeca (1550–1600)*. Mexico City: Fondo de Cultura Económica, 1977.

Powell, Philip Wayne. *Soldiers, Indians, and Silver*. Berkeley: University of California Press, 1969.

Priestley, Herbert Ingram. *José de Gálvez: Visitor-General of New Spain (1765–1771)*. Berkeley: University of California Press, 1916.

Quezada, Noemí. "Cosmovisión, sexualidad e Inquisición." In *Inquisición novohispana*, edited by Noemí Quezada, Martha Eugenia Rodríguez, and Marcela Suárez. 2 vols. Mexico City: Universidad Nacional Autónoma de México, Universidad Autónoma Metropolitana, 2000.

————. "La brujería: Salud y enfermedad. Nuevas perspectivas teóricas."
Lecture presented at the Escuela Nacional de Antropología e Historia,
Mexico City, April 27, 2001.

Quezada, Noemí, Martha Eugenia Rodríguez, and Marcela Suárez, eds.
Inquisición novohispana, 2 vols. Mexico City: Universidad Nacional
Autónoma de México, Universidad Autónoma Metropolitana, 2000.

Radding, Cynthia. "Crosses, Caves, and *Matachinis*: Divergent Appropriations
of Catholic Discourse in Northwestern New Spain." *The Americas* 55,
2 (1998): 177–201.

————. *Entre el desierto y la sierra: Las naciones O'odham y Tegüima de Sonora,
1530–1840*. Mexico City: Instituto Nacional Indigenista, Centro de
Investigaciones y Estudios Superiores en Antropología Social, 1995.

————. "Nomads and Villagers of Northeastern Mexico and Eastern Bolivia," X
Meeting of Mexican Historians, Dallas–Fort Worth, 21 November 1999.

————. *Wandering Peoples: Colonialism, Ethnic Spaces, and Ecological Frontiers
in Northwestern Mexico, 1700–1850*. Durham, N.C.: Duke University
Press, 1997.

Ramos Arizpe, Miguel. "Memoria presentada a las Cortes de Cádiz." In *Miguel
Ramos Arizpe, Discursos, memorias, e informes*, edited by Vito Alessio Robles.
Mexico City: Universidad Nacional Autónoma de México, 1942.

Reff, Daniel. *Disease, Depopulation and Culture Change in Northwestern New
Spain, 1518–1764*. Salt Lake City: University of Utah Press, 1991.

Richmond, Douglas. "The Legacy of African Slavery in Colonial Mexico,
1519–1810." *Journal of Popular Culture* 35, 2 (2001): 1–16.

Ricklis, Robert A. *The Karankawa Indians of Texas: An Ecological Study of
Cultural Tradition and Change*. Austin: University of Texas Press, 1996.

Riley, Carroll L. *The Frontier People: The Greater Southwest in the Protohistoric
Period*. Rev. and expanded ed. Albuquerque: University of New Mexico
Press, 1987.

Riley, James D. "Status and Residence: The Labradores of Tlaxcala and the
City of Puebla, 1680–1800." Paper read at the VII Conference of Mexican
and United States Historians. Oaxaca, October 22–26, 1985.

Rodríguez Casado, Vicente. *Primeros años de dominación española en la Luisiana*.
Madrid: Consejo Superior de Investigaciones Científicas, 1942.

Rollings, Willard H. *The Osage: An Ethnohistorical Study of Hegemony on the
Prairie-Plains*. Columbia: University of Missouri Press, 1992.

Roucek, Joseph. *Social Control*. 2nd ed. Reprint, Westport, Conn.: Greenwood
Press, 1970.

Rubial, Antonio. "Catalina de Erauso o el travestismo tolerado." *Historias* 43 (1999).

Sahlins, Marshall. *Stone Age Economics*. Chicago: Aldine-Atherton, 1972.

Sala-Molins, Louis. *Le Code Noir, ou le Calvaire de Canaan; Records of the States of the United States of America: Louisiana, 1678–1810*. Paris: Presses Universitaires de France, 1987.

Sánchez García, José Hermenegildo. *Crónica del Nuevo Santander*. Mexico City: Consejo Nacional para la Cultura y las Artes, 1990.

Sánchez Ortega, María Elena. "Sorcery and Eroticism in Love Magic." In *Cultural Encounters: The Impact of the Inquisition in Spain and the New World*, edited by M. E. Perry and A. J. Cruz. Berkeley: University of California Press, 1991.

Sandos, James A. "Between Crucifix and Lance: Indian-White Relations in California, 1769–1848." In *Contested Eden: California before the Gold Rush*, edited by Ramón Gutiérrez and Richard Orsi. Berkeley: University of California Press, 1998.

———. "Christianization among the Chumash: An Ethnohistoric Approach." *American Indian Quarterly* 15, 1 (1991): 65–89.

———. "Junípero Serra's Canonization and the Historical Record." *American Historical Review* 93, 5 (1988): 1253–69.

Santa María, Vicente de. *Relación histórica de la Colonia del Nuevo Santander*. Annotated and edited by Ernesto de la Torre Villar. Mexico City: Universidad Nacional Autónoma de México, 1973.

Scardaville, Michael C., and Jesús María Belmonte. "Florida in the Late First Spanish Period: The Griñan Report." *El Escribano* 16 (1979): 1–24.

Schafer, Daniel L. "'A Swamp of an Investment?': Richard Oswald's British East Florida Plantation Experiment." In *Colonial Plantations and Economy in Florida*, edited by Jane G. Landers. Gainesville: University Press of Florida, 2000.

Schafer, Judith Kelleher. *Slavery, the Civil Law, and the Supreme Court of Louisiana*. Baton Rouge: Louisiana State University Press, 1994.

Schmitt, Karl, and Iva Osanai Schmitt. *Wichita Kinship, Past and Present*. Norman: University Book Exchange, 1953.

Schroeder, Susan, Stephanie Wood, and Robert Haskett, eds. *Indian Women of Colonial Mexico*. Norman: University of Oklahoma Press, 1997.

Schwartz, Stuart B. "Spaniards, *Pardos*, and the Missing Mestizos: Identities and Racial Categories in the Early Hispanic Caribbean." *New West Indian Guide* 70, 1–2 (1997): 5–19.

Secoy, Frank Raymond. *Changing Military Patterns on the Great Plains (17th Century through Early 19th Century)*. Monographs of the American Ethnological Society, vol. 21. Locust Valley, N.Y.: J. J. Augustin Publisher, 1953.

Seed, Patricia. *To Love, Honor and Obey in Colonial Mexico: Conflicts Over Marriage Choice, 1574–1821*. Stanford: Stanford University Press, 1988.

Sheridan, Cecilia. *Anónimos y desterrados: La contienda por el "sitio que llaman de Quauyla," siglos XVI–XVIII*. Mexico: CIESAS, Miguel Angel Porrúa, 2000.

———. "'Indios amigos': Estrategias militares en la frontera noreste novohispana." In *Memorias del Primer Congreso Internacional sobre fuerzas militares en Iberoamérica, siglos XVIII–XIX*. Mexico: Universidad Veracruzana, forthcoming.

———. "Indios Madrineros: Colonizadores tlaxcaltecas en el noreste novohis-pano." *Estudios de Historia Novohispana* 24 (2001): 15–51.

———. *El suave yugo del evangelio: Las misiones franciscanas de Río Grande en el periodo colonial*. Saltillo, Mexico: Universidad Autónoma de Coahuila; Centro de Estudios Sociales y Humanísticos, A.C., and Instituto Coahuilense de Cultura, 1999.

Sheridan, Thomas E., ed. *Empire of Sand: The Seri Indians and the Struggle for Spanish Sonora, 1645–1803*. Tucson: University of Arizona Press, 1999.

Simmons, Marc. *The Last Conquistador: Juan de Oñate and the Settling of the Far Southwest*. Norman: University of Oklahoma Press, 1991.

———. "Settlement Patterns in Colonial New Mexico." In *New Spain's Far Northern Frontier: Essays on Spain in the American West, 1540–1821*, edited by David J. Weber. Albuquerque: University of New Mexico Press, 1979.

Simpson, Leslie Byrd. *The Encomienda in New Spain*. Rev. and enlarged ed. Berkeley: University of California Press, 1966.

Sites, Paul. *Control: The Basis of Social Order*. New York: Dunellen Publishing Co., 1973.

Sleeper-Smith, Susan. *Indian Women and French Men: Rethinking Cultural Encounter in the Western Great Lakes*. Amherst: University of Massachusetts Press, 2001.

Socolow, Susan. *The Women of Colonial Latin America*. New York: Cambridge University Press, 2000.

———. "Women of the Frontier, Buenos Aires, 1740–1810." In *Contested Ground: Comparative Frontiers in the Greater Southwest and the Río de la Plata*, edited by Donna J. Guy and Thomas E. Sheridan. Tucson: University of Arizona Press, 1998.

Solano Costa, Fernando. "La emigración acadiana a la Luisiana española (1783–1785)." *Cuadernos de historia Jerónimo Zurita* 2, 7 (1954): 82–125.

Spada Suárez, Rosa. *El travestismo femenino en "Don Gil de las calzas verdes" de Tirso de Molina.* Mexico City: Instituto Nacional de Antropología e Historia, 1998.

Spear, Jennifer. "'They Need Wives': Métissage and the Regulation of Sexuality in French Louisiana, 1699–1730." In *Sex, Love, Race: Crossing Boundaries in North American History,* edited by Martha Hodes. New York: New York University Press, 1999.

Spicer, Edward H., *Cycles of Conquest: The Impact of Spain, Mexico, and the United States on the Indians of the Southwest, 1533–1960.* Tucson, University of Arizona Press, 1962.

———. *The Yaquis: A Cultural History.* Tucson: University of Arizona Press, 1980.

Stephens, Thomas M. *Dictionary of Latin American Racial and Ethnic Terminology.* Gainesville: University of Florida Press, 1989.

Stern, Peter. "Marginals and Acculturation in Frontier Society." In *New Views of Borderlands History,* edited by Robert H. Jackson. Albuquerque: University of New Mexico Press, 1998.

Stern, Steve. *The Secret History of Gender: Women, Men and Power in Late Colonial Mexico.* Chapel Hill: University of North Carolina Press, 1995.

Stoddard, Ellwyn R., Richard L. Nostrand, and Jonathan P. West. *Borderlands Sourcebook: A Guide to the Literature on Northern Mexico and the American Southwest.* Norman: University of Oklahoma Press, 1983.

Strauss, Claude Lévi. *The Elementary Structures of Kinship.* Edited by Rodney Needham. Translated by James Harle Bell and John Richard von Sturmer. Rev. ed. Boston: Beacon Press, 1969.

Suárez, Marcela. "Sexualidad, Inquisición y herejía en la Nueva España de las Luces." In *Inquisición novohispana,* edited by Noemí Quezada, Martha Eugenia Rodríguez, and Marcela Suárez. 2 vols. Mexico City: Universidad Nacional Autónoma de México, Universidad Autónoma Metropolitana, 2000.

Surrey, Nancy M. M. *The Commerce of Louisiana during the French Régime, 1699–1763.* New York: Columbia University, 1916.

Swann, Michael. *Tierra Adentro: Settlement and Society in Colonial Durango.* Boulder, Colo.: Westview Press, 1982.

Swanton, John R. *Source Material on the History and Ethnology of the Caddo Indians.* Bureau of American Ethnology Bulletin 132. Washington, D.C.: Smithsonian Institution, 1942.

Taylor, William B. *Magistrates of the Sacred: Priests and Parishioners in Eighteenth-Century Mexico*. Stanford: Stanford University Press, 1996.

Temple, Thomas Workman, II. "Toypurina the Witch and the Indian Uprising at San Gabriel." *Masterkey* 32 (1958): 136–52.

TePaske, John Jay. *The Governorship of Spanish Florida, 1700–1763*. Durham, N.C.: Duke University Press, 1964.

Texada, David Ker. "The Administration of Alejandro O'Reilly as Governor of Louisiana, 1769–1770." Ph.D. diss., Louisiana State University, 1968.

———. *Alejandro O'Reilly and the New Orleans Rebels*. Lafayette: Center for Louisiana Studies, University of Southwestern Louisiana, 1970.

Thomas, Alfred Barnaby. *Teodoro de Croix and the Northern Frontier of New Spain, 1776–1783*. Norman: University of Oklahoma Press, 1941.

Torres Ramírez, Bibiano. *Alejandro O'Reilly en Indias*. Seville: Escuela de Estudios Hispano-Americanos, 1969.

Torres-Reyes, Ricardo. *The British Siege of St. Augustine, 1740*. Denver: Denver Service Center (National Park Service), 1972.

Tudisco, A. Jeff. *Class and Caste in Village India*. San Francisco: Field Educational Publications, 1969.

Twinam, Ann. *Public Lives, Private Secrets: Gender, Honor, Sexuality, and Illegitimacy in Colonial Spanish America*. Stanford: Stanford University Press, 1999.

Ulloa, Jorge Juan, and Antonio de Ulloa. "Eighteenth-Century Spanish American Towns: African and Afro-Hispanic Life and Labor in Cities and Suburbs." In *The African in Latin America*, edited by Anne Pescatello. New York: Alfred A. Knopf, 1975.

Usner, Daniel H. *Indians, Settlers, and Slaves in a Frontier Exchange Economy: The Lower Mississippi Valley before 1783*. Chapel Hill: University of North Carolina for the Institute of Early American History and Culture, 1992.

Valdés, Carlos Manuel. *La gente del mezquite: Los nómadas del noreste en la colonia*. Mexico City: Centro de Investigaciones y Estudios Superiores en Antropología Social, 1995.

Valdés, Carlos Manuel, and Ildefonso Dávila del Bosque. *Esclavos negros en Saltillo: Siglos XVII a XIX*. Saltillo, Mexico: Ayuntamiento de Saltillo and Universidad Autónoma de Coahuila, 1989.

Van Kirk, Sylvia. *Many Tender Ties: Women in Fur Trade Society, 1670–1870*. Norman: University of Oklahoma Press, 1980.

Van Young, Eric. "Sectores medios rurales en el México de los Borbones: El interior de Guadalajara en el siglo XVII." *Revista Latinoamericana de Historia Económica y Social* 8 (1986), 99–117.

Velasco, Sherry. *The Lieutenant Nun: Transgenderism, Lesbian Desire and Catalina de Erauso*. Austin: University of Texas Press, 2000.

Viqueira Albán, Juan Pedro, Sonya Lipsett-Rivera, and Sergio Rivera Ayala. *Propriety and Permissiveness in Bourbon Mexico*. Wilmington, Del.: Scholarly Resources, 1999.

Wade, Peter. *Race and Ethnicity in Latin America*. London: Pluto Press, 1997.

Weber, David J. *The Spanish Frontier in North America*. New Haven, Conn.: Yale University Press, 1992.

Weber, David J., and Jane M. Rausch, eds. *Where Cultures Meet: Frontiers in Latin American History*. Wilmington, Del.: Scholar Resources, 1994.

Webre, Stephen. "The Problem of Slavery in Spanish Louisiana, 1769–1803." *Louisiana History* 25, 2 (1982): 117–35.

West, Robert. *Sonora: Its Geographical Personality*. Austin: University of Texas Press, 1993.

Wheelwright, Julie. *Amazons and Military Maids: Women Who Dressed as Men in the Pursuit of Life, Liberty, and Happiness*. Boston: Pandor, 1989.

Whitaker, Arthur Preston. "Antonio de Ulloa." *Hispanic American Historical Review* 15, 2 (1935): 155–94.

———. "The Commerce of Louisiana and the Floridas at the End of the Eighteenth Century." *Hispanic American Historical Review* 8, 2 (1928): 190–203.

———. *Documents Relating to the Commercial Policy of Spain in the Floridas, with Incidental Reference to Louisiana*. DeLand: Florida State Historical Society, 1931.

———. "James Wilkinson's First Descent to New Orleans in 1787." *Hispanic American Historical Review* 7, 1 (1928): 82–97.

———. *The Mississippi Question, 1795–1803: A Study in Trade, Politics, and Diplomacy*. Reprint, Gloucester, Mass.: Peter Smith, 1962.

———. "New Light on the Treaty of San Lorenzo: An Essay in Historical Criticism." *Mississippi Valley Historical Review* 15, 4 (1929): 435–54.

———. "Reed and Forde, Merchant Adventurers of Philadelphia: Their Trade with Spanish New Orleans." *Pennsylvania Magazine of History and Biography* 61 (1937): 237–62.

———. "The Retrocession of Louisiana in Spanish Policy." *American Historical Review* 39, 3 (1934): 454–76.

———. *Spanish American Frontier, 1783–1795: The Westward Movement and the Spanish Retreat in the Mississippi Valley*. Reprint, Gloucester, Mass.: Peter Smith, 1962.

Williams, E. Russ. *Filhiol and the Founding of Spanish Poste d'Ouachita: The Ouachita Valley in Colonial Louisiana, 1783–1804*. Monroe, La.: Privately published, 1982.

Winston, James E. "The Causes and Results of the Revolution of 1768 in Louisiana." *Louisiana Historical Quarterly* 15, 2 (1932): 181–213.

Winzerling, Oscar William. *Acadian Odyssey*. Baton Rouge: Louisiana State University Press, 1955.

Wolf, Eric R. *Europe and the People without History*. Berkeley: University of California Press, 1982.

Wood, Peter H. *Black Majority: Negroes in South Carolina from 1690 through the Stono Rebellion*. New York: W. W. Norton, 1974.

Wright, Irene. "Dispatches of Spanish Officials Bearing on the Free Negro Settlement of Gracia Real de Santa Teresa de Mose." *Journal of Negro History* 9, 2 (1924): 144–93.

Wu, Celia. "The Population of the City of Querétaro in 1791." *Journal of Latin American Studies* 16, 2 (1984): 277–307.

Wunder, John R., and Pekka Hämäläinen. "Of Lethal Places and Lethal Essays." *American Historical Review* 104, 3 (1999): 1229–34.

Young, Raymond A. "Pinckney's Treaty—A New Perspective." *Hispanic American Historical Review* 43, 4 (1963): 526–35.

Zavala, Silvio. "Los esclavos en el Norte de México Siglo XVI." In *El Norte de México y el Sur de los Estados Unidos: Tercera Reunión de Mesa Redonda sobre Problemas Antropológicos de México y Centro América*. México: Sociedad Mexicana de Antropología, 1943.

Zitomersky, Joseph. "The Form and Function of French–Native American Relations in Early Eighteenth-Century French Colonial Louisiana." In *Proceedings of the Fifteenth Meeting of the French Colonial Historical Society, Martinique and Guadaloupe, May 1989*, edited by Patricia Galloway and Philip P. Boucher. New York: University Press of America, 1992.

Contributors

Juliana Barr earned her Ph.D. from the University of Wisconsin-Madison and currently serves as an assistant professor at the University of Florida. She is completing a book manuscript entitled *Peace Came in the Form of a Woman: The Power Relations of Spanish and Indian Nations in the Early Southwestern Borderlands*. Her other publications include an essay in the July 2004 issue of the *William and Mary Quarterly* entitled "A Diplomacy of Gender: Rituals of First Contact in the 'Land of the Tejas'" and an essay, "The Palette of Fear at San Sabá" in James Brooks, ed., *Presidios y Indios: Negotiating Conquest in the Spanish Borderlands*, which will be published in 2005.

José Cuello obtained his Ph.D. in Latin American history from the University of California at Berkeley in 1981. He directed the Center for Chicano-Boricua Studies at Wayne State University in Detroit from 1989 through 2001. He examines colonial and north Mexican themes through the prism of Saltillo. Key essays are found in *El norte, el noreste y Saltillo en la historia de México* published in 1990. He has written on United States Latino history, and on student academic self-empowerment and academic/community activism and has now returned to work on colonial Latin America.

Susan M. Deeds is Professor of History at Northern Arizona University, a member of the board of directors of the Mexico-North Research Network, and a coauthor of *The Course of Mexican History* (7th ed., Oxford University Press, 2003). Among her publications on the colonial Mexican north are *Defiance and Deference in Colonial Mexico: Indians under Spanish Rule in Nueva Vizcaya* (University of Texas Press, 2003), and numerous articles on missions, labor, rebellions, and other interactions between indigenous groups and Spaniards in today's Chihuahua, Durango, and Sinaloa.

Jesús F. de la Teja is professor of history at Texas State University—San Marcos. His research interests focus on the northeastern frontier of Spanish colonial Mexico and he is the author of numerous publications, including *San Antonio de Béxar: A Community on New Spain's Northern Frontier* (Austin, 1995) and coauthor of *Texas: Crossroads of North America* (Boston, 2004), a college-level survey of the state's history. In addition to his research activities, he has served as a consultant on development of the Texas State History Museum and serves as book review editor of the *Southwestern Historical Quarterly*.

Gilbert C. Din, professor emeritus of Fort Lewis College, Durango, Colorado, studied Latin American history at the University of California, Berkeley, and at the University of Madrid, Spain. He chose Spanish Louisiana as his field of historical inquiry, in which he has published more than fifty articles and seven books. His most recent book-length study, *Spaniards, Planters, and Slaves: The Spanish Regulation of Slavery in Louisiana, 1763–1803* (College Station, Tex., 1999), won the Louisiana Historical Association's 2000 Kemper and Leila Williams Prize in Louisiana history.

Ross Frank is an Associate Professor in the Department of Ethnic Studies, University of California at San Diego. His areas of research focus on comparative modes of cultural change among European and Native American groups, and he has published *From Settler to Citizen: New Mexican Economic Development and the Creation of Vecino Society, 1750–1820* (Berkeley, 2000), which won the New Mexico Historical Society's 2002 Gaspar Pérez de Villagrá Award. The study documented rapid growth in the late colonial New Mexican economy leading to *vecino* cultural florescence and strained relations with the Río Grande pueblos. Forthcoming work will document and analyze the *Tribal Digital Village*, a project created by the eighteen tribes in San Diego County to build a wireless internet backbone serving tribal education, language, and culture. Frank also directs the *Plains Indian Ledger Art Digital Publishing Project*, a cooperative effort to web-publish volumes of Plains Indian drawings done on paper between 1860 and 1900.

Alfredo Jiménez has served as Dean of the Faculty of Philosophy and Letters and Director of the Institute of Educational Sciences, as well as Director of the Department of American Anthropology, Universidad de Sevilla. He is Professor Emeritus at the Department of American History, Universidad de Sevilla. He has conducted extensive field work in Andalucía, New Mexico, and Guatemala, and has led joint international projects as codirector with the Department of Anthropology, University of Pennsylvania, and the Spanish Colonial Research Center, University of New Mexico. His books include: *Los Hispanos de Nuevo México* (Seville, 1974) and *Biografía de un campesino andaluz: La historia oral como etnografía* (Seville, 1978). He is the compiler of *Antropología histórica: La Audiencia de Guatemala en el siglo XVI* (Seville, 1997), and editor of *Handbook of Hispanic Cultures in the United States: History* (Houston, 1994). Jiménez is a member of the Real Academia Sevillana de Buenas Letras, Academia de Geografía e Historia de Guatemala, and Academia Norteamericana de la Lengua Española, New York.

Jane Landers is Associate Dean of the College of Arts and Science and Associate Professor of History at Vanderbilt University. She is the author of *Black Society in Spanish Florida* (Urbana, 1999), editor of *Colonial Plantations and Economy of Florida* (Gainesville, 2000) and *Against the Odds: Free Blacks in the Slave Societies of the Americas* (London, 1996), and coeditor of *The African American Heritage of Florida* (Gainesville, 1995). She has published essays on the African history of the Hispanic Southeast and of the circum-Caribbean in *The American Historical Review*, *Slavery and Abolition*, *The New West Indian Guide*, *The Americas*, and *Colonial Latin American Historical Review*.

Patricia Osante earned her Ph.D. in history at the Universidad Nacional Autónoma de México (UNAM). She works as a researcher in the Historical Institute of Research and coordinates the Northern Mexican History Seminar at the same university. In addition, she manages the coordination of the History Master granted by the Universidad Autónoma de Tamaulipas (UAT). She is the author of several books, including *Orígenes del Nuevo Santander, 1748–1772* (Ciudad Victoria, 1997) and *Testimonio de la causa formada en contra del coronel Don José de Escandón* (Ciudad Victoria, 2000). She has published diverse articles and critical reviews in Mexico, as well as in foreign journals, specializing on the processes of settlement that occurred during the colonial era in New Spain's northern frontier.

Cynthia Radding is Professor of History and Director of the Latin American and Iberian Institute of the University of New Mexico. From 1995 to 2004, she was associate professor of history at the University of Illinois at Urbana-Champaign, whose Research Board financed part of the scholarship that produced the chapter in this book. Radding works on ethnohistory and environmental history of frontier regions in Latin America, focus on northwestern Mexico and eastern Bolivia. Her books include *Wandering Peoples: Colonialism, Ethnic Spaces, and Ecological Frontiers in Northwestern Mexico, 1700–1850* (Durham, N.C., 1997), which won the American Society for Ethnohistory's 1998 Erminie Wheeler-Voegelin Award, and *Landscapes of Power and Identity: Comparative Borderlands in the Sonoran Desert and the Forests of Amazonia, 1700–1860* (Durham, forthcoming 2005).

James A. Sandos is Farquhar Professor of the Southwest at the University of Redlands in southern California. His publications include: *Converting California: Indians and Franciscans in the Missions* (New Haven, 2004); "Between Crucifix and Lance: Indian-white Relations in California, 1769–1848," in *Contested Eden: California before the Gold Rush*, ed. Ramón Gutiérrez and Richard Orsi (Berkeley, 1998); and "Junípero Serra's Canonization and the Historical Record," *American Historical Review* (December, 1988), which won the Hubert B. Herring Award for Best Article Published in the Field of Latin American Studies by the Pacific Coast Council on Latin American Studies.

Cecilia Sheridan works as a researcher in the Saltillo, Coahuila, branch of the Centro de Investigaciones y Estudios Superiores en Antropologia Social. She is the author of *Anónimos y desterrados: La contienda por el "sitio que llaman de Quauyla," siglos XVI–XVIII* (México, 2000) and *El "yugo suave del evangelio": Las misiones franciscanas de Río Grande en el período colonial* (México, 1999). Her research interests include indigenous groups of northern Mexico, water and the environment, and the processes of conquest and colonization in northeastern Mexico. Current projects include a study on the Indian cultures of northeastern Mexico and the causes for their disappearance and a study of Coahuila during the first federalist period in post-independence Mexico.

Index

Additional italicized terms can be found in the glossary beginning on page 277.
abuse of power, 269
Acadians, 50
Acuña, José de, 109
Adams-Onis Treaty, 42
Africans. *See* blacks
Afro-Spanish Florida, 31
agricultural settlements, 142
Agüero, José Carlos de, 13, 22*n* 7, 124
Alazapa Indians, 137, 140–41, 143
Alberto, Solange, 100
alcades ordinarios (magistrates), 4, 51
alcaldes de barrio (justices of the peace), 51
alcaldes mayores (district magistrate): abuse of power, 269; vs. *cabildo*, 209; candidates for, 82; and *encomendero-labradores*, conflict between, 208; political and judicial authorities, 4; role of, 184–85
alcaldías mayores (minor territorial divisions), 4
alcoholism, 264
alguaciles, 185
alliances: French-Indian, 156, 159; Indian-Indian, 128–29, 131–33; Spanish-Indian, 159; of Toboso Indians, 136–137
Alonso (of the Nonoxe nation), 135
Altamira, Marqués de, 243
Álvarez, Salvador, 130
Amaru, Tupac, 25*n* 36
American-born Spaniards, 7

Amerindians. *See* Indians
Ancheta, Antonio de, 188–89
Anglo-Americans, 64–65
Angolan slaves, 31
Anza, Juan Bautista de: alliances developed by, 79–80; banishment of Beitia, 87–88; militia system developed by, 84
Apaches. *See also* Lipan Apaches: alliances of, 146*n* 22; captive exchanges, 163, 165; and Comanches, 80; Spanish relations with, 168
Apalachees, 29, 30
apostasy, 99
arbitrio judicial (personal discretion), 40
Arizpe, Miguel Ramos, 209
Arkansas Post, 65
Armenta, Antonio, 90
army. *See* military system
Asevedo, Pedro Lorenzo de, 44*n* 17
Atotonilco, 130
Aubrey, Charles-Philippe, 53
Audiencia of Guadalajara, 7
audiencias (judicial/administrative units), 4
autonomy, 30
Avilés, Pedro Menéndez de, 28
ayuntamiento (municipal council), 4, 8

backsliding, 263
banditry, 103
Bando de Buen Gobierno edict, 37

banishment, 47*n* 43, 262
baptism, 217, 262, 263
Barbadillo y Victoria, Francisco, 138
Barberena, Francisco de, 249*n* 26
barrera (barrier), 63
Barrera, Roque de la, 235
Barrera y Garza, Tomás Sánchez
    de la, 237
barrier, 63
Barrios y Jáuregui, Jacinto de, 157
behavior, deviant political, 10
Beitia, Antonio, 87–88
Beltrán, Gonzalo Aguirre, 100
Bernal, Cayetano, 89
blacks: census of, 216; classification
    of, 211; deliverance of, 31; free
    blacks, 62–63; in militia, 33;
    persons of pure African descent,
    7; racial consolidation of, 203;
    registration of, 36; rites to, by
    priests, 59; as slaves, 215
blancos (whites), 215
blasphemy, 104
Bonaparte, Napoleon, 67
bond, 13
Borrego, José Vázquez, 236, 249*n* 26
Bourbon Reforms, 210, 247, 254
branding, 13
bravery ranking, 166
bride-service societies, 156, 167
British (English speakers), 36
brotherhood, 161
Bryan, Hugh and Jonathan, 31
Bushnell, Amy Turner, 28
Bustillo y Zevallos, Antonio, 146*n* 22

caballerías, 233
cabeceras (head villages), 187
Cabeza Indians, 133–34
cabildo (town council): vs. *alcaldes
    mayores*, 209; development of,
    182; in Florida, 29; functions of,
    4, 186; in New Orleans, 51, 56,

    58–61, 73*n* 32; in Saltillo, 208;
    in Sonora, 184; vs. Spanish
    military, 189
cabildo fund, 60
cabildos abiertos (municipal forums
    open to the elite), 61
caciques (headmen), 30, 181
cacomites, 97
Caddos: and Apaches, 150; Franciscan
    missionaries, 151; illicit trade
    with, 171; and Osages, 66;
    Spanish relations with, 154, 168
Cadelo, Isidro, 90
Cajuns, 50
Calderón, Felipe de, 109
calidad, 211–12
Calleja, Félix, 123
Camacho, Pedro, 139
camino real (royal road), 103
Camorlinga, Diego, 188–89
Canary Islanders, 63, 229–30, 245
Cantillana, Agustín Sánchez de, 111
capellanías (chaplaincies), 215
captive exchanges, 154, 163, 165
captives, 164–66, 193–94
Carlos III, 52, 254
Carmen, María del, 256
Caro, José Ximénez, 10
Carolina, 30
Carondelet, 61, 62, 66
Casa-Calvo, Marqués de, 61
castas: degraded nature of, 35; persons
    of mixed racial groups, 7; in
    Saltillo, 206
casta system, 91, 201; in New Mexico,
    83; subdivisions of, 211
castas limpias, 211, 214
castizo, 225*n* 39
Catholic Church. *See also* Franciscan
    missionaries; Jesuits; The
    Inquisition: conflict between
    Crown and, 5, 89–90, 254;
    control mechanisms of, 14;

as ecclesiastical institution, 20; excommunication, 14, 15; French, on slavery, 59; jurisdiction of, 258; offenses against, 99; power to shame, 106; relationships of Crown and, 5

caución juratoria (bond), 13

causa criminal (criminal suit), 38

celibacy, 110–11, 264

censuses, 87, 216, 253

Cervantes, Fernando, 105

Chacón, Fernando, 77, 90

chaplaincies, 215

Charles III, King of Spain, 16

chichimecas, 206

Chiso Indians, 135

choirmasters, 185

Chouteau, Auguste, 66

citizenship categories, 201

city government, 29, 51

civic life, 28

civil authority, 241

class systems, 204

clientela (mutual obligation between patrons and dependents), 37

Coahuiltecan, 151, 169

coartación (permission for slaves to "buy themselves"), 60, 61, 62

Cocoyome Indians, 132–34

Code Noir, 58

Code Noir ou Loi Municipale, 61

code of privileges and exemptions, 51, 234

coercion, 20, 235, 245

Cohahuila, 164

Collier, Jane Fishburne, 156, 167

colonization: bureaucracy, 20; character of colonists, 228; colonization policy, 124; courts, 13; domination by, 203; elite in, 123; by families, 231–35, 245; legislation, 243; Nuevo Santander, 231–35; policies of, 124; recolonization of Mexico, 210–11; social control of the colonizer, 271

Comanches: and Apaches, 80; captives taken from, 164; effect of, on frontier, 8; enemies of, 149; peace with, 159; Spanish relations with, 80, 168; ties with French, 158

comisarios de barrio (neighborhood commissioners), 27, 38

Commandancy General, 7

community, 151

community harmony, 259–60

común (community), 151, 182

Concha, Fernando de la, 77–78, 88

concubinage, 34

confession, 19–20

conflicts. *See also* Crown: definition of, 23*n* 15; from the elite, 3; resolution of, 40; source of, 2

congregas. See reducción

constructed identities, 218

Contreras, Juan, 135

contrition, 107

control. *See also* social controls: mechanisms of, Church, 14; military and social, 9

control system of slave market, 129

conversion, 263, 266

conversos (suspect Jewish converts), 99

conviction, 20

cooperation, 50, 67

Cope, Douglas, 217

Coronado, Francisco Vázquez de, 9

corregidores (political and judicial authorities), 4

corregimientos (minor territorial divisions), 4

Cortés, Gregorio Ortiz, 191

Cortés, Hernán, 9

Coser, Lewis, 23*n* 15

councilmen, 51

Council of the Indies, 12, 15, 22*n* 3

councilors, 4
countryside, 8
court cases, 101
cowboys, 98, 267
coyotes (mestizos), 214, 216–17, 225*n* 39
Creek, 33
Creoles, 54
criminal suit, 38
criollos: as an economic class, 214; intermediate racial category, 203; military and intellectual elite, 3, 7; representative of, 210
Crosby, Maria, 39
cross-cultural reliance, 112
Crown: vs. Church for control, 89–90; communications with, 21; conflict between Church and, 5, 89–90, 254; conflicts, source of, 5; control of, 1; as an institution, 21; relationships of Church and, 5
Cuello, José, 34, 39
Cuencamé, 10
Cuervo y Valdés, Don Francisco, 18
cultivation systems, 183
Cunca'ac (Seris), 181
curanderos, 109
currency redemption, 53–54
Cusihuiriachi, 97–98, 108
customary law, 40
Cutter, Charles, 40

Darien anti-slavery petition of 1739, 44*n* 20
debt peonage, 208
decent society. See *gente decente*
degraded nature, 35
Delvaux, Jean, 65
demographic shift, 83
derecho (customary law), 40
deterritorialization, 126, 129, 142

devil and devil worshiping: as alter ego to patriarchy, 106; experiences with, 97; phallic imagery, 104
Din, Gilbert, 31
diplomatic gifts, 162
diseases, 151
dissidents, 51
distribution, 97, 184, 208
district commandants, 51
district magistrate, 82
divorce, 255, 257
doctrina (mission), 32
dominance, 150
domination, 112
doncellas guerreras (warrior maidens), 102
dormitory, 266
Drake, Francis, 30

economic behavior, 79–80
economic class, 214
economics, 152
economic slavery, 209
Eiasiquiche, 149
el campo (countryside), 8
elections, 187, 269
emic, 15, 24*n* 25
encomendero-labradores, 206, 208
encomiendas (grants of Indian labor/tribute), 122, 129, 206
encomienda system: abuses of, 137–38; method of control in, 140–41
endogamous unions, 216
endogamy, 218
English speakers, 36
Enrique, Agueda, 38, 46*n* 43
entradas (expeditions), 10, 30
equal-but-separate, 207
equidad (justice), 40
Erauso, Catalina de, 100–101, 102, 104

Escandón y Helguera, José de, 124, 232, 233, 242
escolta (mission guard), 267–68
escribanos (scribes), 8
españoles americanos (American-born Spaniards), 7, 203
españoles europeos (European Spaniards), 7, 19, 203
ethnic-racial designations, 83
ethnogenesis, 126
ethnography, 2
etic, 24*n* 25
European Spaniards, 7, 19, 203
evacuation to Cuba, 42
evangelization, 180
excommunication, 14, 15
expeditions, 10, 30
extended kinship group, 37
extermination policy, 241

Fabela, Antonia de la, 111
fact-finding inquiry, 40
Fages, Eulalia Callis de, 255–59
Fages, Pedrito, 256
Fages, Pedro, 254–59, 265
Fajardo, Guajardo, 17
family bonds, 161
family colonization, 231–35, 245
female agency, 102
feminist resistance, 262
Fernandéz, José, 38
flogging, 13, 268, 274*n* 24
Florida: actions against by United States, 41; Afro-Spanish, development of, 31; *Bando de Buen Gobierno* edict, 37; defense of, 33; missions expansion in, 29; racial mixing in, 34; revolts of Indians in, 29; second occupation of, 35; *Sociedad de Castas*, 34; Spanish control of, 27
forced distribution of goods on credit, 86–87

forced labor drafts, 97
forts, 8
Franciscan missionaries: behavior of, 88; control of, 238–39; disqualification of, 243; ethnic-racial designations by, 83; in Sonora, 183; in Texas, 151; and vecinos, conspiracies between, 88
free blacks, 62–63
freedmen, 32
French Creoles, 52
French traders, 158
frontier: Crown control of, 7; method of expanding, 142; natural and cultural, 182–83; strategies for conquering, 122
frontier character, 100
fuero (code of privileges and exemptions), 51, 234
fuero tribunals, 68–69*n* 5

Gabrielino Indians, 261–62
gachupines, 203
Galloway, Patricia, 160
Gálvez, Bernardo de, 57
Gálvez, José de, 10, 61, 265
gambling, 108
Gavilanes Indians, 135–36
gender and political culture, 192–93
gender differences, 112
gender identification, 261
gender norms, 100–101, 110–15
gender ratios, 205
general populace, 211–12
gente decente (decent society), 211–12
gente de color quebrado (people of broken color), 27
gente de razón, 86, 211
gentiles: census of, 189; effects of conversion on, 269–70; and runaways, 266
geographical mobility, 106
Georgians, 33

gift exchange, 161, 162
gobernaciones (kingdoms or
    provinces), 4
Godoy, Manuel, 67
Golpazos, Juana, 96, 105
Gonzales, Josefa, 18
governance. *See also* under *alcaldes*:
    elections, 187, 269; native
    councils, 184–86; native
    institutions, 152
governor, 184–85
graffiti, 270
Gran Chichimeca, 227
grants of Indian labor/tribute,
    122, 129
Gresham's law, 54
Griffen, William, 130
Grimarest, Enrique de, 191
Guacuanquacis, 177
Guadalajara, Tomás de, 96, 98
Guajardo Fajardo, Diego, 15
Guerrero, Antonio, 89
Guevara, Antonio Ladrón de, 18, 140
Guzmán, Nuño Beltrán de, 9

Harpe, Bérnard de la, 155
headmen, 30, 181
head of household, 8
head villages, 187
healing, 99
hechicería (witchcraft), 100
Héctor, Francisco Luis, 57
heresy, 16, 27, 99
Hevia y Valdés, Bishop, 17
Hocio, Francisco, 90
Hoebel, E. Adamson, 166, 167
hombres ricos y ponderosos (rich and
    powerful men), 8
honor: dimensions of, 171; husbands
    responsibility for, 39; loss of, 257;
    male, 167; between societies,
    153; in Spanish value system, 6
honorific status, 219

Horruytiner, Pedro Lamberto, 45*n* 22
horse sales, 80–81
hostage exchange, 166
housing construction, 81
Humaña, Gutiérrez de, 10
hunter-gather communities: effect
    of Spanish population on,
    131; extermination of, 247;
    integration of, 122, 227, 244;
    as labor source, 266; resistance
    by, 132, 231

Iberia. *See* Spain
idolatry, 16
Ildefonso, Dávila, 215
immersion system of conversion, 266
immigrants, 63
immigration policy, 64
incest, 18
Indian emancipation, 269
Indian leaders: elected offices, 188;
    military rankings, 188
Indian mobility, 124, 126, 130–31
Indians. *See also* under *specific
    tribe*: aiding Spanish in native
    conquest, 133; alliances against
    Spanish, 131–33; alliances
    amongst, 128–29; alliance with
    Spain, 79–80; attacks by, 131–32,
    227; as children of the King, 174;
    code of conduct towards, 265;
    conflict between internal groups,
    191; conflicts amongst, 141;
    control of, by missionaries, 232;
    control over, 122; demography
    of, 270; equality with Spanish,
    207; extinction of, 125; Florida,
    revolts of, 29; as frontier settlers,
    121; group names, 125, 143–44;
    The Inquisition and, 101; labor
    by, 97, 139; land distribution to,
    269; land grants to, 134–35;
    as migratory workers, 207;
    military conquest over, 122;
    movement of, 193; property

rights suppressed, 246; reduction efforts towards, 29; relationships amongst tribes, 80; resistance of, 270; subjugation of, 254; territory of, 126–27; uprising threats, 261; urban, 34
Indian women: abuses of, 140; in court cases, 101; rape of, 158, 265; role of, 154; treatment of, 255, 265; work of, 266
indigenous office holding, 191
indios, 201
indios bárbaros, 8, 156
indios bozales, 32
indios de pueblo (Pueblo Indians). *See* Pueblo Indians
indios ladinos, 44*n* 17
inferiority, 271
infidelity, 255
inheritance laws, 209
The Inquisition: as an agent of social control, 24–25*n* 28, 99–104; impact of, 16; jurisdiction of, 101; murder investigation by, 98–99; in New Spain, 25*n* 29
inspections, 24*n* 22
institutions. *See also* Catholic Church; Crown
Interior Provinces, 7
intermarriage, 154, 155
internal economy, 60
internalization, 25*n* 37
intimidation policy, 235
investors, 246
Isleños (Canary Islanders), 63

Jackson, Andrew, 41
Jacobins, 57
Jémez Pueblo, 90
Jesuits: expulsion of, 16, 183; missionary efforts of, 183, 196*n* 3; in social order, 16
Jesús María, Francisco Casañas de, 158

Jewish converts, 99
José, Nicolás, 261–63
judges, 4
judicial/administrative units, 4
judicial review, 14
juez de agua, 191
juicio de residencia (judicial review), 14
juridical system. *See* laws and legal system
justice, 40
justices of the peace, 51
justicias, 185

Karankawan Indians, 151, 169, 170
Kardiner, Abram, 167
kinship, 153

labor. *See also* encomienda system; slavery: forced labor drafts, 97, 184; hunter-gather communities as source of, 266; by Indians, 97, 139; settlers obligation for, 241; wage labor, 208
labor migration, 96, 97
labor scarcity, 227
Lafora, Nicolás de, 24*n* 22
land conflicts, 188–90
land distribution, 238, 242–44, 269, 274–75*n* 26
land written from or about, 11
languages, 33
Larios, Juan, 134
Larrea, Juan Bautista de, 134
la tierra (land written from or about), 11
Law of the Indies, 233
laws and legal system: access to, 241; courts and judges, 50; *derecho* (customary law), 40; Indian women in court cases, 101; inheritance laws, 209; judicial administration, 40; *juicio de residencia* (judicial review), 14; jurisdiction of church, 258;

justices of the peace, 51; *justicias*, 185; lawsuit appeals, 81–82; *ley* (written law), 40; and order, 37; parallel, 211; racial discrimination of, 212; Spanish, and religious traditions, 37; Spanish juridical system, 51

Lemos, Manuel Gayoso de, 64

León, Miguel de, 147*n* 42

León, Alonso de, 139–40

lesbians, 102

ley (written law), 40

Leyva de Bonilla, Francisco, 10

Liberty (slave), 41

ligado (tied), 109, 111

Lima, 3

Lipan Apaches, 149–52, 158, 169

literacy, 82, 187, 193

Llul, Pedro, 39

lobos, 214, 225*n* 39

Lorenzo, Esteban, 11

Loreto, George, 191

Louisiana: Anglo-Americans in, 64–65; control in, Spanish, 52; legal system in, 50–51; local resident of Spain, 53; planters' views on slavery, 58; population of, 49; Spanish disposal of, 67; Spanish policy within, 50; trade with European countries, 56–57

Louis XV, King of France, 52, 55

love magic, 107–10, 112

machismo, 106

mador, 185

magic, 104

magistrates, 4, 51

mala raza, 214

maleficiado (bewitched), 109

male rank, 156

manumission, 62

marital preferences, 218–19

maroons, 60

marriages: among cousins, 215; among Spanish elite, 213–14; endogamous unions, 216, 218; to formalize racial identities, 217; interclass, 205; intermarriage, 154, 155; between mulattos and Spanish, 213; polygamous, 270; promises of, 208; records of, 214; to soldiers, 263

Martínez, Antonio, 190

Mascorta, José Antonio, 191

Massanet, Damián, 158

matrilineal societies, 160

mayordomo (overseer), 268

McCaa, Robert, 217–18

médicos (physicians), 8

Medina, Ysidora de, 101

Menchaca, Miguel Jorge, 173

mercantile regulations, 52, 54, 56

Merino, Juan Pérez, 147*n* 42

mestizaje (miscegenation), 34, 83, 201

mestizos (persons of Spanish-Indian parentage), 7, 203, 214, 225*n* 39

Mexican Independence, 210–11

Mexico City, 3

migration: New World, 19; spontaneous, 227; stimulation of, 229

migratory workers, 207

military and intellectual elite, 3, 7

military system: attacks on presidio-mission complex, 170; authority of, 241; control over soldiers, 242; *escolta* (mission guard), 268; within holy sanctuaries, 15; military conquest, 122; military *fuero*, 234; military organization, 84; militias, 33, 124; militia system, 84–85; *presidiales* (soldiers), 8; presidial system, 188; *presidios* (forts), 8; Pueblo Indians cooperation with, 84; size of army, 51–52; soldiers' pay, 53; as source of prestige and social status, 84; Spanish army, 177

Miller, William Ian, 171*n* 8
mining centers: Indians as slaves in, 206; lure of, 227, 244; as source of cultural exchange, 108; Spanish control in, 96
minor territorial divisions, 4
Miró, Esteban, 64
miscegenation. *See also sistema de castas* (caste system): censuses, 7; concubinage vs. marriage, 34; ethnic-racial designations, 83; and racial identities, 204
misdemeanors, 17
mission, 32
missionaries. *See also* Franciscan missionaries; Jesuits: in Alta California, 264; control of Indians by, 232
mission communities, 184
mission guard, 267–68
mission Indians, 266
mission-presidio system, 232
missions. *See also* Toboso Indians: control of, 240; development of, 253; expansion in Florida, 29; goals of, 268–69; liquidation of, 246; under protection of villas, 243; as refuge, 128; resistance to, 151, 164, 169, 170*n* 1; San Miguel de las Bocas, 97
Mission San Antonio Galindo, 140
Mission San Buenaventura, 134
mission system, 127
mistreatment of Indians, 10
mixed marriages, 194
mobility: geographical limitations, 106; Indian, 124, 126, 130–31; Indians as migratory workers, 207; movement of Indians, 193; movement regulations in New Mexico, 86; reducción limiting, 182; regulation of travel, 105–6
monjería (dormitory), 266
Montalbán, Juan Pérez de, 103

Montero, Manuel, 262
Montero, Regina Josefa, 262
Montiano, Manuel de, 32, 45*n* 22
Moore, James, 30
Mora, Manuel García de la, 88
Morales, Luis de, 18
morality, 14, 16, 18
Morfi, Juan Agustín, 24*n* 22, 78, 129, 155
morisco, 225*n* 39
Morro Castle, 55
Mose, 32, 33
mulatos (persons of Spanish-black parentage), 7, 203, 216–17
mulatos libres, 214
municipal council, 4, 8
municipal forums open to the elite, 61
murder, 98, 101

Natchitoches, 65
native councils, 184–86
natural elites, 82–83
naturales (natives), 82
Nava, General Pedro de, 173
Navarette, Melchor de, 44*n* 19
negros (blacks). *See* blacks
neighborhood commissioners, 27, 38
Nentvig, Juan, 185–86
New Mexico: casta system in, 83; demographic shift in, 83; forces within the province of, 77–78; movement regulations in, 86; tools for social control in, 90
New Orleans, 52
New Spain: natural and cultural frontiers in, 182–83; northern frontier, social control on, 9; society in, 8; viceroyalty of, 3
nijoras, 194
nomadic raiders, 181
Noperi, Gerónimo, 192
Noperi, Ignacio, 191–92
Noriega, Francisco de, 96

Noriega, Matiás, 255
Nueva Galicia, 9
Nueva Vizcaya, 22n 5, 96
Nuevo León, 10, 123
Nuevo Santander, 123, 229, 231–35

obraje (textile workshop), 90
occupational structure, 219
officers, 65
Oglethorpe, James, 33
oidores (audencia judges), 4
Oliván Rebolledo, Juan de, 138
Oñate, Juan de, 9
Opata, 33
O'Reilly, Alejandro, 55, 56
Osage nation, 65–66
Osages, 155
Osanai, Iva, 167
ostracism, 47n 44
overseer, 268

Pacheco, Rafael Martínez, 177
pacification, 228
Padilla, Juan Antonio, 168
Palóu, Francisco, 258
Pardiñas (governor), 135, 136
parentela (extended kinship group), 37
Parker, Susan R., 34, 36
Parral, 24n 24, 96
Parsons, Elsie Clews, 161
Paterno, Severo, 89
patriarchal order, 114
patriarchal system, 106, 259–60
Patriot War of 1812, 41
Patronato Réal, 5
Payeras, Mariano, 270–71
peace negotiations, 136
peculium (property), 60
Pedrote, 133
peer pressure, 37
penal hacienda, 90
Peñalosa, Sosa, 11
peninsulares (European Spaniards),
    7, 19, 203

perjury, 82
personal discretion, 40
persons of mixed racial groups, 7
persuasion, 20, 233–35, 245, 254
Peru, 3
peyote, 105, 108
Pfefferkorn, Ignaz, 185
physicians, 8
piezas, 194
Pima Indians, 188–90
Pinckney's Treaty, 64, 67
pioneers, 33
piracy, 30
Pitt-Rivers, Julian, 171
plebe (the general populace), 211–12
policies: colonization, 124; coopera-
    tion, 67; extermination, 241;
    immigration, 64; intimidation,
    235; within Louisiana, 50;
    settlement, 232; subjugation, 241
policy for control, 180–81
political and judicial authorities, 4
political culture and gender, 192–93
politics, cross-cultural, 154
polygamy, 270
polygyny, 177
Pope, 5
popular uprisings, 11
Porres, Ambrosio Espinosa de, 12
Portolá, Gaspar de, 265
presidiales (soldiers), 8
presidial system, 188
presidio-mission complex, 170
presidios (forts), 8
Prestamero, Juan de, 190
priests: baptism rites, 263; behavior
    of, 88; conflicts amongst, 15;
    control of, 14; conversion, 266;
    conversion of runaways by, 33;
    life of, 264; in mission life, 187,
    191–92, 266–67; protest of
    Indian abuse, 265; racial records
    by, 214; rites to blacks by, 59; vs.
    secular control, 208, 269; social
    control by, 267–68; from Spanish
    elite, 215

probanza de méritos y servicios (record of merits and services), 12
Protestantism, 31
Pruneda, Luis de, 137
Pueblo Indians: individual identity of, 87; naming conventions, 87; petitions for removal of alcaldes mayores, 86; social and economic relations with, 78; vs. vecinos, 79, 85
Pueblo Revolt of 1680, 9
Pujol, Juan, 248*n* 8
purity of blood, 201, 207, 215

Quapaws, 66
Quintanilla, Juliana, 139
Quintanilla Hevia y Valdés, Diego de, 15
Qui Te Sain, 160

race in religious terms, 211
racial categories, 217
racial domination, 203
racial drift, 218
racial endogamy, 207, 216
racial identities: and miscegenation, 204; and privileged position, 213
racial ideology, 211–12
racialized social structures, 201
racial labels, 225*n* 39
racial passing, 217
racial principal, 204–5
racial purity, 205
racial variability, 218
Radding, Cynthia, 33
raiding economies, 144*n* 8
Ramos, Francisco, 109
Ramos, María, 109
rancherías, 133, 166, 180, 183
rancheros (small farmers), 210
ranchos (small mixed-farms), 121
rape: of Indians, 158; of Indian women, 265

reales (mining centers). *See* mining centers
Réal y Supremo Consejo de Indias (Supreme Royal Council of the Indies), 4, 6
rebellion, 122
Recopilación de leyes de Indias, 243
record of merits and services, 12
reducción: of Atotonilco, 130; *congregas*, 129, 137–38; differential effects of, 193; policy for control, 180–81; republic of Indians, 182
reduction efforts toward Indians, 29
reforms, 19
refugees, 63–64
regidores (councilmen), 4, 51
registration of blacks, 36
relaciones (narratives of important events), 4
relationships: of Crown and Church, 5; within and between societies in Texas, 153
religious conversion, 122–23
religious spectacle, 107
Rengel, José Antonio, 257–58
Rentería, Matías de, 96–98, 105
repartimiento (distribution), 97, 184, 208
repartimiento de efectos (forced distribution of goods on credit), 86–87
representative, 210
república de españoles, 211
república de indios, 207, 211
reputation loss, 17
revolts and uprisings. *See also* Toboso Indians: of Creoles, 54; of Florida Indians, 29; folk cultures of resistance, 104–8; French, 55; Indian rebellion, 103; Pueblo revolt of 1680, 9; Tepehuanes and Tarahumaras, 8–9
Rey, Alfonso, 173
Rey, Félix del, 55, 56

Reyes, Antonio de los, 257–58
Ripperdá, Governor, 162
ritual, 154
Rivadeneira, Antonio Balcarcel, 134
rivalries, 192–93
Rivera, Joaquín José de, 189
Rivera, Pedro de, 24n 22, 230
Roberto (slave), 41
Rodríguez, Francisco Xavier, 55, 56
royal road, 103
Rubí, Marqués de, 24n 22
Ruiz del Moral, Romualdo, 45n 22
runaway slaves, 33, 60

Salas, Bartolomé de, 108
Saltillo: decline of, 208; economic
    recovery of, 209–10; history of,
    205–10; racial identities in, 217;
    racial mixtures in, 34; recoloniza-
    tion of, 210–11; sistema de castas,
    204
Samaniego, Juan Ignacio Gil, 191,
    198n 27
San Agustín, 28
San Antonio, 164
San Buenaventura y Tejada, Francisco
    de, 31
Sánchez, Nereo, 90
sanctions, 17
sanctuary: holy, immunity within,
    15; immunity within holy
    sanctuaries, 31
Sandoval, Felipe de, 177
San Estaban pueblo, 207
San Luis de Talimali (Tallahassee), 29
San Miguel de las Bocas, 97
San Saba, 149
Santa Elena, 28
Santiago, 133
Schmitt, Karl, 167
scribes, 8
secularization, 269
seditious meetings, 90
Seed, Patricia, 218

Seguí, Juan, 38, 46–47n 43-44
self-confessions, 107
Seno Mexicano, 245
Sepúlveda, Francisco García de, 139
Serra, Junípero: Alta California, 254;
    Indian conversions, 266; vs.
    Pedro Fages, 258
servants, 214
settlement policy, 232
settlements: consolidation of indige-
    nous, 180–81; inducement for,
    233–34, 235
sexual abuses, 215
sexual relations, 156
sexual scandals, 254–55
shame: Catholic Church's power to,
    106–7; vs. guilt, 268
silver, 97
silver discoveries, 131
silver mining, 227
silver mining town, 96
sistema de castas (caste system): as a
    racial principal, 204–5; in Saltillo,
    201; white slavery under, 216
sitios, 233
slave market, 129
slavery: abuse within, 59; after French
    Revolution, 58; French Catholic
    Church on, 59; laws regarding,
    61–62; in mining centers, 206;
    Spanish law regarding, 59;
    Spanish practices, 60
slaves: Angolan, 31; Indians as, 137,
    148n 44, 175, 206; legal treat-
    ment of, 40, 41; Louisiana popu-
    lation levels, 49; rights of, 61;
    runaway, 33, 60; of various races
    and genders, 215–16
small farmers, 210
small mixed towns, 121
small settlements, 187
social controls: backward social
    control, 14; of the colonizer, 271;
    division of groups for, 211; in
    elites, 254; evacuation to Cuba,

42; flexibility as a form of, 56;
and immigrants, 63; limited
by violence, 113; by limiting
population movement, 96; limits
to, 264; method of imposition,
203–4; militia system as, 84–85;
by moral admonitions, 106–7;
native councils as vehicle for,
186; native institutions of, 152;
in the northern provinces, 77;
over hunter gatherers, 208;
policies, 15; racialized system of,
216; religious spectacle for, 107;
and slavery, 57–63; by supression
of racial identities, 220; theory, 2;
through alliance and diplomacy,
153; tools for, 82–83, 90; virtuous
life as form of, 264–65; white, 50
social hierarchy, 212
social honor, 219
socialization, 25n 37
social networks, 112
social order, 91
social structure, 7
sociedad de castas (caste system), 34,
201. See also *sistema de castas*
sodality groups, 161
Sola, Lázaro, 90
soldiers, 8
Sonaran missions, 187
Sonora, 179
sorcery, 107
Sosa, Francisco de, 137
Sosa, Gaspar Castaño de, 10
Soto, Antonia de: as female agency,
102; introduction to magic, 105;
masquerading as a man, 95–100
Spain. *See also* Crown; laws and legal
system; military system: governing of empire by, 3; hierarchy
within, 267; inheritance laws,
209; reimposition of rule by, 56;
settlements by, 127
Spanish colonization, 123
Spanish Florida, 41

St. Augustine: destruction of, 30;
economic and social ranks in, 34
St. Louis, 65
Stono Rebellion, 31
subjugation policy, 241
sumaria (fact-finding inquiry), 40
Superior Council, 53, 54, 55
Supreme Royal Council of the
Indies, 4, 6
suppression of racial identities, 220
syndic, 51

Tamarón y Romeral, Bishop Pedro,
13, 24n 22
Tapiz, Pedro, 18
Tarahumaras, 9
Tecolote, Francisco, 133, 135,
145n 14
temastianes, 185
Tepehuanes, 8
territoriality: changes in, 130–31,
137–38; negotiating, 135
Tesgüino, 193
tesha (brother), 161
Tewa Pueblos, 88
Texas, 149
thievery, 13
tied (romantically), 109, 111
Tienda de Cuervo, José, 237
time, 12, 15
timekeeping, 266
Tlaxcaltecans, 8, 229
Toboso Indians, 129–35, 136–37,
142–43
topiles, 184–86
town council, 182, 208
Toypurina, 261–62
trade: in guns and horses, 159; lack
of, 159; Spanish as source of, 161
traders, 158
transgenderism, 102
transvestites, 100–101, 102
trasalvo, 225n 39

travel movement. *See* mobility
Treaty of San Lorenzo, 64, 67
Treviño, Antonio, 149, 170
tributary groups, 211
tribute, 162, 184
Tuerto, Felipe, 135–36

Uchise, 33
Ulloa, Antonio de, 53, 54, 55
Unzaga, Luis de, 56
Unzaga Ibarrola, Domingo de, 249*n* 26
uprisings. *See* revolts and uprisings

Valcárcel, Domingo, 157, 242–43
Valdés, Carlos Manuel, 215
Valdés, José Mariano, 173*n* 16
Valdés, Luis de, 13
values, 2
value system, 6
vaqueros (cowboys), 98, 267
Varela, Juan Manuel, 192
vecinos (head of household): character of, 78; described, 92; economic behavior by, 79–80; as electorate, 8; and Franciscan missionaries, conspiracies between, 88; vs. Pueblo Indians, 85; vs. Pueblo Indians, vices of, 79; responding in development of new social order, 91
Velázquez, Diego, 9
Velázquez, Juan, 10
Veracruz, 9
Vial, Pedro (Pierre), 173
viceroyalties, 3–4, 22*n* 2
Vidal, Nicolás María, 62

vida política (civic life), 28
Villanueva, Cristina de, 109
Villanueva, Juan Núñez de, 109
villas, 233
violence, 152
virreinato (viceroyalty), 22*n* 2
visitas (small settlements), 187

wage labor, 208
warfare, 113, 122, 132. *See also* military system
warrior bond, 161
warrior maidens, 102
warrior prestige, 160
Whitefield, George, 31
whites, 215–16
white slavery, 216
Wichitas, 149, 158, 159, 164, 168
wife-stealing, 166, 167, 177
Wilkinson, James, 64
witchcraft, 100
witchcraft cases, 99–100, 104–5, 107
women: as captives, 164–66, 193–94; colonial elite, 261; Indian, in court cases, 101; masquerading as men, 95; moral obligations of, 255; murder by, 98, 101; in patriarchal order in the frontier, 113; power over men, 111; roles of, 193; sexual power of, 257; as slaves, 215
written law, 40

Zacatecas, 23*n* 10, 244
Zavala, Martín de, 139
Zepeda, Nicolás de, 97
Zorrilla, Atanasio, 191